THIS

TIME

IS

DIFFERENT

THIS TIME IS DIFFERENT

*Eight Centuries
of Financial Folly*

CARMEN M. REINHART
KENNETH S. ROGOFF

Princeton University Press

Princeton and Oxford

Thirteenth printing, and first paperback printing, 2011
Paperback ISBN 978-0-691-15264-6

The Library of Congress has cataloged the cloth edition of this book as follows

Reinhart, Carmen M.
This time is different : eight centuries of financial folly /
Carmen M. Reinhart, Kenneth S. Rogoff.
p.   cm.
Includes bibliographical references and index.
ISBN 978-0-691-14216-6 (hardcover : alk. paper)
1. Financial crises—Case studies.   2. Fiscal policy—
Case studies.   3. Business cycles—Case studies.
I. Rogoff, Kenneth S.   II. Title.
HB3722.R45   2009
338.5′42—dc22
2009022616

British Library Cataloging-in-Publication Data is available

This book has been composed in Goudy text
with Trade Gothic and Century italic by
Princeton Editorial Associates, Inc., Scottsdale, Arizona

Printed on acid-free paper. ∞

Printed in the United States of America

17   19   20   18   16

To William Reinhart,
Juliana Rogoff,
and Gabriel Rogoff

CONTENTS

CONTENTS

6

External Default through History   86

PART III
The Forgotten History of Domestic Debt and Default   101

7

The Stylized Facts of Domestic Debt and Default   103

8

Domestic Debt: The Missing Link Explaining
External Default and High Inflation   119

9

Domestic and External Default:
Which Is Worse? Who Is Senior?   128

CONTENTS

CONTENTS

PART VI
What Have We Learned? 275

17

Reflections on Early Warnings, Graduation,
Policy Responses, and the Foibles of Human Nature 277

TABLES

Figures

Boxes

PREFACE

This book provides a quantitative history of financial crises in their various guises. Our basic message is simple: We have been here before. No matter how different the latest financial frenzy or crisis always appears, there are usually remarkable similarities with past experience from other countries and from history. Recognizing these analogies and precedents is an essential step toward improving our global financial system, both to reduce the risk of future crisis and to better handle catastrophes when they happen.

If there is one common theme to the vast range of crises we consider in this book, it is that excessive debt accumulation, whether it be by the government, banks, corporations, or consumers, often poses greater systemic risks than it seems during a boom. Infusions of cash can make a government look like it is providing greater growth to its economy than it really is. Private sector borrowing binges can inflate housing and stock prices far beyond their long-run sustainable levels, and make banks seem more stable and profitable than they really are. Such large-scale debt buildups pose risks because they make an economy vulnerable to crises of confidence, particularly when debt is short term and needs to be constantly refinanced. Debt-fueled booms all too often provide false affirmation of a government's policies, a financial institution's ability to make outsized profits, or a country's standard of living. Most of these booms end badly. Of course, debt instruments are crucial to all economies, ancient and modern, but balancing the risk and opportunities of debt is always a challenge, a challenge policy makers, investors, and ordinary citizens must never forget.

In this book we study a number of different types of financial crises. They include sovereign defaults, which occur when a government fails to meet payments on its external or domestic debt obligations or both. Then there are banking crises such as those the world has experienced in spades in the late 2000s. In a typical major banking crisis, a nation finds that a significant part of its banking sector has become insolvent after heavy investment losses, banking panics, or both. Another important class of crises consists of exchange rate crises such as those that plagued Asia, Europe, and Latin America in the 1990s. In the quintessential exchange rate crisis, the value of a country's currency falls precipitously, often despite a government "guarantee" that it will not allow this to happen under any circumstances. We also consider crises marked by bouts of very high inflation. Needless to say, unexpected increases in inflation are the de facto equivalent of outright default, for inflation allows all debtors (including the government) to repay their debts in currency that has much less purchasing power than it did when the loans were made. In much of the book we will explore these crises separately. But crises often occur in clusters. In the penultimate text chapter of the book we will look at situations—such as the Great Depression of the 1930s and the latest worldwide financial crisis—in which crises occur in bunches and on a global scale.

Of course, financial crises are nothing new. They have been around since the development of money and financial markets. Many of the earliest crises were driven by currency debasements that occurred when the monarch of a country reduced the gold or silver content of the coin of the realm to finance budget shortfalls often prompted by wars. Technological advances have long since eliminated a government's need to clip coins to fill a budget deficit. But financial crises have continued to thrive through the ages, and they plague countries to this day.

Most of our focus in this book is on two particular forms of crises that are particularly relevant today: sovereign debt crises and banking crises. Both have histories that span centuries and cut across regions. Sovereign debt crises were once commonplace among the now advanced economies that appear to have "graduated" from periodic bouts of government insolvency. In emerging markets, however, recurring (or serial) default remains a chronic and serious disease. Banking crises, in contrast, remain a recurring problem everywhere. They are an equal-opportunity menace, affecting rich and poor countries alike. Our banking crisis investigation takes us on a tour from bank runs and bank failures in Europe during the Napoleonic Wars to the recent global financial crises that began with the U.S. subprime crisis of 2007.

Our aim here is to be expansive, systematic, and quantitative: our empirical analysis covers sixty-six countries over nearly eight centuries. Many important books have been written about the history of international financial crises,[1] perhaps the most famous of which is Kindleberger's 1989 book *Manias, Panics and Crashes*.[2] By and large, however, these earlier works take an essentially narrative approach, fortified by relatively sparse data.

Here, by contrast, we build our analysis around data culled from a massive database that encompasses the entire world and goes back as far as twelfth-century China and medieval Europe. The core "life" of this book is contained in the (largely) simple tables and figures in which these data are presented rather than in narratives of personalities, politics, and negotiations. We trust that our visual quantitative history of financial crises is no less compelling than the earlier narrative approach, and we hope that it may open new vistas for policy analysis and research.

Above all, our emphasis is on looking at long spans of history to catch sight of "rare" events that are all too often forgotten, although they turn out to be far more common and similar than people seem to think. Indeed, analysts, policy makers, and even academic economists have an unfortunate tendency to view recent experience through the narrow window opened by standard data sets, typically based on a narrow range of experience in terms of countries and time periods. A large fraction of the academic and policy literature on debt and default draws conclusions based on data collected since 1980, in no small part because such data are the most readily accessible. This approach would be fine except for the fact that financial crises have much longer cycles, and a data set that covers twenty-five years simply cannot give one an adequate perspective on the risks of alternative policies and investments. An event that was rare in that twenty-five-year span may not be all that rare when placed in a longer historical context. After all, a researcher stands only a one-in-four chance of observing a "hundred-year flood" in twenty-five years' worth of data. To even begin to think about such events, one needs to compile data for several centuries. Of course, that is precisely our aim here.

In addition, standard data sets are greatly limited in several other important respects, especially in regard to their coverage of the types of government debt. In fact, as we shall see, historical data on domestically issued government debt is remarkably difficult to obtain for most countries, which have often been little more transparent than modern-day banks with their off–balance sheet transactions and other accounting shenanigans.

The foundations of our analysis are built on a comprehensive new database for studying international debt and banking crises, inflation, and currency crashes and debasements. The data come from Africa, Asia, Europe, Latin America, North America, and Oceania (data from sixty-six countries in all, as previously noted, plus selected data for a number of other countries). The range of variables encompasses, among many other dimensions, external and domestic debt, trade, national income, inflation, exchange rates, interest rates, and commodity prices. The data coverage goes back more than eight hundred years, to the date of independence for most countries and well into the colonial period for several. Of course, we recognize that the exercises and illustrations that we provide here can only scratch the surface of what a data set of this scope and scale can potentially unveil.

Fortunately, conveying the details of the data is not essential to understanding the main message of this book: we have been here before. The instruments of financial gain and loss have varied over the ages, as have the types of institutions that have expanded mightily only to fail massively. But financial crises follow a rhythm of boom and bust through the ages. Countries, institutions, and financial instruments may change across time, but human nature does not. As we will discuss in the final chapters of this book, the financial crisis of the late 2000s that originated in the United States and spread across the globe—which we refer to as the Second Great Contraction—is only the latest manifestation of this pattern.

We take up the latest crisis in the final four chapters before the conclusion, in which we review what we have learned; the reader should find the material in chapters 13–16 relatively straightforward and self-contained. (Indeed, readers interested mainly in lessons of history for the latest crisis are encouraged to jump directly to this material in a first reading.) We show that in the run-up to the sub-prime crisis, standard indicators for the United States, such as asset price inflation, rising leverage, large sustained current account deficits, and a slowing trajectory of economic growth, exhibited virtually all the signs of a country on the verge of a financial crisis—indeed, a severe one. This view of the way into a crisis is sobering; we show that the way out can be quite perilous as well. The aftermath of systemic banking crises involves a protracted and pronounced contraction in economic activity and puts significant strains on government resources.

The first part of the book gives precise definitions of concepts describing crises and discusses the data underlying the book. In the construction of our data set we have built heavily on the work of earlier scholars. However, our data set also includes a considerable amount of new material from diverse primary and secondary sources. In addition to providing a systematic dating of external debt and exchange rate crises, the appendixes to this book catalog dates for domestic inflation and banking crises. The dating of sovereign defaults on domestic (mostly local-currency) debt is one of the more novel features that rounds out our study of financial crises.

The payoff to this scrutiny comes in the remaining parts of the book, which apply these concepts to our expanded global data set. Part II turns our attention to government debt, chronicling hundreds of episodes of default by sovereign nations on their debt to external creditors. These "debt crises" have ranged from those related to mid-fourteenth-century loans by Florentine financiers to England's Edward III to German merchant bankers' loans to Spain's Hapsburg Monarchy to massive loans made by (mostly) New York bankers to

Latin America during the 1970s. Although we find that during the modern era sovereign external default crises have been far more concentrated in emerging markets than banking crises have been, we nevertheless emphasize that even sovereign defaults on external debt have been an almost universal rite of passage for every country as it has matured from an emerging market economy to an advanced developed economy. This process of economic, financial, social, and political development can take centuries.

Indeed, in its early years as a nation-state, France defaulted on its external debt no fewer than eight times (as we show in chapter 6)! Spain defaulted a mere six times prior to 1800, but, with seven defaults in the nineteenth century, surpassed France for a total of thirteen episodes. Thus, when today's European powers were going through the emerging market phase of development, they experienced recurrent problems with external debt default, just as many emerging markets do today.

From 1800 until well after World War II, Greece found itself virtually in continual default, and Austria's record is in some ways even more stunning. Although the development of international capital markets was quite limited prior to 1800, we nevertheless catalog the numerous defaults of France, Portugal, Prussia, Spain, and the early Italian city-states. At the edge of Europe, Egypt, Russia, and Turkey have histories of chronic default as well.

One of the fascinating questions raised in our book is why a relatively small number of countries, such as Australia and New Zealand, Canada, Denmark, Thailand, and the United States, have managed to avoid defaults on central government debt to foreign creditors, whereas far more countries have been characterized by serial default on their external debts.

Asian and African financial crises are far less researched than those of Europe and Latin America. Indeed, the widespread belief that modern sovereign default is a phenomenon confined to Latin America and a few poorer European countries is heavily colored by the paucity of research on other regions. As we shall see, precommunist China repeatedly defaulted on international debts, and modern-day India and Indonesia both defaulted in the 1960s, long before the first postwar round of Latin defaults. Postcolonial Africa has a default record that looks as if it is set to outstrip that of any previously emerging market region. Overall, we find that a systematic quantitative examination of the postcolonial default records of Asia and Africa debunks the notion that most countries have avoided the perils of sovereign default.

The near universality of default becomes abundantly clear in part II, where we begin to use the data set to paint the history of default and financial crises in broad strokes using tables and figures. One point that certainly jumps out from the analysis is that the fairly recent (2003–2008) quiet spell in which governments have generally honored their debt obligations is far from the norm.

The history of domestic public debt (i.e., internally issued government debt) in emerging markets, in particular, has largely been ignored by contemporary scholars and policy makers (even by official data providers such as the International Monetary Fund), who seemed to view its emergence at the beginning of the twenty-first century as a stunning new phenomenon. Yet, as we will show in part III, domestic public debt in emerging markets has been extremely significant during many periods and in fact potentially helps resolve a host of puzzles pertaining to episodes of high inflation and default. We view the difficulties one experiences in finding data on government debt as just one facet of the general low level of transparency with which most governments maintain their books. Think of the implicit guarantees given to the massive mortgage lenders that ultimately added trillions to the effective size of the U.S. national debt in 2008, the trillions of dollars in off–balance sheet transactions engaged in by the Federal Reserve, and the implicit guarantees involved in taking bad assets off bank balance sheets, not to mention unfunded pension and medical liabilities. Lack of transparency is endemic in government debt, but the difficulty of finding basic historical data on central government debt is almost comical.

Part III also offers a first attempt to catalog episodes of overt default on and rescheduling of domestic public debt across more than a century. (Because so much of the history of domestic debt has largely been forgotten by scholars, not surprisingly, so too has its history of default.) This phenomenon appears to be somewhat rarer than external default but is far too common to justify the extreme assumption that governments always honor the nominal face value of domestic debt, an assumption that dominates the economics literature. When overt default on domestic debt does occur, it appears to occur in situations of greater duress than those that lead to pure external default—in terms of both an implosion of output and a marked escalation of inflation.

Part IV broadens our discussion to include crises related to banking, currency, and inflation. Until very recently, the study of banking crises has typically focused either on earlier historical experiences in advanced countries, mainly the banking panics before World War II, or on modern-day experiences in emerging markets. This dichotomy has perhaps been shaped by the belief that for advanced economies, destabilizing, systemic, multicountry financial crises are a relic of the past. Of course, the recent global financial crisis emanating out of the United States and Europe has dashed this misconception, albeit at great social cost.

The fact is that banking crises have long plagued rich and poor countries alike. We reach this conclusion after examining banking crises ranging from Denmark's financial panic during the Napoleonic Wars to the recent first global financial crisis of the twenty-first century. The incidence of banking crises proves to be remarkably similar in the high- and the middle- to low-income countries. Banking crises almost invariably lead to sharp declines in tax revenues as well as significant increases in government spending (a share of which is presumably dissipative). On average, government debt rises by 86 percent during the three years following a banking crisis. These indirect fiscal consequences are thus an order of magnitude larger than the usual costs of bank bailouts.

Episodes of treacherously high inflation are another recurrent theme. No emerging market country in history has managed to escape bouts of high inflation. Indeed, there is a very strong parallel between our proposition that few countries have avoided serial default on external debt and the proposition that few countries have avoided serial bouts of high inflation. Even the United States has had a checkered history, including in 1779, when the inflation rate approached 200 percent. Early on across the world, as already noted, the main device for defaulting on government obligations was that of debasing the content of the coinage. Modern currency presses are just a technologically advanced and more efficient approach to achieving the same end. As a consequence, a clear inflationary bias throughout history emerges. Starting in the twentieth century, inflation spiked radically higher. Since then, inflation crises have stepped up to a higher plateau. Unsurprisingly, then, the more modern period also has seen a higher incidence of exchange rate crashes and larger median changes in currency values. Perhaps more surprising, and made visible only by a broader historical context, are the early episodes of pronounced exchange rate instability, notably during the Napoleonic Wars.

Just as financial crises have common macroeconomic antecedents in asset prices, economic activity, external indicators, and so on, so do common patterns appear in the sequencing (temporal order) in which crises unfold, the final subject of part IV.

The concluding chapter offers some reflections on crises, policy, and pathways for academic study. What is certainly clear is that again and again, countries, banks, individuals, and firms take on excessive debt in good times without enough awareness of the risks that will follow when the inevitable recession hits. Many players in the global financial system often dig a debt hole far larger than they can reasonably expect to escape from, most famously the United States and its financial system in the late 2000s. Government and government-guaranteed debt (which, due to deposit insurance, often implicitly includes bank debt) is certainly the most problematic, for it can accumulate massively and for long periods without being put in check by markets, especially where regulation prevents them from effectively doing so. Although private debt certainly plays a key role in many crises, government debt is far more often the unifying problem across the wide range of financial crises we examine. As we stated earlier, the fact that basic data on domestic debt are so opaque and difficult to obtain is proof that governments will go to great lengths to hide their books when things are going wrong, just as financial insti-

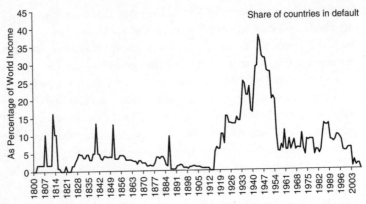

Figure P.1. Sovereign external debt, 1800–2008: Percentage of countries in external default or restructuring weighted by their share of world income.

tutions have done in the contemporary financial crisis. We see a major role for international policy-making organizations, such as the International Monetary Fund, in providing government debt accounts that are more transparent than those available today.

Our immersion in the details of crises that have arisen over the past eight centuries and in data on them has led us to conclude that the most commonly repeated and most expensive investment advice ever given in the boom just before a financial crisis stems from the perception that "this time is different." That advice, that the old rules of valuation no longer apply, is usually followed up with vigor. Financial professionals and, all too often, government leaders explain that we are doing things better than before, we are smarter, and we have learned from past mistakes. Each time, society convinces itself that the current boom, unlike the many booms that preceded catastrophic collapses in the past, is built on sound fundamentals, structural reforms, technological innovation, and good policy.

Given the sweeping data on which this book has been built, it is simply not possible to provide textural context to all the hundreds of episodes the data encompass. Nevertheless, the tables and figures speak very powerfully for themselves of the phenomenal recurrent nature of the problem. Take figure P.1, which shows the percentage of countries worldwide, weighted by GDP, that have been in a state of default on their external debt at any time.

The short period of the 2000s, represented by the right-hand tail of the chart, looks sufficiently benign. But was it right for so many policy makers to declare by 2005 that the problem of sovereign default on external debt had gone into deep remission? Unfortunately, even before the ink is dry on this book, the answer will be clear enough. We hope that the weight of evidence in this book will give future policy makers and investors a bit more pause before next they declare, "This time is different." It almost never is.

ACKNOWLEDGMENTS

A book so long in the making generates many debts of gratitude. Among those who helped is Vincent Reinhart, who consulted on the economic and statistical content and edited and re-edited all the chapters. He also provided the anecdote that led to the book's title. Vincent worked for the Federal Reserve for almost a quarter century. Back around the time of the collapse of the hedge fund Long-Term Capital Management in 1998, which seemed like a major crisis then but seems less so given recent events, he attended a meeting of the board of governors with market practitioners. A trader with an un-characteristically long memory explained, "More money has been lost because of four words than at the point of a gun. Those words are 'This time is different.'"

A special debt of gratitude is owed to Jane Trahan for her ex-tremely helpful and thorough editing of the manuscript, and to our editor at Princeton University Press, Seth Ditchik, for his suggestions and editorial guidance throughout this process. Ethan Ilzetzki, Fer-nando Im, Vania Stavrakeva, Katherine Waldock, Chenzi Xu, and Jan Zilinsky provided excellent research assistance. We are also grate-ful to Peter Strupp and his colleagues at Princeton Editorial Associ-ates for skillfully negotiating all the technical details of producing this volume.

PREAMBLE: SOME INITIAL INTUITIONS ON FINANCIAL FRAGILITY AND THE FICKLE NATURE OF CONFIDENCE

This book summarizes the long history of financial crises in their many guises across many countries. Before heading into the deep waters of experience, this chapter will attempt to sketch an economic framework to help the reader understand why financial crises tend to be both unpredictable and damaging. As the book unfolds, we will take other opportunities to guide interested readers through the related academic literature when it is absolutely critical to our story. Rest assured that these are only short detours, and those unconcerned with economic theory as an engine of discovery can bypass these byways.

As we shall argue, economic theory proposes plausible reasons that financial markets, particularly ones reliant on leverage (which means that they have thin capital compared to the amount of assets at stake), can be quite fragile and subject to crises of confidence.[1] Unfortunately, theory gives little guidance on the exact timing or duration of these crises, which is why we focus so on experience.

Perhaps more than anything else, failure to recognize the precariousness and fickleness of confidence—especially in cases in which large short-term debts need to be rolled over continuously—is the key factor that gives rise to the this-time-is-different syndrome. Highly indebted governments, banks, or corporations can seem to be merrily rolling along for an extended period, when *bang!*—confidence collapses, lenders disappear, and a crisis hits.

The simplest and most familiar example is bank runs (which we take up in more detail in the chapter on banking crises). We talk about banks for two reasons. First, that is the route along which the academic literature developed. Second, much of our historical data set applies to the borrowing of banks and of governments. (Other large and liquid participants in credit markets are relatively new entrants to the world of finance.) However, our examples are quite illustrative of a broader phenomenon of financial fragility. Many of the same general principles apply to these market actors, whether they be government-sponsored enterprises, investment banks, or money market mutual funds.

Banks traditionally borrow at short term. That is, they borrow in the form of deposits that can be redeemed on relatively short notice. But the loans they make mostly have a far longer maturity and can be difficult to convert into cash on short notice. For example, a bank financing the expansion of a local hardware store might be reasonably confident of repayment in the long run as the store expands its business and revenues. But early in the expansion, the bank may have no easy way to call in the loan. The store owner simply has insufficient revenues, particularly if forced to make payments on principal as well as interest.

A bank with a healthy deposit base and a large portfolio of illiquid loans may well have bright prospects over the long term. However, if for some reason, depositors all try to withdraw their funds at once—say, because of panic based on a false rumor that the bank has lost money gambling on exotic mortgages—trouble ensues. Absent a way to sell its illiquid loan portfolio, the bank might simply not be able to pay off its panicked depositors. Such was the fate of the banks in the classic movies *It's a Wonderful Life* and *Mary Poppins*. Those movies were rooted in reality: many banks have shared this fate, particularly when the government has not fully guaranteed bank deposits.

The most famous recent example of a bank run is the run on the United Kingdom's Northern Rock bank. Panicked depositors, not satisfied with the British government's partial insurance scheme, formed long queues in September 2007. The broadening panic eventually forced the British government to take over the bank and more fully back its liabilities.

Other borrowers, not just banks, can suffer from a crisis of confidence. During the financial crisis that started in the United States in 2007, huge financial giants in the "shadow banking" system outside regulated banks suffered similar problems. Although they borrowed mainly from banks and other financial institutions, their vulnerability was the same. As confidence in the investments they had made fell, lenders increasingly refused to roll over their short-term loans, and they were forced to throw assets on the market at fire-sale prices. Distressed sales drove prices down further, leading to further losses and downward-spiraling confidence. Eventually, the U.S. government had to step in to try to prop up the market; the drama is still unfolding, and the price tag for resolution continues to mount.

Governments can be subject to the same dynamics of fickle expectations that can destabilize banks. This is particularly so when a government borrows from external lenders over whom it has relatively little influence. Most government investments directly or indirectly involve the long-run growth potential of the country and its tax base, but these are highly illiquid assets. Suppose, for example, that a country has a public debt burden that seems manageable given its current tax revenues, growth projections, and market interest rates. If the market becomes concerned that a populist fringe candidate is going to win the next election and raise spending so much that the debt will become difficult to manage, investors may suddenly balk at rolling over short-term debt at rates the country can manage. A credit crisis unfolds.

Although these kinds of scenarios are not everyday events, over the long course of history and the broad range of countries we cover in this book, such financial crises occur all too frequently. Why cannot big countries, or even the world as a whole, find a way to put a stop to crises of confidence, at least premature ones? It is possible, but there is a rub. Suppose a world government agency provided expansive deposit insurance to protect every worthy borrower from panics. Say there was a super-sized version of the International Monetary Fund (IMF), today's main multilateral lender that aims to help emerging markets when they run into liquidity crises. The problem is that if one provides insurance to everyone everywhere, with no conditions, some players are going to misbehave. If the IMF lent too much with too few conditions, the IMF itself would be bankrupt in short order, and financial crises would be unchecked. Complete insurance against crises is neither feasible nor desirable. (Exactly this conundrum will face the global financial community in the wake of the latest financial crisis, with the IMF's lending resources having been increased fourfold in response to the crisis while, at the same time, lending conditionality has been considerably relaxed.)

What does economic theory have to say about countries' vulnerability to financial crises? For concreteness, let us focus for now on governments, the main source of the crises examined in this book. Economic theory tells us that if a government is sufficiently frugal, it is not terribly vulnerable to crises of confidence. A government does not have to worry too much about debt crises if it consistently runs fiscal surpluses (which happens when tax receipts exceed expenditures), maintains relatively low debt levels, mostly borrows at longer-term maturities (say ten years or more), and does not have too many hidden off–balance sheet guarantees.

If, in contrast, a government runs large deficits year after year, concentrating its borrowing at shorter-term maturities (of say one year or less), it becomes vulnerable, perhaps even at debt-burden levels that seemingly should be quite manageable. Of course, an ill-intentioned government could try to reduce its vulnerability by attempting to issue large amounts of long-term debt. But most likely, markets would quickly catch on and charge extremely high interest rates on any long-dated borrowing. Indeed, a principal reason that some governments choose to borrow at shorter maturities instead of longer maturities is precisely so that they can benefit from lower interest rates as long as confidence lasts.

Economic theory tells us that it is precisely the fickle nature of confidence, including its dependence on the public's expectation of future events, that makes it so difficult to predict the timing of debt crises. High debt levels lead, in many mathematical economics models, to "multiple equilibria" in which the debt level might be sustained

—or might not be.[2] Economists do not have a terribly good idea of what kinds of events shift confidence and of how to concretely assess confidence vulnerability. What one does see, again and again, in the history of financial crises is that when an accident is waiting to happen, it eventually does. When countries become too deeply indebted, they are headed for trouble. When debt-fueled asset price explosions seem too good to be true, they probably are. But the exact timing can be very difficult to guess, and a crisis that seems imminent can sometimes take years to ignite. Such was certainly the case of the United States in the late 2000s. As we show in chapter 13, all the red lights were blinking in the run-up to the crisis. But until the "accident," many financial leaders in the United States—and indeed many academics—were still arguing that "this time is different."

We would like to note that our caution about excessive debt burdens and leverage for governments is different from the admonitions of the traditional public choice literature of Buchanan and others.[3] The traditional public finance literature warns about the shortsightedness of governments in running fiscal deficits and their chronic failure to weigh the long-run burden that servicing debt will force on their citizens. In fact, excessive debt burdens often generate problems in the nearer term, precisely because investors may have doubts about the country's will to finance the debt over the longer term. The fragility of debt can be every bit as great a problem as its long-term tax burden, at times even greater.

Similar fragility problems arise in other crisis contexts that we will consider in this book. One of the lessons of the 1980s and 1990s is that countries maintaining fixed or "highly managed" exchange rate regimes are vulnerable to sudden crises of confidence. Speculative attacks on fixed exchange rates can blow up overnight seemingly stable long-lived regimes. During the period of the successful fix, there is always plenty of this-time-is-different commentary. But then, as in the case of Argentina in December 2001, all the confidence can collapse in a puff of smoke. There is a fundamental link to debt, however. As Krugman famously showed, exchange rate crises often have their roots in a government's unwillingness to adopt fiscal and monetary policies consistent with maintaining a fixed exchange rate.[4] If speculators realize the government is eventually going to run out of the resources needed to back the currency, they will all be looking to time their move out of the currency in anticipation of the eventual crash. Public debts do not always have to be explicit; contingent government guarantees have been at the crux of many a crisis.

Certainly countries have ways of making themselves less vulnerable to crises of confidence short of simply curtailing their borrowing and leverage. Economic theory suggests that greater transparency helps. As the reader shall see later on, governments tend to be anything but transparent when it comes to borrowing. And as the financial crisis of the late 2000s shows, private borrowers are often little better unless government regulation forces them to be more transparent. A country with stronger legal and regulatory institutions can certainly borrow more. Indeed, many scholars consider Britain's development of superior institutions for making debt repayment credible a key to its military and development successes in the eighteenth and nineteenth centuries.[5] But even good institutions and a sophisticated financial system can run into problems if faced with enough strains, as the United States has learned so painfully in the most recent crisis.

Finally, there is the question of why financial crises tend to be so painful, a topic we take up mainly in the introduction to chapter 10 on banking crises. In brief, most economies, even relatively poor ones, depend on the financial sector to channel money from savers (typically consumers) to investment projects around the economy. If a crisis paralyzes the banking system, it is very difficult for an economy to resume normal economic activity. Ben Bernanke famously advanced bank collapse as an important reason that the Great Depression of the 1930s lasted so long and hit so hard. So financial crises, particularly those that are large and difficult to resolve, can have profound effects. Again, as in the case of multiple equilibria and financial fragility, there is a large economic theory literature on the topic.[6] This strong connection between financial markets and real economic activity, particularly when financial markets cease to function, is what has made so many of the crises we consider in this book such spectacular historic events. Consider, in contrast, the collapse of the tech stock bubble in 2001. Although technology stocks soared and collapsed, the effect on the real economy was only the relatively mild recession of 2001. Bubbles are far more dangerous when they are fueled by debt, as in the case of the global housing price explosion of the early 2000s.

Surely, the Second Great Contraction—as we term the financial crisis of the late 2000s, which has spread to nearly every region—will have a profound effect on economics, particularly the study of linkages between financial markets and the real economy.[7] We hope some of the facts laid out in this book will be helpful in framing the problems that the new theories need to explain, not just for the recent crisis but for the multitude of crises that have occurred in the past, not to mention the many that have yet to unfold.

THIS

TIME

IS

DIFFERENT

- PART I -

FINANCIAL CRISES:
AN OPERATIONAL PRIMER

The essence of the this-time-is-different syndrome is simple. It is rooted in the firmly held belief that financial crises are things that happen to other people in other countries at other times; crises do not happen to us, here and now. We are doing things better, we are smarter, we have learned from past mistakes. The old rules of valuation no longer apply. Unfortunately, a highly leveraged economy can unwittingly be sitting with its back at the edge of a financial cliff for many years before chance and circumstance provoke a crisis of confidence that pushes it off.

- 1 -

VARIETIES OF CRISES
AND THEIR DATES

Because this book is grounded in a quantitative and historical analysis of crises, it is important to begin by defining exactly what constitutes a financial crisis, as well as the methods—quantitative where possible—by which we date its beginning and end. This chapter and the two that follow lay out the basic concepts, definitions, methodology, and approach toward data collection and analysis that underpin our study of the historical international experience with almost any kind of economic crisis, be it a sovereign debt default, banking, inflation, or exchange rate crisis.

Delving into precise definitions of a crisis in an initial chapter rather than simply including them in a glossary may seem somewhat tedious. But for the reader to properly interpret the sweeping historical figures and tables that follow later in this volume, it is essential to have a sense of how we delineate what constitutes a crisis and what does not. The boundaries we draw are generally consistent with the existing empirical economics literature, which by and large is segmented across the various types of crises we consider (e.g., sovereign debt, exchange rate). We try to highlight any cases in which results are conspicuously sensitive to small changes in our cutoff points or where we are particularly concerned about clear inadequacies in the data. This definition chapter also gives us a convenient opportunity to expand a bit more on the variety of crises we take up in this book.

The reader should note that the crisis markers discussed in this chapter refer to the measurement of crises within individual countries. Later on, we discuss a number of ways to think about the international dimensions of crises and their intensity and transmission, culminating in our definition of a global crisis in chapter 16. In addition to reporting on one country at a time, our root measures of crisis thresholds report on only one type of crisis at a time (e.g., exchange rate crashes, inflation, banking crises). As we emphasize, particularly in chapter 16, different varieties of crises tend to fall in clusters, suggesting that it may be possible, in principle, to have systemic definitions of crises. But for a number of reasons, we prefer to focus on the simplest and most transparent delineation of crisis episodes, especially because doing otherwise would make it very difficult to make broad comparisons across countries and time. These definitions of crises are rooted in the existing empirical literature and referenced accordingly.

We begin by discussing crises that can readily be given strict quantitative definitions, then turn to those for which we must rely on more qualitative and judgmental analysis. The concluding section defines *serial default* and the *this-time-is-different syndrome*, concepts that will recur throughout the remainder of the book.

Crises Defined by Quantitative Thresholds: Inflation, Currency Crashes, and Debasement

Inflation Crises

We begin by defining inflation crises, both because of their universality and long historical significance and because of the relative simplicity and clarity with which they can be identified. Because we are interested in cataloging the extent of default (through inflating debt away) and not only its frequency, we will attempt to mark not only the beginning of an inflation or currency crisis episode but its duration as well. Many high-inflation spells can best be described as chronic—lasting many years, sometimes dissipating and sometimes plateauing at an intermediate level before exploding. A number of studies, including our own earlier work on classifying post–World War II exchange rate arrangements, use a twelve-month inflation threshold of 40 percent or higher as the mark of a high-inflation episode. Of course, one can argue that the effects of inflation are pernicious at much lower levels of inflation, say 10 percent, but the costs of sustained moderate inflation are not well established either theoretically or empirically. In our earlier work on the post–World War II era, we chose a 40 percent cutoff because there is a fairly broad consensus that such levels are pernicious; we discuss general inflation trends and lower peaks where significant. Hyperinflations—inflation rates of 40 percent *per month*—are of modern vintage. As we will see in chapter 12 on inflation crises (especially in table 12.3), Hungary in 1946 (Zimbabwe's recent experience notwithstanding) holds the record in our sample.

For the pre–World War I period, however, even 40 percent *per annum* is too high an inflation threshold, because inflation rates were much lower then, especially before the advent of modern paper currency (often referred to as "fiat" currency because it has no intrinsic value and is worth something only because the government declares by fiat that other currencies are not legal tender in domestic transactions). The median inflation rates before World War I were well below those of the more recent period: 0.5 percent per annum for 1500–1799 and 0.71 percent for 1800–1913, in contrast with 5.0 percent for 1914–2006. In periods with much lower average inflation rates and little expectation of high inflation, much lower inflation rates could be quite shocking and traumatic to an economy—and therefore considered crises.[1] Thus, in this book, in order to meaningfully incorporate earlier periods, we adopt an inflation crisis threshold of 20 percent per annum. At most of the main points at which we believe there were inflation crises, our main assertions appear to be reasonably robust relative to our choice of threshold; for example, our assertion that there was a crisis at any given point would stand up had we defined inflation crises using a lower threshold of, say, 15 percent, or a higher threshold of, say, 25 percent. Of course, given that we are making most of our data set available online, readers are free to set their own threshold for inflation or for other quantitative crisis benchmarks.

Currency Crashes

In order to date currency crashes, we follow a variant of an approach introduced by Jeffrey Frankel and Andrew Rose, who focus exclusively on large exchange rate depreciations and set their basic threshold (subject to some caveats) as 25 percent per annum.[2] This definition is the most parsimonious, for it does not rely on other variables such as reserve losses (data governments often guard jealously —sometimes long delaying their publication) and interest rate hikes (which are not terribly meaningful in financial systems under very heavy government control, which was in fact the case for most countries until relatively recently). As with inflation, the 25 percent threshold that one might apply to data from the period after World War II—at least to define a severe exchange rate crisis—would be too high for the earlier period, when much smaller movements constituted huge surprises and were therefore extremely disruptive. Therefore, we define as a currency crash an annual depreciation in excess of 15 percent. Mirroring our treatment of inflation episodes, we are concerned here not only with the dating of the initial crash (as in Frankel and Rose as well as Kaminsky and Reinhart) but with the full period in which annual depreciations exceeded the threshold.[3] It is hardly surprising that the largest crashes shown in table 1.1 are similar in timing and order of magnitude to the profile for inflation crises. The "honor" of the record currency crash, however, goes not to Hungary (as in the case of inflation) but to Greece in 1944.

Currency Debasement

The precursor of modern inflation and foreign exchange rate crises was currency debasement during the long era in which the principal means of exchange was metallic coins. Not surprisingly, debasements were particularly frequent and large during wars, when drastic reductions in the silver content of the currency sometimes provided sovereigns with their most important source of financing.

In this book we also date currency "reforms" or conversions and their magnitudes. Such conversions form a part of every hyperinflation episode in our sample; indeed it is not unusual to see that there were several conversions in quick succession. For example, in its struggle with hyperinflation, Brazil had no fewer than four currency conversions from 1986 to 1994. When we began to work on this book, in terms of the magnitude of a single conversion, the record holder was China, which in 1948 had a conversion rate of three million to one. Alas, by the time of its completion, that record was surpassed by

TABLE 1.1
Defining crises: A summary of quantitative thresholds

Crisis type	Threshold	Period	Maximum (percent)
Inflation	An annual inflation rate of 20 percent or higher. We examine separately the incidence of more extreme cases in which inflation exceeds 40 percent per annum.	1500–1790 1800–1913 1914–2008	173.1 159.6 9.63E+26[a]
Currency crash	An annual depreciation versus the U.S. dollar (or the relevant anchor currency— historically the U.K. pound, the French franc, or the German DM and presently the euro) of 15 percent or more.	1800–1913 1914–2008	275.7 3.37E+9
Currency debasement: Type I	A reduction in the metallic content of coins in circulation of 5 percent or more.	1258–1799 1800–1913	−56.8 −55.0
Currency debasement: Type II	A currency reform whereby a new currency replaces a much-depreciated earlier currency in circulation.	The most extreme episode is the recent Zimbabwean conversion at a rate of ten billion to one.	

[a]In some cases the inflation rates are so large (as in Hungary in 1946, for example) that we are forced to use scientific notation. Thus, E+26 means that we have to add zeroes and move the decimal point twenty-six places to the right in the 9.63 entry.

Zimbabwe with a ten-billion-to-one conversion! Conversions also follow spells of high (but not necessarily hyper) inflation, and these cases are also included in our list of modern debasements.

The Bursting of Asset Price Bubbles

The same quantitative methodology could be applied in dating the bursting of asset price bubbles (equity or real estate), which are commonplace in the run-up to banking crises. We discuss these crash episodes involving equity prices in chapter 16 and leave real estate crises for future research.[4] One reason we do not tackle the issue here is that price data for many key assets underlying financial crises, particularly housing prices, are extremely difficult to come by on a long-term cross-country basis. However, our data set does include housing prices for a number of both developed and emerging market countries over the past couple of decades, which we shall exploit later in our analysis of banking crises.

Crises Defined by Events: Banking Crises and External and Domestic Default

In this section we describe the criteria used in this study to date banking crises, external debt crises, and domestic debt crisis counterparts, the last of which are by far the least well documented and understood. Box 1.1 provides a brief glossary to the key concepts of debt used throughout our analysis.

Banking Crises

With regard to banking crises, our analysis stresses events. The main reason we use this approach has to do with the lack of long-range time series data that would allow us to date banking or financial crises quantitatively along the lines of inflation or currency crashes. For example, the relative price of bank stocks (or financial institutions relative to the market) would be a logical indicator to examine. However, doing this is problematic, particularly for the earlier part of our sample and for developing countries, where many domestic banks do not have publicly traded equity.

Another idea would be to use changes in bank deposits to date crises. In cases in which the beginning of a banking crisis has been marked by bank runs and withdrawals, this indicator would work well, for example in dating the numerous banking panics of the

---

BOX 1.1
Debt glossary

External debt   The total debt liabilities of a country with foreign creditors, both official (public) and private. Creditors often determine all the terms of the debt contracts, which are normally subject to the jurisdiction of the foreign creditors or to international law (for multilateral credits).

Total government debt (total public debt)   The total debt liabilities of a government with both domestic and foreign creditors. The "government" normally comprises the central administration, provincial governments, federal governments, and all other entities that borrow with an explicit government guarantee.

Government domestic debt   All debt liabilities of a government that are issued under and subject to national jurisdiction, regardless of the nationality of the creditor or the currency denomination of the debt; therefore, it includes government foreign-currency domestic debt, as defined below. The terms of the debt contracts can be determined by the market or set unilaterally by the government.

Government foreign-currency domestic debt   Debt liabilities of a government issued under national jurisdiction that are nonetheless expressed in (or linked to) a currency different from the national currency of the country.

Central bank debt   Not usually included under government debt, despite the fact that it usually carries an implicit government guarantee. Central banks usually issue such debt to facilitate open market operations (including sterilized intervention). Such debts may be denominated in either local or foreign currency.

1800s. Often, however, banking problems arise not from the liability side but from a protracted deterioration in asset quality, be it from a collapse in real estate prices (as in the United States at the outset of the 2007 subprime financial crisis) or from increased bankruptcies in the nonfinancial sector (as in later stages of the financial crisis of the late 2000s). In this case, a large increase in bankruptcies or nonperforming loans could be used to mark the onset of the crisis. Unfortunately, indicators of business failures and nonperforming loans are usually available sporadically, if at all, even for the modern period in many countries. In any event, reports of nonperforming loans are often wildly inaccurate, for banks try to hide their problems for as long as possible and supervisory agencies often look the other way.

Given these data limitations, we mark a banking crisis by two types of events: (1) bank runs that lead to the closure, merging, or takeover by the public sector of one or more financial institutions (as in Venezuela in 1993 or Argentina in 2001) and (2) if there are no runs, the closure, merging, takeover, or large-scale government assistance of an important financial institution (or group of institutions) that marks the start of a string of similar outcomes for other financial institutions (as in Thailand from 1996 to 1997). We rely on existing studies of banking crises and on the financial press. Financial stress is almost invariably extremely great during these periods.

There are several main sources for cross-country dating of crises. For the period after 1970, the comprehensive and well-known studies by Caprio and Klingebiel—the most updated version of which covers the period through 2003—are authoritative, especially in terms of classifying banking crises into systemic versus more benign categories. Kaminsky and Reinhart, and Jácome (the latter for Latin America), round out the sources.[5] In addition, we draw on many country-specific studies that pick up episodes of banking crisis not covered by the multicountry literature; these country-specific studies make an important contribution to this chronology.[6] A summary discussion of the limitations of this event-based dating approach is presented in table 1.2. The years in which the banking crises began are listed in appendixes A.3 and A.4 (for most early episodes it is difficult to ascertain exactly how long the crisis lasted).

External Debt Crises

External debt crises involve outright default on a government's external debt obligations—that is, a default on a payment to creditors of a loan issued under another country's jurisdiction, typically (but not always) denominated in a foreign currency, and typically held mostly by foreign creditors. Argentina holds the record for the largest default; in 2001 it defaulted on more than $95 billion in external

TABLE 1.2
Defining crises by events: A summary

Type of crisis	Definition and/or criteria	Comments
Banking crisis Type I: systemic (severe) Type II: financial distress (milder)	We mark a banking crisis by two types of events: (1) bank runs that lead to the closure, merging, or takeover by the public sector of one or more financial institutions and (2) if there are no runs, the closure, merging, takeover, or large-scale government assistance of an important financial institution (or group of institutions) that marks the start of a string of similar outcomes for other financial institutions.	This approach to dating the beginning of banking crises is not without drawbacks. It could date crises too late, because the financial problems usually begin well before a bank is finally closed or merged; it could also date crises too early, because the worst of a crisis may come later. Unlike in the case of external debt crises (see below), which have well-defined closure dates, it is often difficult or impossible to accurately pinpoint the year in which the crisis ended.
Debt crisis External	A sovereign default is defined as the failure of a government to meet a principal or interest payment on the due date (or within the specified grace period). These episodes include instances in which rescheduled debt is ultimately extinguished in terms less favorable than the original obligation.	Although the time of default is accurately classified as a crisis year, in a large number of cases the final resolution with the creditors (if it ever did take place) seems indeterminate. For this reason we also work with a crisis dummy that picks up only the first year.
Domestic	The definition given above for an external debt crisis applies. In addition, domestic debt crises have involved the freezing of bank deposits and/or forcible conversions of such deposits from dollars to local currency.	There is at best some partial documentation of recent defaults on domestic debt provided by Standard and Poor's. Historically, it is very difficult to date these episodes, and in many cases (such as those of banking crises) it is impossible to ascertain the date of the final resolution.

debt. In the case of Argentina, the default was managed by reducing and stretching out interest payments. Sometimes countries repudiate the debt outright, as in the case of Mexico in 1867, when more than $100 million worth of peso debt issued by Emperor Maximilian was repudiated by the Juarez government. More typically, though, the government restructures debt on terms less favorable to the lender than were those in the original contract (for instance, India's little-known external restructurings in 1958–1972).

External defaults have received considerable attention in the academic literature from leading modern-day economic historians, such as Michael Bordo, Barry Eichengreen, Marc Flandreau, Peter Lindert, John Morton, and Alan Taylor.[7] Relative to early banking crises (not to mention domestic debt crises, which have been all but ignored in the literature), much is known about the causes and consequences of these rather dramatic episodes. The dates of sovereign defaults and restructurings are those listed and discussed in chapter 6. For the period after 1824, the majority of dates come from several Standard and Poor's studies listed in the data appendixes. However, these are incomplete, missing numerous postwar restructurings and early defaults, so this source has been supplemented with additional information.[8]

Although external default dates are, by and large, clearly defined and far less contentious than, say, the dates of banking crises (for which the end is often unclear), some judgment calls are still required, as we discuss in chapter 8. For example, in cataloging the number of times a country has defaulted, we generally categorize any default that occurs two years or less after a previous default as part of the same episode. Finding the end date for sovereign external defaults, although easier than in the case of banking crises (because a formal agreement with creditors often marks the termination), still presents a number of issues.

Although the time of default is accurately classified as a crisis year, in a large number of cases the final resolution with the creditors (if it ever was achieved) seems interminable. Russia's 1918 default following the revolution holds the record, lasting sixty-nine years. Greece's default in 1826 shut it out of international capital markets for fifty-three consecutive years, and Honduras's 1873 default had a comparable duration.[9] Of course, looking at the full default episode is useful for characterizing borrowing or default cycles, calculating "hazard" rates, and so on. But it is hardly credible that a spell of fifty-three years could be considered a crisis—even if those years were not exactly prosperous. Thus, in addition to constructing the country-specific dummy variables to cover the entire episode, we have employed two other qualitative variables aimed at encompassing the core crisis period surrounding the default. The first of these records only the year of default as a crisis, while the second creates a seven-year window centered on the default date. The rationale is that neither the three years that precede a default nor the three years that follow it can be considered a "normal" or "tranquil" period. This technique allows analysis of the behavior of various economic and financial indicators around the crisis on a consistent basis over time and across countries.

Domestic Debt Crises

Domestic public debt is issued under a country's own legal jurisdiction. In most countries, over most of their history, domestic debt has been denominated in the local currency and held mainly by residents. By the same token, the overwhelming majority of external public debt—debt under the legal jurisdiction of foreign governments—has been denominated in foreign currency and held by foreign residents.

Information on domestic debt crises is scarce, but not because these crises do not take place. Indeed, as we illustrate in chapter 9, domestic debt crises typically occur against a backdrop of much worse economic conditions than the average external default. Usually, however, domestic debt crises do not involve powerful external creditors. Perhaps this may help explain why so many episodes go unnoticed in the mainstream business and financial press and why studies of such crises are underrepresented in the academic literature. Of course, this is not always the case. Mexico's much-publicized near-default in 1994–1995 certainly qualifies as a "famous" domestic default crisis, although not many observers may realize that the bulk of the problem debt was technically domestic and not external. In fact, the government debt (in the form of *tesobonos,* mostly short-term debt instruments repayable in pesos linked to the U.S. dollar), which was on the verge of default until the country was bailed out by the International Monetary Fund and the U.S. Treasury, was issued under domestic Mexican law and therefore was part of Mexico's domestic debt. One can only speculate that if the *tesobonos* had not been so widely held by nonresidents, perhaps this crisis would have received far less attention. Since 1980, Argentina has defaulted three times on its domestic debt. The two domestic debt defaults that coincided with defaults on external debt (1982 and 2001) attracted considerable international attention. However, the large-scale 1989 default that did not involve a new default on external debt—and therefore did not involve nonresidents—is scarcely known in the literature. The many defaults on domestic debt that occurred during the Great Depression of the 1930s in both advanced economies and developing ones are not terribly well documented. Even where domestic defaults are documented in official volumes on debt, it is often only footnotes that refer to arrears or suspensions of payments.

Finally, some of the domestic defaults that involved the forcible conversion of foreign currency deposits into local currency have occurred during banking crises, hyperinflations, or a combination of the two (defaults in Argentina, Bolivia, and Peru are in this list). Our approach to constructing categorical variables follows that previously described for external debt default. Like banking crises and unlike external debt defaults, for many episodes of domestic default the endpoint for the crisis is not easily established.

Other Key Concepts

Serial Default

Serial default refers to multiple sovereign defaults on external or domestic public (or publicly guaranteed) debt, or both. These defaults may occur five or fifty years apart, and they can range from wholesale default (or repudiation) to partial default through rescheduling (usually stretching interest payments out at more favorable terms for the debtor). As we discuss in chapter 4, wholesale default is actually quite rare, although it may be decades before creditors receive any type of partial repayment.

The This-Time-Is-Different Syndrome

The essence of the this-time-is-different syndrome is simple.[10] It is rooted in the firmly held belief that financial crises are things that happen to other people in other countries at other times; crises do not happen to us, here and now. We are doing things better, we are smarter, we have learned from past mistakes. The old rules of valuation no longer apply. The current boom, unlike the many booms that preceded catastrophic collapses in the past (even in our country), is built on sound fundamentals, structural reforms, technological innovation, and good policy. Or so the story goes.

In the preamble we have already provided a theoretical rationale for the this-time-is-different syndrome based on the fragility of highly leveraged economies, in particular their vulnerability to crises of confidence. Certainly historical examples of the this-time-is-different syndrome are plentiful. It is not our intention to provide a catalog of these, but examples are sprinkled throughout the book. For example, box 1.2 exhibits a 1929 advertisement that embodies the spirit of "this time is different" in the run-up to the Great Depression, and box 6.2 explores the Latin American lending boom of the 1820s, which marked the first debt crisis for that region.

A short list of the manifestations of the syndrome over the past century is as follows:

1. The buildup to the emerging market defaults of the 1930s

Why was this time different?

The thinking at the time: There will never again be another world war; greater political stability and strong global growth will be sustained indefinitely; and debt burdens in developing countries are low.

BOX 1.2
The this-time-is-different syndrome on the eve of the Crash of 1929

FAMOUS WRONG GUESSES
IN HISTORY
when all Europe guessed wrong

The date—October 3rd, 1719. The scene—*Hotel de Nevers*, Paris. A wild mob—fighting to be heard. "Fifty shares!" "I'll take two hundred!" "Five hundred!" "A thousand here!" "Ten thousand!"

Shrill cries of women. Hoarse shouts of men. Speculators all—exchanging their gold and jewels or a lifetime's meager savings for magic shares in John Law's Mississippi Company. Shares that were to make them rich overnight.

Then the bubble burst. Down—down went the shares, Facing utter ruin, the frenzied populace tried to "sell". Panic-stricken mobs stormed the *Banque Royale*. No use! The bank's coffers were empty. John Law had fled. The great Mississippi Company and its promise of wealth had become but a wretched memory.

Today you need not guess.

HISTORY sometimes repeats itself—but not invariably. In 1719 there was practically no way of finding out the *facts* about the Mississippi venture. How different the position of the investor in 1929!

Today, it is inexcusable to buy a "bubble" —inexcusable because unnecessary. For now every investor—whether his capital consists of a few thousands or mounts into the millions —has at his disposal facilities for obtaining the *facts*. Facts which—as far as is humanly possible—eliminate the hazards of speculation and substitute in their place sound principles of investment.

STANDARD STATISTICS

200 VARICK ST.
New York, New York (now the home of Chipotle Mexican Grill)

Saturday Evening Post, September 14, 1929

Note: This advertisement was kindly sent to the authors by Professor Peter Lindert.

The major combatant countries in World War I had built up enormous debts. Regions such as Latin America and Asia, which had escaped the worst ravages of the war, appeared to have very modest and manageable public finances. The 1920s were a period of relentless global optimism, not dissimilar to the five-year boom that preceded the worldwide financial crisis that began in the United States in mid-2007. Just as global peace was an important component of the 2000s dynamic, so was the widely held view that the experience of World War I would not soon be repeated.

In 1929, a global stock market crash marked the onset of the Great Depression. Economic contraction slashed government resources as global deflation pushed up interest rates in real terms. What followed was the largest wave of defaults in history.

2. The debt crisis of the 1980s

Why was this time different?

The thinking at the time: Commodity prices are strong, interest rates are low, oil money is being "recycled," there are skilled technocrats in government, money is being used for high-return infrastructure investments, and bank loans are being made instead of bond loans, as in the interwar period of the 1920s and 1930s. With individual banks taking up large blocks of loans, there will be incentive for information gathering and monitoring to ensure the monies are well spent and the loans repaid.

After years of secular decline, the world experienced a boom in commodity prices in the 1970s; commodity-rich Latin America seemed destined to reap enormous profits as world growth powered higher and higher prices for scarce material resources. Global inflation in the developed world had led to a long period of anomalously low real interest rates in rich countries' bond markets. And last but not least, there had been essentially no new defaults in Latin America for almost a generation; the last surge had occurred during the Great Depression.

Many officials and policy economists spoke very approvingly of the loans from Western banks to developing countries. The banks were said to be performing an important intermediation service by taking oil surpluses from the Organization of Petroleum Exporting Countries and "recycling" them to developing countries. Western banks came into the loop because they supposedly had the lending and monitoring expertise necessary to lend en masse to Latin America and elsewhere, reaping handsome markups for their efforts.

The 1970s buildup, like so many before it, ended in tears. Steeply higher real interest rates combined with a collapse of global commodity prices catalyzed Mexico's default in August 1983, and shortly thereafter the defaults of well over a dozen other major emerging markets, including Argentina, Brazil, Nigeria, the Philippines, and Turkey. When the rich countries moved to tame inflation in the early 1980s, steep interest rate hikes by the central banks hugely raised the carrying costs of loans to developing countries, which were typically indexed to short-term rates (why that should be the case is an issue we address in the chapter on the theory of sovereign debt). With the collapse of global demand, commodity prices collapsed as well, falling by 70 percent or more from their peak in some cases.

3. The debt crisis of the 1990s in Asia

Why was this time different?   *The thinking at the time: The region has a conservative fiscal policy, stable exchange rates, high rates of growth and saving, and no remembered history of financial crises.*

Asia was the darling of foreign capital during the mid-1990s. Across the region, (1) households had exceptionally high savings rates that the governments could rely on in the event of financial stress, (2) governments had relatively strong fiscal positions so that most borrowing was private, (3) currencies were quasi-pegged to the dollar, making investments safe, and (4) it was thought that Asian countries never have financial crises.

In the end, even a fast-growing country with sound fiscal policy is not invulnerable to shocks. One huge weakness was Asia's exchange rate pegs against the dollar, which were often implicit rather than explicit.[11] These pegs left the region extremely vulnerable to a crisis of confidence. And, starting in the summer of 1997, that is precisely what happened. Governments such as Thailand's ultimately suffered huge losses on foreign exchange intervention when doomed efforts to prop up the currency failed.[12] Korea, Indonesia, and Thailand among others were forced to go to the International Monetary

Fund for gigantic bailout packages, but this was not enough to stave off deep recessions and huge currency depreciations.

4. The debt crisis of the 1990s and early 2000s in Latin America

Why was this time different?

The thinking at the time: The debts are bond debts, not bank debts. (Note how the pendulum swings between the belief that bond debt is safer and the belief that bank debt is safer.) With orders of magnitude more debt holders in the case of bonds than in the case of international banks, countries will be much more hesitant to try to default because renegotiation would be so difficult (see instance 2 earlier).

During the early 1990s, international creditors poured funds into a Latin American region that had only just emerged from a decade of default and stagnation. The credit had been channeled mainly through bonds rather than banks, leading some to conclude that the debts would be invulnerable to renegotiation. By spreading debt claims out across a wide sea of bond holders, it was claimed, there could be no repeat of the 1980s, in which debtor countries had successfully forced banks to reschedule (stretch out and effectively reduce) debt repayments. Absent the possibility of renegotiation, it would be much harder to default.

Other factors were also at work, lulling investors. Many Latin American countries had changed from dictatorships to democracies, "assuring greater stability." Mexico was not a risk because of the North American Free Trade Agreement, which came into force in January 1994. Argentina was not a risk, because it had "immutably" fixed its exchange rate to the dollar through a currency board arrangement.

Eventually, the lending boom of the 1990s ended in a series of financial crises, starting with Mexico's December 1994 collapse. What followed included Argentina's $95 billion default, the largest in history at that time; Brazil's financial crises in 1998 and 2002; and Uruguay's default in 2002.

5. The United States in the run-up to the financial crisis of the late 2000s (the Second Great Contraction)

Why was this time different?

The thinking at the time: Everything is fine because of globalization, the technology boom, our superior financial system, our better understanding of monetary policy, and the phenomenon of securitized debt.

Housing prices doubled and equity prices soared, all fueled by record borrowing from abroad. But most people thought the United States could never have a financial crisis resembling that of an emerging market.

The final chapters of this book chronicle the sorry tale of what unfolded next, the most severe financial crisis since the Great Depression and the only one since World War II that has been global in scope. In the intervening chapters we will show that the serial nature of financial crises is endemic across much of the spectrum of time and regions. Periods of prosperity (many of them long) often end in tears.

- 2 -

DEBT INTOLERANCE:
THE GENESIS OF SERIAL DEFAULT

Debt intolerance is a syndrome in which weak institutional structures and a problematic political system make external borrowing a tempting device for governments to employ to avoid hard decisions about spending and taxing.

This chapter lays out a statistical framework for thinking about serial default in terms of some countries' inability to resist recurrent exposure to debt default relapses. The reader wishing to avoid the modest amount of technical discussion in the next two chapters can readily skip ahead to the chapter on external default without any important loss of continuity.

Debt intolerance is defined as the extreme duress many emerging markets experience at external debt levels that would seem quite manageable by the standards of advanced countries. The duress typically involves a vicious cycle of loss in market confidence, spiraling interest rates on external government debt, and political resistance to repaying foreign creditors. Ultimately, default often occurs at levels of debt well below the 60 percent ratio of debt to GDP enshrined in Europe's Maastricht Treaty, a clause intended to protect the euro system from government defaults. Safe debt thresholds turn out to depend heavily on a country's record of default and inflation.[1]

Debt Thresholds

This chapter constitutes a first pass at understanding why a country might be vulnerable to recurrent default, then proceeds to form a quantitative measure of vulnerability to marginal rises in debt, or "debt intolerance."

Few macroeconomists would be surprised to learn that emerging market countries with overall ratios of public debt to GNP above, say, 100 percent run a significant risk of default. Even among advanced countries, Japan's debt of about 170 percent of its GNP (depending on the debt definition used) is considered problematic (Japan holds massive foreign exchange reserves, but even its net level of debt of about 94 percent of GNP is still very high).[2] Yet emerging market default can and does occur at ratios of external debt to GNP that are far lower than these, as some well-known cases of external debt default illustrate (e.g., Mexico in 1982, with a ratio of debt to GNP of 47 percent, and Argentina in 2001, with a ratio of debt to GNP slightly above 50 percent).

Our investigation of the debt thresholds of emerging market countries begins by chronicling all episodes of default or restructuring of external debt for middle-income countries for the years 1970–2008, where default is defined along the lines described in chapter 1 on definitions of default.[3] This is only our first pass at listing sovereign default dates. Later we will look at a far broader range of countries across a far more sweeping time span. Table 2.1 records the external debt default dates. For each middle-income country, the table lists the first year of the default or restructuring episode and the ratios of external debt to GNP and external debt to exports at the end of the year of the credit event, that is, when the technical default began.[4] Obviously the aforementioned defaults of Mexico in 1982 and Argentina in 2001 were not exceptions, nor was the most recent default, that of Ecuador in 2008. Table 2.2, which is derived from table 2.1, shows that external debt exceeded 100 percent of GNP in only 16 percent of the default or restructuring episodes, that more than half of all defaults occurred at levels below 60 percent, and that there were defaults against debt levels that were below 40 percent of GNP in nearly 20 percent of the cases.[5] (Arguably, the thresholds of external debt to GNP reported in table 2.1 are biased upward because the ratios of debt to GNP corresponding to the years of the credit events are driven up by the real depreciation in the ex-

TABLE 2.1
External debt at the time of default: Middle-income countries, 1970–2008

	Year of default or restructuring	Ratio of external debt to GNP at the end of the year of default or restructuring	Ratio of external debt to exports at the end of the year of default or restructuring
Albania	1990	16.6	98.6
Argentina	1982	55.1	447.3
	2001	50.8	368.1
Bolivia	1980	92.5	246.4
Brazil	1983	50.1	393.6
Bulgaria	1990	57.1	154.0
Chile	1972	31.1	n.a.
	1983	96.4	358.6
Costa Rica	1981	136.9	267.0
Dominican Republic	1982	31.8	183.4
Ecuador	1984	68.2	271.5
	2000	106.1	181.5
	2008	20.0	81.0
Egypt	1984	112.0	304.6
Guyana	1982	214.3	337.7
Honduras	1981	61.5	182.8
Iran	1992	41.8	77.7
Iraq	1990	n.a.	n.a.
Jamaica	1978	48.5	103.9
Jordan	1989	179.5	234.2
Mexico	1982	46.7	279.3
Morocco	1983	87.0	305.6
Panama	1983	88.1	162.0
Peru	1978	80.9	388.5
	1984	62.0	288.9
Philippines	1983	70.6	278.1
Poland	1981	n.a.	108.1
Romania	1982	n.a.	73.1
Russian Federation	1991	12.5	n.a.
	1998	58.5	109.8
South Africa	1985	n.a.	n.a.
Trinidad and Tobago	1989	49.4	103.6
Turkey	1978	21.0	374.2
Uruguay	1983	63.7	204.0
Venezuela	1982	41.4	159.8
Yugoslavia	1983	n.a.	n.a.
Average		69.3	229.9

Sources: Reinhart, Rogoff, and Savastano (2003a), updated based on World Bank (various years), *Global Development Finance*.

Notes: Income groups are defined according to World Bank (various years), *Global Development Finance*. n.a., not available. Debt stocks are reported at end of period. Hence, taking the ratio of debt to GNP at the end of the default year biases ratios *upward*, because in most cases defaults are accompanied by a sizable depreciation in the real exchange rate.

TABLE 2.2

External debt at the time of default: Frequency distribution, 1970–2008

Range of ratios of external debt to to GNP at the end of the first year of default or restructuring (percent)	Percentage of total defaults or restructurings in middle-income countries
< 40	19.4
41–60	32.3
61–80	16.1
81–100	16.1
>100	16.1

Sources: Table 2.1 and authors' calculations.

Notes: Income groups are defined according to World Bank (various years), *Global Development Finance*. These shares are based on the cases for which we have data on the ratios of debt to GNP. All cases marked "n.a." in Table 2.1 are excluded from the calculations.

change rate that typically accompanies such events as locals and foreign investors flee the currency.

We next compare profiles of the external indebtedness of emerging market countries with and without a history of defaults. Figure 2.1 shows the frequency distribution of external debt to GNP for the two groups of countries over 1970–2008. The two distributions are very distinct and show that defaulters borrow more than nondefaulters (even though their ratings tend to be worse at equal levels of debt). The gap between external debt ratios in emerging market countries with and without a history of default widens further when ratios of external debt to exports are considered. It appears that those that risk default the most when they borrow (i.e., those that have the highest debt intolerance levels) borrow the most, especially when measured in terms of exports, their largest source of foreign exchange. It should be no surprise, then, that so many capital flow cycles end in an ugly credit event. Of course, it takes two to tango, and creditors must be complicit in the this-time-is-different syndrome.

We can use these frequency distributions to ask whether there is a threshold of external debt to GNP for emerging economies beyond which the risk of experiencing extreme symptoms of debt intolerance rises sharply. (But this will be only a first step because, as we

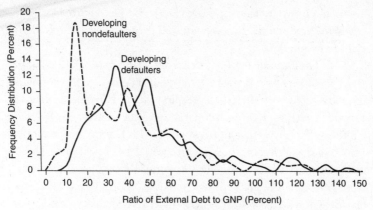

Figure 2.1. Ratios of external debt to GNP:
Defaulters and nondefaulters, 1970–2008.
Sources: Reinhart, Rogoff, and Savastano (2003a), updated based
on International Monetary Fund, *World Economic Outlook,* and
World Bank (various years), *Global Development Finance.*

shall see, differing levels of debt intolerance imply very different thresholds for various individual countries.) In particular, we high-light that countries' repayment and inflation histories matter significantly; the worse the history, the less the capacity to tolerate debt. Over half of the observations for countries with a sound credit history are at levels of external debt to GNP below 35 percent (47 percent of the observations are below 30 percent). By contrast, for those countries with a relatively tarnished credit history, levels of external debt to GNP above 40 percent are required to capture the majority of observations. Already from tables 2.1 and 2.2, and without taking into account country-specific debt intolerance factors, we can see that when the external debt levels of emerging markets are above 30–35 percent of GNP, risks of a credit event start to increase significantly.[6]

Measuring Vulnerability

To operationalize the concept of debt intolerance—to find a way to quantitatively measure a country's fragility as a foreign borrower—

we focus on two indicators: the sovereign ratings reported by *Institutional Investor* and the ratio of external debt to GNP (or of external debt to exports).

The *Institutional Investor* ratings (IIR), which are compiled twice a year, are based on survey information provided by economists and sovereign risk analysts at leading global banks and securities firms. The ratings grade each country on a scale from zero to 100, with a rating of 100 given to countries perceived as having the lowest likelihood of defaulting on their government debt obligations.[7] Hence, one may construct the variable 100 minus IIR as a proxy for default risk. Unfortunately, market-based measures of default risk (say, based on prices at which a country's debt trades on secondary markets) are available only for a much smaller range of countries and over a much shorter sample period.[8]

The second major component of our measure of a country's vulnerability to lapse or relapse into external debt default consists of total external debt, scaled alternatively by GNP and exports. Our emphasis on total external debt (public plus private) in this effort to identify a sustainable debt is due to the fact that historically much of the government debt in emerging markets was external, and the small part of external debt that was private before a crisis often became public after the fact.[9] (Later, in chapter 8, we will extend our analysis to incorporate domestic debt, which has become particularly important in the latest crisis given the large stock of domestic public debt issued by the governments of many emerging markets in the early 2000s prior to the crisis.) Data on domestic private debt remain elusive.

Table 2.3, which shows the panel pairwise correlations between the two debt ratios and the *Institutional Investor* measures of risk for a large sample of developing economies, also highlights the fact that the different measures of risk present a very similar picture of different countries' relative rankings and of the correlation between risk and debt. As expected, the correlations are uniformly positive in all regional groupings of countries, and in most instances they are statistically significant.

TABLE 2.3
Risk and debt: Panel pairwise correlations, 1979–2007

	100 – *Institutional Investor* ratings (IIR)
Correlations with ratio of external debt to GDP	
Full sample of developing countries	0.45*
Africa	0.33*
Emerging Asia	0.54*
Middle East	0.14
Western Hemisphere	0.45*
Correlations with ratio of external debt to exports	
Full sample of developing countries	0.63*
Africa	0.56*
Emerging Asia	0.70*
Middle East	0.48*
Western Hemisphere	0.47*

Sources: Reinhart, Rogoff, and Savastano (2003a), updated based on World Bank (various years), *Global Development Finance*, and *Institutional Investor*.

Note: An asterisk (*) denotes that the correlation is statistically significant at the 95 percent confidence level.

Clubs and Regions

We next use the components of debt intolerance (IIR and external debt ratios) in a two-step algorithm mapped in figure 2.2 to define creditors' "clubs" and regions of vulnerability. We begin by calculating the mean (47.6) and standard deviation (25.9) of the ratings for 90 countries for which *Institutional Investor* published data over 1979–2007, then use these metrics to loosely group countries into three clubs. Those countries that over the period 1979–2007 had an average IIR at or above 73.5 (the mean plus one standard deviation) form club A, a club that comprises countries that enjoy virtually continuous access to capital markets—that is, all advanced economies. As their repayment history shows (see chapter 8), these countries are the least debt intolerant. The club at the opposite extreme, club C, is comprised of those countries whose average IIR is below 21.7 (the mean minus one standard deviation).[10] This "cut-off" club includes countries whose primary sources of external financing are grants and official loans; countries in this club are so debt intolerant that markets only sporadically give them opportunities to borrow. The remaining countries are in club B, the main focus of our analysis, and exhibit varying degrees of vulnerability due to debt intolerance. These countries occupy the "indeterminate" region of theoretical debt models, the region in which default risk is nontrivial and where self-fulfilling runs are a possible trigger to a crisis. (We will return many times to the theme of how both countries and banks can be vulnerable to loss of creditor confidence, particularly when they depend on short-term finance through loans or deposits.) Club B is large and includes both countries that are on the cusp of "graduation" and those that may be on the brink of default. For this intermediate group of countries—whose debt intolerance is not so high that they are simply shut out of debt markets—the degree of leverage obviously affects their risk.

Hence, in our second step we use our algorithm to further subdivide the indeterminate club B into four groups ranging from the least to the most vulnerable to symptoms of debt intolerance. The least vulnerable group includes the (type I) countries with a 1979–2007 average IIR above the mean (47.6) but below 73.5 and a ratio of external debt to GNP below 35 percent (a threshold that, as we have discussed, accounts for more than half the observations of nondefaulters over 1970–2008). The next group includes (type II) countries with an IIR above the mean but a ratio of external debt to GNP that is above 35 percent. This is the second least vulnerable group, that is, the group second least likely to lapse into an external debt crisis. The group that follows encompasses (type III) countries with an IIR below the mean but above 21.7 and an external debt below 35 percent of GNP. Finally, the most debt-intolerant group—the group most vulnerable to an external debt crisis—is comprised of those (type IV) countries with an IIR below the mean and external debt levels above 35 percent of GNP. Countries in the type IV group can easily get bounced into the no-access club. For example, in early 2000 Argentina's IIR was about 44 and its ratio of external debt to

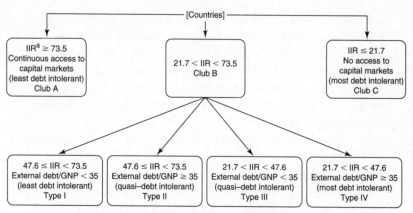

Figure 2.2. Definition of debtors' clubs and external debt intolerance regions.
[a]IIR, average long-term value for *Institutional Investor* ratings.

GNP was 51 percent, making it a type IV country. But by 2003 Argentina's rating had dropped to about 15, indicating that the country had "reverse-graduated" to club C. As we shall see (chapter 17), countries do not graduate to higher clubs easily; indeed, it can take many decades of impeccable repayment and sustained low debt levels to graduate from club B to club A. Falling from grace (moving to a more debt-intolerant range) is not a new phenomenon. It remains to be seen whether after the latest crisis club A loses some members.

The simple point underlying these definitions and groupings is that countries with a history of institutional weakness leading to recurrent default (as reflected in low IIR ratings) tend to be at high risk of experiencing "symptoms" of debt intolerance even at relatively low levels of debt. But both the "patient's" vulnerability to debt and the dose of debt are relevant to the risk of symptoms (default).

Reflections on Debt Intolerance

The sad fact related in our work is that once a country slips into being a serial defaulter, it retains a high and persistent level of debt intolerance. Countries can and do graduate, but the process is seldom fast or easy. Absent the pull of an outside political anchor (e.g., the European Union for countries like Greece and Portugal), recovery may take decades or even centuries. As of this writing, even the commitment device of an outside political anchor must be regarded as a promising experimental treatment in overcoming debt intolerance, not a definitive cure.

The implications of debt intolerance are certainly sobering for sustainability exercises that aim to see if, under reasonable assumptions about growth and world interest rates, a country can be expected to shoulder its external debt burdens. Such sustainability exercises are common, for example, in calculating how much debt reduction a problem debtor country needs to be able to meet its obligations on its remaining debt. Failure to take debt intolerance into account tends to lead to an underestimation of how easily unexpected shocks can lead to a loss of market confidence—or of the will to repay—and therefore to another debt collapse.

Is debt intolerance something a country can eventually surmount? Or is a country with weak internal structures that make it intolerant to debt doomed to follow a trajectory of lower growth and higher macroeconomic volatility? At some level, the answer to the second question has to be yes, but constrained access to international capital markets is best viewed as a symptom, not a cause, of the disease.

The institutional failings that make a country intolerant to debt pose the real impediment. The basic problem is threefold.

- First, the modern literature on empirical growth increasingly points to "soft" factors such as institutions, corruption, and governance as far more important than differences in ratios of capital to labor in explaining cross-country differences in per capita incomes.
- Second, quantitative methods suggest that the risk-sharing benefits to capital market integration may also be relatively modest. (By "capital market integration" we mean the de facto and de jure integration of a country's financial markets with the rest of the world. By "risk-sharing benefits" we mean benefits in terms of lower consumption volatility.) And these results pertain to an ide-

alized world in which one does not have to worry about gratuitous policy-induced macroeconomic instability, poor domestic bank regulation, corruption, or (not least) policies that distort capital inflows toward short-term debt.[11]

- Third, there is evidence to suggest that capital flows to emerging markets are markedly procyclical (that is, they are higher when the economy is booming and lower when the economy is in recession). Procyclical capital inflows may, in turn, reinforce the tendency in these countries for macroeconomic policies to be procyclical as well. The fact that capital inflows collapse in a recession is perhaps the principal reason that emerging markets, in contrast to rich countries, are often forced to tighten both fiscal policy and monetary policy in a recession, exacerbating the downturn.[12] Arguably, having limited but stable access to capital markets may be welfare improving relative to the boom-bust pattern we so often observe. So the deeply entrenched idea that the growth trajectory of an emerging market economy will be hampered by limited access to debt markets is no longer as compelling as was once thought.

The aforementioned academic literature does not actually paint sharp distinctions between different types of capital flows—for instance, debt, equity, and foreign direct investment (FDI)—or between long-term versus short-term debt. Practical policy makers, of course, are justifiably quite concerned with the exact form that cross-border flows take, with FDI generally thought to have properties preferable to those of debt (FDI tends to be less volatile and to spin off indirect benefits such as technology transfer).[13] We generally share the view that FDI and equity investment are somewhat less problematic than debt, but one wants to avoid overstating the case. In practice, the three types of capital inflows are often interlinked (e.g., foreign firms will often bring cash into a country in advance of actually making plant acquisitions). Moreover, derivative contracts can blur the three categories. Even the most diligent statistical authority may find it difficult to accurately separate different types of foreign capital inflows (not to mention the fact that, when in doubt, some countries prefer to label a particular investment FDI to make their vulnerabilities seem lower). Given these qualifications, however, we still believe that the governments of advanced countries can do more to discourage excessive dependence on risky nonindexed debt relative to other forms of capital flows.[14] Finally, it should be noted that short-term debt—typically identified as the most problematic in terms of precipitating debt crises—facilitates trade in goods and is necessary in some measure to allow private agents to execute hedging strategies. Of course, one can plausibly argue that most of the benefits of having access to capital markets could be enjoyed with relatively modest ratios of debt to GNP.

All in all, debt intolerance need not be fatal to growth and macroeconomic stability, but it is still a serious impediment. However, the evidence on serial default presented in this book suggests that to overcome debt intolerance, policy makers need to be prepared to keep debt levels low for extended periods of time while undertaking more basic structural reforms to ensure that countries can eventually digest higher debt burdens without experiencing intolerance. This applies not only to external debt but also to the reemerging problem of domestic government debt. Policy makers who face tremendous short-term pressures will still choose to engage in high-risk borrowing, and for the right price, markets will let them. But understanding the basic problem should at least guide a country's citizens, not to mention international lending institutions and the broader international community, in making their own decisions.

In our view, developing a better understanding of the problem of serial default on external debt obligations is essential to designing better domestic and international economic policies with regard to crisis prevention and resolution. Although further research is needed, we believe a good case can be made that debt intolerance can be captured systematically by a relatively small number of variables, principally a country's own history of default and high inflation. Debt-intolerant countries face surprisingly low thresholds for external borrowing, beyond which risks of default or restructuring become significant. With the explosion of domestic borrowing that occurred at the turn of the twenty-first century, on which we present new data in this book, the thresholds for external debt almost certainly fell even from the low levels of a decade earlier, as we shall discuss in chapter 11. Our initial results suggest that the same factors that determine external debt intolerance, not to mention other manifestations of debt intolerance such as domestic dollarization (de facto or de jure substitution of a foreign currency for transactions or indexation of financial instruments), are also likely to impinge heavily on domestic debt intolerance.

Finally, whereas debt-intolerant countries need badly to find ways to bring their ratios of debt to GNP to safer ground, doing so is not easy. Historically, the cases in which countries have escaped high ratios of external debt to GNP, via either rapid growth or sizable and prolonged repayments, have been very much the exception.[15] Most large reductions in external debt among emerging markets have been achieved via restructuring or default. Failure to recognize the difficulty in escaping a situation of high debt intolerance simply through growth and gently falling ratios of debt to GNP is one of the central errors underlying many standard calculations employed both by the private sector and by official analysts during debt crises.

At the time of this writing, many emerging markets are implementing fiscal stimulus packages that mirror efforts in the advanced economies in order to jump-start their economies. Our analysis suggests that in the "shadow of debt intolerance" such measures must be viewed with caution, for widening deficits leave countries uncomfortably close to debt thresholds that have been associated with severe debt-servicing difficulties. Going forward, after the global financial crisis of the late 2000s subsides, a challenge will be to find ways to channel capital to debt-intolerant countries in nondebt form to prevent the cycle from repeating itself for another century to come.

- 3 -

A GLOBAL DATABASE
ON FINANCIAL CRISES
WITH A LONG-TERM VIEW

One would think that with at least 250 sovereign external default episodes during 1800–2009 and at least 68 cases of default on domestic public debt, it would be relatively straightforward to find a comprehensive long-range time series on public sector debt. Yet this is not the case; far from it. Government debt is among the most elusive of economic time series.

Having defined crises and taken a first pass at analyzing vulnerability to serial default, we now turn to the core of the book, the data set. It is this lode of information that we mine in various ways to explain events. This chapter presents a broad-brush description of the comprehensive database used in this study and evaluates its main sources, strengths, and limitations. Further documentation on the coverage and numerous sources of individual time series by country and by period is provided in appendixes A.1 and A.2. Those are devoted, respectively, to the macroeconomic time series used and the public debt data (which together form the centerpiece of our analysis).

This chapter is organized as follows. The first section describes the compilation of the family of time series that are brought together from different major and usually well-known sources. These series include prices, modern exchange rates (and earlier metal-based ones), real GDP, and exports. For the recent period, the data are primarily found in standard large-scale databases. For earlier history we relied on individual scholars or groups of scholars.[1] Next we describe the data that are more heterogeneous in both their sources and their methodologies. These are series on government finances and individual efforts to construct national accounts—notably nominal and real GDP, particularly before 1900. The remaining two sections are devoted to describing the particulars of building a cross-country, multicentury database on public debt and its characteristics, as well as the various manifestations and measurements of economic crises. Those include domestic and external debt defaults, inflation and banking crises, and currency crashes and debasements. Constructing the database on public domestic and external debt can best be described as having been more akin to archaeology than to economics. The compilation of crisis episodes has encompassed the use of both mechanical rules of thumb to date a crisis as well as arbitrary judgment calls on the interpretation of historical events as described by the financial press and scholars in the references on which we have drawn, which span more than three centuries.

Prices, Exchange Rates, Currency Debasement, and Real GDP

Prices

Our overarching ambition in this analysis is to document the incidence and magnitude of various forms of expropriation or default through the ages. No such study would be complete without taking stock of expropriation through inflation. Following the rise of fiat (paper) currency, inflation became the modern-day version of currency "debasement," the systematic degradation of metallic coins that was a favored method of monarchs for seizing resources before the development of the printing press. To measure inflation, we generally rely on consumer price indexes or their close relative, cost-of-living indexes. For the modern period, our data sources are primarily the standard databases of the International Monetary Fund: *International Financial Statistics* (IFS) and *World Economic Outlook* (WEO). For pre–World War II coverage (usually from early 1900s or late 1800s), *Global Financial Data* (GFD), several studies by Williamson,[2] and the Oxford Latin American Economic History Database (OXLAD) are key sources.[3]

For earlier periods in the eight centuries spanned by our analysis, we rely on the meticulous work of a number of economic historians who have constructed such price indexes item by item, most often by city rather than by country, from primary sources. In this regard, the scholars participating in the Global Price and Income History Group project at the University of California–Davis and their counterparts at the Dutch International Institute of Social History have been an invaluable source of prices in Asia and Europe.[4] Again, the complete references by author to this body of scholarly work are given in the data appendixes and in the references. For colonial America, *Historical Statistics of the United States* (HSOUS, recently updated) provides the U.S. data, while Richard Garner's Economic History Data Desk: Economic History of Latin America, the United States and the New World, 1500–1900, covers key cities in Latin America.[5]

On the Methodology Used in Compiling Consumer Price Indexes

When more than one price index is available for a country, we work with the simple average. This approach is most useful when there are price series for more than one city for the same country, such as in the pre-1800s data. When no such consumer price indexes are available, we turn to wholesale or producer price indexes (as, for example, for China in the 1800s and the United States in the 1720s). Absent any composite index, we fill in the holes in coverage with individual commodity prices. These almost always take the form of wheat prices for Europe and rice prices for Asia. We realize that a single commodity (even if it is the most important one) is a relative price rather than the aggregate we seek, so if for any given year we have at least one consumer (or cost-of-living) price series and the price of wheat (or rice), we do not average the two but give full weight to the composite price index. Finally, from 1980 to the present, the International Monetary Fund's *World Economic Outlook* dominates all other sources, because it enforces uniformity.

Exchange Rates, Modern and Early, and Currency Debasement

The handmaiden to inflation is, of course, currency depreciation. For the period after World War II, our primary sources for exchange rates are IFS for official rates and *Pick's Currency Yearbooks* for market-based rates, as quantified and documented in detail by Reinhart and Rogoff.[6] For modern prewar rates GFD, OXLAD, HSOUS, and the League of Nations' *Annual Reports* are the primary sources. These are sometimes supplemented with scholarly sources for individual countries, as described in appendix A.1. Less modern are the exchange rates for the late 1600s through the early 1800s for a handful of European currencies, which are taken from John Castaing's *Course of Exchange*, which appeared twice a week (on Tuesdays and Fridays) from 1698 through the following century or so.[7]

We calculated the earlier "silver-based" exchange rates (trivially) from the time series provided primarily by Robert Allen and Richard Unger, who constructed continuous annual series on the silver content of currencies for several European currencies (for other sources see individual tables in the data appendixes, which list individual authors).[8] The earliest series, for Italy and England, begins in the mid-thirteenth century. As described in appendix A.1.4, these series are the foundation for dating and quantifying the "debasement crises"—the precursors of modern devaluations, as cataloged and discussed in chapter 11.

Real GDP

To maintain homogeneity inasmuch as it is possible for such a large sample of countries over the course of approximately two hundred years, we employ as a primary source Angus Maddison's data, spanning 1820–2003 (depending on the country), and the version updated through 2008 by the Groningen Growth and Development Centre's Total Economy Database (TED).[9] GDP is calculated on the basis of purchasing power parity (PPP) in 1990.[10] TED includes, among other things, series on levels of real GDP, population, and GDP per capita for up to 125 countries from 1950 to the present. These countries represent about 96 percent of the world's population. Because the smaller and poorer countries are not in the database, the sample represents an even larger share of world GDP (99 percent). We do not attempt to include in our study aggregate measures of real economic activity prior to 1800.[11]

To calculate a country's share of world GDP continuously over the years, we sometimes found it necessary to interpolate the Maddison data. (By and large, the interpolated GDP data are used only in forming weights and percentages of global GDP. We do not use them for dating or calibrating crises.) For most countries, GDP is reported only for selected benchmark years (e.g., 1820, 1850, 1870). Interpolation took three forms, ranging from the best or preferred practice to the most rudimentary. When we had actual data for real GDP (from either official sources or other scholars) for periods for which the Maddison data are missing and periods for which both series are available, we ran auxiliary regressions of the Maddison GDP series on the available GDP series for that particular country in order to interpolate the missing data. This allowed us to maintain cross-country comparability, enabling us to aggregate GDP by region or worldwide. When no other measures of GDP were available to fill in the gaps, we used the auxiliary regressions to link the Maddison measure of GDP to other indicators of economic activity, such as an output index or, most often, central government revenues—for which we have long-range continuous time series.[12] As a last resort, if no potential regressors were available, we used interpolation to connect the dots of the missing Maddison data, assuming a constant annual growth rate in between the reported benchmark years. Although this method of interpolation is, of course, useless from the vantage point of discerning any cyclical pattern, it still provides a reasonable measure of a particular country's share of world GDP, because this share usually does not change drastically from year to year.

Exports

As is well known, export data are subject to chronic misinvoicing problems because exporters aim to evade taxes, capital controls, and currency restrictions.[13] Nevertheless, external accounts are most often available for a far longer period and on a far more consistent basis than are GDP accounts. In spite of problems resulting from misinvoicing, external accounts are generally considered more reliable than most other series on macroeconomic activity. The postwar export series used in this study are taken from the International Monetary Fund (IMF), whereas the earlier data come primarily from GFD and OXLAD. Official historical statistics and assorted academic studies listed in appendix A.1 complement the main databases. Trade balances provide a rough measure of the country-specific capital flow cycle, particularly for the earlier periods, from which data on capital account balances are nonexistent. Exports are also used to scale debt, particularly external debt.

Government Finances and National Accounts

Public Finances

Data on government finances are primarily taken from Mitchell for the pre-1963 period and from Kaminsky, Reinhart, and Végh and sources they have cited for the more recent period.[14] The Web pages of the central banks and finance ministries of the many countries in our sample provide the most up-to-date data. For many of the countries in our sample, particularly in Africa and Asia, the time series on central government revenues and expenditures date back to the colonial period. Details on individual country coverage are presented in appendix table A.1.7. In nearly all cases, the Mitchell data go back to the 1800s, enabling us to calculate ratios of debt to revenue for many of the earlier crises.

The European State Finance Database, which brings together data provided by many authors, is an excellent source for the larger European countries for the pre-1800 era, because it offers considerable detail on government revenues and expenditures, not to mention extensive bibliographical references.

National Accounts

Besides the standard sources, such as the IMF, the United Nations, and the World Bank, which provide data on national accounts for the post–World War II period (with different starting points depending on the country), we consult other multicountry databases such as OXLAD for earlier periods. As with other time series used in this study, the national account series (usually for the period before World War I) build on the efforts of many scholars around the world, such as Brahmananda for India, Yousef for Egypt, and Baptista for Venezuela.[15]

Public Debt and Its Composition

As we have already emphasized, finding data on domestic public debt is remarkably difficult. Finding data on defaults on domestic debt is, not surprisingly, even more problematic. In this volume we catalog more than seventy instances of outright default on domestic debt dating back to the early 1800s. Yet even this tally is probably a considerable understatement.[16]

For the advanced economies, the most comprehensive data come from the Organisation for Economic Co-operation and Development (OECD), which provides time series on general government debt since 1980. However, these data have several important limitations. They include only a handful of emerging markets. For many advanced economies (Greece, Finland, France, and the United Kingdom, to name a few), the data actually begin much later, in the 1990s, so the OECD data on public debt provide only a relatively short time series. Moreover, only total debt is reported, with no particulars provided regarding the composition of debt (domestic versus foreign) or its maturity (long-term versus short-term). Similarly, to consider the IMF's well-known *World Economic Outlook* database as extending to public debt requires a stretch of the imagination.[17] Data are provided only for the G-7 and only from 1980 onward (out of 180 countries covered in the WEO).

The most comprehensive data on public debt come from the World Bank's *Global Development Finance* (GDF, known previously as the World Debt Tables). It is an improvement on the other databases in that it begins (for most countries) in 1970 and provides extensive detail on the particulars of external debt. Yet GDF also has serious limitations. No advanced economies are included in the database (nor are newly industrialized countries, such as Israel, Korea, or Singapore) to facilitate comparisons. Unlike data from the IMF and the World Bank for exchange rates, prices, government finances, and so on, the database includes no data prior to 1970. Last but certainly not least, these data cover only external debt. In a few countries, such as Côte d'Ivoire or Panama, external debt is a sufficient statistic on government liabilities because the levels of domestic public debt are relatively trivial. As we shall show in chapter 7, however, domestic debt accounts for an important share of total government debt for most countries. The all-country average share oscillated between 40 and 80 percent during 1900–2007.[18]

In search of the elusive data on total public debt, we examined the archives of the global institutions' predecessor, the League of Nations, and found that its *Statistical Yearbook: 1926–1944* collected information on, among other things, public domestic and external debt. Although neither the IMF nor the World Bank continued this practice after the war, the newly formed United Nations (UN) inherited the data collected by the League of Nations, and in 1948 its Department of Economic Affairs published a special volume on public debt spanning 1914–1946. From that time onward, the UN continued to collect and publish the domestic and external debt data on an annual basis in the same format used by its prewar predecessor in its *Statistical Yearbook*. As former colonies became independent nations, the database expanded accordingly. This practice continued until 1983, at which time the domestic and external public debt series were discontinued altogether. In total, these sources yield time series that span 1914–1983 for the most complete cases. They cover advanced and developing economies. For the most part, they also disaggregated domestic debt into long-term and short-term components. To the best of our knowledge, these data are not available electronically in any database; hence, obtaining it required going to the original publications. These data provide the starting point for our public debt series, which have been (where possible) extended to the period prior to 1914 and since 1983.

For data from the period prior to 1914 (including several countries that were then colonies), we consulted numerous sources, both country-specific statistical and government agencies and individual scholars.[19] Appendix A.2 provides details of the sources by country and time period. In cases for which no public debt data are available for the period prior to 1914, we approximated the foreign debt stock by reconstructing debt from individual international debt issues. These debenture (debt not secured by physical collateral or assets) data also provide a proximate measure of gross international capital inflows. Many of the data come from scholars including Miller, Wynne, Lindert and Morton, and Marichal, among others.[20] From these data we construct a foreign debt series (but it does not include total debt).[21] This exercise allows us to examine standard debt ratios for default episodes of several newly independent nations in Latin America as well as Greece and important defaults such as that of China in 1921 and those of Egypt and Turkey in the 1860s and 1870s. These data are most useful for filling holes in the early debt time series when countries first tap international capital markets. Their usefulness (as measures of debt) is acutely affected by repeated defaults, write-offs, and debt restructurings that introduce disconnects between the amounts of debt issued and the subsequent debt stock.[22]

For some countries (or colonies in the earlier period) for which we have only relatively recent data for total public debt but have reliable data going much further back on central government revenues and expenditures, we calculate and cumulate fiscal deficits to provide a rough approximation of the debt stock.[23]

To update the data for the time since 1983, we rely mostly on GDF for external debt, with a few valuable recent studies facilitating the update.[24] Last but certainly not least are the official government sources themselves, which are increasingly forthcoming in providing domestic debt data, often under the IMF's 1996 *Special Data Dissemination Standard*, prominently posted at the IMF's official Web site.[25]

Global Variables

We label two types of variables "global." The first are those that are genuinely global in scope, such as world commodity prices. The second type consists of key economic and financial indicators for the world's financial centers during 1800–2009 that have exerted a true global influence (in modern times, the U.S. Federal Reserve's target policy interest rate is such an example). For commodity prices, we have time series since the late 1700s from four different core sources (see appendix A.1). The key economic indicators include the current account deficit, real and nominal GDP, and short- and long-term interest rates for the relevant financial center of the time (the United Kingdom prior to World War I and the United States since then).

Country Coverage

Table 3.1 lists the sixty-six countries in our sample. We include a large number or African and Asian economies, whereas previous studies of the same era typically included at most a couple of each. Overall, our data set includes thirteen African countries, twelve Asian countries, nineteen European countries, and eighteen Latin American countries, plus North America and Oceania. (Our sample excludes many of the world's poorest countries, which by and large cannot borrow meaningful amounts from private sector lenders and virtually all of which have effectively defaulted even on heavily subsidized government-to-government loans. This is an interesting subject for another study, but here we are mainly interested in financial flows that, at least in the first instance, had a substantial market element.)[26]

As the final column of table 3.1 illustrates, our sample of sixty-six countries indeed accounts for about 90 percent of world GDP. Of course, many of these countries, particularly those in Africa and Asia, have become independent nations only relatively recently (see column 2). These recently independent countries have not been exposed to the risk of default for nearly as long as, say, the Latin American countries, and we have to calibrate our intercountry comparisons accordingly.

Table 3.1 flags which countries in our sample may be considered "default virgins," at least in the narrow sense that they have never outright failed to meet their external debt repayment obligations or rescheduled on even one occasion. One conspicuous grouping of countries includes the high-income Anglophone nations, Australia, Canada, New Zealand, and the United States. (The mother country, England, defaulted in earlier eras, as we have already noted.) In addition, none of the Scandinavian countries, Denmark, Finland, Norway, and Sweden, has defaulted, nor has Belgium or the Netherlands. And in Asia, Hong Kong, Korea, Malaysia, Singapore, Taiwan, and Thailand have all avoided external default. Admittedly, two of these countries, Korea and Thailand, managed to avoid default only through massive IMF loan packages during the last debt crisis of the 1990s and otherwise suffered much of the same trauma as a typical defaulting country. Of the default-free Asian countries, only Thailand existed as an independent state before the end of World War II; others have had the potential for default for only a relatively short time. Default or restructuring of domestic public debt would significantly reduce the "default virgin" list, among other things eliminating the United States from the roster of nondefaulters. For example, the abrogation of the gold clause in the United States in 1933, which meant that public debts would be repaid in fiat currency rather than gold, constitutes a restructuring of nearly all the government's domestic debt. Finally, one country from Africa, Mauritius, has never defaulted or restructured.

It is notable that the nondefaulters, by and large, are all hugely successful growth stories. This begs the question "Do high growth rates help avert default, or does averting default beget high growth rates?" Certainly we see many examples in world history in which very rapidly growing countries ran into trouble when their growth slowed.

Of course, governments can achieve de facto partial default on nominal bond debt simply through unanticipated bursts of inflation, as we discuss later, in chapters 11 and 12. Governments have

TABLE 3.1
Countries' share of world GDP, 1913 and 1990

Region and country	Year of independence (if after 1800)	Share of world real GDP (1990 Geary-Khamis dollars)	
		1913	1990
Africa			
Algeria	1962	0.23	0.27
Angola	1975	0.00	0.03
Central African Republic	1960	0.00	0.01
Côte d'Ivoire	1960	0.00	0.06
Egypt	1831	0.40	0.53
Kenya	1963	0.00	0.10
Mauritius*	1968	0.00	0.03
Morocco	1956	0.13	0.24
Nigeria	1960	0.00	0.40
South Africa	1910	0.36	0.54
Tunisia	1957	0.06	0.10
Zambia	1964	0.00	0.02
Zimbabwe	1965	0.00	0.05
Asia			
China		8.80	7.70
Hong Kong*		n.a.	n.a.
India	1947	7.47	4.05
Indonesia	1949	1.65	1.66
Japan		2.62	8.57
Korea*	1945	0.34	1.38
Malaysia*	1957	0.10	0.33
Myanmar	1948	0.31	0.11
Philippines	1947	0.34	0.53
Singapore*	1965	0.02	0.16
Taiwan*	1949	0.09	0.74
Thailand*		0.27	0.94
Europe			
Austria		0.86	0.48
Belgium*	1830	1.18	0.63
Denmark*		0.43	0.35
Finland*	1917	0.23	0.31
France		5.29	3.79
Germany		8.68	4.67
Greece	1829	0.32	0.37
Hungary	1918	0.60	0.25
Italy		3.49	3.42
Netherlands*		0.91	0.95

(continued)

TABLE 3.1 Continued

Region and country	Year of independence (if after 1800)	Share of world real GDP (1990 Geary-Khamis dollars)	
		1913	1990
Europe (continued)			
Norway*	1905	0.22	0.29
Poland	1918	1.70	0.72
Portugal		0.27	0.40
Romania	1878	0.80	0.30
Russia		8.50	4.25
Spain		1.52	1.75
Sweden		0.64	0.56
Turkey		0.67	1.13
United Kingdom		8.22	3.49
Latin America			
Argentina	1816	1.06	0.78
Bolivia	1825	0.00	0.05
Brazil	1822	0.70	2.74
Chile	1818	0.38	0.31
Colombia	1819	0.23	0.59
Costa Rica	1821	0.00	0.05
Dominican Republic	1845	0.00	0.06
Ecuador	1830	0.00	0.15
El Salvador	1821	0.00	0.04
Guatemala	1821	0.00	0.11
Honduras	1821	0.00	0.03
Mexico	1821	0.95	1.91
Nicaragua	1821	0.00	0.02
Panama	1903	0.00	0.04
Paraguay	1811	0.00	0.05
Peru	1821	0.16	0.24
Uruguay	1811	0.14	0.07
Venezuela	1830	0.12	0.59
North America			
Canada*	1867	1.28	1.94
United States*		18.93	21.41
Oceania			
Australia*	1901	0.91	1.07
New Zealand*	1907	0.21	0.17
Total sample: 66 countries		93.04	89.24

Sources: Correlates of War (n.d.), Maddison (2004).

Note: An asterisk (*) denotes no sovereign external default or rescheduling history. n.a., not available. Several of these countries that have avoided external default (such as the United States) have not escaped from a default or rescheduling of their domestic debt. (See chapter 7.)

many ways to partially default on debts, and many types of financial crises over the years have taken their character from the government's choice of financing and default vehicle. The fact that government debt can be a common denominator across disparate types of crises will become even more clear when we take up the links between crises in chapter 16.

- PART II -

SOVEREIGN EXTERNAL DEBT CRISES

Most countries in all regions have gone through a prolonged phase as serial defaulters on debt owed to foreigners.

A Digression on the Theoretical Underpinnings of Debt Crises

In this book we chronicle hundreds of episodes in which sovereign nations have defaulted on their loans from external creditors. These "debt crises" range from defaults on mid-fourteenth-century loans made by Florentine financiers to England's Edward III to those on massive loans from (mostly) New York bankers to Latin America during the 1970s. Why do countries seem to run out of money so often? Or do they?

Former Citibank chairman (1967–1984) Walter Wriston famously said, "Countries don't go bust." In hindsight, Wriston's comment sounded foolish, coming just before the great wave of sovereign defaults in the 1980s. After all, he was the head of a large bank that had deeply invested across Latin America. Yet, in a sense, the Citibank chairman was right. Countries do not go broke in the same sense that a firm or company might. First, countries do not usually go out of business. Second, country default is often the result of a complex cost-benefit calculus involving political and social considerations, not just economic and financial ones. Most country defaults happen long before a nation literally runs out of resources.

In most instances, with enough pain and suffering, a determined debtor country can usually repay foreign creditors. The question most leaders face is where to draw the line. The decision is not always a completely rational one. Romanian dictator Nikolai Ceauşescu single-mindedly insisted on repaying, in the span of a few years, the debt of $9 billion owed by his poor nation to foreign banks during the 1980s debt crisis. Romanians were forced to live through cold winters with little or no heat, and factories were forced to cut back because of limited electricity.

Few other modern leaders would have agreed with Ceauşescu's priorities. The Romanian dictator's actions are especially puzzling given that the country could presumably have renegotiated its debt burden, as most other developing countries eventually succeeded in doing during the crisis of the 1980s. By the same token, modern convention holds that a debtor country should not have to part with rare national treasures to pay off debts. During Russia's financial crisis in 1998, no one contemplated for a moment the possibility that Moscow might part with art from the Hermitage museum simply to appease Western creditors.[1]

The fact that lenders depend on a sovereign nation's willingness to repay, not simply its ability to repay, implies that sovereign bankruptcy is a distinctly different animal than corporate bankruptcy. In corporate or individual bankruptcy, creditors have well-defined rights that typically allow them to take over many of the debtor's assets and put a lien on a share of its future income. In sovereign bankruptcy, creditors may be able to do the same on paper, but in practice their enforcement power is very limited.

This chapter provides an analytical framework that allows us to think more deeply about the underpinnings of international debt markets. Our goal here is to provide not a comprehesive survey of this extensive literature but a broad overview of issues.[2] Readers mainly interested in understanding the historical experience might choose to skip this chapter. In some respects, however, the analysis of this chapter lies at the heart of everything that follows. Why on earth do foreign creditors ever trust countries to repay their debt anyway, especially when they have been burned so regularly in the past? Why would domestic residents in emerging markets ever entrust their money to banks or local currency when they, too, have been burned so often? Why do explosions of global inflation occur sometimes, such as in the early 1990s, when forty-five countries had inflation rates over 20 percent, and not during other periods, such as the early 2000s, when only a couple had such high inflation rates?

These are not simple questions, and they are the subject of huge debate among economists. We do not come close to providing complete answers; the social, political, and economic problems underpinning default are simply too complex. If future generations of researchers do resolve these issues, perhaps the topic of this book will become moot and the world will finally reach an era in which we can say, "This time really *is* different." However, history is littered with instances in which people declared premature victory over such thorny issues.

We first concentrate on what is perhaps the most fundamental "imperfection" of international capital markets, the lack of a supernational legal framework for enforcing debt contracts across borders. This is an abstract way of saying that if the government of Argentina (a country sporting a famous history of serial default) borrows money from a U.S. bank and then defaults, the bank's options for direct enforcement of its claims are limited. To sharpen our discussion of the international aspects of the problem, we will temporarily ignore political and economic divisions within the borrowing country and simply treat it as a unified actor. Thus we will ignore domestic public debt (debt borrowed by the government from its own citizens or from local banks).

It may seem strange to those unfamiliar with economic modeling to group a government and its population together as a unified actor. In altogether too many countries, governments can be kleptocratic and corrupt, with national policies dictated by the political elite rather than by the average citizen. Indeed, political disunity is often a key driver of sovereign defaults and financial crises. The fact that the U.S. subprime crisis became much worse in the run-up to the country's 2008 election is quite typical. Preelection posturing and postelection uncertainty routinely exacerbate the challenge of developing a coherent and credible policy response. Brazil's massive 2002 financial crisis was sparked in no small part by investors' concerns regarding a shift from the centrist government of then-president Fernando Henrique Cardoso to the more populist policies of the opposition leader Luiz Inácio Lula da Silva. The irony, of course, is that the left-leaning winner ultimately proved more conservative in his macroeconomic governance than investors had feared or, perhaps, some of his supporters had hoped.

Sovereign Lending

If the reader has any doubt that willingness to pay rather than ability to pay is typically the main determinant of country default, he or she need only peruse our earlier table 2.2. The table shows that more than half of defaults by middle-income countries occur at levels of external debt relative to GDP below 60 percent, when, under normal circumstances, real interest payments of only a few percent of income would be required to maintain a constant level of debt relative to GDP, an ability that is usually viewed as an important indicator of sustainability. Expressed as a percentage of exports or government revenues, of course, payments would typically be several times higher, as we will illustrate later. But even so, a workout would be manageable over time in most cases except during wartime, especially if the country as a whole were clearly and credibly committed to gradually increasing exports over time to a level commensurate with eventual full repayment.

The centrality of willingness to pay rather than ability to pay is also clear when one looks back several hundred years to international lending during the sixteenth, seventeenth, and eighteen centuries (what we term the early period of default). Back then, the major borrowers were countries such as France and Spain, which commanded great armies of their own. Foreign investors could hardly have expected to collect through force. As Michael Tomz reminds us, during the colonial era of the nineteenth century, superpowers did periodically intervene to enforce debt contracts.[3] Britain routinely bullied and even occupied countries that failed to repay foreign debts (for example, it invaded Egypt in 1882 and Istanbul in the wake of Turkey's 1876 default). Similarly, the United States' "gunboat diplomacy" in Venezuela, which began in the mid-1890s, was motivated in part by debt repayment concerns. And the U.S. occupation of Haiti beginning in 1915 was rationalized as necessary to collect debt. (Box 5.2 explains how debt problems led the independent nation of Newfoundland to lose its sovereignty.)

In the modern era, however, the idea of using gunboat diplomacy to collect debts seems far-fetched (in most cases). The cost-benefit analysis simply does not warrant governments' undertaking such huge expenses and risks, especially when borrowing is typically diversified across Europe, Japan, and the United States, making the incentives for an individual country to use military force even weaker.

What carrots or sticks, then, can foreign creditors actually hold over sovereign borrowers? This question was first posed coherently in a classic paper by Jonathan Eaton and Mark Gersovitz, who argued that in a changing and uncertain world there is a huge benefit to countries in having access to international capital markets.[4] In early times, capital market access might have enabled countries to get food during times of an exceptionally bad harvest. In modern times, countries may need to borrow to fight recessions or to engage in highly productive infrastructure projects.

Eaton and Gersovitz argued that the benefits of continued capital market access could induce governments to maintain debt repayments absent any legal system whatsoever to force their cooperation. They based their analysis on the conjecture that governments need to worry about their "reputation" as international borrowers. If reneging on debt damages their reputation, governments will not do so lightly. The Eaton and Gersovitz approach is appealing to economic theorists, especially because it is relatively institution-free. (That is, the theory is "pure" in that it does not depend on the particulars of government, such as legal and political structures.) In principle, the theory can explain sovereign borrowing in the Middle Ages as well as today. Note that the reputation argument does not say simply that countries repay their debts now so they can borrow even more in the future. If that were the case, international borrowing would be a Ponzi scheme with exploding debt levels.[5]

This "reputation approach" has some subtle problems. If the whole edifice of international lending were built simply on reputation, lending markets might be even more fragile than they actually are. Surely fourteenth-century Italian financiers must have realized that England's Edward III might die from battle or disease. What would have become of their loans if Edward's successor had had very different goals and aspirations? If Edward had successfully conquered France, what need would he have had for the lenders in the future?[6]

If institutions really do not matter, why, over most of history, has the external debt of emerging markets been denominated largely in foreign currency and written so that it is adjudicated in foreign courts?

Bulow and Rogoff raised another important challenge to the notion that institutions and international legal mechanisms are unimportant in international lending.[7] Countries may, indeed, be willing to repay debts to maintain their right to borrow in the future. But at some point, England's debt burden would have had to reach a point at which the expected value of repayments on existing debt exceeded any future borrowing. At some point, a country must reach its debt limit. Why wouldn't Edward III (or his successor) have simply declared the Italian debts null and void? Then England could have used any payments it *might* have made to its financiers to build up gold reserves that could be used if it experienced a shortfall in the future.

The reputation approach therefore requires some discipline. Bulow and Rogoff argue that in modern times sophisticated investing strategies (e.g., those used in foreign stock markets) might offer as good, or almost as good, a hedge against default as any potential stream of foreign lending. In another work, Bulow and Rogoff contend that instead of relying simply on reputation, repayment of much foreign borrowing, especially by emerging markets, might be enforced by the legal rights of creditors in the lenders' own countries.[8] If a country tried to move to self-insurance, many of the investments it might need to make would involve overseas purchases. Creditors might not be able to seize assets directly in the borrowing country, but, armed with sufficient legal rights, they might well be able to seize the borrower's assets abroad, particularly in their own countries, but potentially also in other countries with highly developed legal systems. Of course, the right to seize assets abroad will also make it difficult for a defaulting country to borrow from other international lenders. If a country defaults on foreign bank A and then attempts to borrow from foreign bank B, bank B has to worry whether bank A will attempt to enforce its prior claim when it comes time for the country to repay. In this sense, the reputation and legal approaches are not so different, though the resemblance can become significant when it comes to policy questions about how to design and operate the international financial system. For example, establishing an international bankruptcy court to replace domestic courts may be virtually irrelevant if legal rights are of little consequence in any event.

Emphasizing legal rights also leads one to focus on other costs besides being cut off from future borrowing. A government contemplating default on international loans must also contemplate the potential disruption to its trade that will result from the need to reroute trade and financing to circumvent creditors. Fourteenth-century England depended on selling wool to Italian weavers, and Italy was the center of the trade in spices, which England desired to import. Default implied making future trade with and through Italy difficult, and surely this would have been costly. Nowadays, trade and finance are even more closely linked. For example, most trade, both within and across countries, is extremely dependent on very short-term bank credits to finance goods during shipment but prior to receipt. If a country defaults on large long-term loans, creditor banks can exert significant pressure against any entity that attempts to finance trade credits. Countries can deal with this problem to some extent by using government foreign exchange reserves to help finance their trade. But governments are typically ill equipped to monitor trade loans at the microeconomic level, and they cannot easily substitute their own abilities for bank expertise. Last but not least, creditors can enforce in creditor countries' courts claims that potentially allow them to seize any defaulter country's goods (or assets) that cross their borders. Bulow and Rogoff argue that, in practice, creditors and debtors typically negotiate a partial default so that one seldom actually observes such seizures.

At some level, neither the reputation-based model of Eaton and Gersovitz nor the institutional approach of Bulow and Rogoff seems quite adequate to explain the scale and size of international lending or the diversity of measures creditors bring to bear in real-life default situations. Trade depends not only on legal conventions but also on political resistance to tariff wars and on a broader exchange of people and information to sustain business growth and development.

Indeed, whereas a country's reputation for repayment may have only limited traction if construed in the narrow sense defined by Eaton and Gersovitz, its reputation interpreted more broadly—for instance, for being a reliable partner in international relations—may be more significant.[9] Default on debt can upset delicate balances in national security arrangements and alliances, and most countries typically have important needs and issues.

In addition to loans, foreign direct investment (FDI) (for example, when a foreign company builds a plant in an emerging market) can also be important to development. A foreign company that wants to engage in FDI with a defaulting country will worry about having its plant and equipment seized (a prominent phenomenon during the 1960s and 1970s; examples include Chile's seizure of its copper mines from American companies in 1977 and the nationalization of foreign oil companies' holdings in the early 1970s by the Organization of Petroleum-Exporting Countries). A debt default will surely cast a pall over FDI, costing the debtor country not only the capital flows but also the knowledge transfer that trade economists find typically accompanies FDI.[10]

In sum, economists can find arguments to explain why countries are able to borrow abroad despite the limited rights of creditors. But the arguments are surprisingly complex, suggesting that sustainable debt levels may be fragile as well. Concerns over future access to capital markets, maintaining trade, and possibly broader international relations all support debt flows, with the relative emphasis and weights depending on factors specific to each situation. That is, even if lenders cannot directly go in and seize assets as in a conventional domestic default, they still retain leverage sufficient to entice a country to repay loans of at least modest size. We can dismiss, however, the popular notion that countries pay back their debts so that they can borrow even more in the future. Ponzi schemes cannot be the foundation for international lending; they must eventually collapse.

How does the limited leverage of foreign creditors relate to the fragility of confidence we emphasized in the preamble? Without going into great detail, it is easy to imagine that many of the models and frameworks we have been alluding to produce highly fragile equilibria in the sense that there are often multiple outcomes that can be quite sensitive to small shifts in expectations. This fragility comes through in many frameworks but is most straightforwardly apparent in cases in which highly indebted governments need to continuously roll over short-term funding, to which we will turn next.

Illiquidity versus Insolvency

We have emphasized the important distinction between willingness to pay and ability to pay. Another important concept is the distinction between a country that faces a short-term funding problem and one that is not willing and/or able to service its debts indefinitely. In most of the literature, this distinction is typically described as the difference between "illiquidity and insolvency." Of course, the reader now understands that this literal analogy between country and corporate debt is highly misleading. A bankrupt corporation may simply not be able to service its debts in full as a going concern. A country defaulter, on the other hand, has typically made a strategic decision that (full) repayment is not worth the necessary sacrifice.

Often governments borrow internationally, either at relatively short horizons of one to three years or at longer horizons, at interest rates linked to short-term international debt. Why borrowing tends to be relatively short term is a topic of its own. For example, Diamond and Rajan contend that lenders want the option of being able to discipline borrowers that "misbehave," that is, fail to invest resources, so as to enhance the probability of future repayment.[11] Jeanne argues that because short-term borrowing enhances the risk of a financial crisis (when often debt cannot be rolled over), countries are forced to follow more disciplined policies, improving economic performance for debtor and creditor alike.[12] For these and other related reasons, short-term borrowing often carries a significantly lower interest rate than longer-term borrowing. Similar arguments have been made about borrowing in foreign currency units.

In either event, when a country borrows short term, not only is it faced with financing interest payments (either through its own resources or through new borrowing) but it must also periodically roll over the principal. A liquidity crisis occurs when a country that is both willing and able to service its debts over the long run finds itself temporarily unable to roll over its debts. This situation is in contrast to what is sometimes casually labeled an "insolvency" problem, one in which the country is perceived to be unwilling or unable to repay over the long run. If a country is truly facing merely a liquidity crisis, a third party (for example, a multilateral lending organization such as the International Monetary Fund) can, in principle, make a short-term bridge loan, with no risk, that will keep the borrower on its feet and prevent it from defaulting. Indeed, if creditors were fully convinced that a country had every intention of repaying its debts over the longer term, the debtor would hardly be likely to run into a short-term liquidity problem ever again.

Sachs illustrates an important caveat.[13] Suppose that the money a country borrows is provided by a large group of lenders, each of which is small individually. It may be in the collective interest of the lenders to roll over short-term debt. Yet it can also produce equilibrium if all lenders refuse to roll over the debt, in which case the borrowing country will be forced into default. If no single lender can provide enough money for the country to meet its payments, there may be both a "default" and a "no-default" equilibrium. The example given by Sachs is, of course, a very good illustration of the theme of financial fragility and the vulnerability of debtors to the "this-time-is-different" syndrome. A borrower can merrily roll along as long as lenders have confidence, but if for some (possibly extraneous) reason confidence is lost, then lending collapses, and no individual lender has the power or inclination to stave it off.

The concept of illiquidity versus insolvency is one we already illustrated in the preamble with bank runs and one that we will see again in other guises. Technically speaking, countries can sometimes be exposed to "multiple equilibria," implying that the difference between a case in which a country defaults and one in which it does not default can sometimes be very small. For a given structure of debt and assuming all actors are pursuing their self-interest, there can be very different outcomes depending on expectations and confidence.

Theorists have developed many concrete examples of situations in which default can occur as a result of a "sunspot" that drives a country from a no-default to a default equilibrium.[14] The possible existence of multiple equilibria and the idea that investors may temporarily become skittish about a country can also play an important role in rationalizing intervention into sovereign lending crises by the governments of creditor countries and international institutions. The danger, of course, is that it is not always easy to distinguish between a default that was inevitable—in the sense that a country is so highly leveraged and so badly managed that it takes very little to force it into default—and one that was not—in the sense that a country is fundamentally sound but is having difficulties sustaining confidence because of a very temporary and easily solvable liquidity problem. In the heat of a crisis, it is all too tempting for would-be rescuers (today notably multilateral lenders such as the IMF) to persuade themselves that they are facing a confidence problem that can be solved with short-term bridge loans, when in fact they are confronting a much more deeply rooted crisis of solvency and willingness to pay.

Partial Default and Rescheduling

Until now, we have somewhat glossed over the point of exactly what constitutes default. In practice, most defaults end up being partial, not complete, albeit sometimes after long negotiations and much acrimony. Creditors may not have the leverage (from whatever source) to enforce full repayment, but they typically do have enough leverage to get at least something back, often a significant share of what they are owed. Even the most famous cases of total default have typically ended in partial repayment, albeit often quite small and many decades later. Russia's Bolshevik government refused to repay Tsarist debts in 1918, but when Russia finally re-entered the debt markets sixty-nine years later, it had to negotiate a token payment on its defaulted debt.

In most cases, though, partial repayment is significant and not a token, with the amount repaid presumably determined by the types of complex cost-benefit considerations we have already been discussing. Precisely because partial repayment is often the result of long and contentious negotiations, interested bystanders often get sucked in. For example, Bulow and Rogoff show how well-intentioned third parties such as international lending institutions (e.g., the IMF) or the governments of creditor countries may be gamed into making side payments to facilitate a deal, much as a realtor may cut her commission to sell a house.[15] Country borrowers and their creditors potentially have bargaining power vis-à-vis outside parties if failed negotiations interfere with trade and cause broader problems in the global financial system, such as contagion to other borrowers.[16] As we have noted, the creation of the IMF since World War II has coincided with shorter but more frequent episodes of sovereign default. This phenomenon is quite consistent with the view that default episodes occur even more frequently than they otherwise might, because both lenders and borrowers realize that in a pinch they can always count on subsidies from the IMF and the governments of creditor countries. (Later literature has come to term this gaming of third parties with deep pockets the "moral hazard" of international lending.)

A bargaining perspective on sovereign default also helps explain why, in addition to outright defaults (partial or complete), we include "reschedulings" in our definition of sovereign defaults. In a typical rescheduling, the debtor forces its creditors to accept longer repayment schedules and often interest rate concessions (relative to market interest rates). The ratings agencies (including Moody's and Standard and Poor's) rightly regard these episodes as negotiated partial defaults in which the agreed rescheduling minimizes the deadweight costs of legal fees and other expenditures related to a more acrimonious default in which a country and its creditors simply walk away from the table, at least for a time. Our data set does make a distinction between reschedulings and outright defaults, although from a theoretical perspective the two are quite similar.

One final but critical point is this: the fact that countries sometimes default on their debt does not provide prima facie evidence that investors were irrational. For making loans to risky sovereigns, investors receive risk premiums sometimes exceeding 5 or 10 percent per annum. These risk premiums imply that creditors receive compensation for occasional defaults, most of which are only partial anyway. Indeed, compared to corporate debt, country defaults often lead to much larger recoveries, especially when official bailouts are included.

We do not want to overemphasize the rationality of lenders. In fact, there are many cases in which the very small risk premiums charged sovereign nations are hardly commensurate with the risks involved. High-risk borrowers, of course, not only have to face interest rate risk premiums on their borrowing but often bear significant deadweight costs if debt problems amplify recessions in the event of default. For borrowers the this-time-is-different mentality may be even more costly than for creditors, but again we will need to revisit this issue in a broader calculus of default.

Odious Debt

Another deep philosophical issue, in principle relevant to thinking about international lending, surrounds the notion of "odious debt." In the Middle Ages, a child could be sent to debtors' prison if his parents died in debt. In principle, this allowed the parent to borrow more (because the punishment for failure to repay was so great), but today the social norms in most countries would view this transfer of debt as thoroughly unacceptable. But of course nations do borrow intertemporally, and the children of one generation may well have to pay off the debts of their parents. At the end of World War II, the gross domestic debt of the United States reached more than 100 percent of GDP, and it took several decades to bring it down to a more normal 50 percent of GDP.

The doctrine of odious debt basically states that when lenders give money to a government that is conspicuously kleptomaniacal and corrupt, subsequent governments should not be forced to honor it. Jayachandran and Kremer argue that one can modify standard reputation models of debt to admit a convention of not honoring odious debt, and that this can be welfare improving.[17] However, there is quite a bit of controversy about whether odious debt can be clearly delineated in practice. Everyone might agree that if the leaders of a country engaged in genocide were to borrow to finance their military, the lenders should recognize the debt as odious and at risk of default in the event of a regime change. However, one can imagine global bureaucrats arguing over, say, whether debt issued by the United States is odious debt, in which case, of course, the concept would not provide sufficient discrimination to be useful in practice. The practical guidelines regarding odious debt must be sufficiently narrowly construed so as to be implementable. In practice, though, weaker versions of odious debt do, perhaps, have some relevance. The circumstances under which a debt burden is accumulated can affect a debtor's view of "fairness," and therefore its willingness to pay. On occasion, the international community may also be willing to treat debtors more gently in these circumstances (at the very least by giving them greater access to subsidized bridge loans).

Domestic Public Debt

If the theory of external sovereign debt is complex, the theory of domestic public debt is even more so. For the purposes of this discussion, we will assume that domestic public debt is denominated in domestic currency, adjudicated within the issuing country, and held by domestic residents. Of these three strictures, the only one that is really absolute in our definition in chapter 1 is the assumption that the debt is adjudicated by domestic authorities. Beginning, perhaps, with Argentina's U.K. pound–denominated "internal" bonds of the late nineteenth century, there have been a number of historical examples in which domestic debt has been indexed to foreign currency (mostly famously the *tesobono* debt issued by Mexico in the early 1990s and the precedents noted in box 7.1), and in recent years that phenomenon has become more prevalent. As more emerging markets have moved to liberalize their capital markets, it has become increasingly common for foreign residents to hold domestic public debt. The nuance that both foreign and domestic residents may hold a certain type of debt can be relevant, but we will set this nuance aside to simplify our discussion.[18]

Domestic debt is debt a country owes to itself. In Robert Barro's famous Ricardian model of debt, domestic public debt does not matter at all, for citizens simply increase their savings when debt goes up to offset future taxes.[19] Barro's analysis, however, presumes that debt will always be honored, even if savings patterns are not homogeneous and debt repayments (as opposed to repudiations) favor some groups at the expense of others. This presumption begs the question as to why political outcomes do not periodically lead countries to default on domestic debt, and assumes away the question as to why anyone lends to governments in the first place. If old people hold most of a country's debt, for example, why don't young voters periodically rise up and vote to renege on the debt, starting anew with a lower tax for the young at the cost of less wealth for the elderly?

One of the more startling findings in part III of this book, on domestic debt, is that such outright defaults occur far more often than one might imagine, albeit not quite as often as defaults on sovereign external debt. Governments can also default on domestic public debt through high and unanticipated inflation, as the United States and many European countries famously did in the 1970s.

What, then, anchors domestic public debt? Why are domestic bondholders paid anything at all? North and Weingast argue that a government's ability to establish political institutions that sustain large amounts of debt repayment constitutes an enormous strategic advantage by allowing a country to marshal vast resources, especially in wartime.[20] They argue that one of the most important outcomes of England's "glorious revolution" of the late 1600s was precisely a framework to promote the honoring of debt contracts, thereby conferring on England a distinct advantage over rival France. France, as we shall see, was at the height of its serial default era during this period. The Crown's ability to issue debt gave England the huge advantage of being able to marshal the resources needed to conduct warfare in an era in which combat was already becoming extremely capital intensive.

In democracies, Kotlikoff, Persson, and Svensson suggest that domestic debt markets might be a convention that can be sustained through reputation, much as in the Eaton and Gersovitz model of sovereign external debt.[21] Tabellini, in a related article, suggests that debt might be sustainable if young voters care sufficiently about older voters.[22] All of these theories, and others for the case in which the government is a monarchy rather than a democracy, are built around the assumption that debt markets are self-sustaining conventions in which the costs and benefits narrowly match up to ensure continuous functioning. Yet, as we have discussed, the incentives for repayment of any kind of government debt probably involve broader issues than just the necessity of smoothing out tax receipts and consumption. Just as failure to honor sovereign debt might conceivably trigger broader responses in international relations outside the debt arena, so might domestic default trigger a breakdown in the social compact that extends beyond being able to borrow in the future. For one thing, in many economies government debt is not simply a means for governments to smooth tax receipts but a store of value that helps maintain the liquidity of credit markets. Governments may periodically default on their debts, but in most countries the record of private firms is even worse.

Financial repression can also be used as a tool to expand domestic debt markets. In China and India today, most citizens are extremely limited as to the range of financial assets they are allowed to hold, with very low-interest bank accounts and cash essentially the only choices. With cash and jewelry at high risk of loss and theft and very few options for accumulating wealth to pay for retirement, healthcare, and children's education, citizens still put large sums in banks despite the artificially suppressed returns. In India, banks end up lending large amounts of their assets directly to the government, which thereby enjoys a far lower interest rate than it probably would in a liberalized capital market. In China, the money goes via directed lending to state-owned enterprises and infrastructure projects, again at far lower interest rates than would otherwise obtain. This kind of financial repression is far from new and was particularly prevalent in both advanced and emerging market economies during the height of international capital controls from World War II through the 1980s.

Under conditions of financial repression, governments can, of course, potentially obtain very large amounts of resources by exploiting to the fullest their monopoly over savings vehicles. However, as we will show later, domestically issued debt has flourished in many emerging markets even when financial repression has been quite limited, for example, during the decades before World War II. ·

We will defer further discussion of domestic debt until we look at the issue empirically in chapters 7–9. There we will also show that there is an important interaction between sovereign debt and domestic debt. Again, as in the case of sovereign external debt, the issue of multiple equilibria often arises in models of domestic debt.[23]

Conclusions

In this chapter we have given a brief overview of the key concepts governing sovereign debt and default, as well as other varieties of crises including currency and banking crises. This chapter, while admittedly abstract, has addressed fundamental questions about international financial crises. We will return to some of these themes later in the book as our expansive new data set helps to cast light on some of the more difficult questions.

In many regards, the theoretical work on the underpinnings of international lending and capital markets raises the question of why defaults are not more frequent. Even Venezuela, the modern-day sovereign default champion, with ten episodes since it achieved independence in 1830, still averages eighteen years between new defaults. If crises recurred almost continuously, the this-time-is-different mentality would seldom manifest itself: every time would be the same, borrowers and lenders would remain constantly on edge, and debt markets would never develop to any significant degree, certainly not to the extent that spectacular crashes are possible. But of course, economic theory tells us that even a relatively fragile economy can roll along for a very long time before its confidence bubble bursts, sometimes allowing it to dig a very deep hole of debt before that happens.

- 5 -

CYCLES OF SOVEREIGN DEFAULT
ON EXTERNAL DEBT

*P*olicy makers should not have been overly cheered by the absence of major external sovereign defaults from 2003 to 2009 after the wave of defaults in the preceding two decades. Serial default remains the norm, with international waves of defaults typically separated by many years, if not decades.

Recurring Patterns

We open our tour of the panorama of financial crises by discussing sovereign default on external debt, which, as we have just been analyzing theoretically, occurs when a government defaults on debt owed to foreigners. (Some background on the historical emergence of sovereign debt markets is provided in box 5.1.)

Figure 5.1 plots the percentage of all independent countries in a state of default or restructuring during any given year between 1800 and 2008 (for which our data set is most complete). For the world as a whole (or at least those countries with more than 90 percent of global GDP, which are represented by our data set), the relatively short period of few defaults before the late 2000s can be seen as typical of the lull that follows large global financial crises. Aside from such lulls, there are long periods when a high percentage of all countries are in a state of default or restructuring. Indeed, figure 5.1 reveals five pronounced peaks or default cycles.

The first such peak was during the Napoleonic Wars. The second ran from the 1820s through the late 1840s, when at times nearly half the countries in the world were in default (including all

---

BOX 5.1

The development of international sovereign debt markets
in England and Spain

Modern debt institutions as we now understand them evolved gradually. This was particularly the case with domestic borrowing, in which the relationship between taxes, repayments, and power was historically often blurred. Loans were typically highly nontransparent, with ill-specified interest rates and re-payment schedules and often no specific dates on which principal repayments would be made. A king's promise to "repay" could often be removed as easily as the lender's head. Borrowing was frequently strongly coercive in nature. Early history is replete with examples of whole families who were slaughtered simply to seize their lands and other wealth. In thirteenth-century France, the Templars (of Crusades fame) were systematically exiled by the French kings, who seized their wealth.

In medieval times, the church enforced usury laws that were intended to prevent Christians from lending to each other at interest. Of course, non-Christians, especially Jews, were allowed to lend, but this gave sovereigns ac-cess to only a very small pool of their nation's total funds. In order to gain access to larger wealth pools, borrowers (sometimes with the help of theolo-gians) had to think of ways to try to circumvent church law. During this period, international lending markets were sometimes helped by the device of having a borrower repay in a stronger, more stable currency than was spec-ified in the original loan, perhaps repaying in currency that was not being as aggressively debased. Of course, such devices are tantamount to paying in-terest, yet they were often viewed as acceptable.

By far the most sophisticated early financial markets appeared in the Italian city-states of Genoa, Florence, and Venice in the late thirteenth cen-tury. (See, for example, the excellent discussions of MacDonald or Ferguson.)[1] Early loans took the guise of "repayable taxes," but soon the system evolved to the point at which sovereign loans were sufficiently transparent that a sec-ondary market developed.

As historian Carlo Cipolla has emphasized, the first true interna-tional debt crisis had its roots in loans made by Italian merchants to England starting in the late thirteenth century.[2] In that era, it was Italy that was the developed financial center and England the developing nation rich in natu-ral resources, especially sheep's wool. As we have already discussed, a sequence of Italian loans helped finance various stages of a long series of wars between England and France. When Edward III of England defaulted in 1340 after a series of military failures, the news reached Florence quickly. Because the ma-jor banks had lent heavily to Edward, a bank run hit Florence's economy. The whole affair played out in slow motion by modern standards, but one major Italian lender, the Peruzzi Bank, went bankrupt in 1343, and another, the

69

Bardi Bank, did in 1346. Thus England, like so many emerging markets in later eras, went through the trauma of sovereign external default (and more than once) before it eventually "graduated" to the status of nondefaulter. Before its graduation, England was to experience several more episodes of government debt restructurings; however, these more recent credit events involved only domestic debt—as we will document.

Indeed, England did not truly cast off its status as a serial defaulter until the Glorious Revolution in 1688, which led to a substantial strengthening of Parliament's power. As North and Weingast argued in their seminal work, this provided, for the first time, a self-renewing institution that stood behind British debt. Weingast further argued that the Bank of England, by providing a bureaucratic "delegated monitor" to oversee the government's debt service, provided the key instrument through which Parliament expressed its power.[3] Certainly a number of other factors helped support Britain's success, including the government's practice of using short-term debt to finance wars, then converting the debt to longer-term debt after each war's conclusion. Short-term financing of wars makes sense, of course, because uncertainty over the war's conclusion forces the government to pay a premium, which it will not want to lock in. The issuance of long-term debt also facilitated an active secondary market that helped make English debt liquid, a point underscored by Carlos et al.[4] Finally, it cannot be overemphasized that one of the main factors underlying England's relatively pristine repayment record is the country's remarkable success in its many wars. As we have already seen with regard to the early British monarchs, nothing causes debt failure to the extent that war failure does. We will return to the issue of graduation toward the end of this book.

Prior to 1800, few nations other than England had achieved the capacity to build up significant international debts and then default on them. To achieve large-scale serial default requires a sufficient store of wealth to keep convincing each new generation of creditors that the earnings needed to repay the debt will eventually be available (that this time it will be different) and that the country is sufficiently stable to ensure that it will be around to make the payments. After 1800, thanks to rapid global income growth in the wake of the Industrial Revolution as well as to Britain's capacity for spinning off excess savings, many countries began to fulfill the wealth criteria. Prior to 1800, aside from the early Italian cities, plus Portugal and Prussia on one occasion each, only France and Spain commanded the resources and stability to engage in big-time international defaults. And default they did, Spain six times by our count and France eight, as we illustrate in this chapter.

Spain's first string of defaults, in 1557, 1560, 1575, and 1596 under Philip II (1556–1598), have been extensively studied and debated by economic historians, as have the later and far uglier episodes that occurred under Philip II's successors in 1607, 1627, and 1647. The Spanish experience illustrates a number of issues that have continually recurred in later cases of serial default. Spain is also extremely important historically as the last country to threaten the domination of Europe until Napoleon.

Prior to the sixteenth century, Spain was sufficiently diffuse and its regions' finances sufficiently tenuous that large-scale international borrowing was not feasible. The discovery of the New World changed all that. Spectacular lodes of silver were found in Mexico and Peru, with truly massive amounts beginning to arrive in Europe by the 1540s. The huge increase in revenues greatly enhanced the power of the king, who was no longer so reliant on domestic tax revenues, which required the cooperation of Parliament. At the same time, the influx of precious metals, especially silver, had a huge inflationary impact on prices in Europe.

Spain's newfound wealth made it relatively easy for its monarchs to raise money by borrowing, and borrow they did. Leveraging seemed to make sense given the possibility of dominating Europe. King Philip's various military adventures against the Turks and the Dutch, and then his truly disastrous decision to launch the "Invincible Armada" against England, all required huge sums of money. Financiers including wealthy Flemish, German, and Portuguese investors, Spanish merchants, and especially Italian bankers were willing to lend significant sums to Spain given a sufficient risk premium. At any one time, the Spanish Crown typically owed its creditors roughly half of a year's revenues, although on occasion the amount exceeded two years' income. Of course, as we summarize in table 6.1, Spain did indeed default on its debts, repeatedly.

of Latin America). The third began in the early 1870s and lasted for two decades. The fourth began in the Great Depression of the 1930s and extended through the early 1950s, when again nearly half of all countries stood in default.[5] The final default cycle in the figure encompasses the debt crises of the 1980s and 1990s in the emerging markets.

Indeed, when one weights countries by their share of global GDP, as in figure 5.2, the lull in defaults after 2002 stands out even more against the preceding century. Only the two decades before World War I—the halcyon days of the gold standard—exhibited tranquility anywhere close to that of 2003–2008.[6] Looking forward, one cannot fail to note that whereas one- and two-decade lulls in defaults are not at all uncommon, each lull has invariably been followed by a new wave of defaults.

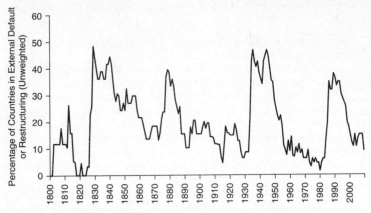

Figure 5.1. Sovereign external debt: Countries in external
default or restructuring, unweighted, 1800–2008.
Sources: Lindert and Morton (1989); Suter (1992); Purcell and
Kaufman (1993); Reinhart, Rogoff, and Savastano (2003a);
MacDonald (2006); and Standard and Poor's.
Notes: The sample includes all countries, out of a total of sixty-six
listed in table 1.1, that were independent states in the given year.

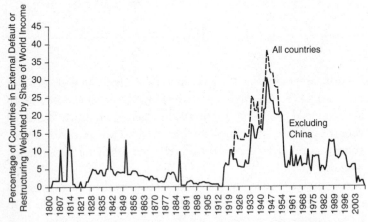

Figure 5.2. Sovereign external debt: Countries in external default or
restructuring, weighted by share of world income, 1800–2008.
Sources: Lindert and Morton (1989); Suter (1992); Purcell and
Kaufman (1993); Reinhart, Rogoff, and Savastano (2003a);
Maddison (2004); MacDonald (2006); and Standard and Poor's.
Notes: The sample includes all countries, out of a total of sixty-six listed in
table 1.1, that were independent states in the given year. Three sets of GDP
weights are used, 1913 weights for the period 1800–1913, 1990 weights for
the period 1914–1990, and 2003 weights for the period 1991–2008.

Figure 5.2 also shows that the years just after World War II were the peak, by far, of the largest default era in modern world history. By 1947, countries representing almost 40 percent of global GDP were in a state of default or rescheduling. This situation was partly a result of new defaults produced by the war but also partly due to the fact that many countries never emerged from the defaults surrounding the Great Depression of the 1930s.[7] By the same token, the defaults during the Napoleonic Wars are seen to have been as important as those in any other period. Outside of the crisis following World War II, only the peak of the 1980s debt crisis nears the levels of the early 1800s.

As we will see when we look at the experiences of individual countries in chapter 6, serial default on external debt—that is, repeated sovereign default—is the norm throughout every region in the world, including Asia and Europe.

Default and Banking Crises

A high incidence of global banking crises has historically been associated with a high incidence of sovereign defaults on external debt. Figure 5.3 plots the (GDP-weighted) share of countries experiencing a banking crisis against the comparably calculated share of countries experiencing a default or restructuring in their external debt (as in figure 5.2). Sovereign defaults began to climb with the onset of World War I (as did banking crises) and continued to escalate during the Great Depression and World War II (when several advanced economies joined the ranks of the defaulters). The decades that followed were relatively quiet until debt crises swept emerging markets beginning in the 1980s and 1990s.[8]

The channels through which global financial turbulence could prompt more sovereign debt crises in emerging markets are numerous and complex. Some of these channels are as follows:

- Banking crises in advanced economies significantly drag down world growth. The slowing, or outright contraction, of economic activity tends to hit exports especially hard, limiting the avail-

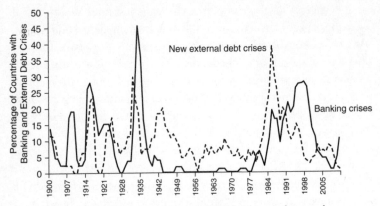

Figure 5.3. Proportion of countries with banking and external
debt crises: All countries, 1900–2008 (unweighted).
Sources: Lindert and Morton (1989); Suter (1992);
Purcell and Kaufman (1993); Kaminsky and Reinhart (1999);
Bordo et al. (2001); Macdonald (2003); Reinhart, Rogoff,
and Savastano (2003a); Maddison (2004); Caprio et al. (2005);
Jácome (2008); and Standard and Poor's.
Notes: New external debt crises refers to the first year of
default. Sample size includes all countries. The figure shows
a three-year moving average.

ability of hard currency to the governments of emerging markets
and making it more difficult to service their external debt.

- Weakening global growth has historically been associated with declining world commodity prices. These reduce the export earnings
  of primary commodity producers and, accordingly, their ability to
  service debt.
- Banking crises in global financial centers (and the credit crunches
  that accompany them) produce a "sudden stop" of lending to
  countries at the periphery (using the term popularized by Guillermo
  Calvo).[9] Essentially, capital flows from the "north" dry up in a manner unrelated to the underlying economic fundamentals in emerging
  markets. With credit hard to obtain, economic activity in emerging market economies contracts and debt burdens press harder
  against declining governmental resources.

74

- Banking crises have historically been "contagious" in that investors withdraw from risk-taking, generalize the experience of one country to others, and reduce their overall exposure as their wealth declines. The consequences are clearly deleterious for emerging markets' ability both to roll over and to service external sovereign debt.
- Banking crisis in one country can cause a loss of confidence in neighboring or similar countries, as creditors look for common problems.

As of this writing, it remains to be seen whether the global surge in financial sector turbulence of the late 2000s will lead to a similar outcome in the sovereign default cycle. The precedent in figure 5.3, however, appears discouraging on that score. A sharp rise in sovereign defaults in the current global financial environment would hardly be surprising.

Default and Inflation

If a global surge in banking crises indicates a likely rise in sovereign defaults, it may also signal a potential rise in the share of countries experiencing high inflation. Figure 5.4, on inflation and default (1900–2007), illustrates the striking positive co-movement of the share of countries in default on debt and the share experiencing high inflation (defined here as an annual rate above 20 percent). Because inflation represents a form of partially defaulting on government liabilities that are not fully indexed to prices or the exchange rate, this observed co-movement is not entirely surprising.[10]

As chapter 12 illustrates, default through inflation became more commonplace over the years as fiat money displaced coinage as the principal means of exchange. In effect, even when we focus on the post-1900 era of fiat money (Figure 5.4), this pattern is evident. That is, a tight relationship between inflation and outright external default is of fairly modern vintage. For 1900–2007, the simple pair-

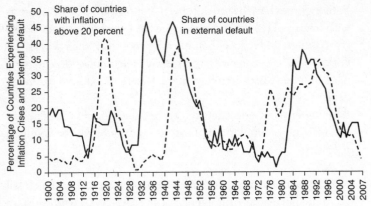

Figure 5.4. Inflation crises and external default, 1900–2007.
Sources: For the share of countries in default, see the sources
for figure 5.1. The sources for inflation are too numerous to list
here but are given in appendix A.1 by country and period.
Notes: Inflation crises are years in which the annual inflation rate
exceeds 20 percent per annum. The probabilities of both inflation
and default are simple unweighted averages. Correlations: 1900–2007,
0.39; excluding the Great Depression, 0.60; 1940–2007, 0.75.

wise correlation coefficient is 0.39; for the years after 1940, the correlation nearly doubles to 0.75.

This increased correlation can probably be explained by a
change in the willingness of governments to expropriate through various channels and the abandonment of a gold (or other metallic)
standard rather than by a change in macroeconomic influences. In
Depression-era defaults, deflation was the norm. To the extent that
such price-level declines were unexpected, debt burdens became
even more onerous and detrimental to economic performance. This
relationship is the essence of Irving Fisher's famous "debt-deflation"
theory.[11] As a corollary to that theory, an adverse economy presumably makes sovereign default more likely. In contrast, a higher background rate of inflation makes it less likely that an economy will be
pushed into a downward deflationary spiral. That defaults and infla-

tion moved together positively in the later part of the post–World War II period probably indicates that governments are now more willing to resort to both to lighten their real interest burdens.

Inflation conditions often continue to worsen after an external default.[12] Shut out from international capital markets and facing collapsing revenues, governments that have not been able to restrain their spending commensurately have, on a recurring basis, resorted to the inflation tax, even in its most extreme hyperinflationary form.

Global Factors and Cycles of Global External Default

We have already seen from figures 5.1 and 5.2 that global financial conflagration can be a huge factor in generating waves of defaults. Our extensive new data set also confirms the prevailing view among economists that global economic factors, including commodity prices and interest rates in the countries that are financial centers, play a major role in precipitating sovereign debt crises.[13]

We employed a range of real global commodity price indexes over the period 1800–2008 to assess the degree of co-movement of defaults and commodity prices. Peaks and troughs in commodity price cycles appear to be leading indicators of peaks and troughs in the capital flow cycle, with troughs typically resulting in multiple defaults.

As Kaminsky, Reinhart, and Végh have demonstrated for the postwar period and Aguiar and Gopinath have recently modeled, emerging market borrowing tends to be extremely procyclical.[14] Favorable trends in countries' terms of trade (meaning high prices for primary commodities) typically lead to a ramping up of borrowing. When commodity prices drop, borrowing collapses and defaults step up. Figure 5.5 is an illustration of the commodity price cycle, split into two periods at World War II. As the upper panel of the figure broadly suggests for the period from 1800 through 1940 (and as econometric testing corroborates), spikes in commodity prices are almost invariably followed by waves of new sovereign defaults. The lower panel of figure 5.5 calibrates the same phenomenon for the 1940s through the 2000s. Although the association can be seen in the post–World War II period, it is less compelling.

As observed earlier, defaults are also quite sensitive to the global capital flow cycle. When flows drop precipitously, more coun-

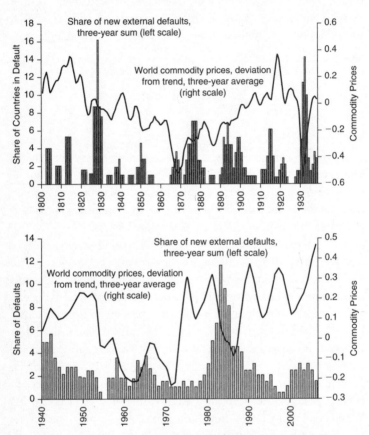

Figure 5.5. Commodity prices and new external defaults, 1800–2008.
Sources: Gayer et al. (1953); Boughton (1991); *The Economist* (2002); International Monetary Fund (various years), *World Economic Outlook;* and the authors' calculations based on the sources listed in appendixes A.1 and A.2.
Notes: "New external defaults" refers to the first year of default. Because of the marked negative downward drift in commodity prices during the sample period, prices are regressed against a linear trend so as to isolate the cycle.

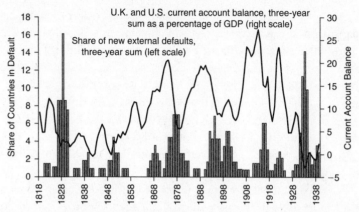

Figure 5.6. Net capital flows from financial centers and external default, 1818–1939.
Sources: Imlah (1958), Mitchell (2003a, 2003b), Carter et al. (2006),
and the Bank of England.
Notes: The current account balance for the United Kingdom and the United States
is defined according to the relative importance (albeit in a simplistic, arbitrary way)
of these countries as the financial centers and primary suppliers of capital to the
rest of the world: for 1818–1913, the United Kingdom receives a weight of 1
(United States, 0); for 1914–1939, both countries' current accounts are equally
weighted; for the period after 1940, the United States receives a weight equal to 1.

tries slip into default. Figure 5.6 documents this association by plotting the current account balance of the financial centers (the United
Kingdom and the United States) against the number of new defaults
prior to the breakdown of Bretton Woods. There is a marked visual
correlation between peaks in the capital flow cycle and new defaults
on sovereign debt. The financial centers' current accounts capture
the pressures of the "global savings glut," for they give a net measure
of excess center-country savings rather than the gross measure given
by the capital flow series in our data set.

An even stronger regularity found in the literature on modern
financial crises is that countries experiencing sudden large capital inflows are at high risk of experiencing a debt crisis.[15] The preliminary evidence here suggests that the same is true over a much broader sweep of
history, with surges in capital inflows often preceding external debt crises
at the country, regional, and global levels since 1800, if not before.

We recognize that the correlations captured by these figures are merely illustrative and that different default episodes involve many different factors. But aside from illustrating the kind of insights that can be achieved from such an extensive data set, the figures do bring into sharp relief the vulnerabilities of countries to global business cycles. The problem is that crisis-prone countries, particularly serial defaulters, tend to overborrow in good times, leaving them vulnerable during the inevitable downturns. The pervasive view that "this time is different" is precisely why this time usually is *not* different and why catastrophe eventually strikes again.

The capital flow cycle illustrated in figure 5.6 can be seen even more tellingly in case studies of individual countries, but we do not have the space here to include these.

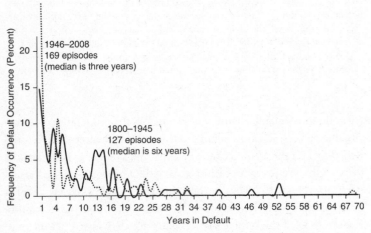

Figure 5.7. Duration of external default episodes, 1800–2008.
Sources: Lindert and Morton (1989); Suter (1992); Purcell and Kaufman (1993); Reinhart, Rogoff, and Savastano (2003a); MacDonald (2006); Standard and Poor's; and the authors' calculations.
Notes: The duration of a default episode is the number of years from the year of default to the year of resolution, be it through restructuring, repayment, or debt forgiveness. The Kolmogorov-Smirnov test for comparing the equality of two distributions rejects the null hypothesis of equal distributions at the 1 percent level of significance.

The Duration of Default Episodes

Another noteworthy insight from the "panoramic view" has to do with the observation that the median duration of default episodes in the post–World War II period has been half their length during 1800–1945 (three years versus six years, as shown in figure 5.7).

The charitable interpretation of this fact is that crisis resolution mechanisms have improved since the bygone days of gunboat diplomacy. After all, Newfoundland lost nothing less than its sovereignty when it defaulted on its external debts in 1936, ultimately becoming a Canadian province (see box 5.2); Egypt, among other countries, became a British "protectorate" following default.

A more cynical explanation points to the possibility that when bailouts are facilitated by multilateral lending institutions such as the International Monetary Fund, creditors are willing to cut more

---

BOX 5.2
External default penalized: The extraordinary case of
Newfoundland, 1928–1933

Just as governments sometimes broker a deal to have a healthy bank take over a bankrupt one, Britain pushed sovereign but bankrupt Newfoundland to be absorbed by Canada.

Newfoundland's fiscal march toward default between 1928 and 1933 can be summarized as follows:

Year	Total public debt (millions)	Ratio of debt to revenue	Interest payments as a share of revenues
1920	n.a.	n.a.	0.20
1928	79.9	8.4	0.40
1929	85.5	8.6	0.39
1930	87.6	7.6	0.36
1931	87.6	9.0	0.44

Year	Total public debt (millions)	Ratio of debt to revenue	Interest payments as a share of revenues
1932	90.1	11.4	0.59
1933	98.5	12.6	1.58

Sources: Baker (1994); League of Nations (various years), *Statistical Yearbook;* and the authors' calculations.

Note: The ratio of total debt to revenue at the time of external default, for an average of 89 episodes, is 4.2. n.a., not available.

Specific events hastened this march:

Time frame or date	Event
1928–1933	Fish prices collapsed by 48 percent, newsprint prices by 35 percent. The value of total exports fell by 27 percent over the same period, imports by 44 percent.[16]
Early 1931	Debt service difficulties began in earnest when the government had to borrow to service its debts.
February 17, 1933	The British government appointed a commission to examine the future of Newfoundland and in particular on the financial situation and the prospects therein.
October 4, 1933	The first recommendation of the commission was to suspend the existing form of government until such time as the island became self-supporting again.
December 21, 1933	The Loan Act was passed giving up sovereignty to avoid the certainty of default.

      Between 1928 and 1933, government revenues, still largely derived from customs duties, declined and the ratio of debt to revenue climbed (see the above table). Also, demands for relief payments were increasing, occasioned by the failures of fisheries in 1930–1932. The cost of debt servicing was becoming unbearable.

      Well before debt servicing difficulties became manifest in 1931, Newfoundland's fiscal finances were treading on precarious ground. Persistent fiscal deficits throughout the relatively prosperous 1920s had led to mounting (mostly external) debts. The ratio of public debt to revenues, around 8 at the outset of the Great Depression, was twice as high as the ratios of debt to revenue in about ninety default episodes! By 1932, interest payments alone absorbed the lion's share of revenues. A default seemed inevitable. Technically (and only technically), Newfoundland did not default.

As David Hale observes: "The Newfoundland political history of the 1930s is now considered to be a minor chapter in the history of Canada. There is practically no awareness of the extraordinary events which occurred there. The British parliament and the parliament of a self-governing dominion agreed that democracy should be subordinate to debt. The oldest parliament in the British Empire, after Westminster, was abolished and a dictatorship was imposed on 280,000 English-speaking people who had known seventy-eight years of direct democracy. The British government then used its constitutional powers to steer the country into a federation with Canada."[17]

Though not quite to the same extreme as Newfoundland, Egypt, Greece, and Turkey sacrificed partial sovereignty (as regards government finance, at least) to England following their nineteenth-century defaults. The United States established a fiscal protectorate in the Dominican Republic in 1907 in order to control the customs house, and then it occupied the country in 1916. The United States also intervened in Haiti and Nicaragua to control the customs houses and obtain revenue for debt servicing. Such were the days of gunboat diplomacy.

---

slack to their serially defaulting clients. The fact remains that, as Eichengreen observes in several contributions, the length of time separating default episodes in the more recent period (since World War II) has been much shorter. Once debt is restructured, countries are quick to releverage (see the discussion of the Brady plan countries in box 5.3).[18]

BOX 5.3

External default penalized? The case of the missing "Brady bunch"

Is it realistic to assume that a problem debtor country can achieve a "debt reversal" from a high ratio of debt to GDP to a low ratio simply through growth, without a substantial debt write-down? One attempt to do so was the issuance of Brady bonds, U.S. dollar–denominated bonds issued by an emerging market, collateralized by U.S. Treasury zero-coupon bonds. Brady bonds arose from an effort in the 1980s to reduce the debt of developing countries that were frequently defaulting on loans. The bonds were named for Treasury Secretary Nicholas Brady, who promoted the program of debt reduction. Participating countries were Argentina, Brazil, Bulgaria, Costa Rica, the Dominican Republic, Ecuador, Jordan, Mexico, Morocco, Nigeria, Peru, the Philippines, Poland, Uruguay, and Vietnam.

Identifying Debt Reversals

To identify episodes of large debt reversals for middle- and low-income countries over the period 1970–2000, Reinhart, Rogoff, and Savastano selected all episodes in which the ratio of external debt to GNP fell 25 percentage points or more within any three-year period, then ascertained whether the decline in the ratio was caused by a decrease in the numerator, an increase in the denominator, or some combination of the two.[19] The algorithm they used yielded a total of fifty-three debt reversal episodes for the period 1970–2000, twenty-six of them corresponding to middle-income countries and another twenty-seven to low-income countries.

The Debt Reversal Episodes

Of the twenty-two debt reversals detected in middle-income countries with emerging markets, fifteen coincided with some type of default or restructuring of external debt obligations. In six of the seven episodes that did not coincide with a credit event, the debt reversal was effected mainly through net debt repayments; in only one of these episodes (Swaziland, 1985) did the debt ratio decline primarily because the country "grew" out of its debts! Growth was also the principal factor explaining the decline in debt ratios in three of the fifteen default or restructuring cases: those of Morocco, Panama, and the Philippines. Overall, this exercise shows that countries typically do not grow out of their debt burden, providing yet another reason to be skeptical of overly sanguine standard sustainability calculations for debt-intolerant countries.

Of those cases involving credit events, Egypt and Russia obtained (by far) the largest reduction in their nominal debt burden in their restructuring deals. Two Asian countries that experienced crises (Korea and Thailand) engineered the largest debt repayments among the episodes in which a credit event was avoided.

Conspicuously absent from the large debt reversal episodes were the well-known Brady restructuring deals of the 1990s. Although the algorithm used by Reinhart, Rogoff, and Savastano picks up Bulgaria, Costa Rica, Jordan, Nigeria, and Vietnam, larger countries such as Brazil, Mexico, and Poland do not show up in the debt reversal category.

The Puzzle of the Missing "Brady Bunch": An Episode of Fast Releveraging

Reinhart, Rogoff, and Savastano traced the evolution of external debt in the seventeen countries whose external obligations were restructured under the umbrella of the Brady deals in the late 1980s. From this analysis of the profile of external debt, it became clear why the debt reversal algorithm used by

Reinhart, Rogoff, and Savastono did not pick up twelve of the seventeen Brady deals:

- In ten of those twelve cases, the decline in the ratio of external debt to GNP produced by the Brady restructurings was smaller than 25 percentage points. In fact, in Argentina and Peru, three years after the Brady deal the ratio of debt to GNP was higher than it had been in the year prior to the restructuring!
- By the year 2000, seven of the seventeen countries that had undertaken a Brady-type restructuring (Argentina, Brazil, Ecuador, Peru, the Philippines, Poland, and Uruguay) had ratios of external debt to GNP that were higher than those they had experienced three years after the restructuring, and by the end of 2000 four of those countries (Argentina, Brazil, Ecuador, and Peru) had debt ratios that were higher than those recorded prior to the Brady deal.
- By 2003, four members of the Brady bunch (Argentina, Côte D'Ivoire, Ecuador, and Uruguay) had once again defaulted on or restructured their external debt.
- By 2008, less than twenty years after the deal, Ecuador had defaulted twice. A few other members of the Brady group may follow suit.

In the chapter that follows, we document the extensive evidence of the repeated (or serial) nature of the default cycle by country, region, and era. In so doing we include some famous episodes as well as little-documented cases of default or restructuring in the now-advanced economies and in several Asian countries.

- 6 -

EXTERNAL DEFAULT
THROUGH HISTORY

Today's emerging market countries did not invent serial default—that is, repeated sovereign default. Rather, a number of today's now-wealthy countries had similar problems when they were emerging markets. Serial default on external debts is the norm throughout every region in the world, including Asia and Europe.

The perspective offered by the scale (across time) and scope (across countries) of our data set provides an important payoff in understanding defaults: it allows us to see that virtually all countries have defaulted on external debt at least once, and many have done so several times during their emerging market-economy phase, a period that typically lasts at least one or two centuries.

The Early History of Serial Default:
Emerging Europe, 1300–1799

Today's emerging markets can hardly claim credit for inventing serial default. Table 6.1 lists the number of defaults, including the default years, between 1300 and 1799 for a number of now-rich European countries (Austria, England, France, Germany, Portugal, and Spain).

Spain's defaults established a record that as yet remains unbroken. Indeed, Spain managed to default seven times in the nineteenth century alone after having defaulted six times in the preceding three centuries.

With its string of nineteenth-century defaults, Spain took the mantle for most defaults from France, which had abrogated its debt obligations on eight occasions between 1500 and 1800. Because

TABLE 6.1
The early external defaults: Europe, 1300–1799

Country	Years of default	Number of defaults
Austria	1796	1
England	1340, 1472, 1594*	2*
France	1558, 1624, 1648, 1661, 1701, 1715, 1770, 1788	8
Germany (Prussia)	1683	1
Portugal	1560	1
Spain	1557, 1575, 1596, 1607, 1627, 1647	6

Sources: Reinhart, Rogoff, and Savastano (2003a) and sources cited therein, MacDonald (2006).

Note: The asterisk (*) denotes our uncertainty at this time about whether England's default was on domestic or external debt.

during episodes of external debt default the French monarchs had a habit of executing major domestic creditors (an early and decisive form of "debt restructuring"), the population came to refer to these episodes as "bloodletting."[1] The French finance minister Abbe Terray, who served from 1768 to 1774, even opined that governments should default at least once every hundred years in order to restore equilibrium.[2]

Remarkably, however, despite the trauma the country experienced in the wake of the French Revolution and the Napoleonic Wars, France eventually managed to emerge from its status as a serial defaulter. France did not default in the nineteenth or twentieth century, nor has it (so far, anyway) in the twenty-first century. Therefore, France may be considered among the first countries to "graduate" from serial default, a subject considered in more detail in box 6.1. Austria and Portugal defaulted only once in the period up to 1800, but each then defaulted a handful of times during the nineteenth century, as we will see.

Two centuries after England defaulted under Edward III, King Henry VIII engaged in an epic debasement of the currency, effectively defaulting on all the Crown's domestic debts. Moreover, he seized all

---

BOX 6.1
France's graduation after eight external defaults, 1558–1788

French finances were thoroughly unstable prior to 1500, thanks in part to spectacular periodic debasements of the currency. In 1303 alone, France debased the silver content of its coins by more than 50 percent. At times, French revenues from currency manipulation exceeded that from all other sources.[3]

The French monarchy began to run up debts starting in 1522 with Francis I. Eventually, as a result of both extremely opaque financial accounting and continuing dependence on short-term finance, France found itself quite vulnerable when Philip II of Spain upset financial markets with his decision to default in 1557. Just as in modern financial markets, where one country's default can spread contagiously to other countries, the French king, Henry II, soon found himself unable to roll over short-term debt. Henry's efforts to reassure lenders that he had no intention to follow Philip's example by defaulting helped for a while, but by 1558 France had also been forced to default. The crash of 1557–1560 was an event of international scope, radiating throughout much of Europe.[4]

France's immediate problem in 1558 may have been the Spanish default, but its deeper problem was its failure to develop a less opaque system of finances. For example, Francis I systematically sold public offices, in effect giving away future tax revenues in exchange for upfront payments. Corruption was rampant. As a result of the center's loss of control over tax revenue, France found itself constantly rocked by defaults, including many smaller ones in addition to the eight defaults listed in table 6.1.

The War of the Spanish Succession (1701–1714) led to an explosion of debts that especially crippled France, given the difficulties the center faced in ramping up tax revenues. These massive war debts led to some of the most studied and celebrated financial experimentation in history, including the Mississippi and South Sea bubbles memorialized in Charles Kindleberger's classic book on bubbles, manias, and panics.[5]

The final French defaults of the eighteenth century occurred in 1770 and 1788.[6] The default in 1770 followed the Seven Years' War (1756–1763), in which financially better-developed England simply escalated (requiring ever-greater government resources) beyond the capacity of the financially underdeveloped French government to keep up.

Technically, 1788 was the year of France's last default, although, as we will see, postrevolutionary France experienced an epic hyperinflation that effectively led to the elimination of virtually all debts, public and private. Still, what is remarkable about the further course of French history is how the country managed to graduate and avoid further outright defaults.

the Catholic Church's vast lands. Such seizures, often accompanied by executions, although not strictly bond defaults, certainly qualify as reneging on sovereign obligations if not exactly international debt.

Capital Inflows and Default:
An "Old World" Story

The capital flow cycle emerges strikingly in figure 6.1, which is based on seventeenth-century Spain. The figure illustrates how defaults often follow in the wake of large spikes in capital inflows (which often roll in during the euphoria that accompanies the sense that "this time is different").

External Sovereign Default after 1800:
A Global Picture

Starting in the nineteenth century, the combination of the development of international capital markets and the emergence of a number of new nation-states led to an explosion in international defaults.

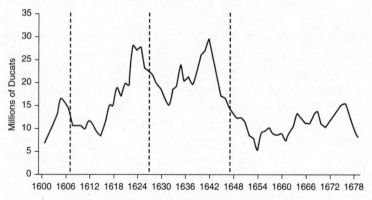

Figure 6.1. Spain: Defaults and loans to the Crown,
1601–1679 (three-year moving sum).
Sources: Gelabert (1999a, 1999b), European State Finance Database (Bonney n.d.).
Note: Defaults of 1607, 1627, and 1647 are represented by vertical lines.

Table 6.2 lists nineteenth-century episodes of default and rescheduling in Africa, Europe, and Latin America. We have already explained in chapter 4 why, from a theoretical perspective, debt reschedulings are effectively negotiated partial defaults. The issue is so fundamental here that we feel obliged to expand further, particularly underscoring why rescheduling is also akin to outright default from a practical perspective

Practitioners rightly view reschedulings as negotiated partial defaults for essentially two reasons. The first reason, of course, is that debt reschedulings often involve reducing interest rates, if not principal. Second, and perhaps more important, international debt reschedulings typically saddle investors with illiquid assets that may not pay off for decades. This illiquidity is a huge cost to investors, forcing them to hold a risky asset, often with compensation far below the market price of risk. True, investors that have held on to defaulted sovereign debt for a sufficient number of years—sometimes decades—have often eventually earned a return similar to what they would have earned by investing in relatively risk-free bonds issued by financial centers (the United Kingdom or, later, the United States) over the same period. Indeed, a number of papers have been written showing precisely such calculations.[7]

Although the similarity of these earnings is interesting, it is important to underscore that the right benchmark is the return on high-risk illiquid assets, not highly liquid low-risk assets. It is no coincidence that in the wake of the U.S. subprime mortgage debt crisis of 2007, subprime debt sold at a steep discount relative to the expected value of future repayments. Investors rightly believed that if they could pull their money out, they could earn a much higher return elsewhere in the economy provided they were willing to take illiquid positions with substantial risk. And of course they were right. Investing in risky illiquid assets is precisely how venture capital and private equity, not to mention university endowments, have succeeded (until the late 2000s) in earning enormous returns. By contrast, debt reschedulings at negotiated below-market interest rates impose risk on the creditor with none of the upside of, say, a venture capital investment. Thus, the dis-

TABLE 6.2

External default and rescheduling: Africa, Europe, and Latin America, nineteenth century

Country, date of independence[a]	Years of default and rescheduling			
	1800–1824	1825–1849	1850–1874	1875–1899
Africa				
Egypt, 1831				1876
Tunisia			1867	
Europe				
Austria-Hungary	1802, 1805, 1811, 1816		1868	
France	1812			
Germany				
Hesse	1814			
Prussia	1807, 1813			
Schleswig-Holstein			1850	
Westphalia	1812			
Greece, 1829		1826, 1843	1860	1893
The Netherlands	1814			
Portugal		1828, 1837, 1841, 1845	1852	1890
Russia		1839		1885
Spain	1809, 1820	1831, 1834	1851, 1867, 1872	1882
Sweden	1812			
Turkey				1876
Latin America				
Argentina, 1816		1827		1890
Bolivia, 1825				1875
Brazil, 1822				1898
Chile, 1818		1826		1880
Colombia, 1819		1826	1850, 1873	1880
Costa Rica, 1821		1828	1874	1895
Dominican Republic, 1845			1872	1892, 1897, 1899
Ecuador, 1830		1826	1868	1894
El Salvador, 1821		1828		1898
Guatemala, 1821		1828		1876, 1894, 1899
Honduras, 1821		1828	1873	
Mexico, 1821		1827, 1833, 1844	1866	1898
Nicaragua, 1821		1828		1894
Paraguay, 1811			1874	1892
Peru, 1821		1826		1876
Uruguay, 1811				1876, 1891
Venezuela, 1830		1826, 1848	1860, 1865	1892, 1898

Sources: Standard and Poor's, Purcell and Kaufman (1993), Reinhart, Rogoff, and Savastano (2003a) and sources cited therein.

[a]The years are shown for those countries that became independent during the nineteenth century.

tinction between debt reschedulings—negotiated partial defaults—and outright defaults (which typically end in partial repayment) is not a sharp one.

Table 6.2 also lists each country's year of independence. Most of Africa and Asia was colonized during this period, giving Europe and Latin America a substantial head start on the road to fiscal profligacy and default. The only African countries to default during this period were Tunisia (1867) and Egypt (1876). Austria, albeit not quite so prolific as Spain, defaulted a remarkable five times. Greece, which gained its independence only in 1829, made up for lost time by defaulting four times. Default was similarly rampant throughout the Latin American region, with Venezuela defaulting six times and Colombia, Costa Rica, the Dominican Republic, and Honduras defaulting four times.

Looking down the columns of table 6.2 also gives us a first glimpse of the clustering of defaults regionally and internationally. Note that a number of countries in Europe defaulted during or just after the Napoleonic Wars, whereas many countries in Latin America (plus their mother country, Spain) defaulted during the 1820s (see box 6.2 for a summary of Latin America's early days in international markets). Most of these defaults were associated with Latin America's wars of independence. Although none of the subsequent clusterings have been quite so pronounced in terms of the number of countries involved, notable episodes of global default occurred from the late 1860s to the mid-1870s and again from the mid-1880s through the early 1890s. We look at this clustering a bit more systematically later.

Next we turn to the twentieth century. Table 6.3 shows defaults in Africa and Asia, including the many newly colonized countries. Nigeria, despite its oil riches, has defaulted a stunning five times since achieving independence in 1960, more often than any other country over the same period. Indonesia has defaulted four times. Morocco, counting its first default in 1903 during an earlier era of independence, also defaulted three times in the twentieth century. India prides itself on having escaped the Asian crisis of the 1990s

---

BOX 6.2
Latin America's early days in international capital markets, 1822–1825

Borrowing by the newly independent (or newly invented) nations of Latin America between 1822 and 1825 is reflected in the following table:

State	Total value of bonds issued in London, 1822–1825 (£)
Argentina (Buenos Aires)	3,200,000
Brazil	1,000,000
Central America	163,300
Chile	1,000,000
Gran Colombia (Colombia, Ecuador, Venezuela)	6,750,000
Mexico	6,400,000
Peru	1,816,000
Poyais	200,000

Sources: Marichal (1989) and the authors.

The volatile and often chaotic European financial markets of the Napoleonic Wars had settled down by the early 1820s. Spain had, in quick succession, lost colony after colony in Central and South America, and the legendary silver and gold mines of the New World were up for grabs.

Forever engaged in an endless quest for higher yields, London bankers and investors were swept away by silver fever. The great demand in Europe for investment opportunities in Latin America, coupled with new leaders in Latin America desperate for funds to support the process of nation building (among other things), produced a surge in lending from (mostly) London to (mostly) Latin American sovereigns.[8]

According to Marichal, by mid-1825 twenty-six mining companies had been registered in the *Royal Exchange*. Any investment in Latin America became as coveted as South Sea shares (by 1825 already infamous) had been a century earlier. In this "irrationally exuberant" climate, Latin American states raised more than 20 million pounds during 1822–1825.

"General Sir" Gregor MacGregor, who had traveled to Latin America and fought as a mercenary in Simon Bolivar's army, seized the opportunity to convince fellow Scots to invest their savings in the fictitious country of Poyais. Its capital city, Saint Joseph (according to the investment prospectus circulated at the time), boasted "broad boulevards, colonnaded buildings, and a splendid domed cathedral." Those who were brave and savvy enough to cross the Atlantic and settle Poyais would be able to build sawmills to exploit the native forests and establish gold mines.[9] London bankers were also impressed with such prospects of riches, and in 1822 MacGregor (the Prince of

Poyais) issued a bond in London for £160,000 at a price of issue to the public of £80, well above the issue price for the first Chilean bond floated.[10] The interest rate of 6 percent was the same as that available to Buenos Aires, Central America, Chile, Greater Colombia, and Peru during that episode. Perhaps it is just as well that Poyais faced the same borrowing terms as the real sovereigns, for the latter would all default on their external debts during 1826–1828, marking the first Latin American debt crisis.

(thanks in part to massive capital controls and financial repression). In point of fact, it has been forced to reschedule its external debt three times since independence, albeit not since 1972. Although China did not default during its communist era, it did default on external debt in both 1921 and 1939.

Thus, as table 6.3 illustrates, the notion that countries in Latin America and low-income Europe were the only ones to default during the twentieth century is an exaggeration, to say the least.

Table 6.4 looks at Europe and Latin America, regions in which, with only a few exceptions, countries were independent throughout the twentieth century. Again, as in the earlier tables, we see that country defaults tend to come in clusters, including especially the period of the Great Depression, when much of the world went into default; the 1980s debt crisis; and the 1990s debt crisis. The last of these episodes saw somewhat fewer technical defaults thanks to massive intervention by the official community, particularly the International Monetary Fund and the World Bank. Whether these massive interventions were well advised is a different issue that we will set aside here. Notable in table 6.4 are Turkey's five defaults, Peru's six, and Brazil's and Ecuador's seven. Other countries, too, have had as many defaults.

So far we have focused on the number of defaults, but this measure is somewhat arbitrary. Default episodes can be connected, particularly if the terms of debt restructuring are harsh and make relapse into default almost inevitable. In these tables we have tried to exclude obviously connected episodes, so when a follow-on default occurs within two years of an earlier one, we count the two defaults

TABLE 6.3
Default and rescheduling: Africa and Asia, twentieth century to 2008

Country, date of independence[a]	Years of default and rescheduling			
	1900–1924	1925–1949	1950–1974	1975–2008
Africa				
Algeria, 1962				1991
Angola, 1975				1985
Central African Republic, 1960				1981, 1983
Côte d'Ivoire, 1960				1983, 2000
Egypt				1984
Kenya, 1963				1994, 2000
Morocco, 1956	1903			1983, 1986
Nigeria, 1960				1982, 1986, 1992, 2001, 2004
South Africa, 1910				1985, 1989, 1993
Zambia, 1964				1983
Zimbabwe, 1965			1965	2000
Asia				
China	1921	1939		
Japan		1942		
India, 1947			1958, 1969, 1972	
Indonesia, 1949			1966	1998, 2000, 2002
Myanmar, 1948				2002
The Philippines, 1947				1983
Sri Lanka, 1948				1980, 1982

Sources: Standard and Poor's, Purcell and Kaufman (1993), Reinhart, Rogoff, and Savastano (2003a) and sources cited therein.

[a]The years are shown for those countries that became independent during the twentieth century.

as one episode. However, to gain further perspective into countries' default histories, we next look at the number of years each country has spent in default since it achieved independence.

We begin by tabulating the results for Asia and Africa in table 6.5. For each country, the table gives the year of independence,

TABLE 6.4
Default and rescheduling: Europe and Latin America, twentieth century to 2008

Country, date of independence[a]	Years of default and rescheduling			
	1900–1924	1925–1949	1950–1974	1975–2008
Europe				
Austria		1938, 1940		
Germany		1932, 1939		
Greece		1932		
Hungary, 1918		1932, 1941		
Poland, 1918		1936, 1940		1981
Romania		1933		1981, 1986
Russia	1918			1991, 1998
Turkey	1915	1931, 1940		1978, 1982
Latin America				
Argentina			1951, 1956	1982, 1989, 2001
Bolivia		1931		1980, 1986, 1989
Brazil	1902, 1914	1931, 1937	1961, 1964	1983
Chile		1931	1961, 1963, 1966, 1972, 1974	1983
Colombia	1900	1932, 1935		
Costa Rica	1901	1932	1962	1981, 1983, 1984
Dominican Republic		1931		1982, 2005
Ecuador	1906, 1909, 1914	1929		1982, 1999, 2008
El Salvador	1921	1932, 1938		
Guatemala		1933		1986, 1989
Honduras				1981
Mexico	1914	1928		1982
Nicaragua	1911, 1915	1932		1979
Panama, 1903		1932		1983, 1987
Paraguay	1920	1932		1986, 2003
Peru		1931	1969	1976, 1978, 1980, 1984
Uruguay	1915	1933		1983, 1987, 1990, 2003
Venezuela				1983, 1990, 1995, 2004

Sources: Standard and Poor's, Purcell and Kaufman (1993), Reinhart, Rogoff, and Savastano (2003a) and sources cited therein.

Note: The World War II external debts of the Allied countries to the United States were repaid only by mutual agreement, notably that of the United Kingdom. Technically, this debt forgiveness constitutes a default.

[a]The years are shown for those countries that became independent during the twentieth century.

TABLE 6.5
The cumulative tally of default and rescheduling: Africa and Asia,
year of independence to 2008

Country	Share of years in default or rescheduling since independence or 1800[a]	Total number of defaults and/or reschedulings
Africa		
Algeria	13.3	1
Angola	59.4	1
Central African Republic	53.2	2
Côte d'Ivoire	48.9	2
Egypt	3.4	2
Kenya	13.6	2
Mauritius	0.0	0
Morocco	15.7	4
Nigeria	21.3	5
South Africa	5.2	3
Tunisia	5.3	1
Zambia	27.9	1
Zimbabwe	40.5	2
Asia		
China	13.0	2
Hong Kong	0.0	0
India	11.7	3
Indonesia	15.5	4
Japan	5.3	1
Korea	0.0	0
Malaysia	0.0	0
Myanmar	8.5	1
The Philippines	16.4	1
Singapore	0.0	0
Sri Lanka	6.8	2
Taiwan	0.0	0
Thailand	0.0	0

Sources: Authors' calculations, Standard and Poor's, Purcell and Kaufman (1993), Reinhart, Rogoff, and Savastano (2003a) and sources cited therein.

[a]For countries that became independent prior to 1800, the calculations are for 1800–2008.

the total number of defaults and reschedulings (using our measure), and the share (percentage) of years since 1800 (or since independence, if more recent) the country has spent in a state of default or rescheduling. It is notable that, although there have been many defaults in Asia, the typical default has been resolved relatively quickly. Only China, India, Indonesia, and the Philippines spent more than 10 percent of their independent lives in default (though of course on a population-weighted basis, those countries make up most of the region). Africa's record is far worse, with several countries having spent roughly half their time in default. Certainly one of the main reasons that African defaults are less celebrated than, say, Latin American defaults is that the debts of African countries have typically been relatively small and the systemic consequences less acute. These circumstances have not made the consequences any less painful for Africa's residents, of course, who must bear the same costs in terms of sudden fiscal consolidation and reduced access to credit, often accompanied by higher interest rates and exchange rate depreciation.

Table 6.6 gives the same set of statistics for Europe and Latin America. Greece, as noted, has spent more than half the years since 1800 in default. A number of Latin American countries spent roughly 40 percent of their years in default, including Costa Rica, the Dominican Republic, Mexico, Nicaragua, Peru, and Venezuela.

The same prevalence of default has been seen across most European countries, although there has been a great deal of variance, depending especially on how long countries have tended to remain in default (compare serial debtor Austria, which has tended to emerge from default relatively quickly, with Greece, which lived in a perpetual state of default for over a century). Overall, one can see that default episodes, while recurrent, are far from continuous. This wide spacing no doubt reflects adjustments that debtors and creditors make in the wake of each default cycle. For example, today many emerging markets are following quite conservative macroeconomic policies. Over time, though, this caution usually gives way to optimism and profligacy, but only after a long lull.

One way of summarizing the data in tables 6.5 and 6.6 is to look at a timeline giving the number of countries in default or re-

TABLE 6.6

The cumulative tally of default and rescheduling: Europe, Latin America, North America, and Oceania, year of independence to 2008

Country	Share of years in default or rescheduling since independence or 1800[a]	Total number of defaults and/or reschedulings
Europe		
Austria	17.4	7
Belgium	0.0	0
Denmark	0.0	0
Finland	0.0	0
France	4.3	9
Germany	13.0	8
Greece	50.6	5
Hungary	37.1	7
Italy	3.4	1
The Netherlands	6.3	1
Norway	0.0	0
Poland	32.6	3
Portugal	10.6	6
Romania	23.3	3
Russia	39.1	5
Spain	23.7	13
Sweden	0.0	0
Turkey	15.5	6
United Kingdom	0.0	0
Latin America		
Argentina	32.5	7
Bolivia	22.0	5
Brazil	25.4	9
Chile	27.5	9
Colombia	36.2	7
Costa Rica	38.2	9
Dominican Republic	29.0	7
Ecuador	58.2	9
El Salvador	26.3	5
Guatemala	34.4	7
Honduras	64.0	3
Mexico	44.6	8
Nicaragua	45.2	6

(*continued*)

TABLE 6.6 Continued

Country	Share of years in default or rescheduling since independence or 1800[a]	Total number of defaults and/or reschedulings
Latin America (*continued*)		
Panama	27.9	3
Paraguay	23.0	6
Peru	40.3	8
Uruguay	12.8	8
Venezuela	38.4	10
North America		
Canada	0.0	0
United States	0.0	0
Oceania		
Australia	0.0	0
New Zealand	0.0	0

Sources: The authors' calculations, Standard and Poor's, Purcell and Kaufman (1993), Reinhart, Rogoff, and Savastano (2003a) and sources cited therein.

[a]For countries that became independent prior to 1800, the calculations are for 1800–2008.

structuring at any given time. We have already seen such a timeline in figure 5.1 in terms of the total number of countries and in figure 5.2 in terms of the share of world income. These figures illustrate the clustering of defaults in an even more pronounced fashion than do our debt tables that mark first defaults.

Later, in chapter 16, we will take a deeper and more systematic look at what truly constitutes a global financial crisis.

- PART III -

THE FORGOTTEN HISTORY OF DOMESTIC DEBT AND DEFAULT

For most countries, finding data, even a couple of decades old, on domestic public debt is an exercise in archaeology.

- 7 -

THE STYLIZED FACTS OF
DOMESTIC DEBT AND DEFAULT

*D*omestic debt is a large portion of countries' total debt; for the sixty-four countries for which we have long-range time series, domestic debt averages almost two-thirds of total public debt. For most of the sample, these debts have typically carried a market interest rate except during the era of financial repression after World War II.

Domestic and External Debt

In part I we discussed the surprisingly exotic nature of our long-range sixty-four-country data set on domestic debt. Indeed, only recently have a few groups of scholars begun constructing data for the contemporary period.[1]

Figure 7.1 plots the share of domestic debt in total public debt for 1900–2007. It ranges between 40 and 80 percent of total debt. (See appendix A.2 for data availability by country.) Figures 7.2 and 7.3 break this information out by regions. The numbers in these figures are simple averages across countries, but the ratios are also fairly representative of many of the emerging markets in the sample (including now-rich countries such as Austria, Greece, and Spain when they were still emerging markets).[2] As the graphs underscore, our data set includes significant representation from every continent, not just a handful of Latin American and European countries, as is the case in most of the literature on external debt.

Of course, the experience has been diverse. For advanced economies, domestic debt accounts for the lion's share of public sector liabilities. At the other extreme, in some emerging markets, especially

Figure 7.1. Domestic public debt as a share of total debt:
All countries, 1900–2007.
Sources: The League of Nations, the United Nations,
and other sources listed in appendix A.2.

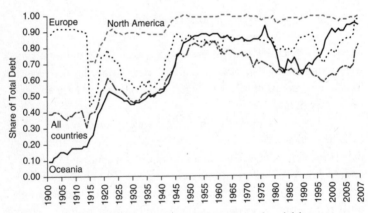

Figure 7.2. Domestic public debt as a share of total debt:
Advanced economies, 1900–2007.
Sources: The League of Nations, the United Nations,
and other sources listed in appendix A.2.

in the 1980s and 1990s, domestic debt markets were dealt a brutal blow by many governments' propensity to inflate (sometimes leading to hyperinflation). For instance, in the years following the hyperinflation of 1989 to 1990, domestic debt accounted for 10 to 20 percent of Peru's

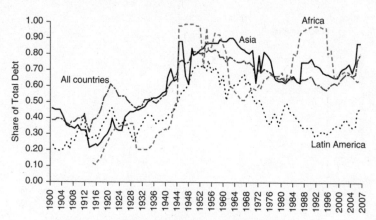

Figure 7.3. Domestic public debt as a share of total debt:
Emerging market economies, 1900–2007.
Sources: The League of Nations, the United Nations,
and other sources listed in appendix A.2.

public debt. Yet this was not always so. The early entries in the League of Nations data from the end of World War I show that Peru's domestic debt at the time accounted for about two-thirds of its public sector debt, as was then the case for many other countries in Latin America. Indeed, the share was even higher in the 1950s, when the world's financial centers were not engaged in much external lending.

Maturity, Rates of Return,
and Currency Composition

In addition to showing that domestic public debt is a large portion of total debt, the data also dispel the belief that until recently emerging markets (and developing countries) had never been able to borrow long term. As figure 7.4 shows, long-term debt constitutes a large share of the total debt stock over a significant part of the sample, at least for the period 1914–1959. For this subperiod, the League of Nations/ United Nations database provides considerable detail on maturity structure. It may come as a surprise to many readers (as it did to us) that the modern bias toward short-term debt is a relatively recent phe-

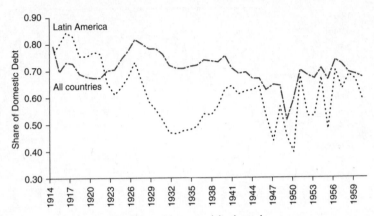

Figure 7.4. Share of domestic debt that is long term:
All countries and Latin America, 1914–1959.
Sources: The League of Nations, the United Nations,
and other sources listed in appendix A.2.

nomenon, evidently a product of the "inflation fatigue" of the 1970s
and 1980s.

Also not particularly novel was the fact that many emerging
markets began paying market-oriented interest rates on their domestic debt in the decade before the 2007 financial crisis. Of course, during the post–World War II era, many governments repressed their
domestic financial markets, with low ceilings on deposit rates and
high requirements for bank reserves, among other devices, such as directed credit and minimum requirements for holding government
debt in pension and commercial bank portfolios. But in fact, interest
rate data for the first half of the twentieth century shows that financial repression was neither so strong nor so universal. As table 7.1
shows for the years 1928–1946 (the period for which we have the best
documentation), interest rates on domestic and external debt issues
were relatively similar, supporting the notion that the interest rates
on domestic public debt were market determined, or at least reflected
market forces to a significant extent.

A final issue has to do with the extent of inflation or foreign
currency indexation. Many observers viewed Mexico's famous issuance of dollar-linked domestic debt in the early 1990s (the so-

TABLE 7.1
Interest rates on domestic and external debt, 1928–1946

Country	Range of interest rates (percent)	
	Domestic debt issues	External debt issues
Argentina	3–6	$3^1/_2$–$4^1/_2$
Australia	2–4	3.375–5
Austria	$4^1/_2$–6	5
Belgium	$3^1/_2$–5	3–7
Bolivia	$^1/_4$–8	6–8
Brazil	4–7	4–7
Bulgaria	4–$6^1/_2$	7–$7^1/_2$
Canada	1–$5^1/_2$	$1^1/_4$–$5^1/_2$
Chile	1–8	$4^1/_2$–7
Colombia	3–10	3–6
Costa Rica	6	5–$7^1/_2$
Denmark	$2^1/_2$–5	$4^1/_2$–6
Ecuador	3	4–8
Egypt	$2^1/_2$–$4^1/_2$	$3^1/_2$–4
Finland	4–$5^1/_2$	$2^1/_2$–7
Germany	$3^1/_2$–7	$5^1/_2$–6
Greece	3–9	3–10
Hungary	$3^1/_2$–5	3–$7^1/_2$
India	3–$5^1/_2$	3–$5^1/_2$
Italy	$3^1/_2$–5	No external debt
Japan	$3^1/_2$–5	4–$6^1/_2$
The Netherlands	$2^1/_2$–6	No external debt
New Zealand	$2^1/_2$–4	$2^1/_2$–5
Nicaragua	5	4–5
Poland	3–7	3–7
Portugal	2.1–7	3–4
Romania	$3^1/_2$–5	4–7
South Africa	$3^1/_2$–6	$3^1/_2$–6
Spain	$3^1/_2$–6	3–4
Sweden	$2^1/_2$–$4^1/_2$	No external debt
Thailand	$2^1/_2$–$4^1/_2$	$4^1/_2$–7
Turkey	$2^1/_2$–$5^1/_2$	$6^1/_2$–$7^1/_2$
United Kingdom	$1^1/_2$–4	No marketable external debt
United States	$1^1/_2$–$2^1/_2$	No external debt
Uruguay	5–7	$3^1/_2$–6
Venezuela	3	3

Source: United Nations (1948).

Notes: Rates on domestic issues are for long-term debt, because this facilitates comparison to external debt, which has a similar maturity profile. The higher interest rates are the most representative.

called *tesobonos*) as a major innovation. As the thinking went, this time was truly different. We know by now that the situation was nothing new; Argentina had issued domestic government bonds in the late 1800s that were denominated in pounds sterling, and Thailand had issued dollar-linked domestic debt in the 1960s. (See box 7.1 for the case studies and the appendixes for sources.)[3]

We can summarize what we know about domestic debt by noting that over most of history, for most countries (especially emerg-

---

BOX 7.1
Foreign currency–linked domestic debt: Thai *tesobonos?*

Our time series on domestic debt covers sixty-four of the sixty-six countries in the sample and begins in 1914 (and in several cases much earlier). During this lengthy period, domestic debt has been almost exclusively (especially prior to the 1990s) denominated in the domestic currency and held predominantly by domestic residents (usually banks). However, there have been notable exceptions that have blurred the lines between domestic and foreign debt. Some examples follow.

Mexican Dollar-Linked Domestic Debt:
The "Infamous" Tesobonos

As part of an inflation stabilization plan, in the late 1980s the Mexican peso was tied to the U.S. dollar via an official preannounced exchange rate band; de facto, it was a peg to the U.S. dollar. In early 1994, the peso came under speculative pressure following the assassination of presidential candidate Luis Donaldo Colosio. To reassure (largely) U.S. investors heavily exposed to Mexican treasury bonds that the government was committed to maintaining the value of the peso, the Mexican authorities began to link to the U.S. dollar its considerable stock of short-term domestic debt by means of "*tesobonos,*" short-term debt instruments repayable in pesos but linked to the U.S. dollar. By December 1994, when a new wave of speculation against the currency broke out, nearly all the domestic debt was dollar denominated. Before the end of the year, the peso was allowed to float; it immediately crashed, and a major episode of the twin currency and banking crises unfolded into early 1995. Had it not been for a then-record bailout package from the International Monetary Fund and the U.S. government, in all likelihood Mexico would have faced default on its sovereign debts. The central bank's dollar reserves had been nearly depleted and would not suffice to cover maturing bonds.

Because the *tesobonos* were dollar linked and held mostly by non-residents, most observers viewed the situation as a replay of August 1982, when Mexico had defaulted on is external debt to U.S. commercial banks. A nontrivial twist in the 1995 situation was that, if default proceedings had been necessary, they would have come under the jurisdiction of Mexican law. This episode increased international awareness of the vulnerabilities associated with heavily relying on foreign currency debt of any sort. The Mexican experience did not stop Brazil from issuing copious amounts of dollar-linked debt during the run-up to its turbulent exit from the *Real* Plan. Surprisingly, Mexico's earlier crisis had not raised concerns about the validity or usefulness of debt sustainability exercises that focused exclusively on external debt. Domestic government debt would continue to be ignored by the multilaterals and the financial industry for nearly another decade.

Argentine U.K. Pound–Denominated "Internal" Bonds of the Late Nineteenth and Early Twentieth Centuries

The earliest emerging market example of modern-day foreign currency–linked domestic debt widely targeted at nonresidents that we are aware of comes from Argentina in 1872.[4] After defaulting on its first loans in the 1820s, Argentina remained mostly out of international capital markets until the late 1860s. With some interruptions, most famously the Barings crisis of 1890, Argentina issued numerous external bonds in London and at least three more placements of domestic (or internal, as these were called) bonds in 1888, 1907, and 1909. Both the external and internal bonds were denominated in U.K. pounds. About a century later, after Argentina had fought (and lost) a long war with chronic high inflation, its domestic debts (as well as its banking sector) would become almost completely dollarized.[5]

Thailand's "Curious" Dollar-Linked Debt of the 1960s

Thailand is not a country troubled by a history of high inflation. Two large devaluations occurred in 1950 and 1954, and they had some moderate inflationary impact, but the situation during the late 1950s and early 1960s could hardly be described as one that would have fostered the need for an inflation hedge, such as indexing debts or issuing contracts to a foreign currency. Yet for reasons that remain a mystery to us, between 1961 and 1968 the Thai government issued dollar-linked domestic debt. During this period, domestic debt accounted for 80–90 percent of all government debt. Only about 10 percent of the domestic debt stock was linked to the U.S. dollar, so at no point in time was the Thai episode a case of significant "liability dollarization." We do not have information as to who were the primary holders of the domestic dollar-linked debt; perhaps such data might provide a clue as to why it came about in the first place.

ing markets), domestic debt has been a large and highly significant part of total debt. Nothing about the maturity structure of these debts or the interest rates paid on them lends justification to the common practice of ignoring them in calculations of the sustainability of external debt or the stability of inflation.

We acknowledge that our data set has important limitations. First, the data generally cover only central government debt. Of course, it would be desirable to have long-range time series on consolidated government debt, including state and local debt and guaranteed debt for quasi-public agencies. Furthermore, many central banks across the world issue debt on their own, often to sterilize foreign exchange intervention.[6] Adding such data, of course, would only expand the perception of how important domestic public debt has been.

We now take up some important potential applications of the data.

Episodes of Domestic Default

Theoretical models encompass a wide range of assumptions about domestic public debt. The overwhelming majority of models simply assume that debt is always honored. These include models in which deficit policy is irrelevant due to Ricardian equivalence.[7] (Ricardian equivalence is basically the proposition that when a government cuts taxes by issuing debt, the public does not spend any of its higher after-tax income because it realizes it will need to save to pay taxes later.) Models in which debt is always honored include those in which domestic public debt is a key input in price level determination through the government's budget constraint and models in which generations overlap.[8] There is a small amount of literature that aims to help us understand why governments honor domestic debt at all.[9] However, the general assumption throughout the literature is that although governments may inflate debt away, outright defaults on domestic public debt are extremely rare. This assumption is in stark contrast to the literature on external public debt, in which the government's incentive to default is one of the main focuses of inquiry.

In fact, our reading of the historical record is that overt de jure defaults on domestic public debt, though less common than external defaults, are hardly rare. Our data set includes more than 70 cases of overt default (compared to 250 defaults on external debt) since 1800.[10] These de jure defaults took place via a potpourri of mechanisms, ranging from forcible conversions to lower coupon rates to unilateral reduction of principal (sometimes in conjunction with a currency conversion) to suspensions of payments. Tables 7.2–7.4 list these episodes. Figure 7.5 aggregates the data, plotting the share of countries in default on domestic debt each year.

Our catalog of domestic defaults is almost certainly a lower bound, for domestic defaults are far more difficult to detect than defaults on international debt. Even the widespread defaults on domestic debt during the Great Depression of the 1930s in both advanced and developing economies are not well documented. As a more recent example, consider Argentina. Between 1980 and 2001, Argentina defaulted three times on its domestic debt. The two defaults that coincided with defaults on external debt (in 1982 and 2001) did attract considerable international attention. However, the large-scale 1989 default, which did not involve a new default on external debt, is scarcely known outside Argentina.

Some Caveats Regarding Domestic Debt

Why would a government refuse to pay its domestic public debt in full when it can simply inflate the problem away? One answer, of course, is that inflation causes distortions, especially to the banking system and the financial sector. There may be occasions on which, despite the inflation option, the government views repudiation as the lesser, or at least less costly, evil. The potential costs of inflation are especially problematic when the debt is relatively short term or indexed, because the government then has to inflate much more aggressively to achieve a significant real reduction in debt service payments. In other cases, such as in the United States during the Great Depression, default (by abrogation of the gold clause in 1933)

TABLE 7.2
Selected episodes of domestic debt default or restructuring, 1740–1921

Country	Dates	Commentary
Argentina	1890	This default also extended to several "internal" bonds. These bonds, although not issued in London, were denominated in a foreign currency (£s) and marketed abroad—the forerunners of the Mexican *tesobonos* of the 1990s.
China	March 1921	A consolidated internal debt plan was used to deal with arrears on most government bonds since 1919.
Denmark	January 1813	During the crisis, foreign debts were serviced but domestic debt was reduced by 39 percent.
Mexico	November 30, 1850	After the restructuring of foreign debt in October of that year, domestic debt, which accounted for 60 percent of total public debt, was cut roughly in half.
Peru	1850	Domestic colonial debts were not canceled; debt prices collapsed, and this debt was finally restructured.
Russia	December 1917– October 1918	Debts were repudiated and gold in all forms was confiscated, followed by confiscation of all foreign exchange.
United Kingdom	1749, 1822, 1834, 1888–1889	These were among several conversions of debt into lower coupon rates. The reductions in rates were mostly 0.5–1.0 percent in these episodes.
United States	January 1790	Nominally, interest was maintained at 6 percent, but a portion of the interest was deferred for ten years.
United States (nine states)	1841–1842	Three states repudiated their debts altogether.
United States (states and many local governments)	1873–1883 or 1884	By 1873, ten states were in default. In the case of West Virginia, settlement was as late as 1919.

Sources: Many sources were used in constructing this table. All are listed in the references.

TABLE 7.3
Selected episodes of domestic debt default or restructuring, late 1920s–1950s

Country	Dates	Commentary
Bolivia	1927	Arrears of interest lasted until at least 1940.
Canada (Alberta)	April 1935	This was the only province to default and the default lasted for about ten years.
China	1932	In this first of several "consolidations," the monthly cost of domestic service was cut in half. Interest rates were reduced to 6 percent (from more than 9 percent), and amortization periods were approximately doubled.
Greece	1932	Interest on domestic debt was reduced by 75 percent starting in 1932; domestic debt was about one-fourth of total public debt.
Mexico	1930s	Service on external debt was suspended in 1928. During the 1930s, interest payments included "arrears of expenditure and civil and military pensions."[a]
Peru	1931	After suspending service on external debt on May 29, Peru made "partial interest payments" on domestic debt.
Romania	February 1933	Redemption of domestic and foreign debt was suspended (except for three loans).
Spain	October 1936– April 1939	Interest payments on external debt were suspended; arrears on domestic debt service accumulated.
United States	1933	The gold clause was abrogated. In effect, the United States refused to pay Panama the annuity in gold that was due to Panama according to a 1903 treaty. The dispute was settled in 1936, when the United States paid the agreed amount in gold *balboas*.

(*continued*)

TABLE 7.3 Continued

Country	Dates	Commentary
United Kingdom[b]	1932	Most of the outstanding debt from World War I was consolidated into a 3.5 percent perpetual annuity.
Uruguay	November 1, 1932– February 1937	After suspending redemption of external debt on January 20, redemptions on domestic debt were likewise suspended.
Austria	December 1945	The schilling was restored, with a limit of 150 per person; the remainder were placed in blocked accounts. In December 1947, large amounts of previously blocked schillings were invalidated and rendered worthless. Fifty percent of deposits were temporarily blocked.
Germany	June 20, 1948	Monetary reform limited each person to 40 Deutschemark, along with partial cancellation and blocking of all accounts.
Japan	March 2, 1946–1952	After inflation, one-to-one exchange of bank notes for new issue was limited to 100 yen per person. Remaining balances were deposited in blocked accounts.
Russia	1947	The monetary reform subjected privately held currency to a 90 percent reduction.
	April 10, 1957	Domestic debt (about 253 billion rubles at the time) was repudiated.

Sources: Many sources were used in constructing this table. All are listed in the references.
[a]League of Nations (various years), *Statistical Abstract*.
[b]World War II debts to the United States were only partially repaid, by mutual agreement. Technically, this debt forgiveness constitutes a default.

TABLE 7.4
Selected episodes of domestic debt default or restructuring, 1970–2008

Country	Dates	Commentary
Africa		
Angola	1976, 1992–2002	
Cameroon	2004	
Congo (Kinshasa)	1979	
Gabon	1999–2005	
Ghana	1979, 1982	The country defaulted on central bank notes (in the context of conversion to a new currency).
Liberia	1989–2006	
Madagascar	2002	
Mozambique	1980	
Rwanda	1995	No external default.
Sierra Leone	1997–1998	
Sudan	1991	
Zimbabwe	2006	With maturities of less than a year for more than 98.5 percent of domestic debt, it was restructured.
Asia		
Mongolia	1997–2000	
Myanmar	1984, 1987	
Sri Lanka	1996	No external default.
Solomon Islands	1995–2004	
Vietnam	1975	
Europe and the Middle East		
Croatia	1993–1996	
Kuwait	1990–1991	
Russia	1998–1999	This was the largest local currency debt default (US$39 billion) since that in Brazil in 1990.
Ukraine	1998–2000	Bond maturities were unilaterally extended.
Western Hemisphere		
Antigua and Barbuda	1998–2005	

(continued)

TABLE 7.4 Continued

Country	Dates	Commentary
Western Hemisphere (*continued*)		
Argentina	1982, 1989–1990, 2002–2005	U.S. dollar–denominated debt was forcibly converted to peso debt.
Bolivia	1982	Deposits in U.S. dollars were forcibly converted into local currency. Foreign currency deposits were again allowed in 1985 as part of the stabilization plan when capital controls were lifted.
Brazil	1986–1987, 1990	Abrogation of inflation-linked indexes was embedded in the original contracts. The largest default (US$62 billion) occurred in 1990.
Dominica	2003–2005	
Dominican Republic	1975–2001	
Ecuador	1999	
El Salvador	1981–1996	This is the only case in Latin America in which a default on domestic debt was *not* accompanied by external default.
Grenada	2004–2005	
Mexico	1982	Dollar deposits were forcibly converted to pesos.
Panama	1988–1989	Domestic suppliers' credit, wages, and civil and military pensions were in arrears.
Peru	1985	Deposits in U.S. dollars were forcibly converted into local currency. Foreign currency deposits were allowed again in 1988.
Surinam	2001–2002	
Venezuela	1995–1997, 1998	

Sources: Many sources were used in constructing this table. All are listed in the references.

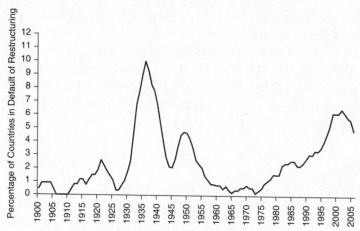

Figure 7.5. Sovereign domestic debt: Percent of countries in default
or restructuring, 1900–2008 (five-year moving average).
Sources: League of Nations; Reinhart, Rogoff, and Savastano
(2003a); Standard and Poor's; and the authors' calculations.
Notes: Unweighted aggregates.

was a precondition for reinflating the economy through expansion-
ary fiscal and monetary policy.

Of course, there are other forms of de facto default (besides
inflation). The combination of heightened financial repression with
rises in inflation was an especially popular form of default from the
1960s to the early 1980s. Brock makes the point that inflation and
reserve requirements are positively correlated, particularly in Africa
and Latin America.[11] Interest rate ceilings combined with inflation
spurts are also common. For example, during the 1972–1976 external debt rescheduling in India, (interbank) interest rates in India
were 6.6 and 13.5 percent in 1973 and 1974, while inflation spurted
to 21.2 and 26.6 percent. These episodes of de facto default through
financial repression are not listed among our de jure credit events.
They count at all only to the extent that inflation exceeds the 20 percent threshold we use to define an inflation crisis.[12]

Clearly, the assumption embedded in many theoretical models, that governments always honor the nominal face value of debt,

is a significant overstatement, particularly for emerging markets past and present. Nevertheless, we also caution against reaching the conclusion at the opposite extreme, that governments can ignore powerful domestic stakeholders and simply default at will (de jure or de facto) on domestic debt. We will now proceed to explore some implications of the overhang of large domestic debt for external default and inflation.

- 8 -

DOMESTIC DEBT: THE MISSING LINK EXPLAINING EXTERNAL DEFAULT AND HIGH INFLATION

Recognizing the significance of domestic debt can go a long way toward solving the puzzle of why many countries default on (or restructure) their external debts at seemingly low debt thresholds. In fact, when previously ignored domestic debt obligations are taken into account, fiscal duress at the time of default is often revealed to be quite severe.

In this chapter we also show that domestic debt may explain the paradox of why some governments seem to choose inflation rates far above any level that might be rationalized by seignorage revenues leveraged off the monetary base. (Loosely speaking, if a government abuses its currency monopoly by promiscuously printing currency, it will eventually drive the demand for its currency down so far that it actually takes in less real revenue from currency creation than it would at a lower level of inflation.) Although domestic debt is largely ignored in the vast empirical literature on high inflation and hyperinflation, we find that in many cases the hidden domestic public debt was at least the same order of magnitude as base money (currency plus private bank deposits at a government's central bank) and sometimes a large multiple of that amount.

Understanding the Debt Intolerance Puzzle

We begin by revisiting the conventional wisdom on external debt default and its implications for debt sustainability exercises and debt default thresholds. Indeed, in the 250 episodes of default on external debt in our database, it is clear that domestic debt loomed large across the vast majority of them. Table 8.1 gives the ratio of both external debt and total debt (including domestic and external liabilities) relative to government revenues on the eve of many of the most notable defaults of the nineteenth and twentieth centuries. We normalize debt by means of government revenues because data on nominal GDP is sketchy or nonexistent for the nineteenth-century default episodes. (For many countries, standard sources do not provide anything close to a continuous time series for GDP for the nineteenth century.)[1] Exports, which make sense as the main basis for assessing a country's ability to service external debt owed to foreigners, are perhaps less important than government revenues once domestic public debt is added to the calculus of debt sustainability.

Looking more broadly at our sample, figure 8.1 is based on the eighty-nine episodes of external default from 1827 to 2003 for which we have full data on external debt, total debt, and revenues. We see that in all regions except Latin America, external debt has typically accounted for less than half of total debt during the year a country has defaulted on external debt; for Latin America, the average ratio has been higher but still only 60 percent.

TABLE 8.1
Debt ratios at the time of default: Selected episodes

Country	Year of default	Ratio of external public debt to revenue	Ratio of total public debt to revenue
Mexico	1827	1.55	4.20
Spain	1877	4.95	15.83
Argentina	1890	4.42	12.46
Germany	1932	0.64	2.43
China	1939	3.10	8.96
Turkey	1978	1.38	2.69
Mexico	1982	3.25	5.06
Brazil	1983	0.83	1.98
Philippines	1983	0.23	1.25
South Africa	1985	0.09	1.32
Russia	1998	3.90	4.95
Pakistan	1998	3.32	6.28
Argentina	2001	1.59	2.62

Sources: See appendixes A.1 and A.2.

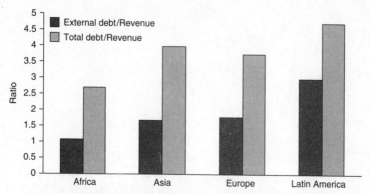

Figure 8.1. Ratios of public debt to revenue during external default:
Eighty-nine episodes, 1827–2003.
Sources: The League of Nations, Mitchell (2003a, 2003b), the
United Nations, and others sources listed in appendixes A.1 and A.2.

Thus, uncovering data on domestic debt suggests at least a partial answer to a basic question asked throughout the literature on international debt: Why do the governments of emerging markets tend to default at such stunningly low levels of debt repayment and ratios of debt to GDP?[2] In chapter 2, for example, we discussed evidence that serial defaulters tend to default at ratios of debt to GDP that are below the upper bound of 60 percent set by the euro area's Maastricht Treaty.[3] In fact, taking into account domestic public debt, the anomaly largely disappears.

Figures 8.2 and 8.3 give us a different perspective on the data by providing the frequency distribution (simple and cumulative) of external debt to GDP and of total debt to GDP across all the episodes of external debt in our sample for which we have full data. As the figures illustrate, the ratios of external debt to government revenue are massed at a much smaller average than are the ratios of total debt to government revenue during the year of an external default, with a mean of 2.4 versus 4.2. This order-of-magnitude difference is consistent across individual episodes (as table 8.1 highlights for some well-known cases). It is also consistent across regions and time.

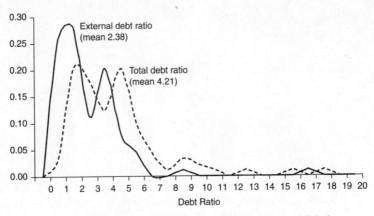

Figure 8.2. Ratios of public debt to revenue during external default:
Frequency of occurrence, 1827–2003.

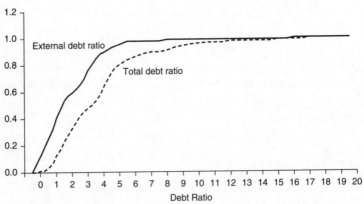

Figure 8.3. Ratios of public debt to revenue during external default:
Cumulative frequency of occurrence, 1827–2003.
Sources: The League of Nations, Mitchell (2003a, 2003b), the United Nations,
other sources listed in appendixes A.1 and A.2, and the authors' calculations.
Note: Kolmogorov-Smirnov, 31.46; significant at 1 percent.

Obviously, if domestic debt were trivial, the frequency distribution of the total debt ratio at the time of default should overlap that of domestic debt. That is, we should find that domestic debt is quite a small share of total debt on the eve of default. But this is hardly the case, and a standard battery of tests rejects this hypothesis across the board.[4]

Domestic Debt on the Eve and in the Aftermath of External Default

Domestic debt is not static around external default episodes. In fact, the precrisis buildup in domestic debt often shows the same frenzied increases in the run-up to external default as foreign borrowing does. The pattern is illustrated in figure 8.4, which depicts debt accumulation during the five years before and during external default across all the episodes in our sample.

Presumably, the co-movement of domestic and foreign debt is a product of the same procyclical behavior of fiscal policy documented by previous researchers.[5] As has been shown repeatedly over time, the governments of emerging markets are prone to treat favorable shocks as permanent, fueling a spree in government spending and borrowing that ends in tears.[6] Figure 8.4 does not continue past the default date. If it did, we would see that countries often continue

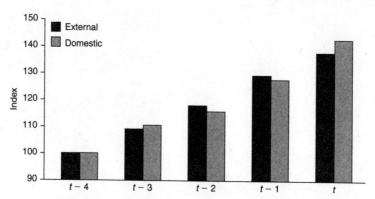

Figure 8.4. The run-up in government domestic and external debt on the eve of external default: Eighty-nine episodes, 1827–2003.
Sources: The League of Nations, the United Nations, and other sources listed in appendixes A.1 and A.2.
Note: The year of the default is indicated by t; $t - 4 = 100$.

to run up domestic public debt after they have been shut off from international capital markets.

Precommunist China (figure 8.5) provides an interesting and instructive example of why domestic debt often builds up in the aftermath of external defaults. Prior to its two major defaults in 1921 and 1939, China's government relied almost exclusively on external debt. But as access to foreign borrowing dried up, the government, still faced with the need to fund itself, was forced to rely on internal domestic borrowing, despite the underdeveloped state of China's financial markets. So it is hardly surprising that public domestic debt exploded in the aftermath of both incidents. By the mid-1940s, China's government relied almost exclusively on domestic debt.

The Literature on Inflation and the "Inflation Tax"

Another area of the literature that has, by and large, ignored domestic debt is the empirical work on high inflation and hyperinflation.

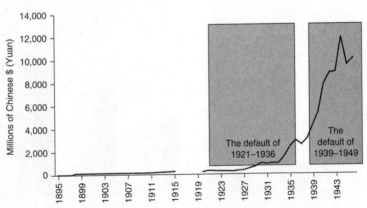

Figure 8.5. Domestic public debt outstanding: China, 1895–1949.
Sources: Huang (1919); Cheng (2003); the United Nations,
Department of Economic Affairs (various years),
Statistical Yearbook, 1948–1984; and the authors' calculations.
Note: Data for 1916–1919 are missing.

Ever since Cagan, researchers have concentrated on a government's incentives to gain seignorage revenues from the monetary base.[7] Indeed, a recurring paradox in this literature has to do with why governments sometimes seem to increase inflation above and beyond the seignorage-maximizing rate. Many clever and plausible answers to this question have been offered, with issues of time consistency and credibility featuring prominently. However, we submit that the presence of significant domestic public debt may be a major factor overlooked, especially considering—as we have already discussed—that a large share of debt was often long term and nonindexed. We do not refer simply to the study of rare hyperinflation episodes but equally to the much more common phenomenon of high and moderately high inflation as studied, for example, by Dornbusch and Fischer and by many others since.[8] Although there are literally hundreds of empirical papers on inflationary finance in developing countries and postconflict economies, domestic debt is rarely mentioned, much less employed in time series analysis.

Defining the Tax Base: Domestic Debt or the Monetary Base?

As in the literature on external debt, the implicit assumption is that domestic public debt is relatively unimportant. But is this a good approximation? Table 8.2 suggests that in many important episodes domestic debt has been a major factor in a government's incentive to allow inflation, if not indeed the dominant one.[9] Thus a comparison of actual inflation rates to any hypothetical "seignorage-maximizing rate," calculated only off the monetary base, may often be beside the point.

For example, we see from table 8.2 that when inflation first spiked to 66 percent in Germany in 1920 after World War I, domestic debt was almost triple the size of the monetary base. In the case of Brazil, domestic debt was almost 20 times the size of the money base.[10]

The importance of domestic debt is hardly confined to episodes of hyperinflation. Table 8.2 lists a number of high-inflation

TABLE 8.2
Inflation and domestic public debt: Selected episodes, 1917–1994

Country	Year	Rate of inflation	Ratio of domestic debt to GDP	Ratio of base money to GDP	Ratio of domestic debt to total domestic liabilities
		Some episodes of hyperinflation			
Argentina	1989	3,079.5	25.6	16.4	61.2
Brazil	1987	228.3	164.9	9.8	94.4
	1990	2,947.7	155.1	7.1	95.6
Germany	1920	66.5	52.6	19.4	73.0
	1923	22,220,194,522.37	0.0	0.0	1.0
		Episodes of high inflation			
Greece	1922	54.2	53.0	34.3	60.7
	1923	72.6	41.3	32.7	55.9
Italy	1917	43.8	79.1	24.1	76.6
	1920	56.2	78.6	23.5	77.1
Japan	1944	26.6	236.7	27.8	89.5
	1945	568.1[a]	266.5	74.4	78.2
Norway	1918	32.5	79.3	86.4	47.9
	1920	18.1	106.9	65.6	62.3
The Philippines	1981	13.1	10.4	6.6	61.1
	1984	46.2	11.0	13.9	44.2
Turkey	1990	60.3	14.7	7.4	66.6
	1994	106.3	20.2	7.1	73.9

Sources: See appendixes A.1 and A.2.
Notes: "Money" and "debt" refer to the levels at the beginning of each episode. The episodes of hyperinflation meet the classic Cagan definition.
[a]This episode does not meet the classic Cagan definition.

episodes as well. Domestic public debt was almost 80 percent of Japan's total domestic liabilities (including currency) in 1945, when inflation went over 500 percent. In all of the cases listed in table 8.2, domestic public debt has been at least the same order of magnitude as the monetary base (with the exception of the case of Norway, where it was slightly below that in 1918).

The "Temptation to Inflate" Revisited

Precise calculations of the gain to governments of inflating away the real value of their debt require considerably more information on the maturity structure of the debt and interest payments than is available in our cross-country data set. A critical piece of knowledge is the extent to which inflation is expected or not. In addition, one needs to understand bank reserve requirements, interest rate regulations, the degree of financial repression, and other constraints to make any kind of precise calculation. But the fact that domestic nominal debt has been so great compared to the base money across so many important episodes of high inflation suggests that debt needs to be given far more attention in future studies.[11]

We have now discussed some of the potential links among external default, inflation, and domestic debt, and emphasized that default through inflation is an important component of the domestic default calculus. In the next chapter we turn our attention to some features of the domestic versus external default cross-country experience that have hitherto remained unexplored.

- 9 -

DOMESTIC AND EXTERNAL DEFAULT: WHICH IS WORSE? WHO IS SENIOR?

We have shown that the amount of domestic debt is large in general, particularly in episodes of external default or high inflation. Clearly, in trying to understand how crises play out, it would be helpful to better understand the relative seniority of domestic and foreign debt. This section is an attempt to provide a first pass in looking at some key characteristics of the data. Clearly, the way crises play out is going to differ across countries and time. Many factors, such as the independence of the central bank and exchange rate regime, are likely to be relevant. Nevertheless, a few simple comparisons of the trajectory of output and inflation during the run-up to and the aftermath of domestic and external defaults are revealing.[1]

Our calculations can be taken as only suggestive for several reasons. One is simply that there is no comprehensive database on overt domestic debt defaults prior to our own, much less on de facto defaults. Although we are confident that we have a relatively complete picture of external defaults and episodes of high inflation in our sample, we simply do not know how many episodes of domestic default we may have missed, even restricting attention to de jure defaults. In this chapter we provide a broad indication of how clear episodes of domestic default or restructuring are hidden in the historical archives. Thus, our list of domestic defaults is surely a lower bound on the actual incidence.

Finally, but worthy of discussion, our approach is systematic in documenting the *incidence* of default but is silent about the *magnitude* of default. Even though our database on public debt can provide valuable insight on the magnitude of the original default or restructuring, it would be a stretch of the imagination to suggest that these data provide a snapshot of the subsequent restructuring nuances or the actual recovery rates. With these caveats in mind, a number of results stand out.

Real GDP in the Run-up to and the Aftermath of Debt Defaults

First, how bad are macroeconomic conditions on the eve of a default? Unambiguously, output declines in the run-up to a default on domestic debt are typically significantly worse than those seen prior to a default on external debt. As highlighted in figures 9.1 and 9.2, the average cumulative decline in output during the three-year run-up to a domestic default crisis is 8 percent. The output decline in the year of the domestic debt crisis alone is 4 percent; the comparable average decline for external debt events is 1.2 percent. To compare the antecedents of domestic and external defaults, we performed a variety of tests for individual years, as well as for the cumulative change in the window prior to default. The latter test comprised a total of 224 observations for domestic crises (that is, the number of annual observations in advance of domestic crises) and 813 for external crashes (again, years multiplied by number of crises).

As noted earlier, the results have to be interpreted with care, for many domestic episodes are twin default crises and, as a consequence, output is also suffering from limited access to external credit (if there is any at all).

Inflation in the Run-up to and the Aftermath of Debt Defaults

The comparable exercise for the inflation rate yields even starker differences (figures 9.3 and 9.4). Inflation during the year of an external default is on average high, at 33 percent.[2] However, inflation truly gallops during domestic debt crises, averaging 170 percent in the year of the default.[3] After the domestic default, inflation remains

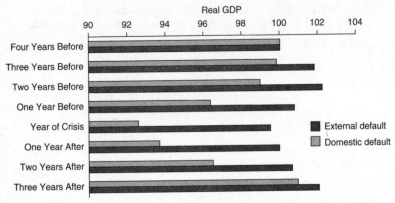

Figure 9.1. Real GDP before, during, and after domestic
and external debt crises, 1800–2008.
Sources: Maddison (2004), Total Economy Database (2008),
and the authors' calculations.
Note: Real GDP is indexed to equal 100 four years before the crisis.

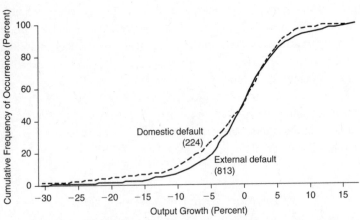

Figure 9.2. Domestic and external debt crises and real GDP, three
years before crisis and year of crisis, 1800–2008.
Sources: Maddison (2004), Total Economy Database (2008),
and the authors' calculations.
Notes: The Kolmogorov-Smirnov test (K-S test) is used to determine whether
two data sets differ significantly. The K-S test has the advantage of making no
assumption about the distribution of data. The test is nonparametric and
distribution free. Here Kolmogorov-Smirnov, 8.79; significant at 1 percent.

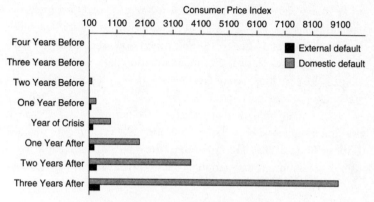

Figure 9.3. Consumer prices before, during, and after
domestic and external debt crises, 1800–2008.
Sources: International Monetary Fund (various years), *International
Financial Statistics* and *World Economic Outlook*; additional sources
listed in appendix A.1; and the authors' calculations.
Note: Consumer prices are indexed to equal 100 four years before the crisis.

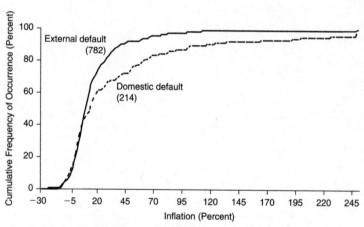

Figure 9.4. Domestic and external debt crises and inflation, three years
before crisis and year of crisis, 1800–2008.
Sources: International Monetary Fund (various years), *International
Financial Statistics* and *World Economic Outlook*; additional sources
listed in appendix A.1; and the authors' calculations.

at or above 100 percent in the following years. Not surprisingly, default through inflation goes hand in hand with domestic default— before, during, and after the more explicit domestic expropriations. The extensive scholarly literature on inflation has been silent on this point.[4] We conclude that overt domestic default tends to occur only in times of severe macroeconomic distress.

A more analytical approach in comparing real GDP growth and inflation across episodes of domestic and external debt defaults is shown in table 9.1. The columns of the table provide sample averages of economic growth and inflation in the run-up to and the after-

TABLE 9.1
Output and inflation around and during debt crises

	Average real GDP growth			Average inflation		
	Domestic	External	Difference	Domestic	External	Difference
$t-3$	−0.2	1.8	−2.0*	35.9	15.6	20.3*
$t-2$	−0.9	0.4	−1.3	38.3	14.6	23.7*
$t-1$	−2.6	−1.4	−1.2	68.0	15.0	53.0*
t (crisis)	−4.0	−1.2	−2.8*	171.2	33.4	137.8*
$t+1$	1.2	0.4	0.8	119.8	38.2	81.6*
$t+2$	3.0	0.7	2.3*	99.2	28.9	70.2*
$t+3$	4.6	1.4	3.2*	140.3	29.1	111.2*
$t-3$ to t	−1.9	−0.1	−1.8*	79.4	19.7	59.7*
$t+1$ to $t+3$	2.9	0.8	2.1*	119.8	32.1	87.7*

Means tests

Kolmogorov-Smirnov tests for the equality of two distributions

	Number of observations		K-S statistic	Number of observations		K-S statistic
	Domestic	External		Domestic	External	
$t-3$ to t and $t+1$ to $t+3$	224	813	8.8*	214	782	20.0*

Sources: International Monetary Fund (various years), *International Financial Statistics* and *World Economic Outlook*; Maddison (2004); Total Economy Database (2008); additional sources listed in appendixes A.1 and A.2; and the authors' calculations.

Notes: Means *t*-tests assume unknown and unequal variances. The year of default is indicated by *t*. An asterisk (*) denotes that the difference is statistically significant at the 1 percent level. The critical value of the Kolmogorov-Smirnov test at the 1 percent significance level is 5.16.

math of defaults on the two types of debt. The bottom row reports the results of a Kolmogorov-Smirnov test, which is a statistical test of the equality of two frequency distributions. Both real growth and inflation behave distinctly differently around domestic defaults than around external ones.

The Incidence of Default on Debts Owed to External and Domestic Creditors

To shed some light on the incidence of expropriation of residents versus nonresidents, we constructed four time series for the period 1800–2006, showing the probability of external default (or the share of countries in our sample that are in external default in a given year); the comparable statistic for domestic default episodes; the probability of an inflation crisis (defined here as the share of countries in any given year during the more than two hundred years of our sample in which the annual rate of inflation exceeded 20 percent); and the sum of the incidence of high inflation and domestic default, which summarizes the expropriation of the holdings of domestic residents.[5]

Figure 9.5 shows the probability of external default versus the comparable statistic for domestic default through either inflation or explicit default. Table 9.2 presents some summary statistics on the underlying data. During the early period and up to World War II, the incidence of external default was higher than it was later.[6] Specifically, for 1800–1939, the probability of external default was about 20 percent versus 12 percent for domestic residents. For the entire sample, there was no statistically significant difference in the incidence of default on debts to domestic creditors versus foreigners. With the widespread adoption of fiat money, inflation apparently became the more expedient form of expropriation. As a result, the incidence of taxing domestic residents increased after World War II.[7]

Figure 9.6 plots the probability of domestic default as a share of the probability of default. A ratio above 0.5 implies that domestic creditors do worse, while a ratio below 0.5 implies that foreigners do worse.

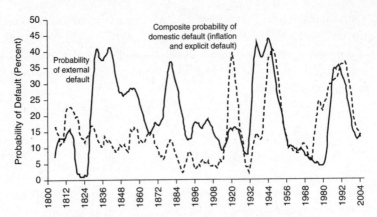

Figure 9.5. Who is expropriated, residents or foreigners?
The probability of domestic and external default, 1800–2006.
Sources: International Monetary Fund (various years), *International Financial Statistics* and *World Economic Outlook*; Maddison (2004); Total Economy Database (2008); additional sources listed in appendix A.1; and the authors' calculations.

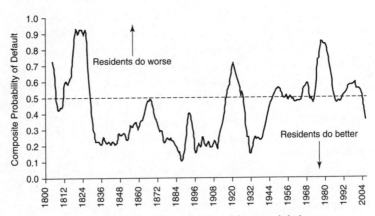

Figure 9.6. Composite probability of domestic default
as a share of the total default probability, 1800–2006.
Sources: International Monetary Fund (various years), *International Financial Statistics* and *World Economic Outlook*; Maddison (2004); Total Economy Database (2008); additional sources listed in appendix A.1; and the authors' calculations.

TABLE 9.2
Who gets expropriated, residents or foreigners? Preliminary tests for the
equality of two proportions (binomial distribution), 1800–2006

	The two samples	1800–2006	1800–1939	1940–2006
$n_1 = n_2$	Number of observations (years) over which the probability of external and domestic default was calculated	207	139	66
p_1	Probability of external default	0.1975	0.2048	0.1823
p_2	Composite probability of domestic default[a]	0.1505	0.1202	0.2138
$p_1 - p_2$	Difference	0.0470	0.0846	−0.0315
Z-test		1.2625	1.9122*	−0.4535
	Significance level	0.1034	0.0279	0.6749
Who was expropriated more, residents or foreigners?		Same	Foreigners	Same

Sources: International Monetary Fund (various years), *International Financial Statistics* and *World Economic Outlook;* Maddison (2004); Total Economy Database (2008); additional sources listed in appendixes A.1 and A.2; and the authors' calculations.

Notes: This table answers the question "Has the likelihood of expropriation of domestic residents increased in the recent period (i.e., from 1800–1939 to 1940–2006)?" The answer is "Yes!" Z-test, 1.4716; level of significance, 0.0706**; the year of default is indicated by t. The test statistic for the equality of two proportions is calculated as follows:

$$Z = \frac{(p_1 - p_2)}{\left\{P(1-P)\left[\frac{1}{n_1} + \frac{1}{n_2}\right]\right\}^{1/2}}, \text{ where } P = \frac{p_1 n_1 + p_2 n_2}{n_1 + n_2}.$$

[a]The composite probability of domestic default is defined as the probability of explicit default of domestic debt plus the probability of an inflation crisis (i.e. default through inflation).

* denotes significance at the 5 percent level.
** denotes significance at the 1 percent level.

Certainly, this admittedly very crude first pass at the evidence does nothing to dissuade us from our prior belief that domestic debt is often held by important political stakeholders in debtor countries and cannot always be lightly dismissed as strictly junior debt, a point highlighted by Allan Drazen.[8]

Table 9.2 allows us to look more systematically at the difference in the treatment of domestic residents and foreigners over time. It reports sample averages of the probability of domestic and external defaults for the entire period from 1800 to 2006 and two subperiods split at World War II. As is stated in the notes to the table, the probability that domestic residents would be expropriated was higher in the postwar period.

Summary and Discussion of Selected Issues

In the past few chapters we have provided an extensive new cross-country data set on a key macroeconomic variable that governments often manage to keep remarkably hidden from view: domestic public debt. We have also presented what we believe to be the first attempt at a cross-country international catalog of historical defaults on domestic public debt, spanning two centuries and sixty-six countries.

Our first look at the data suggests that researchers need to revisit the empirical literature on the sustainability of external government debt and on governments' incentives to engage in high inflation and hyperinflation, taking into account the newly uncovered data on domestic public debt and, where possible, broader definitions of government or government-guaranteed debt. Of course, how domestic debt impacts inflation and external default will vary across episodes and circumstances. In some cases, domestic debt is eliminated through high inflation; in other cases, governments default on external debt.

How did domestic public debt in emerging markets fall off many economists' radar screens? Many researchers, aware only of the difficulties of emerging markets in issuing debt in the ultra-high-inflation 1980s and 1990s, simply believed that no one would ever voluntarily lend in domestic currency to the kleptocratic government of an emerging market. Surely no one would trust such a government to resist inflating such debt down to nothing. The logical implication was that domestic currency public debt must not exist. True, a few researchers have contemplated the possibility. Alesina and Tabellini, for example, considered a theoretical case in which domestic debt was honored ahead of external debt.[9] But absent any data or even any awareness of the earlier existence of significant quantities of domestic public debt in virtually every country (even during its emerging market phase), these isolated examples have had no great impact on the mainstream academic or policy literature.

The lack of transparency exhibited by so many governments and multilateral institutions in failing to make time series on domestic debt easily available is puzzling. After all, these governments routinely tap domestic and foreign markets to sell debt. In general, uncertainty about a government's past repayment performance is more likely than not going to raise risk premiums on new issuances. Even more puzzling is why global investors do not insist on historical information relevant to the value of securities they may purchase. Any credit card company will want to know a consumer's purchase and repayment history, what kind of debt burdens the consumer has managed in the past, and under what circumstances. Surely historical information is equally relevant to governments.

One can only surmise that many governments do not want capital markets to fully recognize the risks they are running by piling on debt and debt guarantees due to their fear of having to pay much higher financing costs. Publishing historical data will make investors ask why current data cannot be made equally available. Still, one would think a strong case could be made for less profligate governments to open up their books more readily and be rewarded for doing so by lower interest rates. This transparency, in turn, would put pressure on weaker borrowers. Yet today even the United States runs an extraordinarily opaque accounting system, replete with potentially costly off-budget guarantees. In its response to the most recent financial crisis, the U.S. government (including the Federal Reserve Board) took huge off–balance sheet guarantees onto its books, arguably taking on liabilities that, from an actuarial perspective—as evaluated at the time of the bailout—were of the same order of magnitude as, say, expenditures on defense, if not greater. Why so many governments do not make it easier for standard databases to incorporate their debt histories is an important question for future academic and policy research.

From a policy perspective, a plausible case can be made that an international agency would be providing a valuable public good if it could enforce (or at least promote) basic reporting requirements and transparency across countries. Indeed, it is curious that today's multilateral financial institutions have never fully taken up the task of systematically publishing public debt data, especially in light of these agencies' supposed role at the vanguard of warning policy makers and investors about crisis risks. Instead, the system seems to have forgotten about the history of domestic debt entirely, thinking that today's blossoming of internal public debt markets is something entirely new and different.[10] But as our historical data set on domestic central government debt underscores with surprising force, nothing could be further from the truth. Indeed, we have reason to believe that with our data we have only touched the tip of the iceberg in terms of fully understanding public sector explicit and contingent liabilities.

- PART IV -

BANKING CRISES, INFLATION, AND CURRENCY CRASHES

Countries can outgrow a history of repeated bouts with high inflation, but no country yet has graduated from banking crises.

- 10 -

BANKING CRISES

*A*lthough many now-advanced economies have graduated from a history of serial default on sovereign debt or very high inflation, so far graduation from banking crises has proven elusive. In effect, for the advanced economies during 1800–2008, the picture that emerges is one of serial banking crises.

Until very recently, studies of banking crises have focused either on episodes drawn from the history of advanced countries (mainly the banking panics before World War II) or on the experience of modern-day emerging markets.[1] This dichotomy has perhaps been shaped by the belief that for advanced economies, destabilizing, systemic, multicountry financial crises are a relic of the past.[2] Of course, the Second Great Contraction, the global financial crisis that recently engulfed the United States and Europe, has dashed this misconception, albeit at great social cost.

As we will demonstrate in this chapter, banking crises have long impacted rich and poor countries alike. We develop this finding using our core sample of sixty-six countries (plus a broader extended sample for some exercises). We examine banking crises ranging from Denmark's financial panic during the Napoleonic Wars to the recent "first global financial crisis of the twenty-first century." The incidence of banking crises proves to be remarkably similar in both high-income and middle- to low-income countries. Indeed, the tally of crises is particularly high for the world's financial centers: France, the United Kingdom, and the United States. Perhaps more surprising still are the qualitative and quantitative parallels across disparate income groups. These parallels arise despite the relatively pristine modern-day sovereign default records of the rich countries.

For the study of banking crisis, three features of the data set underlying this book are of particular note. First, to reiterate, our data on banking crises go back to 1800. Second, to our knowledge, we are the first to examine the patterns of housing prices around major banking crises in emerging markets, including Asia, Europe, and Latin America. Our emerging market data set facilitates comparisons across both duration and magnitude with the better-documented housing price cycles in the advanced economies, which have long been known to play a central role in financial crises. We find that real estate price cycles around banking crises are similar in duration and amplitude across the two groups of countries. This result is surprising given that almost all other macroeconomic and financial time series (on income, consumption, government spending, interest rates, etc.) exhibit higher volatility in emerging markets.[3] Third, our analysis employs the comprehensive historical data on central government tax revenues and central government debt compiled (as detailed in chapter 3). These data afford a new perspective on the fiscal consequences of banking crises—notably emphasizing the implications for tax revenue and public debt, which are far more substantive than the usual narrower focus in the literature, bailout costs.

We find that banking crises almost invariably lead to sharp declines in tax revenues, while other factors leading to higher deficits can include the operation of automatic fiscal stabilizers, countercyclical fiscal policy, and higher interest payments due to elevated risk premiums and rating downgrades (particularly, but not exclusively, for emerging markets). On average, during the modern era, real government debt rises by 86 percent during the three years following a banking crisis. (That is, if central government debt was $100 billion at the start of a crisis, it would rise to $186 billion after three years, adjusted for inflation.) These fiscal consequences, which include both direct and indirect costs, are an order of magnitude larger than the usual bank bailout costs. The fact that the magnitudes are comparable in advanced and emerging market economies is again quite remarkable. Obviously, both bailout costs and other fiscal costs depend on a host of political and economic factors, especially the policy response and the severity of the real shock that, typically, triggers the crisis.[4]

A Preamble on the Theory of Banking Crises

Banking Crises in Repressed Financial Systems

Our sample includes basically two kinds of banking crises. The first is common in poor developing countries in Africa and elsewhere, although it occasionally surfaces in richer emerging markets, such as Argentina. These crises are really a form of domestic default that governments employ in countries where financial repression is a major form of taxation. Under financial repression, banks are vehicles that allow governments to squeeze more indirect tax revenue from citizens by monopolizing the entire savings and payments system, not simply currency. Governments force local residents to save in banks by giving them few, if any, other options. They then stuff debt into the banks via reserve requirements and other devices. This allows the government to finance a part of its debt at a very low interest rate; financial repression thus constitutes a form of taxation. Citizens put money into banks because there are few other safe places for their savings. Governments, in turn, pass regulations and restrictions to force the banks to relend the money to fund public debt. Of course, in cases in which the banks are run by the government, the central government simply directs the banks to make loans to it.

Governments frequently can and do make the financial repression tax even larger by maintaining interest rate caps while creating inflation. For example, this is precisely what India did in the early 1970s when it capped bank interest at 5 percent and engineered an increase in inflation of more than 20 percent. Sometimes even that action is not enough to satisfy governments' voracious need for revenue savings, and they stop paying their debts entirely (a domestic default). The domestic default forces banks, in turn, to default on their own liabilities so that depositors lose some or all of their money. (In some cases, the government might actually have issued deposit insurance, but in the event of default it simply reneges on that promise, too.)

143

Banking Crises and Bank Runs

True banking crises, of the variety more typically experienced in emerging markets and advanced economies, are a different kind of creature. As we mentioned in the preamble, banks' role in effecting maturity transformation—transforming short-term deposit funding into long-term loans—makes them uniquely vulnerable to bank runs.[5] Banks typically borrow short in the form of savings and demand deposits (which can, in principle, be withdrawn at short notice). At the same time, they lend at longer maturities, in the form of direct loans to businesses, as well as other longer-dated and higher-risk securities. In normal times, banks hold liquid resources that are more than enough to handle any surges in deposit withdrawals. During a "run" on a bank, however, depositors lose confidence in the bank and withdraw en masse. As withdrawals mount, the bank is forced to liquidate assets under duress. Typically the prices received are "fire sale" prices, especially if the bank holds highly illiquid and idiosyncratic loans (such as those to local businesses about which it has far better information than other investors). The problem of having to liquidate at fire sale prices can extend to a far broader range of assets during a systemic banking crisis of the kind we focus on here. Different banks often hold broadly similar portfolios of assets, and if all banks try to sell at once, the market can dry up completely. Assets that are relatively liquid during normal times can suddenly become highly illiquid just when the bank most needs them.

Thus, even if the bank would be completely solvent absent a run, its balance sheet may be destroyed by having to liquidate assets at fire sale prices. In such a case, the bank run is self-fulfilling. That is, it is another example of multiple equilibria, similar in spirit to when a country's creditors collectively refuse to roll over short-term debt. In the case of a bank run, it is depositors who are effectively refusing to roll over debt.

In practice, banking systems have many ways of handling runs. If the run is on a single bank, that bank may be able to borrow from a pool of other private banks that effectively provide deposit insurance to one another. However, if the run affects a broad enough range of institutions, private insurance pooling will not work. An example of such a run is the U.S. subprime financial crisis of 2007, because problematic mortgage assets were held widely in the banking sector. Exchange rate crises, as experienced by so many developing economies in the 1990s, are another example of a systemic financial crisis affecting almost all banks in a country. In crises represented by both of these examples, it is a real loss to the banking system that eventually sets off the shock. The shock may be manageable if confidence in the banking sector is maintained. However, if a run occurs, it can bankrupt the entire system, turning a damaging problem into a devastating one. Diamond and Dybvig argue that deposit insurance can prevent bank runs, but their model does not incorporate the fact that absent effective regulation, deposit insurance can induce banks to take excessive risk.[6]

Bank runs, in general, are simply one important example of the fragility of highly leveraged borrowers, public and private, as discussed in the preamble to this book. The implosion of the U.S. financial system during 2007–2008 came about precisely because many financial firms outside the traditional and regulated banking sector financed their illiquid investments using short-term borrowing. In modern financial systems, it is not only banks that are subject to runs but also other types of financial institutions that have highly leveraged portfolios financed by short-term borrowing.

Why Recessions Associated with Banking Crises Are So Costly

Severe financial crises rarely occur in isolation. Rather than being the trigger of recession, they are more often an amplification mechanism: a reversal of fortunes in output growth leads to a string of defaults on bank loans, forcing a pullback in other bank lending, which leads to further output falls and repayment problems, and so on. Also, banking crises are often accompanied by other kinds of crises, including exchange rate crises, domestic and foreign debt crises, and inflation crises; we will explore the coincidence and timing of crises in more detail in chapter 16. Thus, one should be careful not to interpret this first pass at our long historical data set as definitive evidence of the causal effects of banking crises; there is a relatively new area in which much further work is yet to be done.

That said, the theoretical and empirical literature on how financial crises can impact real activity is extremely broad and well developed. One of the most influential studies was reported in 1983 by Bernanke, who argued that when nearly half of all U.S. banks failed in the early 1930s, it took the financial system a long time to rebuild its lending capacity. According to Bernanke, the collapse of the financial system is a major reason that the Great Depression persisted, on and off, for a decade rather than ending in a year or two as a normal recession does. (Bernanke, of course, became Federal Reserve chairman in 2006 and had a chance to put his academic insights into practice during the Second Great Contraction, which began in 2007.)

In later work with Mark Gertler, Bernanke presented a theoretical model detailing how the presence of imperfections in the financial market due to asymmetric information between lenders and borrowers can result in an amplification of monetary policy shocks.[7] In the Bernanke-Gertler model, a decrease in wealth (due, say, to an adverse productivity shock) has an outsized effect on production as firms are forced to scale back their investment plans. Firms are forced to scale back on investment because, as their retained earnings fall, they must finance a larger share of their investment projects via more expensive external financing rather than by means of relatively cheap internal financing. Recessions cause a loss in collateral that is then amplified through the financial system.

Kiyotaki and Moore trace out a similar dynamic in a richer intertemporal model.[8] They show how a collapse in land prices (such as occurred in Japan beginning in the early 1990s) can undermine a firm's collateral, leading to a pullback in investment that causes a further fall in land prices, and so on.

In his 1983 article, Bernanke emphasized that the collapse of the credit channel in recessions is particularly acute for small and medium-sized borrowers who do not have name recognition and therefore have far less access than larger borrowers to bond and equity markets as an alternative to more relationship-oriented bank finance. Many subsequent papers have confirmed that small and medium-sized borrowers do suffer disproportionately during a recession, with a fair amount of evidence pointing to the bank lending channel as a central element.[9] We will not dwell further on the vast theoretical literature on financial markets and real activity except to say that there is indeed significant theoretical and empirical support for the view that a collapse in a country's banking system can have huge implications for its growth trajectory.[10]

We now turn to the empirical evidence. Given the vulnerability of banking systems to runs, combined with the theoretical and empirical evidence that banking crises are major amplifiers of recessions, it is little wonder that countries experience greater difficulties in outgrowing financial crises than they do in escaping a long history of sovereign debt crises. In the latter it is possible to speak of "graduation," with countries going for centuries without slipping back into default. But thus far, no major country has been able to graduate from banking crises.

Banking Crises: An Equal-Opportunity Menace

As shown earlier, the frequency of default (or restructuring) on external debt is significantly lower in advanced economies than in emerging markets. For many high-income countries, that frequency has effectively been zero since 1800.[11] Even countries with a long history of multiple defaults prior to 1800, such as France and Spain, present evidence of having graduated from serial default on external debt.

The second column in tables 10.1 and 10.2 highlights the vast difference in the experience of sovereign default between emerging markets (notably in Africa and Latin America but even in several countries in Asia) and high-income Western Europe, North America, and Oceania. The third column of tables 10.1 and 10.2 presents the analogous calculation for each country for banking crises (i.e., the number of years in banking crises, according to the extended data set developed here, divided by the number of years since the

TABLE 10.1
Debt and banking crises: Africa and Asia, year of independence to 2008

Country	Share of years in default or rescheduling since independence or 1800	Share of years in a banking crisis since independence or 1800
Africa		
Algeria	13.3	6.4
Angola	59.4	17.6
Central African Republic	53.2	38.8
Côte d'Ivoire	48.9	8.2
Egypt	3.4	5.6
Kenya	13.6	19.6
Mauritius	0.0	2.4
Morocco	15.7	3.8
Nigeria	21.3	10.2
South Africa	5.2	6.3
Tunisia	9.6	9.6
Zambia	27.9	2.2
Zimbabwe	40.5	27.3
Asia		
China	13.0	9.1
India	11.7	8.6
Indonesia	15.5	13.3
Japan	5.3	8.1
Korea	0.0	17.2
Malaysia	0.0	17.3
Myanmar	8.5	13.1
The Philippines	16.4	19.0
Singapore	0.0	2.3
Sri Lanka	6.8	8.2
Taiwan	0.0	11.7
Thailand	0.0	6.7

Sources: Authors' calculations; Purcell and Kaufman (1993); Kaminsky and Reinhart (1999); Bordo et al. (2001); Reinhart, Rogoff, and Savastano (2003a) and sources cited therein; Caprio et al. (2005); Jácome (2008); and Standard and Poor's. See also appendix A.2.

Note: For countries that became independent prior to 1800, the calculations are for 1800–2008.

TABLE 10.2

Debt and banking crises: Europe, Latin America, North America,
and Oceania, year of independence to 2008

Country	Share of years in default or rescheduling since independence or 1800	Share of years in a banking crisis since independence or 1800
Europe		
Austria	17.4	1.9
Belgium	0.0	7.3
Denmark	0.0	7.2
Finland	0.0	8.7
France	0.0	11.5
Germany	13.0	6.2
Greece	50.6	4.4
Hungary	37.1	6.6
Italy	3.4	8.7
The Netherlands	6.3	1.9
Norway	0.0	15.7
Poland	32.6	5.6
Portugal	10.6	2.4
Romania	23.3	7.8
Russia	39.1	1.0
Spain	23.7	8.1
Sweden	0.0	4.8
Turkey	15.5	2.4
United Kingdom	0.0	9.2
Latin America		
Argentina	32.5	8.8
Bolivia	22.0	4.3
Brazil	25.4	9.1
Chile	27.5	5.3
Colombia	36.2	3.7
Costa Rica	38.2	2.7
Dominican Republic	29.0	1.2
Ecuador	58.2	5.6
El Salvador	26.3	1.1
Guatemala	34.4	1.6
Honduras	64.0	1.1
Mexico	44.6	9.7
Nicaragua	45.2	5.4
Panama	27.9	1.9
Paraguay	23.0	3.1

(continued)

TABLE 10.2 Continued

Country	Share of years in default or rescheduling since independence or 1800	Share of years in a banking crisis since independence or 1800
Latin America (*continued*)		
Peru	40.3	4.3
Uruguay	12.8	3.1
Venezuela	38.4	6.2
North America		
Canada	0.0	8.5
United States	0.0	13.0
Oceania		
Australia	0.0	5.7
New Zealand	0.0	4.0

Sources: Authors' calculations; Purcell and Kaufman (1993); Kaminsky and Reinhart (1999); Bordo et al. (2001); Reinhart, Rogoff, and Savastano (2003a) and sources cited therein; Caprio et al. (2005); Jácome (2008); and Standard and Poor's. See also appendix A.2.

country won independence, or since 1800 if it achieved independence earlier). One striking observation from the tables is that the average length of time a country spends in a state of sovereign default is far greater than the average amount of time spent in financial crisis. A country can circumvent its external creditors for an extended period. It is far more costly to leave a domestic banking crisis hanging, however, presumably due to the crippling effects on trade and investment.

Tables 10.3 and 10.4 present a different perspective on the prevalence of banking crises. The second column tallies the number of banking crises (rather than the number of years in crisis) since a country's independence or 1800; the third column narrows the window to the post–World War II period. Several features are worth noting. *For the advanced economies over the full span, the picture that emerges is one of serial banking crises.* The world's financial centers—the United Kingdom, the United States, and France—stand out in this regard, with 12, 13, and 15 episodes of banking crisis since 1800, respectively. The frequency of banking crises dropped off markedly for the advanced economies and the larger emerging markets alike after

World War II. However, all except Portugal experienced at least one postwar crisis prior to the recent episode. When the recent wave of crises is fully factored in, the apparent drop will likely be even less pronounced. Thus, *although many now-advanced economies have graduated from a history of serial default on sovereign debt or very high inflation*

TABLE 10.3
Frequency of banking crises: Africa and Asia, to 2008

Country	Number of banking crises since independence or 1800	Number of banking crises since independence or 1945
Africa		
Algeria	1	1
Angola	1	1
Central African Republic	2	2
Côte d'Ivoire	1	1
Egypt	3	2
Kenya	2	2
Mauritius	1	1
Morocco	1	1
Nigeria	1	1
South Africa[a]	6	2
Tunisia	1	1
Zambia	1	1
Zimbabwe	1	1
Asia		
China	10	1
India[a]	6	1
Indonesia	3	3
Japan	8	2
Korea	3	3
Malaysia	2	2
Myanmar	1	1
The Philippines	2	2
Singapore	1	1
Sri Lanka	1	1
Taiwan	5	3
Thailand	2	2

Sources: Authors' calculations, Kaminsky and Reinhart (1999), Bordo et al. (2001), Caprio et al. (2005), and Jácome (2008). See also appendix A.2.
[a]For South Africa the calculations are for 1850–2008; for India they are for 1800–2008.

TABLE 10.4
Frequency of banking crises: Europe, Latin America,
North America, and Oceania, to 2008

Country	Number of banking crises since independence or 1800	Number of banking crises since independence or 1945
Europe		
Austria	3	1
Belgium	10	1
Denmark	10	1
Finland	5	1
France	15	1
Germany	8	2
Greece	2	1
Hungary	2	2
Italy	11	1
The Netherlands	4	1
Norway	6	1
Poland	1	1
Portugal	5	0
Romania	1	1
Russia	2	2
Spain	8	2
Sweden	5	1
Turkey	2	2
United Kingdom	12	4
Latin America		
Argentina	9	4
Bolivia	3	3
Brazil	11	3
Chile	7	2
Colombia	2	2
Costa Rica	2	2
Dominican Republic	2	2
Ecuador	2	2
El Salvador	2	2
Guatemala	3	2
Honduras	1	1
Mexico	7	2
Nicaragua	1	1
Panama	1	1
Paraguay	2	1
Peru	3	1

TABLE 10.4 Continued

Country	Number of banking crises since independence or 1800	Number of banking crises since independence or 1945
Latin America (*continued*)		
Uruguay	5	2
Venezuela	2	2
North America		
Canada	8	1
United States	13	2
Oceania		
Australia	3	2
New Zealand	1	1

Sources: Authors' calculations, Kaminsky and Reinhart (1999), Bordo et al. (2001), Caprio et al. (2005), and Jácome (2008).

Note: For countries that became independent prior to 1800, the calculations are for 1800–2008.

(*above 20 percent*), *so far graduation from banking crises has proven elusive*. As we will show later, the same applies to currency crashes. Indeed, tables 10.1–10.4 illustrate that despite dramatic differences in recent sovereign default performance, the incidence of banking crises is about the same for advanced economies as for emerging markets. It also should be noted that as financial markets have developed in the smaller, poorer economies, the frequency of banking crises has increased.[12]

Tables 10.5 and 10.6 summarize, by region, the evidence on the number of banking crises and the share of years each region has spent in a banking crisis. Table 10.5 starts in 1800. (The table includes postindependence crises only, which explains why emerging markets have lower cumulative totals.) Table 10.6 gives the evidence for the period since 1945.

Whether the calculations are done from 1800 (table 10.5) or from 1945 (table 10.6), on average there are no significant differences in either the incidence or the number of banking crises between advanced and emerging economies; indeed banking crises plague both sets of countries. In fact, prior to World War II, the ad-

TABLE 10.5

Summary of the incidence and frequency of banking crises,
1800 (or independence) to 2008

Region or group	Share of years in a banking crisis since independence or 1800	Number of banking crises
Africa	12.5	1.7
Asia	11.2	3.6
Europe	6.3	5.9
Latin America	4.4	3.6
Argentina, Brazil, and Mexico	9.2	9.0
North America	11.2	10.5
Oceania	4.8	2.0
Advanced economies	7.2	7.2
Emerging economies	8.3	2.8

Sources: Based on tables 10.1–10.4.

Notes: Advanced economies include Japan, North America, Oceania, and all European countries not listed below as part of emerging Europe. Emerging economies include Africa, all Asian countries except Japan, Latin America, and emerging Europe (Hungary, Poland, Romania, Russia, and Turkey).

TABLE 10.6

Summary of the incidence and frequency of banking crises,
1945 (or independence) to 2008

Region or group	Share of years in a banking crisis since independence or 1945	Number of banking crises
Africa	12.3	1.3
Asia	12.4	1.8
Europe	7.1	1.4
Latin America	9.7	2.0
Argentina, Brazil, and Mexico	13.5	3.0
North America	8.6	1.5
Oceania	7.0	1.5
Advanced economies	7.0	1.4
Emerging economies	10.8	1.7

Sources: Based on tables 10.1–10.4.

Notes: Advanced economies include Japan, North America, Oceania, and all European countries not listed below as part of emerging Europe. Emerging economies include Africa, all Asian countries except Japan, Latin America, and emerging Europe (Hungary, Poland, Romania, Russia, and Turkey).

vanced economies with their more developed financial systems were more prone to banking crises than were many of their smaller low-income counterparts.[13] Of course, it can be plausibly argued that smaller countries used foreign creditors as their bankers, and therefore the string of defaults on external debts might have been domestic banking crises had they more developed financial sectors.

Banking Crises, Capital Mobility, and Financial Liberalization

Also consonant with the modern theory of crises is the striking correlation between freer capital mobility and the incidence of banking crises, as shown in figure 10.1. The figure is highly aggregated, but a breakdown to regional or country-level data reinforces the message of the figure. *Periods of high international capital mobility have repeatedly produced international banking crises, not only famously, as they did in the 1990s, but historically.* The figure plots a three-year moving average of the share of all countries experiencing a banking crisis on the right-hand scale. On the left-hand scale we have graphed the index of international capital mobility, using the same design principle as Obstfeld and Taylor, both updated and cast back in time, to cover our full sample period.[14] Although the Obstfeld-Taylor index may have its limitations, we feel it nevertheless provides a concise summary of complicated forces by emphasizing de facto capital mobility based on actual flows.

For the period after 1970, Kaminsky and Reinhart have presented formal evidence of the link between crises and financial liberalization.[15] In eighteen of the twenty-six banking crises they studied, the financial sector had been liberalized within the preceding five years, usually less. In the 1980s and 1990s, most liberalization episodes were associated with financial crises of varying severity. In only a handful of countries (for instance, Canada) did liberalization of the financial sector proceed smoothly. Specifically, Kaminsky and Reinhart present evidence that the probability of a banking crisis conditional on financial liberalization having taken place is higher than the unconditional probability of a banking crisis. Using

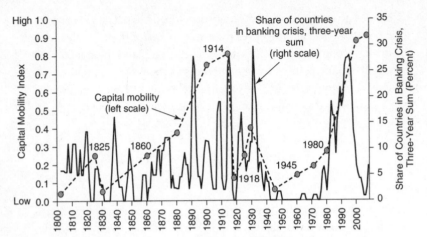

Figure 10.1. Capital mobility and the incidence of banking crises:
All countries, 1800–2008.
Sources: Kaminsky and Reinhart (1999), Bordo et al. (2001),
Obstfeld and Taylor (2004), Caprio et al. (2005), and the authors' calculations.
Notes: This sample includes all countries (even those not in our core sample
of sixty-six). The full listing of the dates of banking crises appears in appendixes
A.3 and A.4. This figure shows that the recovery in equities is far swifter than
that of the housing market. On the left-hand scale we updated our favorite
index of capital mobility, admittedly arbitrary but a concise summary of
complicated forces. The dashed line shows the index of capital mobility
given by Obstfeld and Taylor (2004), backcast from 1800 to
1859 using the same design principle they used.

a fifty-three-country sample for the period 1980–1995, Demirgüç-
Kunt and Detragiache also show, in the context of a multivariate
logit model, that financial liberalization has an independent negative effect on the stability of the banking sector and that this result
is robust across numerous specifications.[16]

The stylized evidence presented by Caprio and Klingebiel suggests that inadequate regulation and lack of supervision at the time of
liberalization may play a key role in explaining why deregulation and
banking crises are so closely entwined.[17] Again, this is a theme across developed countries and emerging markets alike. In the 2000s the United
States, for all its this-time-is-different hubris, proved no exception, for
financial innovation is a variant of the liberalization process.

156

Capital Flow Bonanzas, Credit Cycles, and Asset Prices

In this section we examine some of the common features of banking crises across countries, regions, and time. The focus is on the regularities among cycles in international capital flows, credit, and asset prices (specifically, housing and equity prices).

Capital Flow Bonanzas and Banking Crises

One common feature of the run-up to banking crises is a sustained surge in capital inflows, which Reinhart and Reinhart term a "capital flow bonanza." They delineate a criterion to define a capital flow bonanza (roughly involving several percent of GDP inflow on a multiyear basis), catalog (country-by-country) "bonanza" episodes for 1960–2006, and examine the links between bonanza spells and banking crises.[18] They employ the crises as defined and dated in appendix A.3.[19]

From the dates of banking crises and capital flow bonanzas, two country-specific probabilities can be calculated: the unconditional probability of a banking crisis and the probability of a banking crisis within a window of three years before and after a bonanza year or years—that is, the conditional probability of a crisis. If capital flow bonanzas make countries more crisis prone, the conditional probability of a crisis, $P(\text{Crisis Bonanza})$, should be greater than the unconditional probability, $P(\text{Crisis})$.

Table 10.7 reproduces a subset of the results given by Reinhart and Reinhart that are relevant to banking crises.[20] It presents aggregates of the country-specific conditional and unconditional probabilities for three groups (all countries, high-income countries, and middle- and low-income countries). *The probability of a banking crisis conditional on a capital flow bonanza is higher than the unconditional probability.* The bottom row of table 10.7 provides the share of countries for which $P(\text{Crisis Bonanza}) = P(\text{Crisis})$ as an additional indication of how commonplace it is across countries to see bonanzas associated with a more crisis-prone environment. The majority of countries (61 percent) register a higher propensity to experience a banking crisis around bonanza periods; this percentage would be

TABLE 10.7
The effect of a capital flow bonanza on the probability of a
banking crisis in a sixty-six country sample, 1960–2007

Indicator	Percentage of countries
Probability of a banking crisis	
Conditional on a capital flow bonanza	18.4
(three-year window)	
Unconditional	13.2
Difference	5.2*
Share of countries for which the conditional probability	
is greater than the unconditional probability	60.9

Source: Reinhart and Reinhart (2009, tables 2 and 4), and authors' calculations.
Notes: The window encompasses three years before the bonanza (see Reinhart and Reinhart 2009, table 2), the year (or years if these are consecutive) of the bonanza, and the three years following the episode. The asterisk (*) denotes significance at the 1 percent confidence level.

higher if one were to include post-2007 data in the table. (Many countries that have experienced the most severe banking crises during the late 2000s also ran large sustained current account deficits in the run-up to the crisis. These include many developed countries, such as Iceland, Ireland, Spain, the United Kingdom, and the United States.)

These findings on capital flow bonanzas are also consistent with other identified empirical regularities surrounding credit cycles. Mendoza and Terrones, who examine credit cycles in both advanced and emerging market economies using a very different approach from that just discussed, find that credit booms in emerging market economies are often preceded by surges in capital inflows. They also conclude that, although not all credit booms end in financial crisis, most emerging market crises were preceded by credit booms. They link credit booms to rising asset prices, an issue we turn to next.[21]

Equity and Housing Price Cycles and Banking Crises

In this section we summarize the literature on asset price bubbles and banking crises, extending it to incorporate new data on housing prices in emerging markets, as well as data on the crises that are currently unfolding in advanced economies.

The now-infamous real estate bubble in the United States that began to deflate at the end of 2005 occupies center stage as a culprit in the recent global financial crisis. But the Second Great Contraction is far from unique in that regard. In an earlier work, we documented the trajectory in real housing prices around all the post–World War II banking crises in advanced economies, with particular emphasis on the "Big Five" crises (Spain, 1977; Norway, 1987; Finland and Sweden, 1991; and Japan, 1992).[22] The pattern that emerges is clear: a boom in real housing prices in the run-up to a crisis is followed by a marked decline in the year of the crisis and subsequent years. Bordo and Jeanne, also studying the advanced economies during 1970–2001, found that banking crises tend to occur either at the peak of a boom in real housing prices or right after the bust.[23] Gerdrup presented a compelling narrative of the links between Norway's three banking crises from the 1890s through 1993 and the booms and busts in housing prices.[24]

Table 10.8 illustrates the magnitudes and durations of the downturns in housing prices that have historically accompanied major banking crises in both advanced and emerging economies. Although the links between developed-country banking crises and the housing price cycle have been examined both in our earlier work and in numerous other papers (most frequently case studies), this is the first time systematic evidence has been provided on the behavior of housing prices in emerging market economies around some of their major banking crises. The crisis episodes include the "Big Six" Asian crises of 1997–1998 (Indonesia, Korea, Malaysia, the Philippines, Thailand, and the much-buffeted Hong Kong).

Other episodes in emerging markets have included Argentina's megacrisis in 2001–2002 and Colombia's 1998 crisis, which produced the worst recession since the national income accounts began to be tabulated in the early 1920s. In the conjuncture of recent crises we include Hungary in addition to the advanced economies that have recently had housing market bubbles (Iceland, Ireland, Spain, the United Kingdom, and the United States).[25]

TABLE 10.8
Cycles of real housing prices and banking crises

Country	Year of crisis	Peak	Trough	Duration of downturn	Magnitude of decline (percent)
Advanced economies: The Big Five					
Finland	1991	1989:Q2	1995:Q4	Six years	−50.4
Japan	1992	1991:Q1	Ongoing	Ongoing	−40.2
Norway	1987	1987:Q2	1993:Q1	Five years	−41.5
Spain	1977	1978	1982	Four years	−33.3
Sweden	1991	1990:Q2	1994:Q4	Four years	−31.7
Asian economies: The Big Six					
Hong Kong	1997	1997:Q2	2003:Q2	Six years	−58.9
Indonesia	1997	1994:Q1	1999:Q1	Five years	−49.9
Malaysia	1997	1996	1999	Three years	−19.0
Philippines	1997	1997:Q1	2004:Q3	Seven years	−53.0
South Korea[a]	1997		2001:Q2	Four years	−20.4
Thailand	1997	1995:Q3	1999:Q4	Four years	−19.9
Other emerging economies					
Argentina	2001	1999	2003	Four years	−25.5
Colombia	1998	1997:Q1	2003:Q2	Six years	−51.2
Historic episodes					
Norway	1898	1899	1905	Six years	−25.5
United States	1929	1925	1932	Seven years	−12.6
Current cases					
Hungary	2008	2006	Ongoing	Ongoing	−11.3
Iceland	2007	November 2007	Ongoing	Ongoing	−9.2
Ireland	2007	October 2006	Ongoing	Ongoing	−18.9
Spain	2007	2007:Q1	Ongoing	Ongoing	−3.1
United Kingdom	2007	October 2007	Ongoing	Ongoing	−12.1
United States	2007	December 2005	Ongoing	Ongoing	−16.6

Sources: Bank for International Settlements and the individual country sources described in appendixes A.1 and A.2.
[a]Data series too short to mark peak.

Two features stand out from the summary statistics presented in table 10.8. First is the persistence of the cycle in real housing prices in both advanced economies and emerging markets, typically for four to six years.[26] The second feature that stands out from table 10.8 is that *the magnitudes of the declines in real housing prices around banking crises from peak to trough are not appreciably different in emerging and advanced economies.* This comparability is quite surprising given that most macroeconomic time series exhibit drastically greater volatility in emerging markets; therefore, it merits further attention.[27] Certainly the first results presented here from comparisons of housing price booms and busts around the dates of banking crises appear to provide strong support for the contention that banking crises are an equal-opportunity menace.

The prolonged housing price downturns following financial crises are in stark contrast to the behavior of real equity prices, as illustrated in figure 10.2, in which the pattern of decline and recovery is more V-shaped. (The figure shows only emerging markets, but, as we shall detail later in part V, equity prices exhibit a similar V-shaped recovery in advanced countries.)

The figure shows the evolution of real equity prices from four years prior to a crisis to three years afterward. As the figure makes plain, equity prices typically peak before the year of a banking crisis and decline for two to three years as the crisis approaches and, in the case of emerging markets, in the year following the crisis. The recovery is complete in the sense that three years after the crisis, real equity

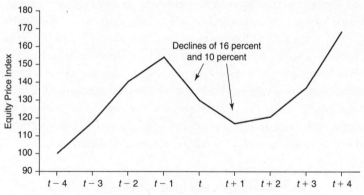

Figure 10.2. Real equity prices and banking crises:
Forty episodes in emerging markets, 1920–2007.
Sources: Global Financial Data (n.d.) and the authors' calculations.
Notes: Four of the forty episodes were from before World War II
(1921–1929). The year of the crisis is indicated by t; $t - 4 = 100$.

prices are on average higher than at the precrisis peak. However, post-crisis Japan offers a sobering counterexample to this pattern, because in that country equity prices only marginally recovered to a much lower peak than the precrisis level and have subsequently continued to drift lower.

One can conjecture that one reason major banking crises are such protracted affairs is that these episodes involve the real estate market's persistent cycle in a way that "pure stock market crashes"—for instance, Black Monday in October 1987 or the bursting of the information technology (IT) bubble in 2001—do not.[28]

Overcapacity Bubbles in the Financial Industry?

Philippon has analyzed the expansion of the financial services sector (including insurance) in the United States, which averaged 4.9 percent of GDP during 1976–1985 and rose to 7.5 percent during 1996–2005.[29] In his paper he argues that this gain was not sustainable and that a decline of at least 1 percent of GDP was probable. In the wake of the subprime crisis, the shrinkage of the financial sector during 2008 and 2009 is proving to be significantly larger. The precrisis explosion and postcollapse implosion of the financial sector surrounding a banking crisis are also not new or unique to the United States.

Figure 10.3 plots the number of banks in the United States in the run-up to and the aftermath of the Great Depression. Perhaps the bubble in equity and real estate prices also extended to the number of financial institutions. This expansion in the number of financial institutions in the run-up to a crisis and contraction in its aftermath have been evident during other banking crises—especially in those cases in which financial liberalization preceded the crisis.

The Fiscal Legacy of Financial Crises Revisited

Looking at the fiscal and growth consequences of banking crises, we again find some surprising parallels between developed countries and emerging markets. Our analysis of the fiscal consequences, in partic-

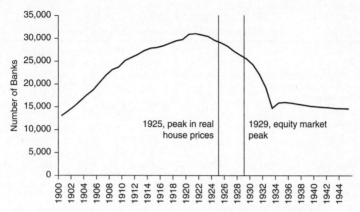

Figure 10.3. The number of banks in the United States, 1900–1945.
Source: Carter et al. (2006).

ular, is a sharp departure from the previous literature, which has focused almost entirely on imputed "bailout costs" to the government, which, as we will argue, are extremely difficult to measure. Instead, we focus on the fiscal costs to the central government, particularly the huge buildup in debt that follows banking crises. We are able to do so by tapping the extensive new cross-country data set on annual domestic debt that underlies the research for this book, data we have already exploited in earlier chapters. These data allow us to show the remarkable surge in debt that occurs in the wake of a crisis.

The Elusive Concept of Bailout Costs

As we have noted, much of the literature on episodes of banking crisis focuses on estimating the ultimate fiscal costs of the bailouts (see, for example, an excellent discussion by Frydl and various papers published by Norges Bank).[30] However, estimates of bailout costs vary markedly across studies, depending on the methodology, and vary even more across time, depending on the length of the horizon used to calculate the fiscal impact of the crisis, a point stressed by Frydl.[31]

Table 10.9 presents the upper and lower bounds of estimates of the bailout costs for some of the better-known banking crises in both advanced and emerging economies in nearly all regions. The

TABLE 10.9
Creative accounting? Bailout costs of banking crises

Country, beginning year	Estimated bailout cost as a percentage of GDP		
	Upper bound	Lower bound	Difference
Argentina, 1981	55.3	4.0	51.3
Chile, 1981	41.2	29.0	12.2
Ghana, 1982	6.0	3.0	3.0
Japan, 1992	24.0	8.0	16.0
Norway, 1987	4.0	2.0	2.0[a]
The Philippines, 1984	13.2	3.0	10.2
Spain, 1977	16.8	5.6	11.2
Sweden, 1991	6.4	3.6	2.8
United States (savings and loan crisis), 1984	3.2	2.4	0.8

Sources: Frydl (1999) and sources cited therein.

[a]Norges Bank (2004) argues that the Norwegian government ultimately made a small profit from the banking resolution.

discrepancies across estimates are large and, in some cases, staggering. Among the "Big Five" crises in advanced economies since World War II, the differences in estimated bailout costs for Japan and Spain, for instance, are 16 and 11 percent of GDP, respectively. Furthermore, as noted by Vale, if the costs are calculated over a longer time horizon after the crisis, the picture that emerges is even more at odds with the higher-end estimates; it shows that the Norwegian government actually made a small profit on the banking resolution due to the later sale of shares in the nationalized banks.[32]

In what follows, we argue that this nearly universal focus on opaque calculations of bailout costs is both misguided and incomplete. It is misguided because there are no widely agreed-upon guidelines for calculating these estimates. It is incomplete because the fiscal consequences of banking crises reach far beyond the more immediate bailout costs. These consequences mainly result from the significant adverse impact that the crisis has on government revenues (in nearly all cases) and the fact that in some episodes the fiscal policy reaction to the crisis has also involved substantial fiscal stimulus packages.

Growth in the Aftermath of Crises

The fact that most banking crises, especially systemic ones, are associated with economic downturns is well established in the empirical literature, although the effects on some key variables, such as housing and government debt and fiscal finances, more broadly, are much less studied.[33] Figure 10.4 shows output for the advanced economies as a group, as well as those that have experienced the "Big Five" crises (Japan, the Nordic countries, and Spain), while figure 10.5 augments this analysis with a comparable summary of the postwar banking crises in emerging markets. As before, t denotes the year of the crisis. Interestingly, the figures show a steeper decline but a somewhat faster comeback in growth for emerging markets than for the advanced economies. It is beyond the scope of this book to ascertain the longer-run growth consequences of banking crises (it is too difficult to delineate the end of banking crises, and growth is simply too complex a subject to mix in here). Nevertheless, this postcrisis pattern is noteworthy because growth (important in its own right) has nontrivial implications for fiscal balances, government debt, and the broader cost and consequences of any financial crisis.

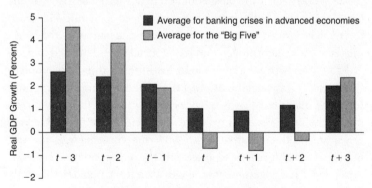

Figure 10.4. Real GDP growth per capita (PPP basis)
and banking crises: Advanced economies.
Sources: Maddison (2004); International Monetary Fund
(various years), *World Economic Outlook;* Total Economy
Database (2008), and the authors' calculations.
Notes: Episodes of banking crisis are listed in appendix A.3.
The year of the crisis is indicated by t.

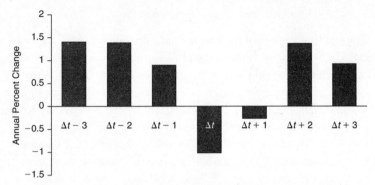

Figure 10.5. Real GDP growth per capita (PPP basis) and banking crises:
Emerging market economies (112 episodes).
Sources: Maddison (2004); International Monetary Fund (various years), *World Economic Outlook;* Total Economy Database; and the authors' calculations.
Notes: Episodes of banking crisis are listed in appendixes A.3 and A.4.
The year of the crisis is indicated by *t*.

Beyond Bailout Costs: The Impact of a Crisis on Revenues and Debt

Since World War II the most common policy response to a systemic banking crisis (in both emerging and advanced economies) has been to engineer (with varying degrees of success) a bailout of the banking sector, whether through purchases of bad assets, directed mergers of bad banks with relatively sound institutions, direct government takeovers, or some combination of these. In many cases such actions have had major fiscal consequences, particularly in the early phases of the crisis. However, as we have emphasized repeatedly, banking crises are protracted affairs with lingering consequences in asset markets—notably real estate prices and the real economy. It is no surprise, then, that government revenues are adversely and significantly impacted by crises.

As noted, several studies have traced the adverse impacts of banking crises on economic activity; what these studies have left unexplored are the direct consequences of the recession on government finances—specifically, tax revenues. Figure 10.6 plots the average pattern in annual real revenue growth three years before, during, and

166

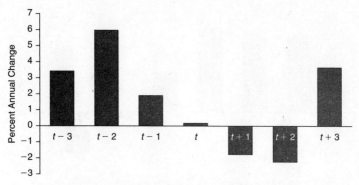

Figure 10.6. Real central government revenue growth
and banking crises: All countries, 1800–1944.
Sources: Revenues are from Mitchell (2003a, 2003b). For the numerous
country-specific sources of prices, see Reinhart and Rogoff (2008a).
Notes: The figure shows that the toll on revenue from crises is not
new. Central government revenues are deflated by consumer prices. There
were a total of eighty-six episodes of banking crisis during 1800–1940 for
which we have revenue data. The year of the crisis is indicated by t.

three years after a crisis for a total of eighty-six banking crises during
1800–1944 for which we have complete revenue data.[34]

A comparable exercise is shown in figure 10.7 for all 138
banking crises since World War II. The patterns of the pre- and postwar samples have not been identical but have been strikingly similar.
Annual revenue growth was robust in the years leading up to the banking crisis, weakened significantly in the year of the crisis, and subsequently posted declines in the years immediately following the onset
of the crisis. For the prewar episodes, revenues declined on average for
two years, while for the postwar crises the revenue slump has extended
to the third year.

Parallels in Revenue Losses between
Emerging Markets and Developed Economies

Again, the parallels in revenue losses between developed countries
and emerging markets have been striking. Figure 10.8 shows the revenue declines surrounding banking crises for the advanced countries
across the entire sample, with the "Big Five" postwar crises listed sep-

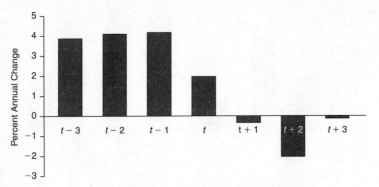

Figure 10.7. Real central government revenue growth
and banking crises: All countries, 1945–2007.
Sources: Revenue information is taken from Mitchell (2003a, 2003b). For the
numerous country-specific sources of prices, see Reinhart and Rogoff (2008a).
Notes: The figure shows that bailout costs are only part of the story of why public
debt surges after a crisis. Central government revenues are deflated by consumer
prices. There were a total of 138 banking crises during 1945–2008 for which we
have revenue data. The year of the crisis is indicated by *t*.

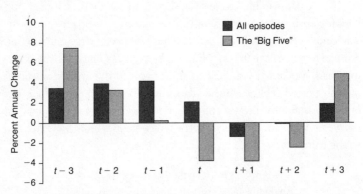

Figure 10.8. Real central government revenue growth
and banking crises: Advanced economies, 1815–2007.
Sources: Revenue information is taken from Mitchell (2003a, 2003b). For the
numerous country-specific sources of prices, see Reinhart and Rogoff (2008a).
Notes: Central government revenues are deflated by consumer prices.
The year of the crisis is indicated by *t*.

arately. Generally revenue growth resumes (from a lower base) starting in the third year after a crisis. Advanced economies exhibit a stronger inclination to resort to stimulus measures to cushion economic activity, as seen most spectacularly in the aggressive use of infrastructure spending in Japan during the 1990s. Emerging markets, more debt intolerant and more dependent on the vagaries of international capital markets for financing, are far less well poised to engage in countercyclical fiscal policy. Nevertheless, the effect of a crisis on the trajectory of taxes is broadly similar between the types of countries. Figure 10.9 shows revenue declines around banking crises for emerging markets for the entire sample. The average revenue drop is actually quite similar to that of the "Big Five" crises, although the recovery is faster—in line with a swifter recovery in growth, as discussed in the preceding section.

Government Debt Buildup in the Aftermath of Banking Crises

To obtain a rough approximation of the impact of a crisis on government finances, we use the historical data on central government debt compiled in appendix A.2, as discussed earlier. It is important

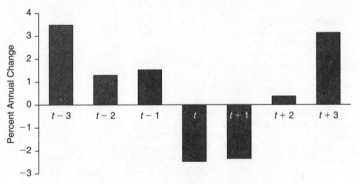

Figure 10.9. Real central government revenue growth
and banking crises: Emerging market economies, 1873–2007.
Sources: Revenue information is from Mitchell (2003a, 2003b). For the
numerous country-specific sources of prices, see appendix A.1.
Notes: The figure shows that the toll on revenue adds to the debt.
Central government revenues are deflated by consumer prices.
The year of the crisis is indicated by *t*.

to note that these data provide only a partial picture, because the entire country, including states and municipalities (not just the central government), is affected by the crisis. Also, typically during these episodes, government-guaranteed debt expands markedly, but this tendency does not show up in the figures for central governments.

With these caveats in mind, figure 10.10 presents a summary of the evolution of debt in the aftermath of some of the major postwar crises in both advanced and emerging markets.

Not surprisingly, taken together, the bailout of the banking sector, the shortfall in revenue, and the fiscal stimulus packages that have accompanied some of these crises imply that there are widening fiscal deficits that add to the existing stock of government debt. What is perhaps surprising is how dramatic the rise in debt is. *If the stock of debt is indexed to equal 100 at the time of the crisis (t), the average experience is one in which the real stock of debt rises to 186 three years after the crisis. That is to say, the real stock of debt nearly doubles.*[35] Such increases in government indebtedness are evident in emerging and advanced economies alike, and extremely high in both. Arguably, the true legacy of banking crises is greater public indebtedness—far

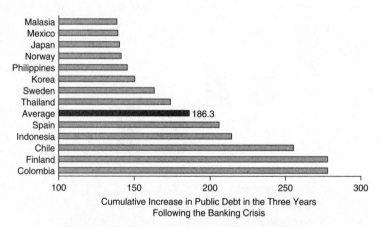

Figure 10.10. The evolution of real public debt following major postwar crises: Advanced and emerging markets.
Source: Reinhart and Rogoff (2008c). *Note:* The stock of debt is indexed to equal 100 in the year of the crisis (central government debt only).

over and beyond the direct headline costs of big bailout packages.[36] (Obviously, as we noted earlier, the rise in public debt depends on a whole range of political and economic factors, including the effectiveness of the policy response and the severity of the initial real economic shock that produced the crisis. Nevertheless, the universality of the large increase in debt is stunning.)

Living with the Wreckage: Some Observations

Countries may, perhaps, "graduate" from serial default on sovereign debt and recurrent episodes of very high inflation (or at least go into remission for extremely long periods), as the cases of Austria, France, Spain, and other countries appear to illustrate. History tells us, however, that graduation from recurrent banking and financial crises is much more elusive. And it should not have taken the 2007 financial crisis to remind us of that fact. Out of the sixty-six countries in our sample, only Austria, Belgium, Portugal, and the Netherlands managed to escape banking crises from 1945 to 2007. During 2008, however, even three of these four countries were among those to engage in massive bailouts.

Indeed, the wave of financial crises that began with the onset of the subprime crisis in the United States in 2007 has dispelled any prior notion among academics, market participants, or policy makers that acute financial crises are either a thing of the past or have been relegated to the "volatile" emerging markets. The this-time-is-different syndrome has been alive and well in the United States, where it first took the form of a widespread belief that sharp productivity gains stemming from the IT industry justified price-earnings ratios in the equity market that far exceeded any historical norm.[37] That delusion ended with the bursting of the IT bubble in 2001. But the excesses quickly reemerged, morphing into a different shape in a different market. The securitization of subprime mortgages combined with a heavy appetite for these instruments in countries such as Germany, Japan, and major emerging markets like China fueled the perception that housing prices would continue to climb forever. The new delusion was that "this time is different" because there were

171

new markets, new instruments, and new lenders. In particular, financial engineering was thought to have tamed risk by better tailoring exposures to investors' appetites. Meanwhile, derivatives contracts offered all manner of hedging opportunities. We now know how the latest popular delusion unraveled. We will return to the more recent financial crisis, the Second Great Contraction, in chapters 13–16.

In sum, historical experience already shows that rich countries are not as "special" as some cheerleaders had been arguing, both when it comes to managing capital inflows and especially when it comes to banking crises. The extensive new data set on which this book is based includes data on housing prices in some key emerging markets as well as data on revenue and domestic debt that date back almost a century for most countries and more for many. Surprisingly, not only are the frequency and duration of banking crises similar across developed countries and middle-income countries; so too are quantitative measures of both the run-up to and the fallout from such crises. Notably, for both groups the duration of declines in real housing prices following financial crises is often four years or more, and the magnitudes of the crashes are comparable. One striking finding is the huge surge in debt that most countries experience in the wake of a financial crisis, with central government debt typically increasing by about 86 percent on average (in real terms) during the three years following the crisis.

This chapter has emphasized the huge costs of recessions associated with systemic banking crises. It is important to emphasize, however, that in the theory of banking crises (discussed briefly in the introduction to this chapter), they are seen as an amplification mechanism and not necessarily as an exogenous causal mechanism. When a country experiences an adverse shock—due, say, to a sudden drop in productivity, a war, or political or social upheaval—naturally banks suffer. The rate of loan default goes up dramatically. Banks become vulnerable to large losses of confidence and withdrawals, and the rates of bank failure rise. Bank failures, in turn, lead to a decrease in credit creation. Healthy banks cannot easily cover the loan portfolios of failed banks, because lending, especially to small and medium-sized businesses, often involves specialized knowledge and relationships.

Bank failures and loan pullbacks, in turn, deepen the recession, caus-ing more loan defaults and bank failures, and so on.

Modern economies depend on sophisticated financial sys-tems, and when banking systems freeze up, economic growth can quickly become impaired or even paralyzed. That is why mass bank failures can be so problematic for an economy and why countries in crisis that fail to fix their financial systems—such as Japan in the 1990s—can find themselves going in and out of recession and per-forming below potential capacity for years.

Although there is a well-developed theory of why banking failures are so problematic in amplifying recessions, the empirical ev-idence we have provided does not, in itself, decisively show that banks are the only problem. The kind of real estate and stock price collapses that surround banking crises, as documented here, would have very substantial adverse effects even in the absence of a bank-ing collapse. As we will see in chapter 16 on the varieties of crisis, many other kinds of crises—including inflation, exchange rate, and domestic and sovereign default crises—often hit in coincidence with banking crises, especially the most severe ones. Thus what we have really shown here is that severe banking crises are associated with deep and prolonged recessions and that further work is needed to es-tablish causality and, more important, to help prioritize policy re-sponses. Nevertheless, the fact that recessions associated with severe banking crises are so consistently deep and share so many character-istics has to serve as a key starting point for future researchers as they attempt to untangle these difficult episodes.

- 11 -

DEFAULT THROUGH DEBASEMENT:
AN "OLD WORLD" FAVORITE

Although inflation really became a commonplace and chronic problem only with the widespread use of paper currency in the early 1900s, students of the history of metal currency know that governments found ways to "extract seignorage" from the currency in circulation long before that. The main device was debasement of the content of the coinage, either by mixing in cheaper metals or by shaving down coins and reissuing smaller ones in the same denomination. Modern currency presses are just a more technologically advanced and more efficient approach to achieving the same end.[1]

Kings, emperors, and other sovereigns have found inventive ways to avoid paying debts throughout recorded history. Winkler gives a particularly entertaining history of early default, beginning with Dionysius of Syracuse in Greece of the fourth century B.C.[2] Dionysius, who had borrowed from his subjects in the form of promissory notes, issued a decree that all money in circulation was to be turned over to the government, with those refusing subject to the pain of death. After he collected all the coins, he stamped each one-drachma coin with a two-drachma mark and used the proceeds to pay off his debts. Although we do not have any data from the period, standard price theory makes the strong presumption that general price levels must have soared in the aftermath of Dionysius's swindle. Indeed, classical monetary theory suggests that, all else equal (including a country's production), prices should double with a doubling of the money supply, meaning an inflation rate of 100 percent. In practice, the level of inflation might have been greater, assuming that the financial chaos and uncertainty that must have hit Syracuse led to a decrease in output at the same time the money supply was being doubled.

Whether or not this innovation had a precedent we do not know. But we do know that the example of Dionysius included several elements that have been seen with startling regularity throughout history. First, inflation has long been the weapon of choice in sovereign defaults on domestic debt and, where possible, on international debt. Second, governments can be extremely creative in engineering defaults. Third, sovereigns have coercive power over their subjects that helps them orchestrate defaults on domestic debt "smoothly" that are not generally possible with international debt. Even in modern times, many countries have enforced severe penalties on those violating restrictions on capital accounts and currency. Fourth, governments engage in massive money expansion, in part because they can thereby gain a seignorage tax on real money balances (by inflating down the value of citizens' currency and issuing more to meet demand). But they also want to reduce, or even wipe out, the real value of public debts outstanding. As noted in chapter 8, as obvious as the domestic debt channel is, it has been neglected in many episodes because the data have not been readily available.

For economists, Henry VIII of England should be almost as famous for clipping his kingdom's coins as he was for chopping off the heads of its queens. Despite inheriting a vast fortune from his father, Henry VII, and even after confiscating the church's assets, he found himself in such desperate need of funds that he resorted to an epic debasement of the currency. This debasement began in 1542 and continued through the end of Henry's reign in 1547 and on into that of his successor, Edward VI. Cumulatively, the pound lost 83 percent of its silver content during this period.[3] (The reader should note that by "debasement" we mean reduction in the silver or gold content of coins, as opposed to inflation, which measures their purchasing power. In a growing economy, a government might be able to slowly debase its coins without lowering their purchasing power because the public will demand more coins as the cost of transactions grows.)

Tables 11.1 and 11.2 provide details on the timing and magnitude of currency debasements across a broad range of European countries in 1258–1799 during the era before the development of paper currency and in the 1800s, the period of transition to paper money.

TABLE 11.1
Expropriation through currency debasement: Europe, 1258–1799

Country, currency	Period covered	Cumulative decline in silver content of currency (percent)	Largest debasement (percent) and year		Share (percentage) of years in which there was a debasement of the currency (a reduction in the silver content)	
					All	15 percent or greater
Austria, Vienna, kreuzer	1371–1499	−69.7	−11.1	1463	25.8	0.0
	1500–1799	−59.7	−12.5	1694	11.7	0.0
Belgium, hoet	1349–1499	−83.8	−34.7	1498	7.3	3.3
	1500–1799	−56.3	−15.0	1561	4.3	0.0
France, livre tournois	1258–1499	−74.1	−56.8	1303	6.2	0.4
	1500–1789	−78.4	−36.2	1718	14.8	1.4
Germany						
Bavaria-Augsburg, pfennig	1417–1499	−32.2	−21.5	1424	3.7	1.2
	1500–1799	−70.9	−26.0	1685	3.7	1.0
Frankfurt, pfennig	1350–1499	−14.4	−10.5	1404	2.0	0.0
	1500–1798	−12.8	−16.4	1500	2.0	0.3
Italy, lira fiorentina	1280–1499	−72.4	−21.0	1320	5.0	0.0
	1500–1799	−35.6	−10.0	1550	2.7	0.0
Netherlands						
Flemish grote	1366–1499	−44.4	−26.0	1488	13.4	5.2
	1500–1575	−12.3	−7.7	1526	5.3	0.0
Guilder	1450–1499	−42.0	−34.7	1496	14.3	6.1
	1500–1799	−48.9	15.0	1560	4.0	0.0
Portugal, reis	1750–1799	−25.6	−3.7	1766	34.7	0.0
Russia, ruble	1761–1799	−42.3	−14.3	1798	44.7	0.0
Spain						
New Castile, maravedis	1501–1799	−62.5	−25.3	1642	19.8	1.3
Valencia, dinar	1351–1499	−7.7	−2.9	1408	2.0	0.0
	1500–1650	−20.4	−17.0	1501	13.2	0.7
Sweden, mark ortug	1523–1573	−91.0	−41.4	1572	20.0	12.0
Turkey, akche	1527–1799	−59.3	−43.9	1586	10.5	3.1
United Kingdom, pence	1260–1499	−46.8	−20.0	1464	0.8	0.8
	1500–1799	−35.5	−50.0	1551	2.3	1.3

Sources: Primarily Allen and Unger (2004) and other sources listed in appendix A.1.

TABLE 11.2

Expropriation through currency debasement: Europe, nineteenth century

Country	Period covered	Cumulative decline in silver content of currency (percent)	Largest debasement (percent) and year		Share (percentage) of years in which there was a debasement of the currency (a reduction in the silver content)	
					All	15 percent or greater
Austria	1800–1860	−58.3	−55.0	1812	37.7	11.5
Germany	1800–1830	−2.2	−2.2	1816	3.2	0.0
Portugal	1800–1855	−12.8	−18.4	1800	57.1	1.8
Russia	1800–1899	−56.6	−41.3	1810	50.0	7.0
Turkey	1800–1899	−83.1	−51.2	1829	7.0	7.0
United Kingdom	1800–1899	−6.1	−6.1	1816	1.0	0.0

Sources: Primarily Allen and Unger (2004) and other sources listed in appendix A.1.

The tables illustrate how strikingly successful monarchs were in implementing inflationary monetary policy via currency debasement. The United Kingdom achieved a 50 percent reduction in the silver content of its currency in 1551, Sweden achieved a debasement of 41 percent in 1572, and Turkey's amounted to 44 percent in 1586. The Russian ruble experienced a debasement of 14 percent in 1798 as part of the country's war-financing effort. The third column of each table looks at cumulative currency debasement over long periods, often adding up to 50 percent or more. Table 11.2 looks at the statistics for European countries during the nineteenth century; outliers include Russia's debasement of 57 percent in 1810 and Austria's of 55 percent in 1812, both related to the economic strains associated with the Napoleonic Wars. In 1829, Turkey managed to reduce the silver content of its coins by 51 percent.

The pattern of sustained debasement emerges strikingly in figure 11.2, which plots the silver content of an equally weighted average of the European currencies in our early sample (plus Russia and

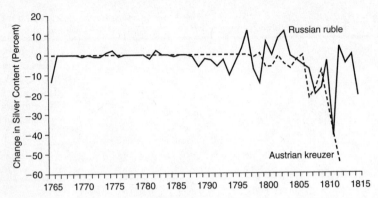

Figure 11.1. Changes in the silver content of the currency, 1765–1815:
Austria and Russia during the Napoleonic Wars.
Sources: Primarily Allen and Unger (2004) and other
sources listed in appendix A.1.3.

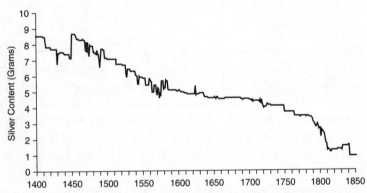

Figure 11.2. The march toward fiat money, Europe, 1400–1850:
The average silver content of ten currencies.
Sources: Primarily Allen and Unger (2004) and other
sources listed in appendix A.1.3.
Notes: In cases in which there was more than one currency
circulating in a particular country (in Spain, for example, we have the
New Castile *maravedi* and the Valencia dinar), we calculate the
simple average. Note that the Napoleonic Wars lasted from
1799 to 1815. In 1812, Austria debased its currency by 55 percent.

Turkey). Figure 11.2 shows what we refer to as "the march toward fiat money" and illustrates that modern inflation is not as different from debasement as some might believe. (The reader will recall that fiat money is currency that has no intrinsic value and is demanded by the public in large part because the government has decreed that no other currency may be used in transactions.)

Perhaps it may seem excessive to devote so much attention here to currency debasement when financial crises have long since moved on to grander and more extravagant schemes. Yet the experience of debasement illustrates many important points. Of course, it shows that inflation and default are nothing new; only the tools have changed. More important, the shift from metallic to paper currency provides an important example of the fact that technological innovation does not necessarily create entirely new kinds of financial crises but can exacerbate their effects, much as technology has constantly made warfare more deadly over the course of history. Finally, our study of debasement reinforces the point that today's advanced economies once experienced the same kind of default, inflation, and debasement traumas that plague many emerging markets today.

- 12 -

INFLATION AND MODERN
CURRENCY CRASHES

If serial default is the norm for a country passing through the emerging market state of development, the tendency to lapse into periods of high and extremely high inflation is an even more striking common denominator.[1] *No emerging market country in history, including the United States (whose inflation rate in 1779 approached 200 percent) has managed to escape bouts of high inflation.*

Of course, the problems of external default, domestic default, and inflation are all integrally related. A government that chooses to default on its debts can hardly be relied on to preserve the value of its country's currency. Money creation and interest costs on debt all enter the government's budget constraint, and in a funding crisis, a sovereign will typically grab from any and all sources.

In this chapter we begin with a helicopter tour (so to speak) of our entire cross-country inflation data set, which, to our knowledge, spans considerably more episodes of high inflation and a broader range of countries than any previously existing body of data. We then go on to look at exchange rate collapses, which are very strongly correlated with episodes of high inflation. In most cases, high inflation and collapsing exchange rates result from a government's abuse of its self-proclaimed monopoly on currency issuance. In the final section of this chapter, we look at how, in the aftermath of high inflation, this monopoly over currency (and sometimes over the broader payments system) often becomes eroded through widespread acceptance and/or indexation of a hard currency alternative, or "dollarization." Just as banking crises have persistent adverse consequences on the economy, so does high inflation.

A key finding that jumps out from our historical tour of inflation and exchange rates is how difficult it is for countries to escape a history of high and volatile inflation. Indeed, there is a strong parallel between escaping a history of high inflation and escaping a history of serial default, and of course the two are often interwined.

An Early History of Inflation Crises

However spectacular some of the coinage debasements reported in tables 11.1 and 11.2, without question the advent of the printing press elevated inflation to a whole new level. Figure 12.1 illustrates the median inflation rate for all the countries in our sample from 1500 to 2007 (we used a five-year moving average to smooth out cycle and measurement errors). The figure shows a clear inflationary bias throughout history (although of course there are always periods of deflation due to business cycles, poor crops, and so on). Starting in the twentieth century, however, inflation spiked radically. (We note that our inflation sample goes back to the 1300s for countries such as

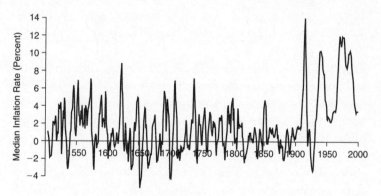

Figure 12.1. The median inflation rate: Five-year moving average for all countries, 1500–2007.
Sources: Given the long period covered and the large number of countries included, consumer prices (or cost-of-living indexes) are culled from many different sources. They are listed in detail by country and period in appendix A.1.

France and England, but in order to achieve a broader and more uniform comparison, we begin here in 1500.)

In the three tables in this chapter we look at country inflation data across the centuries. Table 12.1 presents data for the sixteenth through eighteenth centuries over a broad range of currencies. What is stunning is that every country in both Asia and Europe experienced a significant number of years with inflation over 20 percent during this era, and most experienced a significant number of years with inflation over 40 percent. Take Korea, for example, for which our data set begins in 1743. Korea experienced inflation over 20 percent almost half the time until 1800 and inflation over 40 percent almost a third of the time. Poland, for which our data go back to 1704, experienced similar percentages. Even the United Kingdom had over 20 percent inflation 5 percent of the time, going back to 1500 (and this is probably an underestimate, because official figures of inflation during World War II and its immediate aftermath are widely thought to be well below the levels of inflation that actually prevailed). The New World colonies of Latin America experienced frequent bouts of high inflation long before their wars of independence from Spain.

Modern Inflation Crises: Regional Comparisons

Table 12.2 looks at the years 1800–2007 for thirteen African countries and twelve Asian countries. South Africa, Hong Kong, and Malaysia have notably the best track records in resisting high inflation, though South Africa's record extends back to 1896, whereas Hong Kong's and Malaysia's go back only to 1948 and 1949, respectively.[2]

Most of the countries in Africa and Asia, however, have experienced waves of high and very high inflation. The notion that Asian countries have been immune to Latin American–style high inflation is just as naïve as the notion that Asian countries were immune to default crises up until the Asian financial crisis of the late 1990s. China experienced inflation over 1,500 percent in 1947,[3] and Indonesia over 900 percent in 1966. Even the Asian "tigers,"

TABLE 12.1
"Default" through inflation: Asia, Europe, and the "New World," 1500–1799

Country	Period covered	Share of years in which inflation exceeded		Number of hyperinflations[a]	Maximum annual inflation	Year of peak inflation
		20 percent	40 percent			
Asia						
China	1639–1799	14.3	6.2	0	116.7	1651
Japan	1601–1650	34.0	14.0	0	98.9	1602
Korea	1743–1799	43.9	29.8	0	143.9	1787
Europe						
Austria	1501–1799	8.4	6.0	0	99.1	1623
Belgium	1501–1799	25.1	11.0	0	185.1	1708
Denmark	1749–1799	18.8	10.4	0	77.4	1772
France	1501–1799	12.4	2.0	0	121.3	1622
Germany	1501–1799	10.4	3.4	0	140.6	1622
Italy	1501–1799	19.1	7.0	0	173.1	1527
The Netherlands	1501–1799	4.0	0.3	0	40.0	1709
Norway	1666–1799	6.0	0.8	0	44.2	1709
Poland	1704–1799	43.8	31.9	0	92.1	1762
Portugal	1729–1799	19.7	2.8	0	83.1	1757
Spain	1501–1799	4.7	0.7	0	40.5	1521
Sweden	1540–1799	15.5	4.1	0	65.8	1572
Turkey	1586–1799	19.2	11.2	0	53.4	1621
United Kingdom	1501–1799	5.0	1.7	0	39.5	1587
The "New World"						
Argentina	1777–1799	4.2	0.0	0	30.8	1780
Brazil	1764–1799	25.0	4.0	0	33.0	1792
Chile	1751–1799	4.1	0.0	0	36.6	1763
Mexico	1742–1799	22.4	7.0	0	80.0	1770
Peru	1751–1799	10.2	0.0	0	31.6	1765
United States	1721–1799	7.6	4.0	0	192.5	1779

Sources: Given the long period covered and the large number of countries included, consumer prices (or cost-of-living indexes) are culled from many different sources. They are listed in detail by country and period in appendix A.1.

[a]Hyperinflation is defined here as an annual inflation rate of 500 percent or higher (this is not the traditional Cagan definition).

TABLE 12.2
"Default" through inflation: Africa and Asia, 1800–2008

Country	Beginning of period covered	Share of years in which inflation exceeded		Number of years of hyperinflation[a]	Maximum annual inflation	Year of peak inflation
		20 percent	40 percent			
Africa						
Algeria	1879	24.1	12.0	0	69.2	1947
Angola	1915	53.3	44.6	4	4,416.0	1996
Central African Republic	1957	4.0	0.0	0	27.7	1971
Côte d'Ivoire	1952	7.3	0.0	0	26.0	1994
Egypt	1860	7.5	0.7	0	40.8	1941
Kenya	1949	8.3	3.3	0	46.0	1993
Mauritius	1947	10.0	0.0	0	33.0	1980
Morocco	1940	14.9	4.5	0	57.5	1947
Nigeria	1940	22.6	9.4	0	72.9	1995
South Africa	1896	0.9	0.0	0	35.2	1919
Tunisia	1940	11.9	6.0	0	72.1	1943
Zambia	1943	29.7	15.6	0	183.3	1993
Zimbabwe	1920	23.3	14.0	Ongoing	66,000	
Asia						
China	1800	19.3	14.0	3	1,579.3	1947
Hong Kong	1948	1.7	0.0	0	21.7	1949
India	1801	7.3	1.5	0	53.8	1943
Indonesia	1819	18.6	9.6	1	939.8	1966
Japan	1819	12.2	4.8	1	568.0	1945
Korea	1800	35.3	24.6	0	210.4	1951
Malaysia	1949	1.7	0.0	0	22.0	1950
Myanmar	1872	22.2	6.7	0	58.1	2002
The Philippines	1938	11.6	7.2	0	141.7	1943
Singapore	1949	3.4	0.0	0	23.5	1973
Taiwan	1898	14.7	11.0	0	29.6	1973
Thailand	1821	14.0	7.5	0	78.5	1919

Sources: Given the long period covered and the large number of countries included, consumer prices (or cost-of-living indexes) are culled from many different sources. They are listed in detail by country and period in appendix A.1.

[a]Hyperinflation is defined here as an annual inflation rate of 500 percent or higher (this is not the traditional Cagan definition).

Singapore and Taiwan, experienced inflation well over 20 percent in the early 1970s.

Africa, perhaps not surprisingly, has a considerably worse record. Angola had inflation over 4,000 percent in 1996, Zimbabwe already over 66,000 percent by 2007, putting that country on track to surpass the Republic of the Congo (one of the poor developing countries divorced from global private capital markets that is not included in our sample), which has experienced three episodes of hyperinflation since 1970.[4] And for 2008 Zimbabwe's inflation rate would be seen to have been even worse.

Finally, table 12.3 lists the inflation rates for 1800 through 2008 for Europe, Latin America, North America, and Oceania. The European experiences include the great postwar hyperinflations studied by Cagan.[5] But even setting aside hyperinflations, countries such as Poland, Russia, and Turkey have experienced high inflation an extraordinarily large percentage of the time. In modern times, one does not think of Scandinavian countries as having outsize inflation problems, but they too experienced high inflation in earlier eras. Norway, for example, had an inflation rate of 152 percent in 1812, Denmark 48 percent in 1800, and Sweden 36 percent in 1918. Latin America's post–World War II inflation history is famously spectacular, as the table illustrates, with many episodes of peacetime hyperinflations in the 1980s and 1990s. Latin America's poor performance looks less unique, however, from a broader perspective in terms of countries and history.

Even Canada and United States have each experienced an episode of inflation over 20 percent. Although U.S. inflation never again reached triple digits after the eighteenth century, it did reach 24 percent in 1864, during the Civil War. (Of course, the Confederacy of the South did achieve triple-digit inflation with its currency during the Civil War, which the break-away states ultimately lost.) Canada's inflation rate reached 24 percent as well during 1917. In all of table 12.3, we can see that only New Zealand and Panama have experienced no periods of inflation over 20 percent, although New Zealand's inflation rate reached 17 percent as recently as 1980 and Panama had 16 percent inflation in 1974.

TABLE 12.3
"Default" through inflation: Europe, Latin America, North America, and Oceania, 1800–2008

Country	Beginning of period covered	Share of years in which inflation exceeded		Number of years of hyperinflation[a]	Maximum annual inflation	Year of peak inflation
		20 percent	40 percent			
Europe						
Austria	1800	20.8	12.1	2	1,733.0	1922
Belgium	1800	10.1	6.8	0	50.6	1812
Denmark	1800	2.1	0.5	0	48.3	1800
Finland	1861	5.5	2.7	0	242.0	1918
France	1800	5.8	1.9	0	74.0	1946
Germany	1800	9.7	4.3	2	2.22E + 10	1923
Greece	1834	13.3	5.2	4	3.02E + 10	1944
Hungary	1924	15.7	3.6	2	9.63E + 26	1946
Italy	1800	11.1	5.8	0	491.4	1944
The Netherlands	1800	1.0	0.0	0	21.0	1918
Norway	1800	5.3	1.9	0	152.0	1812
Poland	1800	28.0	17.4	2	51,699.4	1923
Portugal	1800	9.7	4.3	0	84.2	1808
Russia	1854	35.7	26.4	8	13,534.7	1923
Spain	1800	3.9	1.0	0	102.1	1808
Sweden	1800	1.9	0.0	0	35.8	1918
Turkey	1800	20.5	11.7	0	115.9	1942
United Kingdom	1800	2.4	0.0	0	34.4	1800
Latin America						
Argentina	1800	24.6	15.5	4	3,079.5	1989
Bolivia	1937	38.6	20.0	2	11,749.6	1985
Brazil	1800	28.0	17.9	6	2,947.7	1990
Chile	1800	19.8	5.8	0	469.9	1973
Colombia	1864	23.8	1.4	0	53.6	1882
Costa Rica	1937	12.9	1.4	0	90.1	1982
Dominican Republic	1943	17.2	9.4	0	51.5	2004
Ecuador	1939	36.8	14.7	0	96.1	2000
El Salvador	1938	8.7	0.0	0	31.9	1986
Guatemala	1938	8.7	1.4	0	41.0	1990
Honduras	1937	8.6	0.0	0	34.0	1991
Mexico	1800	42.5	35.7	0	131.8	1987
Nicaragua	1938	30.4	17.4	6	13,109.5	1987
Panama	1949	0.0	0.0	0	16.3	1974
Paraguay	1949	32.8	4.5	0	139.1	1952
Peru	1800	15.5	10.7	3	7,481.7	1990

TABLE 12.3 Continued

Country	Beginning of period covered	Share of years in which inflation exceeded		Number of years of hyperinflation[a]	Maximum annual inflation	Year of peak inflation
		20 percent	40 percent			
Latin America (*continued*)						
Uruguay	1871	26.5	19.1	0	112.5	1990
Venezuela	1832	10.3	3.4	0	99.9	1996
North America						
Canada	1868	0.7	0.0	0	23.8	1917
United States	1800	1.0	0.0	0	24.0	1864
Oceania						
Australia	1819	4.8	1.1	0	57.4	1854
New Zealand	1858	0.0	0.0	0	17.2	1980

Sources: Given the long period covered and the large number of countries included, consumer prices (or cost-of-living indexes) are culled from many different sources. They are listed in detail by country and period in appendix A.1.

[a]Hyperinflation is defined here as an annual inflation rate of 500 percent or higher (this is not the traditional Cagan definition).

As in the case of debt defaults, the early years following the 2001 global recession proved to be a relatively quiescent period in terms of very high inflation, although a number of countries (including Argentina, Venezuela, and of course Zimbabwe) did experience problems.[6] Many observers, following the same logic as with external default, have concluded that "this time is different" and that inflation will never return. We certainly agree that there have been important advances in our understanding of central bank design and monetary policy, particularly in the importance of having an independent central bank that places a heavy weight on inflation stabilization. But, as in the case of debt defaults, experience suggests that quiet periods do not extend indefinitely.

Figure 12.2 plots the share of countries that were having inflation crises (defined as an annual inflation rate of 20 percent or higher) in any given year (1800–2007) over four panels for Africa, Asia, Europe, and Latin America, respectively. None of the regions

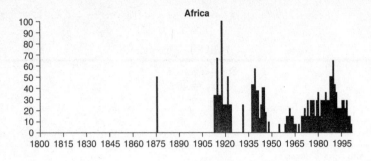

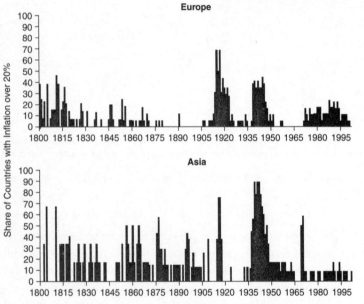

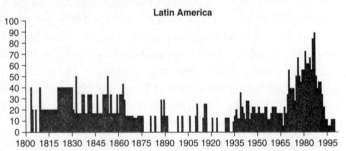

Figure 12.2. The incidence of annual inflation above 20 percent:
Africa, Asia, Europe, and Latin America, 1800–2007.

has had a particularly pristine inflation history. After World War II, the incidence of high inflation has been greater in Africa and Latin America than in other regions, with this trend intensifying during the 1980s and 1990s. The worldwide ebb in inflation is still of modern vintage; we will see if inflation resurfaces again in the years following the financial crisis of the late 2000s, particularly as government debt stocks mount, fiscal "space" (the capacity to engage in fiscal stimulus) erodes, and particularly if a rash of sovereign defaults in emerging markets eventually follows.

Currency Crashes

Having discussed currency debasement and inflation crises, including a long exposé on exchange rate crashes at this stage seems somewhat redundant. Our database on exchange rates is almost as rich as that on prices, especially if one takes into account silver-based exchange rates (see the appendixes for a detailed description). Although we will not go into detail here, a more systematic analysis of the data set will show that, by and large, *inflation crises and exchange rate crises have traveled hand in hand in the overwhelming majority of episodes across time and countries (with a markedly tighter link in countries subject to chronic inflation, where the pass-through from exchange rates to prices is greatest).*

When we look at exchange rate behavior, we can see that probably the most surprising evidence comes from the Napoleonic Wars, during which exchange rate instability escalated to a level that had not been seen before and was not to be seen again for nearly a hundred years. This is starkly illustrated in figures 12.3 and 12.4, with the former depicting the incidence of peak currency depreciation and the latter showing median inflation. The figures also show a significantly

---

Sources: Given the long period covered and the large number of countries included, consumer prices (or cost-of-living indexes) are culled from many different sources. They are listed in detail by country and period in appendix A.1.

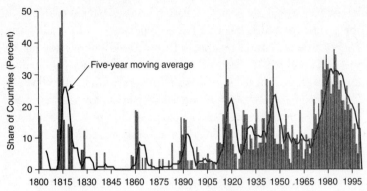

Figure 12.3. Currency crashes: The share of countries with annual
depreciation rates greater than 15 percent, 1800–2007.
Sources: The primary sources are Global Financial Data (n.d.) and Reinhart
and Rogoff (2008a), but numerous others are listed in appendix A.1.
Note: The spike at the left of the figure marks the Napoleonic Wars,
which lasted from 1799 to 1815.

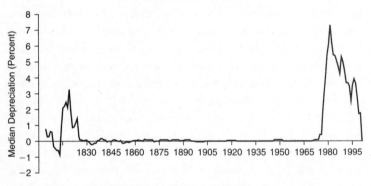

Figure 12.4. Median annual depreciation: Five-year moving
average for all countries, 1800–2007.
Sources: The primary sources are Global Financial Data (n.d.) and Reinhart
and Rogoff (2008a), but numerous others are listed in appendix A.1.
Note: The spike at the left of the figure marks the Napoleonic Wars,
which lasted from 1799 to 1815.

higher incidence of crashes and larger median changes in the more
modern period. This should hardly come as a surprise, given the prominent exchange rate crises in Mexico (1994), Asia (1997), Russia
(1998), Brazil (1999), and Argentina (2001), among other countries.

190

The Aftermath of High Inflation and Currency Collapses

Countries with sustained high inflation often experience dollarization, a huge shift toward the use of foreign currency as a transaction medium, a unit of account, and a store of value. From a practical perspective, this can imply the use of foreign hard currency for trade or, even more prevalently, the indexation of bank accounts, bonds, and other financial assets to foreign currency (what we have termed elsewhere in joint work with Savastano as "liability dollarization").[7] In many cases, a sustained shift toward dollarization is one of the many long-term costs of episodes of high inflation, one that often persists even if the government strives to prevent it. A government that has grossly abused its monopoly over the currency and payments system will often find this monopoly more difficult to enforce in the aftermath. Reducing dollarization and regaining control of monetary policy is often one of the major aims of disinflation policy after a period of elevated inflation. Yet de-dollarization can be extremely difficult. In this short section we digress to look at this important monetary phenomenon.

Successful disinflations generally have not been accompanied by large declines in the degree of dollarization. In fact, the top panel of figure 12.5 shows that the degree of dollarization at the end of the period of disinflation was the same as or higher than at the time of the inflation peak in more than half of the episodes. Moreover, the decrease in the degree of dollarization in many of the other episodes was generally small. This persistence of dollarization is consistent with the evidence on "hysteresis" found by the studies based on a narrower measure of domestic dollarization. In this context, *hysteresis* simply refers to the tendency for a country that has become dollarized to remain so long after the original reasons for the shift (usually excessive inflation on domestic currency) have abated.

The persistence of dollarization is a regularity that tends to be associated with countries' inflation histories. In fact, countries that had repeated bouts of high inflation over the past few decades generally exhibited a higher degree of dollarization in the late 1990s than did countries with better inflationary histories (figure 12.5,

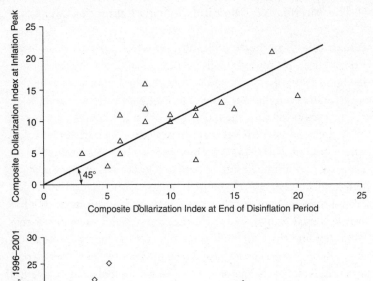

Figure 12.5. The persistence of dollarization.
Source: Reinhart, Rogoff, and Savastano (2003b).
Notes: The top panel shows that disinflation has had no clear effects on the degree of dollarization. "End of disinflation period" is defined as the year when the inflation rate fell below 10 percent. The bottom panel shows that current levels of dollarization are related to a country's history of high inflation. Unconditional probability computed with monthly data on inflation for the period 1958–2001.

lower panel). Interpreting the (unconditional) probability of high inflation used in figure 12.5 as a rough measure of the credibility of a monetary policy gives us some insights as to why achieving low inflation is generally not a sufficient condition for a rapid decrease in the degree of dollarization; namely, a country with a poor inflationary history will need to maintain inflation at low levels for a long period before it can significantly reduce the probability of another inflationary bout.[8] This is yet another parallel to the difficulties a country faces in graduating from debt intolerance.

One can also show a relationship between current levels of dollarization and countries' exchange rate histories. Parallel market exchange rates and pervasive exchange controls have been the norm rather than the exception in countries with histories of high inflation. Conversely, very few countries with hard pegs and unified exchange rates have experienced bouts of high inflation.[9] The evidence thus suggests a link between current levels of dollarization and countries' past reliance on exchange controls and multiple currency practices.

Undoing Domestic Dollarization

We have shown that reducing inflation is generally not sufficient to undo domestic dollarization, at least at horizons of more than five years. Nevertheless, some countries have managed to reduce their degree of domestic dollarization. To identify those countries, it is useful to treat separately cases in which the reduction in domestic dollarization originated in a decline in locally issued foreign currency public debt from those that originated in a decline in the share of foreign currency deposits in broad money.

The few governments in our sample that managed to dedollarize their locally issued foreign currency obligations followed one of two strategies: they either amortized the outstanding debt stock on the original terms and discontinued the issuance of those securities, or they changed the currency denomination of the debt—sometimes, but not always, using market-based approaches. One example of the former strategy is Mexico's decision to redeem in U.S. dollars all the dollar-linked *tesobonos* outstanding at the time of its December 1994 crisis (using the loans it received from the International Monetary Fund and the United States) and to cease issuing domestic foreign

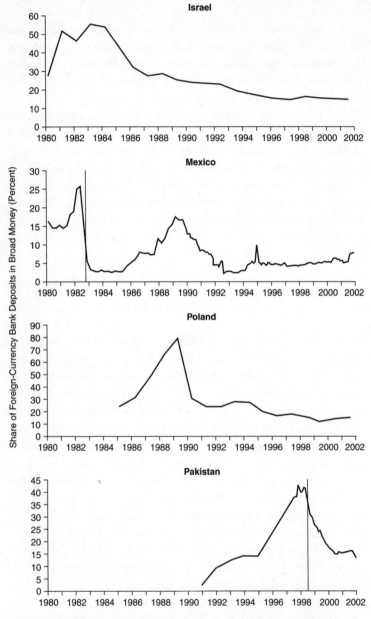

Figure 12.6. The de-dollarization of bank deposits: Israel, Poland,
Mexico, and Pakistan, 1980–2002.

currency–denominated bonds thereafter. A recent example of the latter is Argentina's decision in late 2001 to convert to domestic currency the government bonds that it had originally issued in U.S. dollars (under Argentine law).

Decreases in domestic dollarization caused by declines in the share of foreign currency deposits to broad money are more common in our sample. To identify only those cases in which the reversal of deposit dollarization was large and lasting, we searched for all episodes in which the ratio of foreign currency deposits to broad money satisfied the following three conditions: (1) experienced a decline of at least 20 percent, (2) settled at a level below 20 percent immediately following the decline, and (3) remained below 20 percent until the end of the sample period.

Only four of the eighty-five countries for which we have data on foreign currency deposits met the three criteria during the period 1980–2001: Israel, Poland, Mexico, and Pakistan (figure 12.6). In sixteen other countries, the ratio of foreign currency deposits to broad money declined by more than 20 percent during some portion of 1980–2001. However, in some of these countries—for instance, in Bulgaria and Lebanon—the deposit dollarization ratio settled at a level considerably higher than 20 percent following the decline. And in the majority of the other cases (twelve out of the sixteen) the dollarization ratio initially fell below the 20 percent mark but later rebounded to levels in excess of 20 percent.[10] Some forms of dollarization are even more difficult to eradicate. At present between one-half and two-thirds of mortgage loans in Poland (one of the relatively more successful de-dollarizers) are denominated in a foreign currency, mostly Swiss francs.

In three of the four cases that met our three conditions for a large and lasting decline of the deposit dollarization ratio, the rever-

---

Source: See appendix A.1.
Notes: In the panel on Mexico, the vertical line marks the point, in 1982, at which there was a forcible conversion of foreign currency bank deposits. In the panel on Pakistan, the vertical line marks the point, in 1998, at which there was a forcible conversion of foreign currency bank deposits.

sal started the moment the authorities imposed restrictions on the convertibility of dollar deposits. In Israel, in late 1985 the authorities introduced a one-year mandatory holding period for all deposits in foreign currency, making those deposits substantially less attractive than other indexed financial instruments.[11] By contrast, in Mexico in 1982 and Pakistan in 1998, the authorities forcibly converted the dollar deposits into deposits in domestic currency, using for the conversion an exchange rate that was substantially below (i.e., more appreciated than) the prevailing market rate.

Interestingly, not all the countries that introduced severe restrictions on the availability of dollar deposits managed to lower the deposit dollarization ratio on a sustained basis. Bolivia and Peru adopted measures similar to those of Mexico and Pakistan in the early 1980s, but after some years of extreme macroeconomic instability that took them to the brink of hyperinflation, both countries eventually allowed foreign currency deposits once again, and they have since remained highly dollarized despite their remarkable success in reducing inflation.

Even in the countries where the restrictions on dollar deposits have thus far led to a lasting decline of deposit dollarization, the costs of de-dollarization were far from trivial. In Mexico, capital flight nearly doubled (to about US$6.5 billion per year), bank credit to the private sector fell by almost half in the two years that followed the forced conversion of dollar deposits, and the country's inflation and growth performance remained dismal for several years.[12] As for Pakistan, it is too soon to tell whether its compulsory de-dollarization of 1998 will prove permanent or whether it will eventually be reversed, as was the case in Bolivia and Peru—and in Argentina in its 2001–2002 forcible "pesoization."

This chapter has covered a great deal of ground, etching the highlights of the world's fascinating history of inflation and exchange rate crashes. Virtually every country in the world, particularly during its emerging market phase, has experienced bouts of inflation, often long-lasting and recurrent. Indeed, the history of inflation shows how profoundly difficult it is for countries to permanently graduate from a history of macroeconomic mismanagement without having occasional but very painful relapses. High inflation causes residents to minimize their exposure to further macroeconomic malfeasance for a very long time. Their lower demand for domestic paper currency reduces the base on which the government can secure inflation revenues, making it more painful (in fiscal terms) to restore low inflation. A destabilizing exchange rate dynamic is a natural corollary. In extreme cases, citizens may find ways to more aggressively circumvent the government's currency monopoly by using hard currency, or the government may find itself forced to guarantee the hard currency indexation of bank deposits and other liabilities in an effort to restore the payments system. This weakening of the government's currency monopoly can also take a long time to outgrow.

- PART V -

THE U.S. SUBPRIME MELTDOWN AND THE SECOND GREAT CONTRACTION

How relevant are historical benchmarks for assessing the trajectory of a modern global financial crisis? In this part of the book we draw on our historical data set to develop benchmarks for measuring the severity of the crisis in terms of both the run-up to it and the possible evolution of its aftermath. A few years back, many people would have said that improvements in financial engineering and the conduct of monetary policy had done much to tame the business cycle and limit the risk of financial contagion. But the recent global financial crisis has proven them wrong.

When the "subprime financial crisis" (as it was initially called) began to unfold in the summer of 2007, a cursory reading of the global financial press would have led one to conclude that the world economy was moving through dark and uncharted waters. Indeed, after events took a decided turn for the worse in the early fall of 2008, much of the commentary took on an apocalyptic tone usually reserved for a threat that could potentially end civilization (as we know it). Yet, had policy makers looked at the recent history of financial crises, they would have found that it provided an important qualitative and quantitative perspective on how to gauge the evolution of the crisis.

In the next four chapters we will attempt to do exactly that, drawing on past experiences for analogies and making use of our data set to establish quantitative benchmarks. Because many of our readers may want to begin with the most recent crisis, we have done our best to make this part of the book relatively self-contained, reviewing and repeating main themes from earlier chapters as necessary.

In the first of these chapters, chapter 13, we will begin with an overview of the history of banking crises that is tailored to give the reader a perspective of the current crisis. We will pay particular attention to the debate on the massive global current account imbalances that preceded the crisis and, some would say, helped trigger it. As we will show, the outsized U.S. borrowing from abroad that occurred prior to the crisis (manifested in a sequence of gaping current account and trade balance deficits) was hardly the only warning signal. In fact, the U.S. economy, at the epicenter of the crisis, showed many other signs of being on the brink of a deep financial crisis. Other measures such as asset price inflation, most notably in the real estate sector, rising household leverage, and the slowing output—standard leading indicators of financial crises—all revealed worrisome symptoms. Indeed, from a purely quantitative perspective, the run-up to the U.S. financial crisis showed all the signs of an accident waiting to happen. Of course, the United States was hardly alone in showing classic warning signs of a financial crisis, with Great Britain, Spain, and Ireland, among other countries, experiencing many of the same symptoms.

In the next chapter, chapter 14, we will extend the comparison between the past crises and the recent one by examining the aftermath of severe financial crises. To expand our data set, we will bring in a number of relatively well-known episodes in emerging markets. As we have seen in chapter 10, on banking crises, emerging markets and developed countries experience surprisingly similar outcomes in the wake of financial crises (at least in a number of core areas), so this would seem to be a reasonable exercise. For most of the chapter the crises we use as our comparison group will be postwar crises, but toward the end of the chapter we will make comparisons with the Great Depression. One can plausibly argue that macroeconomic policy was much too passive in the early stages of the Great Depression. Indeed, efforts to maintain balanced budgets in the wake of declining tax revenues were likely deeply counterproductive, while reluctance to abandon the gold standard contributed to deflation in many countries. Still, the comparisons are important because no other financial crisis since the Great Depression has been nearly as global in nature.

In the chapter that follows, chapter 15, we will explore the links that transmit crises across countries, ranging from financial links to trade to common factors such as technology and geopolitical shocks. We will also make a distinction between high-velocity or "fast-and-furious" factors that transmit crises across borders very quickly—for instance, via stock markets—and low-velocity or "slow-burn" factors whereby transmission takes somewhat longer.

In the last of these four chapters, chapter 16, we look at the recent crisis from a global perspective. This chapter will be a culmination of all that has gone before it. Our expansive data set spanning nearly all regions allows us to offer a working definition of a global financial crisis. In addition, our analysis of the different kinds of crises described in this book allows us to develop a new crisis index that essentially aggregates the number of different crises each country is experiencing across the globe. Thus chapter 16 is quite crucial in bringing together the entire spectrum of crises we consider in this book. Even though the most recent crisis does not appear likely to come close to the severity of the Great Depression of the 1930s, readers may nevertheless find the comparisons sobering.

- 13 -

THE U.S. SUBPRIME CRISIS:
AN INTERNATIONAL AND
HISTORICAL COMPARISON

This chapter begins with a broad-brush "pictorial" overview of the global incidence of banking crises through the past century, taking advantage of the expansive amount of data collected for this book. Our aim is to place the international situation of the late 2000s, the "Second Great Contraction," in a broader historical context.[1] We will then go on, in this chapter and the next, to look at how the late-vintage U.S. subprime financial crisis compares with past financial crises. Broadly speaking, we will show that both in the run-up to the recent crisis and in its aftermath (as of the writing of this book), the United States has driven straight down the quantitative tracks of a typical deep financial crisis.

In addition to making our quantitative comparisons in this chapter, we will also discuss the re-emergence of the this-time-is-different syndrome—the insistence that some combination of factors renders the previous laws of investing null and void—that appeared on the eve of the meltdown. This task is not particularly difficult, for the remarks and written works of academics, policy makers, and financial market participants in the run-up to the crisis provide ample evidence of the syndrome. We will place particular emphasis on the debate over whether massive borrowing by the United States from the rest of the world prior to the crisis should have been seen as a critical warning sign.

A Global Historical View of the
Subprime Crisis and Its Aftermath

Before focusing on the Second Great Contraction, which began in 2007, it will be helpful to review the incidence of banking crises over a broader span of history, which we first examined in chapter 10. A closer look at those data shows that the earliest banking crisis in an advanced economy in our sample is that of France in 1802; early crises in emerging markets befell India in 1863, China (in several episodes) during the 1860s–1870s, and Peru in 1873. Because in this chapter we are interested in making broad cross-country comparisons, we will focus mainly on data for the period since 1900, for they are sufficiently rich to allow a systematic empirical treatment.[2]

Figure 13.1 plots the incidence of banking crises among the countries in our sample (which the reader will recall accounts for about 90 percent of world income on the basis of purchasing power parity, or PPP). The graph is, in fact, based on the same data as figure 10.1 except that here we concentrate only on banking crises and not on capital mobility. As before, the figure shows the percentage of all independent countries that experienced a banking crisis in any given year from 1900 through 2008, taking a three-year moving average. As in figure 10.1 and a number of similar figures throughout the book, the tally in figure 13.1 weights countries by their share of global GDP so that crises in larger economies have a greater impact on the overall shape of the graph. This weighted aggregate is meant to provide a measure of the "global" impact of individual banking crises. Therefore, a crisis in the United States or Germany is accorded a much greater weight than a crisis in Angola or Honduras, all of which are part of our sixty-six-country sample. The reader should be aware that although we believe that figure 13.1 gives a fair picture of the proportion of the world in banking crisis at any one time, it is only a rough measure, because banking crises are of varying severity.

As we noted in chapter 10, the highest incidence of banking crises during this 109-year stretch can be found during the worldwide

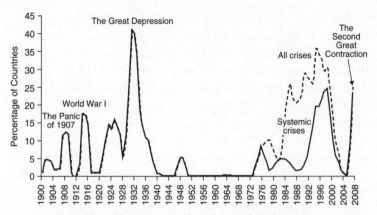

Figure 13.1. The proportion of countries with banking crises,
1900–2008, weighted by their share of world income.
Sources: Kaminsky and Reinhart (1999), Bordo et al. (2001),
Maddison (2004), Caprio et al. (2005), Jácome (2008), and the additional
sources listed in appendix A.3, which provides the dates of banking crises.
Notes: The sample size includes all sixty-six countries listed in table 1.1 that
were independent states in the given year. Three sets of GDP weights are used,
1913 weights for the period 1800–1913, 1990 weights for the period 1914–1990,
and finally 2003 weights for the period 1991–2008. The dotted line indicates
all crises, the solid line systemic crises (for instance, for the 1980s and 1990s,
the crises in the Nordic countries, then Japan, then the rest of Asia). The
entries for 2007–2008 indicate crises in Austria, Belgium, Germany,
Hungary, Japan, the Netherlands, Spain, the United Kingdom, and
the United States. The figure shows a three-year moving average.

Great Depression of the 1930s. Earlier, less widespread "waves" of
global financial stress were evident during and around the Panic of
1907, which originated in New York, as well as the crises accompanying the outbreak of the First World War. Figure 13.1 also reminds
us of the relative calm from the late 1940s to the early 1970s. This
calm may be partly explained by booming world growth but perhaps
more so by the repression of the domestic financial markets (in varying degrees) and the heavy-handed use of capital controls that followed for many years after World War II. (We are not necessarily
implying that such repression and controls are the right approach to
dealing with the risk of financial crises.)

As we also observed in chapter 10, since the early 1970s, financial and international capital account liberalization—reduction and removal of barriers to investment inside and outside a country—have taken root worldwide. So, too, have banking crises.[3] After a long hiatus, the share of countries with banking difficulties first began to expand in the 1970s. The break-up of the Bretton Woods system of fixed exchange rates, together with a sharp spike in oil prices, catalyzed a prolonged global recession, resulting in financial sector difficulties in a number of advanced economies. In the early 1980s, a collapse in global commodity prices, combined with high and volatile interest rates in the United States, contributed to a spate of banking and sovereign debt crises in emerging economies, most famously in Latin America and then Africa. High interest rates raised the cost of servicing large debts, which were often funded at variable interest rates linked to world markets. Falling prices for commodities, the main export for most emerging markets, also made it more difficult for them to service debts.

The United States experienced its own banking crisis, rooted in the savings and loan industry, beginning in 1984 (albeit this was a relatively mild crisis compared to those of the 1930s and the 2000s). During the late 1980s and early 1990s, the Nordic countries experienced some of the worst banking crises the wealthy economies had known since World War II following a surge in capital inflows (lending from abroad) and soaring real estate prices. In 1992, Japan's asset price bubble burst and ushered in a decade-long banking crisis. Around the same time, with the collapse of the Soviet bloc, several formerly communist countries in Eastern Europe joined the ranks of nations facing banking sector problems. As the second half of the 1990s approached, emerging markets faced a fresh round of banking crises. Problems in Mexico and Argentina (in 1994–1995) were followed by the famous Asian crisis of 1997–1998 and then the troubles of Russia and Colombia, among others.[4] That upswing in the banking crisis cycle was closed by Argentina in 2001 and Uruguay in 2002. A brief tranquil period came to an abrupt halt in the summer of 2007 when the subprime crisis in the United States began in earnest, soon transforming itself into a global financial crisis.[5]

As is well known, the U.S. financial crisis of the late 2000s was firmly rooted in the bubble in the real estate market fueled by sustained massive increases in housing prices, a massive influx of cheap foreign capital resulting from record trade balance and current account deficits, and an increasingly permissive regulatory policy that helped propel the dynamic between these factors (a pattern that we will quantify further). To place the housing bubble in historical perspective, figure 13.2 plots the now-famous Case-Shiller housing price index deflated by the GNP deflator (the picture is essentially unchanged if the consumer price index is used).[6] Since 1891, when the price series began, no housing price boom has been comparable in terms of sheer magnitude and duration to that recorded in the years culminating in the 2007 subprime mortgage fiasco. *Between 1996 and 2006 (the year when prices peaked), the cumulative real price increase was about 92 percent—more than three times the 27 percent cumulative increase from 1890 to 1996!* In 2005, at the height of the bubble, real housing prices soared by more than 12 percent (that was about six times the rate of increase in real per capita GDP for that year). Even the prosperous post–World War II decades, when demographic and income trends lent support to housing prices, pale in

Figure 13.2. Real housing prices: United States, 1891–2008.
Sources: Shiller (2005), Standard and Poor's, and U.S. Commerce Department.
Notes: House prices are deflated by the GNP deflator. Real housing prices are indexed to equal 100 in 2000.

comparison to the pre-2007 surge in prices.[7] By mid-2007, a sharp rise in default rates on low-income housing mortgages in the United States eventually sparked a full-blown global financial panic.

The This-Time-Is-Different Syndrome and the Run-up to the Subprime Crisis

The global financial crisis of the late 2000s, whether measured by the depth, breadth, and (potential) duration of the accompanying recession or by its profound effect on asset markets, stands as the most serious global financial crisis since the Great Depression. The crisis has been a transformative moment in global economic history whose ultimate resolution will likely reshape politics and economics for at least a generation.

Should the crisis have come as a surprise, especially in its deep impact on the United States? Listening to a long list of leading academics, investors, and U.S. policy makers, one would have thought the financial meltdown of the late 2000s was a bolt from the blue, a "six-sigma" event. U.S. Federal Reserve Chairman Alan Greenspan frequently argued that financial innovations such as securitization and option pricing were producing new and better ways to spread risk, simultaneously making traditionally illiquid assets, such as houses, more liquid. Hence higher and higher prices for risky assets could be justified.

We could stop here and say that a lot of people were convinced that "this time is different" because the United States is "special." However, given the historic nature of the recent U.S. and global financial collapse, a bit more background will help us to understand why so many people were fooled.

Risks Posed by Sustained U.S. Borrowing from the Rest of the World: The Debate before the Crisis

Chairman Greenspan was among the legion that branded as alarmists those who worried excessively about the burgeoning U.S. current account deficit.[8] Greenspan argued that this gaping deficit, which reached more than 6.5 percent of GDP in 2006 (over $800 billion), was, to a significant extent, simply a reflection of a broader trend toward global financial deepening that was allowing countries to sustain much larger current account deficits and surpluses than in the past. Indeed, in his 2007 book, Greenspan characterizes the sustained U.S. current account deficit as a secondary issue, not a primary risk factor, one that (along with others such as soaring housing prices and the notable buildup in household debt) should not have caused excessive alarm among U.S. policy makers during the run-up to the crisis that began in 2007.[9]

The Federal Reserve chairman was hardly alone in his relatively sanguine view of American borrowing. U.S. Treasury Secretary Paul O'Neill famously argued that it was natural for other countries to lend to the United States given this country's high rate of productivity growth and that the current account was a "meaningless concept."[10]

Greenspan's successor, Ben Bernanke, in a speech he made in 2005, famously described the U.S. borrowing binge as the product of a "global savings glut" that had been caused by a convergence of factors, many of which were outside the control of U.S. policy makers.[11] These factors included the strong desire of many emerging markets to insure themselves against future economic crises after the slew of crises in Latin America and Asia during the 1990s and early 2000s. At the same time, Middle Eastern countries had sought ways to use their oil earnings, and countries with underdeveloped financial systems, such as China, had wanted to diversify into safer assets. Bernanke argued that it was also natural for some developed economies, such as Japan and Germany, to have high savings rates in the face of rapidly aging populations. All these factors together conspired to provide a huge pool of net savings in search of a safe and dynamic resting place, which meant the United States. Of course, this cheap source of funding was an opportunity for the United States. The question authorities might have wrestled with more was "Can there be too much of a good thing?" The same this-time-is-different argument appears all too often in the speeches of policy makers in emerging markets when their countries are experiencing massive capital inflows: "Low rates of return in the rest of the world are simply making investment in our country particularly attractive."

As money poured into the United States, U.S. financial firms, including mighty investment banks such as Goldman Sachs, Merrill Lynch (which was acquired by Bank of America in 2008 in a "shotgun marriage"), and the now defunct Lehman Brothers, as well as large universal banks (with retail bases) such as Citibank, all saw their profits soar. The size of the U.S. financial sector (which includes banking and insurance) more than doubled, from an average of roughly 4 percent of GDP in the mid-1970s to almost 8 percent of GDP by 2007.[12] The top employees of the five largest investment banks divided a bonus pool of over $36 billion in 2007. Leaders in the financial sector argued that in fact their high returns were the result of innovation and genuine value-added products, and they tended to grossly understate the latent risks their firms were taking. (Keep in mind that an integral part of our working definition of the this-time-is-different syndrome is that "the old rules of valuation no longer apply.") In their eyes, financial innovation was a key platform that allowed the United States to effectively borrow much larger quantities of money from abroad than might otherwise have been possible. For example, innovations such as securitization allowed U.S. consumers to turn their previously illiquid housing assets into ATM machines, which represented a reduction in precautionary saving.[13]

Where did academics and policy economists stand on the dangers posed by the U.S. current account deficit? Opinions varied across a wide spectrum. On the one hand, Obstfeld and Rogoff argued in several contributions that the outsized U.S. current account was likely unsustainable.[14] They observed that if one added up all the surpluses of the countries in the world that were net savers (countries in which national savings exceed national investment, including China, Japan, Germany, Saudi Arabia, and Russia), the United States was soaking up more than two out of every three of these saved dollars in 2004–2006. Thus, eventually the U.S. borrowing binge would have to unwind, perhaps quite precipitously, which would result in sharp asset price movements that could severely stress the complex global derivatives system.[15]

Many others took a similarly concerned viewpoint. For example, in 2004 Nouriel Roubini and Brad Setser projected that the U.S. borrowing problem would get much worse, reaching 10 percent of GDP before a dramatic collapse.[16] Paul Krugman (who received a Nobel Prize in 2008) argued that there would inevitably be a "Wile E. Coyote moment" when the unsustainability of the U.S. current account would be evident to all, and suddenly the dollar would collapse.[17] There are many other examples of academic papers that illustrated the risks.[18]

Yet many respected academic, policy, and financial market researchers took a much more sanguine view. In a series of influential papers, Michael Dooley, David Folkerts-Landau, and Peter Garber—"the Deutschebank trio"—argued that the gaping U.S. current account deficit was just a natural consequence of emerging markets' efforts to engage in export-led growth, as well as their need to diversify into safe assets.[19] They insightfully termed the system that propagated the U.S. deficits "Bretton Woods II" because the Asian countries were quasi-pegging their currencies to the U.S. dollar, just as the European countries had done forty years earlier.

Harvard economist Richard Cooper also argued eloquently that the U.S. current account deficit had logical foundations that did not necessarily imply clear and present dangers.[20] He pointed to the hegemonic position of the United States in the global financial and security system and the extraordinary liquidity of U.S. financial markets, as well as its housing markets, to support his argument. Indeed, Bernanke's speech on the global savings glut in many ways synthesized the interesting ideas already floating around in the academic and policy research literature.

It should be noted that others, such as Ricardo Hausmann and Federico Sturzenegger of Harvard University's Kennedy School of Government, made more exotic arguments, claiming that U.S. foreign assets were mismeasured, and actually far larger than official estimates.[21] The existence of this "dark matter" helped explain how the United States could finance a seemingly unending string of current account and trade deficits. Ellen McGrattan of Minnesota and Ed Prescott of Arizona (another Nobel Prize winner) developed a model to effectively calibrate dark matter and found that the explanation might plausibly account for as much as half of the United States' current account deficit.[22]

In addition to debating U.S. borrowing from abroad, economists also debated the related question of whether policy makers should have been concerned about the explosion of housing prices that was taking place nationally in the United States (as shown in the previous section). But again, top policy makers argued that high home prices could be justified by new financial markets that made houses easier to borrow off of and by reduced macroeconomic risk that increased the value of risky assets. Both Greenspan and Bernanke argued vigorously that the Federal Reserve should not pay excessive attention to housing prices, except to the extent that they might affect the central bank's primary goals of growth and price stability. Indeed, prior to joining the Fed, Bernanke had made this case more formally and forcefully in an article coauthored by New York University professor Mark Gertler in 2001.[23]

On the one hand, the Federal Reserve's logic for ignoring housing prices was grounded in the perfectly sensible proposition that the private sector can judge equilibrium housing prices (or equity prices) at least as well as any government bureaucrat. On the other hand, it might have paid more attention to the fact that the rise in asset prices was being fueled by a relentless increase in the ratio of household debt to GDP, against a backdrop of record lows in the personal saving rate. This ratio, which had been roughly stable at close to 80 percent of personal income until 1993, had risen to 120 percent in 2003 and to nearly 130 percent by mid-2006. Empirical work by Bordo and Jeanne and the Bank for International Settlements suggested that when housing booms are accompanied by sharp rises in debt, the risk of a crisis is significantly elevated.[24] Although this work was not necessarily definitive, it certainly raised questions about the Federal Reserve's policy of benign neglect. On the other hand, the fact that the housing boom was taking place in many countries around the world (albeit to a much lesser extent if at all in major surplus countries such as Germany and Japan) raised questions about the genesis of the problem and whether national monetary or regulatory policy alone would be an effective remedy.

Bernanke, while still a Federal Reserve governor in 2004, sensibly argued that it is the job of regulatory policy, not monetary policy, to deal with housing price bubbles fueled by inappropriately weak lending standards.[25] Of course, that argument begs the question of what should be done if, for political reasons or otherwise, regulatory policy does not adequately respond to an asset price bubble. Indeed, one can argue that it was precisely the huge capital inflow from abroad that fueled the asset price inflation and low interest rate spreads that ultimately masked risks from both regulators and rating agencies.

In any event, the most extreme and the most immediate problems were caused by the market for mortgage loans made to "subprime," or low-income, borrowers. "Advances" in securitization, as well as a seemingly endless run-up in housing prices, allowed people to buy houses who might not previously have thought they could do so. Unfortunately, many of these borrowers depended on loans with variable interest rates and low initial "teaser" rates. When it came time to reset the loans, rising interest rates and a deteriorating economy made it difficult for many to meet their mortgage obligations. And thus the subprime debacle began.

The U.S. conceit that its financial and regulatory system could withstand massive capital inflows on a sustained basis without any problems arguably laid the foundations for the global financial crisis of the late 2000s. The thinking that "this time is different"—because this time the U.S. had a superior system—once again proved false. Outsized financial market returns were in fact greatly exaggerated by capital inflows, just as would be the case in emerging markets. What could in retrospect be recognized as huge regulatory mistakes, including the deregulation of the subprime mortgage market and the

2004 decision of the Securities and Exchange Commission to allow investment banks to triple their leverage ratios (that is, the ratio measuring the amount of risk to capital), appeared benign at the time. Capital inflows pushed up borrowing and asset prices while reducing spreads on all sorts of risky assets, leading the International Monetary Fund to conclude in April 2007, in its twice-annual *World Economic Outlook*, that risks to the global economy had become extremely low and that, for the moment, there were no great worries. When the international agency charged with being the global watchdog declares that there are no risks, there is no surer sign that this time *is* different.

Again, the crisis that began in 2007 shares many parallels with the boom period before an emerging market crisis, when governments often fail to take precautionary steps to let steam out of the system; they expect the capital inflow bonanza to last indefinitely. Often, instead, they take steps that push their economies toward greater risk in an effort to keep the boom going a little longer.

Such is a brief characterization of the debate surrounding the this-time-is-different mentality leading up to the U.S. subprime financial crisis. To sum up, many were led to think that "this time is different" for the following reasons:

- The United States, with the world's most reliable system of financial regulation, the most innovative financial system, a strong political system, and the world's largest and most liquid capital markets, was special. It could withstand huge capital inflows without worry.
- Rapidly emerging developing economies needed a secure place to invest their funds for diversification purposes.
- Increased global financial integration was deepening global capital markets and allowing countries to go deeper into debt.
- In addition to its other strengths, the United States has superior monetary policy institutions and monetary policy makers.
- New financial instruments were allowing many new borrowers to enter mortgage markets.

- All that was happening was just a further deepening of financial globalization thanks to innovation and should not be a great source of worry.

The Episodes of Postwar Bank-Centered Financial Crisis

As the list of reasons that "this time is different" (provided by academics, business leaders, and policy makers) grew, so did the similarities of U.S. economic developments to those seen in other precrisis episodes.

To examine the antecedents of the 2007 U.S. subprime crisis (which later grew into the "Second Great Contraction"), we begin by looking at data from the eighteen bank-centered financial crises that occurred in the post–World War II period.[26] For the time being, we will limit our attention to crises in industrialized countries to avoid seeming to engage in hyperbole by comparing the United States to emerging markets. But of course, as we have already seen in chapter 10, financial crises in emerging markets and those in advanced economies are not so different. Later, in chapter 14, we will broaden the comparison set.

The crisis episodes employed in our comparison are listed in table 13.1.

Among the eighteen bank-centered financial crises following World War II, the "Big Five" crises have all involved major declines in output over a protracted period, often lasting two years or more. The worst postwar crisis prior to 2007, of course, was that of Japan in 1992, which set the country off on its "lost decade." The earlier Big Five crises, however, were also extremely traumatic events.

The remaining thirteen financial crises in rich countries represent more minor events that were associated with significantly worse economic performance than usual, but were not catastrophic. For example, the U.S. crisis that began in 1984 was the savings and loan crisis.[27] Some of the other thirteen crises had relatively little impact, but we retain them for now for comparison purposes. It will

215

TABLE 13.1
Post–World War II bank-centered financial crises
in advanced economies

Country	Beginning year of crisis
Severe (systemic) crises: The "Big Five"	
Spain	1977
Norway	1987
Finland	1991
Sweden	1991
Japan	1992
Milder crises	
United Kingdom	1974
Germany	1977
Canada	1983
United States (savings and loan)	1984
Iceland	1985
Denmark	1987
New Zealand	1987
Australia	1989
Italy	1990
Greece	1991
United Kingdom	1991
France	1994
United Kingdom	1995

Sources: Caprio and Klingebiel (1996, 2003), Kaminsky and Reinhart (1999), and Caprio et al. (2005).

soon be clear that the run-up to the U.S. financial crisis of the late 2000s really did not resemble these milder crises, though most policy makers and journalists did not seem to realize this at the time.

A Comparison of the Subprime Crisis with Past Crises in Advanced Economies

In choosing the variables we used to measure the U.S. risk of a financial crisis we were motivated by the literature on predicting financial crises in both developed countries and emerging markets.[28] This literature on financial crises suggests that markedly rising asset prices, slowing real economic activity, large current account deficits, and sustained debt buildups (whether public, private, or both) are important precursors to a financial crisis. Recall also the evidence on capital flow "bonanzas" discussed in chapter 10, which showed that sustained capital inflows have been particularly strong markers for financial crises, at least in the post-1970 period of greater financial liberalization. Historically, financial liberalization or innovation has also been a recurrent precursor to financial crises, as shown in chapter 10.

We begin in figure 13.3 by comparing the run-up in housing prices. Period t represents the year of the onset of the financial crisis. By that convention, period $t - 4$ is four years prior to the crisis, and the graph in each case continues to $t + 3$, except of course in the case of the recent U.S. crisis, which, as of this writing and probably for some time beyond, will remain in the hands of the fates.[29] The figure confirms what case studies have shown, that a massive run-up in housing prices usually precedes a financial crisis. It is a bit disconcerting to note that, according to this figure, the run-up in housing prices in the United States exceeded the average of the "Big Five" financial crises, and the downturn appears to have been sharper (year $t + 1$ is 2008).

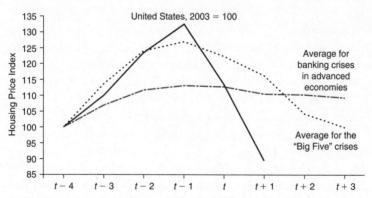

Figure 13.3. Real housing prices and postwar banking crises: Advanced economies. *Sources:* Bank for International Settlements (2005); Shiller (2005); Standard and Poor's; International Monetary Fund (various years), *International Financial Statistics;* and the authors' calculations.
Notes: Consumer prices are used to deflate nominal housing price indices. The year of the crisis is indicated by t; $t - 4 = 100$.

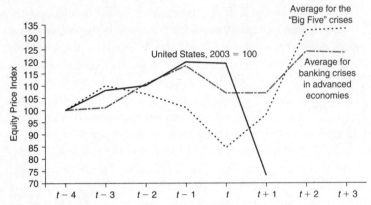

Figure 13.4. Real equity prices and postwar banking crises: Advanced economies.
Sources: Global Financial Data (n.d.); International Monetary Fund (various years), *International Financial Statistics;* and the authors' calculations.
Notes: Consumer prices are used to deflate nominal equity price indices. The year of the crisis is indicated by t; $t-4 = 100$.

In figure 13.4 we look at real rates of growth in equity market price indexes.[30] We see that, going into the crisis, U.S. equity prices held up better than those in either comparison group, perhaps in part because of the Federal Reserve's aggressive countercyclical response to the 2001 recession and in part because of the substantial "surprise element" in the severity of the U.S. crisis. But a year after the onset of the crisis ($t + 1$), equity prices had plummeted, in line with what happened in the "Big Five" financial crises.

In figure 13.5 we look at the trajectory of the U.S. current account deficit, which was far larger and more persistent than was typical in other crises.[31] In the figure, the bars show the U.S. current account trajectory from 2003 to 2007 as a percentage of GDP, and the dashed line shows the average for the eighteen earlier crises. The fact that the U.S. dollar remained the world's reserve currency during a period in which many foreign central banks (particularly in Asia) were amassing record amounts of foreign exchange reserves certainly increased the foreign capital available to finance the record U.S. current account deficits.

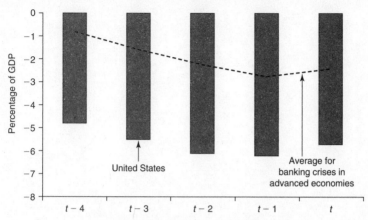

Figure 13.5. Ratio of current account balance to GDP on the
eve of postwar banking crises: Advanced economies.
Sources: International Monetary Fund (various years),
World Economic Outlook; and the authors' calculations.

Financial crises seldom occur in a vacuum. More often than
not, a financial crisis begins only after a real shock slows the pace of
the economy; thus it serves as an amplifying mechanism rather than
a trigger. Figure 13.6 plots real per capita GDP growth on the eve of
banking crises. The U.S. crisis that began in 2007 follows the same
inverted V shape that characterized the earlier crisis episodes. Like
equity prices, the response in GDP was somewhat delayed. Indeed,
in 2007, although U.S. growth had slowed, it was still more closely
aligned with the milder recession pattern of the average for all crises.

In 2008, developments took a turn for the worse, and the
growth slowdown became more acute. At the beginning of 2009, the
consensus—based on forecasts published in the *Wall Street Journal*—
was that this recession would be deeper than the average "Big Five"
experience. Note that in severe Big Five cases, the growth rate has
fallen by more than 5 percent from peak to trough and has remained
low for roughly three years.

Our final figure in this chapter, figure 13.7, illustrates the
path of real public debt (deflated by consumer prices).[32] Increasing

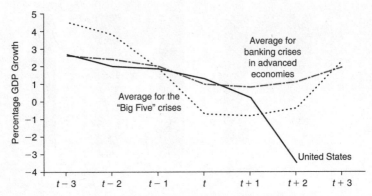

Figure 13.6. Growth in real per capita GDP (PPP basis)
and postwar banking crises: Advanced economies.
Sources: International Monetary Fund (various years),
World Economic Outlook, and *Wall Street Journal*.
Notes: The consensus forecast (–3.5 percent) for 2009 is plotted for the
United States as of July 2009. The year of the crisis is indicated by *t*.

public debt has been a nearly universal precursor of other postwar crises, although, as we will see in chapter 14, the buildup in debt prior to a crisis pales in comparison to its growth after the crisis has begun, for weak growth crushes tax revenues. The U.S. public debt buildup prior to the 2007 crisis was less than the Big Five average. Comparisons across private debt (which we have already alluded to for the United States) would be interesting as well, but unfortunately, comparable data for the range of countries considered here are not easy to obtain. In the case of the United States, the ratio of household debt to household income soared by 30 percent in less than a decade and could well collapse as consumers try to achieve a less risky position as the recession continues.

One caveat to our claim that the indicators showed the United States at high risk of a deep financial crisis in the run-up to 2007: compared to other countries that have experienced financial crises, the United States performed well with regard to inflation prior to 2007. Of course, the earlier crises in developed countries occurred during a period of declining inflation in the rich countries.

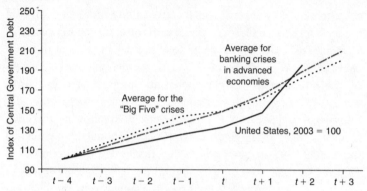

Figure 13.7. Real central government debt and postwar
banking crises: Advanced economies.
Sources: U.S. Treasury Department; International Monetary Fund
(various years), *International Financial Statistics;* appendixes A.1
and A.2 and sources cited therein; and the authors' calculations.
Note: Consumer prices are used to deflate nominal debt. The year
of the crisis is indicated by t; $t - 4 = 100$.

Summary

Why did so many people fail to see the financial crisis of 2007 coming? As to the standard indicators of financial crises, many red lights were blinking brightly well in advance. We do not pretend that it would have been easy to forestall the U.S. financial crisis had policy makers realized the risks earlier. We have focused on macroeconomic issues, but many problems were hidden in the "plumbing" of the financial markets, as has become painfully evident since the beginning of the crisis. Some of these problems might have taken years to address. Above all, the huge run-up in housing prices—over 100 percent nationally over five years—should have been an alarm, especially fueled as it was by rising leverage. At the beginning of 2008, the total value of mortgages in the United States was approximately 90 percent of GDP. Policy makers should have decided several years prior to the crisis to deliberately take some steam out of the system. Unfortunately, efforts to maintain growth and prevent significant sharp stock market declines had the effect of taking the safety valve off the pressure cooker. Of course, even with the epic proportions of this financial crisis, the United States had not defaulted as of the middle of 2009. Were the United States an emerging market, its exchange rate would have plummeted and its interest rates soared. Access to capital markets would be lost in a classic Dornbusch/Calvo–type sudden stop. During the first year following the crisis (2007), exactly the opposite happened: the dollar appreciated and interest rates fell as world investors viewed other countries as even riskier than the United States and bought Treasury securities copiously.[33] But buyer beware! Over the longer run, the U.S. exchange rate and interest rates could well revert to form, especially if policies are not made to re-establish a firm base for long-term fiscal sustainability.

- 14 -

THE AFTERMATH OF FINANCIAL CRISES

In the preceding chapter we presented a historical analysis comparing the run-up to the 2007 U.S. subprime financial crisis with the antecedents of other banking crises in advanced economies since World War II. We showed that standard indicators for the United States, such as asset price inflation, rising leverage, large sustained current account deficits, and a slowing trajectory of economic growth, exhibited virtually all the signs of a country on the verge of a financial crisis—indeed, a severe one. In this chapter we engage in a similar comparative historical analysis focused on the aftermath of systemic banking crises. Obviously, as events unfold, the aftermath of the U.S. financial crisis may prove better or worse than the benchmarks laid out here. Nevertheless, the approach is valuable in itself, because in analyzing extreme shocks such as those affecting the U.S. economy and the world economy at the time of this writing, standard macroeconomic models calibrated to statistically "normal" growth periods may be of little use.

In the previous chapter we deliberately excluded emerging market countries from the comparison set in order not to appear to engage in hyperbole. After all, the United States is a highly sophisticated global financial center. What can advanced economies possibly have in common with emerging markets when it comes to banking crises? In fact, as we showed in chapter 10, the antecedents and aftermath of banking crises in rich countries and in emerging markets have a surprising amount in common. They share broadly similar patterns in housing and equity prices, unemployment, government revenues, and debt. Furthermore, the frequency or incidence of crises does not differ much historically, even if comparisons are limited to the post–World War II period (provided that the ongoing global financial crisis of the late 2000s is taken into account). Thus, in this chapter, as we turn to characterizing the aftermath of severe financial crises, we include a number of recent emerging market cases so as to expand the relevant set of comparators.[1]

Broadly speaking, financial crises are protracted affairs. More often than not, the aftermath of severe financial crises share three characteristics:

- *First*, asset market collapses are deep and prolonged. Declines in real housing prices average 35 percent stretched out over six years, whereas equity price collapses average 56 percent over a downturn of about three and a half years.
- *Second*, the aftermath of banking crises is associated with profound declines in output and employment. The unemployment rate rises an average of 7 percentage points during the down phase of the cycle, which lasts on average more than four years. Output falls (from peak to trough) more than 9 percent on average, although the duration of the downturn, averaging roughly two years, is considerably shorter than that of unemployment.[2]
- *Third*, as noted earlier, the value of government debt tends to explode; it rose an average of 86 percent (in real terms, relative to precrisis debt) in the major post–World War II episodes. As discussed in chapter 10 (and as we reiterate here), the main cause of debt explosions is not the widely cited costs of bailing out and recapitalizing the banking system. Admittedly, bailout costs are difficult to measure, and the divergence among estimates from competing studies is considerable. But even upper-bound estimates pale next to actual measured increases in public debt. In fact, the biggest driver of debt increases is the inevitable collapse in tax revenues that governments suffer in the wake of deep and prolonged output contractions. Many countries also suffer from a spike in the interest burden on debt, for interest rates soar, and in a few cases (most notably that of Japan in the 1990s), countercyclical fiscal policy efforts contribute to the debt buildup. (We note that calibrating differences in countercyclical fiscal policy across countries can be difficult because some countries, such as the Nordic countries, have

powerful built-in fiscal stabilizers through high marginal tax rates and generous unemployment benefits, whereas other countries, such as the United States and Japan, have automatic stabilizers that are far weaker.)

In the last part of the chapter, we will look at quantitative benchmarks from the period of the Great Depression, the last deep global financial crisis prior to the recent one. The depth and duration of the decline in economic activity were breathtaking, even by comparison with severe postwar crises. Countries took an average of ten years to reach the same level of per capita output as they enjoyed in 1929. In the first three years of the Depression, unemployment rose an average of 16.9 percentage points across the fifteen major countries in our comparison set.

Historical Episodes Revisited

The preceding chapter included all the major postwar banking crises in the developed world (a total of eighteen) and put particular emphasis on the ones dubbed the "Big Five" (those in Spain, 1977; Norway, 1987; Finland, 1991; Sweden, 1991; and Japan, 1992). It is quite clear from that chapter, as well as from the subsequent evolution of the 2007 U.S. financial crisis, that the crisis of the late 2000s must be considered a severe Big Five–type crisis by any metric. As a result, in this chapter we will focus on severe systemic financial crises only, including the Big Five crises in developed economies plus a number of famous episodes in emerging markets: the 1997–1998 Asian crises (in Hong Kong, Indonesia, Korea, Malaysia, the Philippines, and Thailand); that in Colombia in 1998; and Argentina's 2001 collapse. These are cases for which we have all or most of the relevant data to allow for meaningful quantitative comparisons across key indicator variables, such as equity markets, housing markets, unemployment, growth, and so on. Central to the analysis are historical housing price data, which can be difficult to obtain and are critical for assessing the recent episode.[3] We also include two earlier historical cases for which we have housing prices: those of Norway in 1899 and the United States in 1929.

The Downturn after a Crisis:
Depth and Duration

In figure 14.1, based on the same data as table 10.8, we again look at the bust phase of housing price cycles surrounding banking crises in the expanded data set. We include a number of countries that experienced crises from 2007 on. The latest crises are represented by bars in dark shading, past crises by bars in light shading. The cumulative decline in real housing prices from peak to trough averages 35.5 percent.[4] The most severe real housing price declines were experienced by Finland, Colombia, the Philippines, and Hong Kong. Their crashes amounted to 50 to 60 percent, measured from peak to trough. The housing price decline experienced by the United States during the latest episode at the time of this writing (almost 28 percent in real terms through late 2008 according to the Case-Shiller index) is already more than twice that registered in the United States during the Great Depression.

Notably, the duration of housing price declines has been quite long lived, averaging roughly six years. Even excluding the extraordinary experience of Japan (with its seventeen consecutive years of real housing price declines), the average remains more than five years. As figure 14.2 illustrates, the equity price declines that accompany banking crises are far steeper than are housing price declines, albeit shorter lived. The shorter duration of a downturn compared with real estate prices is perhaps unsurprising given that equity prices are far less inertial. The average historical decline in equity prices has been 55.9 percent, with the downturn phase of the cycle lasting 3.4 years. As of the end of 2008, Iceland and Austria had already experienced peak-to-trough equity price declines far exceeding the average of the historical comparison group.

226

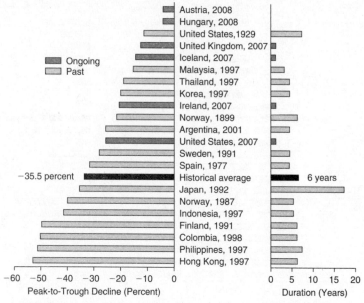

Figure 14.1. Cycles of past and ongoing real house prices and banking crises.
Sources: Appendixes A.1 and A.2 and sources cited therein.
Notes: Each banking crisis episode is identified by country and the beginning
year of the crisis. Only major (systemic) banking crisis episodes are included,
subject to data limitations. The historical average reported does not include
ongoing crisis episodes. For the ongoing episodes, the calculations are based
on data through the following periods: October 2008, monthly, for Iceland
and Ireland; 2007, annual, for Hungary; and Q3, 2008, quarterly, for all
others. Consumer price indexes are used to deflate nominal house prices.

In figure 14.3 we look at increases in unemployment rates
across the historical comparison group. (Because the unemployment
rate is classified as a lagging indicator, we do not include the most recent crisis, although we note that the U.S. unemployment rate has
already risen by 5 percentage points from its bottom value of near 4
percent.) On average, unemployment rises for almost five years, with
an increase in the unemployment rate of about 7 percentage points.
Although none of the postwar episodes has rivaled the rise in un-

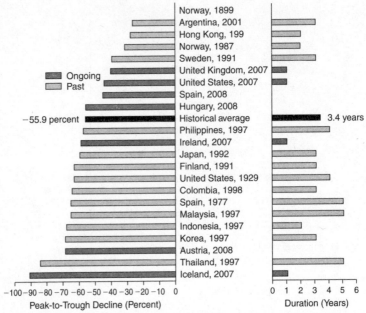

Figure 14.2. Cycles of past and ongoing real equity prices and banking crises.
Sources: Appendixes A.1 and A.2 and sources cited therein.
Notes: Each banking crisis episode is identified by country and the beginning year of the crisis. Only major (systemic) banking crisis episodes are included, subject to data limitations. The historical average reported does not include ongoing crisis episodes. For the ongoing episodes, the calculations are based on data through December 2, 2008. Consumer price indexes are used to deflate nominal equity prices.

employment of more than 20 percentage points experienced by the United States during the Great Depression, the employment consequences of financial crises are nevertheless strikingly large in many cases. For emerging markets the official statistics likely underestimate true unemployment.

Interestingly, figure 14.3 reveals that when it comes to banking crises, the emerging markets, particularly those in Asia, seem to do better in terms of unemployment than the advanced economies. (An exception was seen in the deep recession experienced by Colombia in 1998.) Although there are well-known data issues involved in

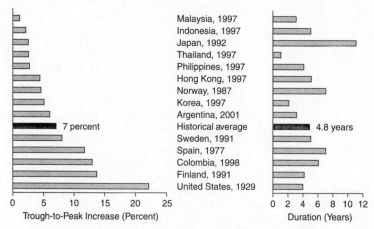

Figure 14.3. Cycles of past unemployment and banking crises.
Sources: Organisation for Economic Co-operation and Development;
International Monetary Fund (various years), *International Financial Statistics;*
Carter et al. (2006); various country sources; and the authors' calculations.
Notes: Each banking crisis episode is identified by country and the
beginning year of the crisis. Only major (systemic) banking crisis episodes
are included, subject to data limitations. The historical average reported
does not include ongoing crisis episodes.

comparing unemployment rates across countries,[5] the relatively poor
performance in advanced countries suggests the possibility that greater
(downward) wage flexibility in emerging markets may help cushion
employment during periods of severe economic distress. The gaps in
the social safety net in emerging market economies, compared to industrial ones, presumably also make workers more anxious to avoid
becoming unemployed.

In figure 14.4 we look at the cycles in real per capita GDP
around severe banking crises. The average magnitude of declines, at
9.3 percent, is stunning. Admittedly, as we noted earlier, for the post–
World War II period, the declines in real GDP have been smaller for
advanced economies than for emerging market economies. A probable explanation for the more severe contractions in emerging
market economies is that they are prone to abrupt reversals in
the availability of foreign credit. When foreign capital comes to a

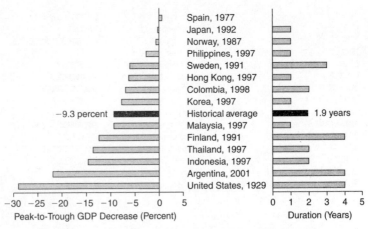

Figure 14.4. Cycles of past real per capita GDP and banking crises.
Sources: Total Economy Database (TED), Carter et al. (2006),
and the authors' calculations.
Notes: Each banking crisis episode is identified by country and the beginning
year of the crisis. Only major (systemic) banking crisis episodes are included,
subject to data limitations. The historical average reported does not include
ongoing crisis episodes. Total GDP in millions of 1990 U.S. dollars
(converted at Geary Khamis PPPs) divided by midyear population.

"sudden stop," to use the phrase popularized by Rudiger Dornbusch
and Guillermo Calvo, economic activity heads into a tailspin.[6]

Compared to unemployment, the cycle from peak to trough
in GDP is much shorter, only two years. Presumably this is partly because potential GDP growth is positive and we are measuring only absolute changes in income, not gaps relative to potential output. Even
so, the recessions surrounding financial crises are unusually long compared to normal recessions, which typically last less than a year.[7] Indeed, multiyear recessions usually occur only in economies that require
deep restructuring, such as that of Britain in the 1970s (prior to the advent of Prime Minister Margaret Thatcher), Switzerland in the 1990s,
and Japan after 1992 (the last due not only to its financial collapse but
also to the need to reorient its economy in light of China's rise). Banking crises, of course, usually require painful restructuring of the financial system and so are an important example of this general principle.

The Fiscal Legacy of Crises

Declining revenues and higher expenditures, owing to a combination of bailout costs and higher transfer payments and debt servicing costs, lead to a rapid and marked worsening in the fiscal balance. The episodes of Finland and Sweden stand out in this regard; the latter went from a precrisis surplus of nearly 4 percent of GDP to a whopping 15 percent deficit-to-GDP ratio. See table 14.1.

Figure 14.5 shows the increase in real government debt in the three years following a banking crisis. The deterioration in government finances is striking, with an average debt increase of more than 86 percent. The calculation here is based on relatively recent data from the past few decades, but recall that in chapter 10 of this book we take advantage of our newly unearthed historical data on domestic debt to show that a buildup in government debt has been a defining characteristic of the aftermath of banking crises for over a century. We look at the percentage increase in debt rather than in

TABLE 14.1
Fiscal deficits (central government balance) as a percentage of GDP

Country, crisis year	Year before the crisis	Peak deficit (year)	Increase or decrease (–) in the fiscal deficit
Argentina, 2001	–2.4	–11.9 (2002)	9.5
Chile, 1980	4.8	–3.2 (1985)	8.0
Colombia, 1998	–3.6	–7.4 (1999)	3.8
Finland, 1991	1.0	–10.8 (1994)	11.8
Indonesia, 1997	2.1	–3.7 (2001)	5.8
Japan, 1992	–0.7	–8.7 (1999)	9.4
Korea, 1997	0.0	–4.8 (1998)	4.8
Malaysia, 1997	0.7	–5.8 (2000)	6.5
Mexico, 1994	0.3	–2.3 (1998)	2.6
Norway, 1987	5.7	–2.5 (1992)	7.9
Spain, 1977[a]	–3.9	–3.1 (1977)	–0.8
Sweden, 1991	3.8	–11.6 (1993)	15.4
Thailand, 1997	2.3	–3.5 (1999)	5.8

Sources: International Monetary Fund (various years), *Government Financial Statistics* and *World Economic Outlook,* and the authors' calculations.

[a]As shown in figure 14.4, Spain was the only country in our sample to show a (modest) increase in per capita GDP growth during the postcrisis period.

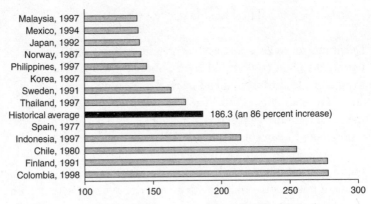

Figure 14.5. The cumulative increase in real public debt in the
three years following past banking crises.
Sources: Appendixes A.1 and A.2 and sources cited therein.
Notes: Each banking crisis episode is identified by country and the beginning year
of the crisis. Only major (systemic) banking crisis episodes are included, subject to
data limitations. The historical average reported does not include ongoing crisis
episodes, which are omitted altogether, because these crises began in 2007 or later,
and the debt stock comparison here is with three years after the beginning of the
banking crisis. Public debt is indexed to equal 100 in the year of the crisis.

debt relative to GDP because sometimes steep output drops compli-
cate the interpretation of debt-to-GDP ratios. We have already emphasized but it bears being stated again, the characteristically huge
buildup in government debt is driven mainly by a sharp falloff in tax
revenue due to the deep recessions that accompany most severe financial crises. The much-ballyhooed bank bailout costs have been,
in several cases, only a relatively minor contributor to the postcrisis
increase in debt burdens.

Sovereign Risk

As shown in figure 14.6, sovereign default, debt restructuring, and/or
near default (avoided by international bailout packages) have been
a part of the experience of financial crises in many emerging markets;
therefore, a decline in a country's credit rating during a crisis hardly

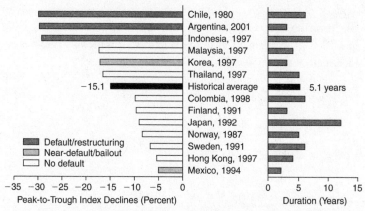

Figure 14.6. Cycles of *Institutional Investor* sovereign ratings and past banking crises.
Sources: Institutional Investor (various years) and the authors' calculations.
Notes: Institutional Investor's ratings range from 0 to 100,
rising with increasing creditworthiness.

comes as a surprise. Advanced economies, however, do not go un-scathed. Finland's sovereign risk rating score went from 79 to 69 in the space of three years, leaving it with a score close to those of some emerging markets! Japan suffered several downgrades from the more famous rating agencies as well.

Comparisons with Experiences from the First Great Contraction in the 1930s

Until now, our comparison benchmark has consisted of postwar financial crises. The quantitative similarities of those crises with the recent crisis in the United States, at least for the run-up and early trajectory, have been striking. Yet, in many ways this "Second Great Contraction" is a far deeper crisis than others in the comparison set, because it is global in scope, whereas the other severe post–World War II crises were either country-specific or at worst regional. Of course, as we will discuss in more detail in chapter 17, policy authorities reacted somewhat hesitantly in the 1930s, which may also

233

explain the duration and severity of the crisis. Nevertheless, given the lingering uncertainty over the future evolution of the crisis of the late 2000s (the Second Great Contraction), it is useful to look at evidence from the 1930s, the First Great Contraction.

Figure 14.7 compares the crises of the 1930s with the deep post–World War II crises in terms of the number of years over which

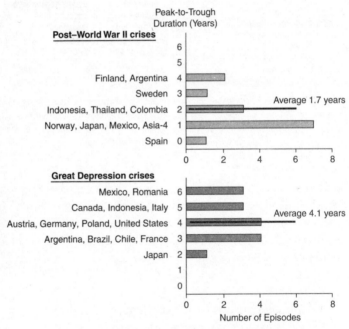

Figure 14.7. The duration of major financial crises: Fourteen Great Depression episodes versus fourteen post–World War II episodes (duration of the fall in output per capita).
Sources: Appendix A.3 and the authors' calculations.
Notes: The fourteen postwar episodes were those in Spain, 1977; Norway, 1987; Finland, 1991; Sweden, 1991; Japan, 1992; Mexico, 1994; Indonesia, Thailand, and (grouped as Asia-4 in the figure) Hong Kong, Korea, Malaysia, and Philippines, all 1997; Colombia, 1998; and Argentina, 2001. The fourteen Great Depression episodes were comprised of eleven banking crisis episodes and three less systemic but equally devastating economic contractions in Canada, Chile, and Indonesia during the 1930s. The banking crises were those in Japan, 1927; Brazil, Mexico, and the United States, all 1929; France and Italy, 1930; and Austria, Germany, Poland, and Romania, 1931.

234

output fell from peak to trough. The upper panel shows postwar crises including those in Colombia, Argentina, Thailand, Indonesia, Sweden, Norway, Mexico, the Philippines, Malaysia, Japan, Finland, Spain, Hong Kong, and Korea—fourteen in all. The lower panel shows fourteen Great Depression crises, including those in Argentina, Chile, Mexico, Canada, Austria, France, the United States, Indonesia, Poland, Brazil, Germany, Romania, Italy, and Japan.

Each half of the diagram forms a vertical histogram. The number of years each country or several countries were in crisis is measured on the vertical axis. The number of countries experiencing a crisis of any given length is measured on the horizontal axis. One sees clearly from the diagram that the recessions accompanying the Great Depression were of much longer duration than the postwar crises. After the war, output typically fell from peak to trough for an average of 1.7 years, with the longest downturn of four years experienced by Argentina and Finland. But in the Depression, many countries, including the United States and Canada, experienced a downturn of four years or longer, with Mexico and Romania experiencing a decrease in output for six years. Indeed, the average length of time over which output fell was 4.1 years in the Great Depression.[8]

It is important to recognize that standard measures of the depth and duration of recessions are not particularly suitable for capturing the epic decline in output that often accompanies deep financial crises. One factor is the depth of the decline, and another is that growth is sometimes quite modest in the aftermath as the financial system resets. An alternative perspective is provided in figure 14.8, which measures the number of years it took for a country's output to reach its precrisis level. Of course, after a steep fall in output, just getting back to the starting point can take a long period of growth. Both halves of the figure are stunning. For the postwar episodes, it took an average of 4.4 years for output to claw its way back to precrisis levels. Japan and Korea were able to do this relatively quickly, at only 2 years, whereas Colombia and Argentina took 8 years. But things were much worse in the Depression, and countries took an average of 10 years to increase their output back to precrisis levels, in part because no country was in a position to "export its way to re-

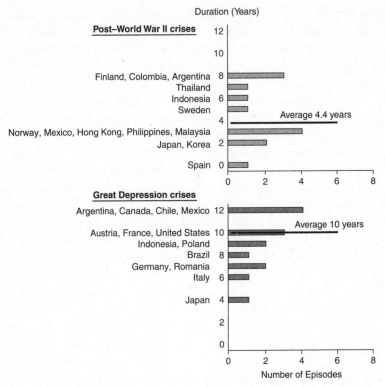

Figure 14.8. The duration of major financial crises:
Fourteen Great Depression episodes versus fourteen post–World War II
episodes (number of years for output per capita to return to its precrisis level).
Sources: Appendix A.3 and the authors' calculations.
Notes: The fourteen postwar episodes were those in Spain, 1977; Norway, 1987;
Finland, 1991; Sweden, 1991; Japan, 1992; Mexico, 1994; Hong Kong, Indonesia,
Korea, Malaysia, the Philippines, and Thailand, all 1997; Colombia, 1998; and
Argentina, 2001. The fourteen Great Depression episodes were comprised of
eleven banking crisis episodes and three less systemic but equally devastating
economic contractions in Canada, Chile, and Indonesia. The banking crises
were those in Japan, 1927; Brazil, Mexico, and the United States, all 1929;
France and Italy, 1930; and Austria, Germany, Poland, and Romania, 1931.
The precrisis level for the Great Depression was that of 1929.

covery" as world aggregate demand imploded. The figure shows, for example, that the United States, France, and Austria took 10 years to rebuild their output to its initial pre-Depression level, whereas Canada, Mexico, Chile, and Argentina took 12. Thus, the Great Depression era sets far more daunting benchmarks for the potential trajectory of the financial crisis of the late 2000s than do the main comparisons we have been making to severe postwar crises.

As we will show in chapter 16, the unemployment increases in the Great Depression were also far greater than those in the severe post–World War II financial crises. The average rate of unemployment increase was about 16.8 percent. In the United States, unemployment rose from 3.2 percent to 24.9 percent.

Finally, in figure 14.9 we look at the evolution of real public debt during the crises of the Great Depression era. Interestingly, public debt grew more slowly in the aftermath of these crises than it did

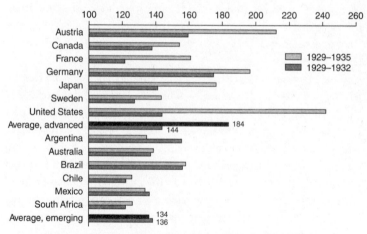

Figure 14.9. The cumulative increase in real public debt three and six years following the onset of the Great Depression in 1929: Selected countries.
Sources: Reinhart and Rogoff (2008b) and sources cited therein.
Notes: The beginning years of the banking crises range from 1929 to 1931. Australia and Canada did not have a systemic banking crisis but are included for comparison purposes, because both also suffered severe and protracted economic contractions. The year 1929 marks the peak in world output and hence is used as the marker for the beginning of the Depression episode.

in the severe postwar crises. In the Depression, it took six years for real public debt to grow by 84 percent (versus half that time in the postwar crises). Some of this difference reflects the very slow policy response that occurred in the Great Depression. It is also noteworthy that public debt in emerging markets did not increase in the later stages (three to six years) following the crises. Some of these emerging markets had already drifted into default (on both domestic and external debts); others may have faced the kind of external constraints that we discussed in connection with debt intolerance and, as such, had little capacity to finance budget deficits.

Concluding Remarks

An examination of the aftermath of severe postwar financial crises shows that these crises have had a deep and lasting effect on asset prices, output, and employment. Unemployment increases and housing price declines have extended for five and six years, respectively. Real government debt has increased by an average of 86 percent after three years.

How relevant are historical benchmarks in assessing the trajectory of a crisis such as the global financial crisis of the late 2000s, the Second Great Contraction? On the one hand, authorities now have arguably more flexible monetary policy frameworks, thanks particularly to a less rigid global exchange rate regime. And some central banks showed an aggressiveness early on by acting in a way that was notably absent in the 1930s or in the latter-day Japanese experience. On the other hand, we would be wise not to push too far the conceit that we are smarter than our predecessors. A few years back, many people would have said that improvements in financial engineering had done much to tame the business cycle and limit the risk of financial contagion. And as we saw in the final section of this chapter, the Great Depression crises were far more traumatic events than even the more severe of the post–World War II crises. In the Depression, it took countries in crisis an average of ten years for real per capita GDP to reach its precrisis level. Still, in the postwar crises it has taken almost four and a half years for output to reach its pre-crisis level (though growth has resumed much more quickly, it has still taken time for the economy to return to its starting point).

What we do know is that after the start of the recent crisis in 2007, asset prices and other standard crisis indicator variables tumbled in the United States and elsewhere along the tracks laid down by historical precedent. It is true that equity markets have since recovered some ground, but by and large this is not out of line with the historical experience (already emphasized in chapter 10) that V-shaped recoveries in equity prices are far more common than V-shaped recoveries in real housing prices or employment. Overall, this chapter's analysis of the postcrisis outcomes for unemployment, output, and government debt provides sobering benchmark numbers for how deep financial crises can unfold. Indeed, our post–World War II historical comparisons were largely based on episodes that were individual or regional in nature. The global nature of the recent crisis has made it far more difficult, and contentious, for individual countries to grow their way out through higher exports or to smooth the consumption effects through foreign borrowing. As noted in chapter 10, historical experience suggests that the brief post-2002 lull in sovereign defaults is at risk of coming to an abrupt end. True, the planned quadrupling of International Monetary Fund (IMF) resources, along with the apparent softening of IMF loan conditions, could have the effect of causing the next round of defaults to play out in slow motion, albeit with a bigger bang at the end if the IMF itself runs into broad repayment problems. Otherwise, as we have mentioned repeatedly, defaults in emerging market economies tend to rise sharply when many countries are simultaneously experiencing domestic banking crises.

- 15 -

THE INTERNATIONAL DIMENSIONS OF THE SUBPRIME CRISIS: THE RESULTS OF CONTAGION OR COMMON FUNDAMENTALS?

In the preceding two chapters we emphasized the similarities between the latest financial crisis (the Second Great Contraction) and previous crises, especially when viewed from the perspective of the United States at the epicenter. Of course, the crisis of the late 2000s is different in important ways from other post–World War II crises, particularly in the ferocity with which the recession spread globally, starting in the fourth quarter of 2008. The "sudden stop" in global financing rapidly extended to small- and medium-sized businesses around the world, with larger businesses able to obtain financing only at much dearer terms than before. The governments of emerging markets are similarly experiencing stress, although as of mid-2009 sovereign credit spreads had substantially narrowed in the wake of massive support by rich countries for the International Monetary Fund (IMF), which we alluded to in the previous chapter.[1]

How does a crisis morph from a local or regional crisis into a global one? In this chapter we emphasize the fundamental distinction between international transmission that occurs due to common shocks (e.g., the collapse of the tech boom in 2001 or the collapse of housing prices in the crisis of the late 2000s) and transmission that occurs due to mechanisms that are really the result of cross-border contagion emanating from the epicenter of the crisis.

In what follows we provide a sprinkling of historical examples of financial crises that swiftly spread across national borders, and we offer a rationale for understanding which factors make it more likely that a primarily domestic crisis fuels rapid cross-border contagion. We use these episodes as reference points to discuss the bunching of banking crises across countries that is so striking in the late-2000s crisis, where both common shocks and cross-country linkages are evident. Later, in chapter 16, we will develop a crisis severity index that allows one to define benchmarks for both regional and global financial crises.

Concepts of Contagion

In defining contagion, we distinguish between two types, the "slow-burn" spillover and the kind of fast burn marked by rapid cross-border transmission that Kaminsky, Reinhart, and Végh label "fast and furious." Specifically, they explain:

> We refer to contagion as an episode in which there are significant *im-mediate* effects in a number of countries following an event—that is, when the consequences are *fast and furious* and evolve over a matter of hours or days. This "fast and furious" reaction is a contrast to cases in which the initial international reaction to the news is muted. The latter cases do not preclude the emergence of gradual and protracted effects that may cumulatively have major economic consequences. We refer to these gradual cases as *spillovers*. *Common* external *shocks*, such as changes in international interest rates or oil prices, are also not *automatically* included in our working definition of contagion.[2]

We add to this classification that common shocks need not all be external. This caveat is particularly important with regard to the recent episode. Countries may share common "domestic" macroeconomic fundamentals, such as housing bubbles, capital inflow bonanzas, increasing private and (or) public leveraging, and so on.

Selected Earlier Episodes

Bordo and Murshid, and Neal and Weidenmier, have pointed out that cross-country correlations in banking crises were also common during 1880–1913, a period of relatively high international capital mobility under the gold standard.[3] In table 15.1 we look at a broader time span including the twentieth century; the table lists the years during which banking crises have been bunched; greater detail on the dates for individual countries is provided in appendix A.3.[4] The famous Barings crisis of 1890 (which involved Argentina and the United Kingdom before spreading elsewhere) appears to have been the first episode of international bunching of banking crises; this was followed by the panic of 1907, which began in the United States and quickly spread to other advanced economies (particularly Denmark, France, Italy, Japan, and Sweden). These episodes are reasonable benchmarks for modern-day financial contagion.[5]

Of course, other pre–World War II episodes of banking crisis contagion pale when compared with the Great Depression, which also saw a massive number of nearly simultaneous defaults of both external and domestic sovereign debts.

Common Fundamentals and the Second Great Contraction

The conjuncture of elements related to the recent crisis is illustrative of the two channels of contagion: cross-linkages and common shocks. Without doubt, the U.S. financial crisis of 2007 spilled over into other markets through direct linkages. For example, German and Japanese financial institutions (and others ranging as far as Kazakhstan) sought more attractive returns in the U.S. subprime market, perhaps owing to the fact that profit opportunities in domestic real estate were limited at best and dismal at worst. Indeed, after the fact, it became evident that many financial institutions outside the United States had nontrivial exposure to the U.S. subprime market.[6] This is a classic channel of transmission or contagion, through which a crisis in one country spreads across international borders. In the present context, however, contagion or spillovers are only part of the story.

That many other countries experienced economic difficulties at the same time as the United States also owed significantly to the

TABLE 15.1
Global banking crises, 1890–2008: Contagion or common fundamentals?

Years of bunching in banking crises	Affected countries	Comments
1890–1891	Argentina, Brazil, Chile, Portugal, the United Kingdom, and the United States	Argentina defaulted and there were runs on all Argentine banks (see della Paolera and Taylor 2001); Baring Brothers faced failure.
1907–1908	Chile, Denmark, France, Italy, Japan, Mexico, Sweden, and the United States	A drop in copper prices undermined the solvency of a trust company (quasi-bank) in New York.
1914	Argentina, Belgium, Brazil, France, India, Italy, Japan, Netherlands, Norway, the United Kingdom, and the United States	World War I broke out.
1929–1931	Advanced economies: Belgium, Finland, France, Germany, Greece, Italy, Portugal, Spain, Sweden, and the United States Emerging markets: Argentina, Brazil, China, India, and Mexico	Real commodity prices collapsed by about 51 percent during 1928–1931. Real interest rates reached almost 13 percent in the United States.
1981–1982	Emerging markets: Argentina, Chile, Colombia, Congo, Ecuador, Egypt, Ghana, Mexico, the Philippines, Turkey, and Uruguay	Between 1979 and 1982, real commodity prices fell about 40 percent. U.S. real interest rates hit about 6 percent— their highest readings since 1933. The decade-long debt crisis in emerging markets began.
1987–1988	Many small, mostly low-income countries; Sub-Saharan Africa was particularly hard hit	These years marked the tail-end of a nearly decade-long debt crisis.
1991–1992	Advanced economies: the Czech Republic, Finland, Greece, Japan, and Sweden	Real estate and equity price bubbles in the Nordic countries and Japan burst;

(continued)

TABLE 15.1 Continued

Years of bunching in banking crises	Affected countries	Comments
	Other countries: Algeria, Brazil, Egypt, Georgia, Hungary, Poland, Romania, and the Slovak Republic	many transition economies coped with liberalization and stabilization.
1994–1995	Argentina, Bolivia, Brazil, Ecuador, Mexico, and Paraguay Others countries: Azerbaijan, Cameroon, Croatia, Lithuania, and Swaziland	The Mexican "tequila crisis" dealt the first blow to the surge in capital inflows to emerging markets since the early 1990s.
1997–1999	Asia: Hong Kong, Indonesia, Malaysia, the Philippines, Taiwan, Thailand, and Vietnam Other countries: Brazil, Colombia, Ecuador, El Salvador, Mauritius, Russia, Turkey, and Ukraine	The second blow was dealt to capital flows to emerging markets.
2007–present	Germany, Hungary, Iceland, Ireland, Japan, Spain, the United Kingdom, the United States, and others	The U.S. subprime real estate bubble—and other real estate bubbles in advanced economies—burst.

Sources: Based on chapters 1–10 of this book.

fact that many of the features that characterized the run-up to the subprime crisis in the United States were present in other advanced economies as well. Two common elements stand out. First, many countries in Europe and elsewhere (Iceland and New Zealand, for example) had their own home-grown real estate bubbles (figure 15.1). Second, the United States was not alone in running large current account deficits and experiencing a sustained "capital flow bonanza," as shown in chapter 10. Bulgaria, Iceland, Ireland, Latvia, New Zealand, Spain, and the United Kingdom, among others, were importing capital from abroad, which helped fuel a credit and asset price boom.[7] These trends, in and of themselves, made these countries vulnerable to the usual nasty consequences of asset market crashes and capital flow reversals—or "sudden stops" à la Dornbusch/Calvo—irrespective of what may have been happening in the United States.

Direct spillovers via exposure to the U.S. subprime markets and common fundamentals of the kind discussed abroad have addi-

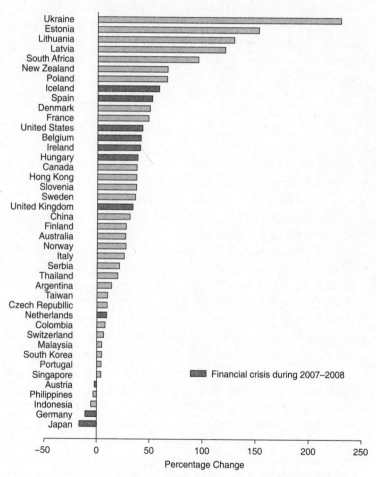

Figure 15.1. Percentage change in real housing prices, 2002–2006.
Sources: Bank for International Settlements and the sources listed in appendix A.1.
Notes: The China data cover 2003–2006.

245

tionally been complemented with other "standard" transmission channels common in such episodes, specifically the prevalence of common lenders. For example, an Austrian bank exposed to Hungary (as the latter encounters severe economic turbulence) will curtail lending not only to Hungary but to other countries (predominantly in Eastern Europe) to which it was already making loans. This will transmit the "shock" from Hungary (via the common lender) to other countries. A similar role was played by a common Japanese bank lender in the international transmission of the Asian crisis of 1997–1998 and by U.S. banks during the Latin American debt crisis of the early 1980s.

Are More Spillovers Under Way?

As noted earlier, spillovers do not typically occur at the same rapid pace associated with adverse surprises and sudden stops in the financial market. Therefore, they tend not to spark immediate adverse balance sheet effects. Their more gradual evolution does not make their cumulative effects less serious, however.

The comparatively open, historically fast-growing economies of Asia, after initially surviving relatively well, were eventually very hard hit by the recessions of the late 2000s in the advanced economies. Not only are Asian economies more export driven than those of other regions, but also their exports have a large manufactured goods component, which makes the world demand for their products highly income elastic relative to demand for primary commodities.

Although not quite as export oriented as Asia, the economies of Eastern Europe have been severely affected by recessions in their richer trading partners in the West. A similar observation can be made of Mexico and Central America, countries that are both highly integrated with and also significantly dependent on workers' remittances from the United States. The more commodity-based economies of Africa and Latin America (as well as the oil-producing nations) felt the effects of the global weakness in demand through its effect on the commodity markets, where prices fell sharply starting in the fall of 2008.

A critical element determining the extent of the damage to emerging markets through these spillover effects is the speed at which the countries of the "north" recover. As cushions in foreign exchange reserves (built in the bonanza years before 2007) erode and fiscal finances deteriorate, financial strains on debt servicing (public and private) will mount. As we have noted, severe financial crises are protracted affairs. Given the tendency for sovereign defaults to increase in the wake of both global financial crises and sharp declines in global commodity prices, the fallout from the Second Great Contraction may well be an elevated number of defaults, reschedulings, and/or massive IMF bailouts.

- 16 -

COMPOSITE MEASURES OF
FINANCIAL TURMOIL

In this book we have emphasized the clustering of crises at several junctures both across countries and across different types of crises. A country experiencing an exchange rate crisis may soon find itself in banking and inflation crises, sometimes with domestic and external default to follow. Crises are also transmitted across countries through contagion or common factors, as we discussed in the previous chapter.

Until now, however, we have not attempted to construct any quantitative index that combines crises regionally or globally. Here, in keeping with the algorithmic approach we have applied to delineating individual financial crisis events, we will offer various types of indexes of financial turbulence that are helpful in assessing the global, regional, and national severity of a crisis.

Our financial turbulence index reveals some stunning information. The most recent global financial crisis—which we have termed the "Second Great Contraction"—is clearly the only global financial crisis that has occurred during the post–World War II period. Even if the Second Great Contraction does not evolve into the Second Great Depression, it still surpasses other turbulent episodes, including the breakdown of Bretton Woods, the first oil shock, the debt crisis of the 1980s in the developing world, and the now-famous Asian crisis of 1997–1998. The Second Great Contraction is already marked by an extraordinarily global banking crisis and by spectacular global exchange rate volatility. The synchronicity of the collapses in housing markets and employment also appears unprecedented since the Great Depression; late in this chapter we will show little-used data from the Great Depression to underscore this comparison.

The index of financial turbulence we develop in this chapter can also be used to characterize the severity of regional crisis, and here we compare the experiences of different continents. The index shows how misinformed is the popular view that Asia does not have financial crises.

This chapter not only links crises globally but also takes on the issue of how different varieties of crisis are linked within a country. Following Kaminsky and Reinhart, we discuss how (sometimes latent) banking crises often lead to currency crashes, outright sovereign default, and inflation.[1]

Finally, we conclude by noting that pulling out of a global crisis is, by nature, more difficult than pulling out of a multicountry regional crisis (such as the Asian financial crisis of 1997–1998). Slow growth in the rest of the world cuts off the possibility that foreign demand will compensate for collapsing domestic demand. Thus, measures such as our index of global financial turbulence can potentially be useful in designing the appropriate policy response.

Developing a Composite Index of Crises: The BCDI Index

We develop our index of crisis severity as follows. In chapter 1 we defined five "varieties" of crises: external and domestic sovereign default, banking crises, currency crashes, and inflation outbursts.[2] Our composite country financial turbulence index is formed by simply summing up the number of types of crises a country experiences in a given year. Thus, if a country did not experience any of our five crises in a given year, its turbulence index for that year would be zero, while in a worst-case scenario (as in Argentina in 2002, for instance) it would be five. We assign such a value for each country for each year. This is what we dub the BCDI index, which stands for banking (systemic episodes only), currency, debt (domestic and external), and inflation crisis index.

Although this exercise captures some of the compounding dimensions of the crisis experience, it admittedly remains an incomplete measure of its severity.[3] If inflation goes to 25 percent per annum (meeting the threshold for a crisis by our definition), it receives the same weight in the index as if it went to 250 percent, which is obviously far more serious.[4] This binary treatment of default is similar to that of the rating agency Standard and Poor's (S&P), which lists countries as either in default or not in default. The S&P index (and ours) take account of debt crisis variables. For example, Uruguay's relatively swift and "market-friendly" restructuring in 2003 is assigned the same value as the drawn-out outright default and major "haircut" successfully imposed on creditors by its larger neighbor, Argentina, during its 2001–2002 default. Nevertheless, indexes such as S&P's have proven enormously useful over time precisely because default tends to be such a discrete event. Similarly, a country that reaches our crisis markers across multiple varieties of crises is almost surely one undergoing severe economic and financial duress.

Where feasible, we also add to our five-crises composite a "Kindleberger-type" stock market crash, which we show separately.[5] In this case, the index runs from zero to six.[6] Although Kindleberger himself did not provide a quantitative definition of a crash, Barro and Ursúa have adopted a reasonable benchmark for defining asset price collapses, which we adopt here. They define a stock market crash as a cumulative decline of 25 percent or more in real equity prices.[7] We apply their methods to the sixty-six countries covered in our sample; the starting dates for equity prices are determined by data availability, as detailed on a country-by-country basis in the data appendixes. Needless to say, our sample of stock market crashes ends with a bang in the cross-country megacrashes of 2008. As in the case of growth collapses, many (if not most) of the stock market crashes have coincided with the crisis episodes described here (chapters 1 and 11). "Most" clearly does not mean all; the Black Monday crash of October 1987 (for example) is not associated with a crisis of any other stripe. False signal flares from the equity market are, of course, familiar. As Samuelson famously noted, "The stock market has predicted nine of the last five recessions."[8] Indeed, although global stock markets continued to plummet during the first part of 2009 (past the end date of our core data set), they then rose markedly in the second quarter of the year, though they hardly returned to their precrisis level.

Beyond sovereign events, there are two other important dimensions of defaults that our crisis index does not capture directly. First, there are defaults on household debt. These defaults, for instance, have been at center stage in the unfolding subprime saga in the United States in the form of the infamous toxic mortgages. Household defaults are not treated separately in our analysis owing to a lack of historical data, even for advanced economies. However, such episodes are most likely captured by our indicator of banking crises. Banks, after all, are the principal sources of credit to households, and large-scale household defaults (to the extent that these occur) impair bank balance sheets.

More problematic is the incidence of corporate defaults, which are in their own right another "variety of crisis." This omission is less of an issue in countries where corporations are bank-dependent. In such circumstances, the same comment made about household default applies to corporate debt. For countries with more developed capital markets, it may be worthwhile to consider widespread corporate default as yet another variety of crisis. As shown in figure 16.1, the United States began to experience a sharp run-up in the incidence of corporate default during the Great Depression well before the government defaulted (the abrogation of the gold clause in 1934). However, it is worth noting that corporate defaults and banking crises are indeed correlated, so our index may partially capture this phenomenon indirectly. In many episodes, corporate defaults have also been precursors to government defaults or reschedulings as governments have tended to shoulder private sector debts.

An Illustration of the Composite at a Country Level

The Argentine crisis of 2001–2002 illustrates how crises may potentially reinforce and overlap one another. The government defaulted on all its debts, domestic and foreign; the banks were paralyzed in a "banking holiday" when deposits were frozen indefinitely; the exchange rate for pesos to U.S. dollars went from one to more than three practically overnight; and prices went from declining (with deflation running at an annual rate of –1 percent or so) to inflating at

251

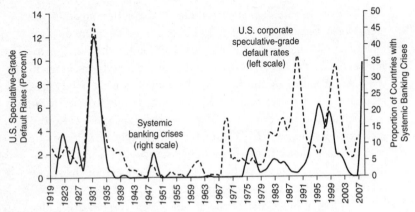

Figure 16.1. The proportion of countries with systemic banking
crises (weighted by their share of world income) and U.S.
corporate speculative-grade default rates, 1919–2008.
Sources: Kaminsky and Reinhart (1999), Bordo et al. (2001), Maddison (2004),
Caprio et al. (2005), Jácome (2008), *Moody's Magazine* (various issues), and
additional sources listed in appendix A.3, which provides banking crises dates.
Notes: The sample includes all sixty-six countries listed in table 1.1 that were
independent states in the given year. Three sets of GDP weights are used, 1913
weights for the period 1800–1913, 1990 weights for the period 1914–1990, and
finally 2003 weights for the period 1991–2008. The entries for 2007–2008 list crises
in Austria, Belgium, Germany, Hungary, Japan, the Netherlands, Spain, the United
Kingdom, and the United States. The figure shows two-year moving averages.

a rate of about 30 percent (by conservative official estimates). We
might add that this episode qualifies as a Barro-Ursúa growth collapse
(per capita GDP fell by about 20 to 25 percent), and real stock prices
crashed by more than 30 percent, along the lines of a Kindleberger-
type crash episode.

World Aggregates and Global Crises

To transition from the experience of individual countries to a world
or regional aggregate, we take weighted averages across all countries
or for a particular region. The weights, as discussed earlier, are given
by the country's share in world output. Alternatively, one can calculate an average tally of crises across a particular country group using
a simple unweighted average. We will illustrate both.

Historical Comparisons

Our aggregate crisis indexes are the time series shown for 1900–2008 in figures 16.2 and 16.3 for the world and for the advanced economies. The advanced economies aggregate comprises the eighteen high-income countries in our sample, while the emerging markets group

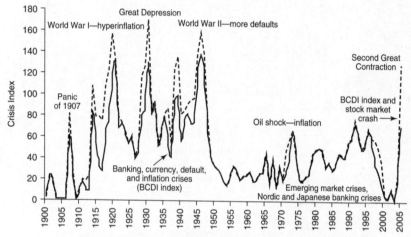

Figure 16.2. Varieties of crises: World aggregate, 1900–2008.
Source: The authors' calculations.
Notes: The figure presents a composite index of banking, currency, sovereign default, and inflation crises and stock market crashes (weighted by their share of world income).The banking, currency, default (domestic and external), and inflation composite (BCDI) index can take a value between zero and five (for any country in any given year) depending on the varieties of crises occurring in a particular year. For instance, in 1998 the index took on a value of 5 for Russia, which was experiencing a currency crash, a banking and inflation crisis, and a sovereign default on both domestic and foreign debt obligations. This index is then weighted by the country's share in world income. This index is calculated annually for the sixty-six countries in the sample for 1800–2008 (shown above for 1900 onward). In addition, we use the definition of a stock market crash given by Barro and Ursúa (2009) for the twenty-five countries in their sample (a subset of the sixty-six-country sample except for Switzerland) for the period 1864–2006; we update their definition of a crash through December 2008 to compile our banking, currency, default (domestic and external), and inflation composite (BCDI +) index. For the United States, for example, the index posts a reading of 2 (banking crisis and stock market crash) in 2008; for Australia and Mexico it also posts a reading of 2 (currency and stock market crash).

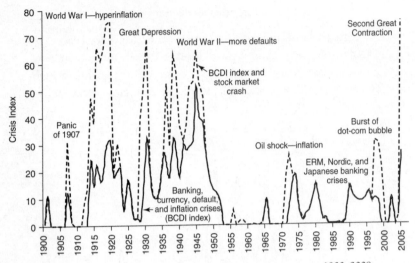

Figure 16.3. Varieties of crises: Advanced economies aggregate, 1900–2008.
Source: The authors' calculations.

Notes: This figure presents a composite index of banking, currency, sovereign default, and inflation crises and stock market crashes, weighted by their share of world income. The banking, currency, default (domestic and external), and inflation composite (BCDI) index can take a value between zero and 5 (for any country in any given year) depending on the varieties of crises taking place in a particular year. For instance, in 1947 the index took on a value of 4 for Japan, which was experiencing a currency crash, an inflation crisis, and a sovereign default on both domestic and foreign debt obligations. This index is then weighted by the country's share in world income. This index is calculated annually for the eighteen advanced economies (includes Austria but not Switzerland) in the Reinhart-Rogoff sample for 1800–2008 (shown above for 1900 onward). In addition, we use the definition of a stock market crash given by Barro and Ursúa (2009) for eighteen advanced economies (includes Switzerland but not Austria) for the period 1864–2006; we update their definition of a crash through December 2008 to compile our banking, currency, default (domestic and external), and inflation composite (BCDI +) index. For the United States and the United Kingdom, for example, the index posts a reading of 2 (banking crisis and stock market crash) in 2008; for Australia and Norway it also posts a reading of 2 (currency and stock market crash). ERM is exchange rate mechanism of the euro system.

aggregates forty-eight entries from Africa, Asia, Europe, and Latin America. The indexes shown are weighted by a country's share in world GDP, as we have done for debt and banking crises.[9] The country indexes (without stock market crashes) are compiled from the time of each country's independence (if after 1800) onward; the index that includes the equity market crashes is calculated based on data availability.

Although inflation and banking crises predated independence in many cases, a sovereign debt crisis (external or internal) is, by definition, not possible for a colony. In addition, numerous colonies did not always have their own currencies. When stock market crashes (shown separately) are added to the BCDI composite, we refer to it as the BCDI +.

Figures 16.2 and 16.3 chronicle the incidence, and to some degree the severity, of varied crisis experiences. A cursory inspection of these figures reveals the very different patterns of the pre–World War II and postwar experiences. This difference is most evident in figure 16.3, which plots the indexes for eighteen advanced economies. The prewar experience was characterized by frequent and severe crisis episodes ranging from the banking crisis–driven "global" panic of 1907 to the debt and inflation crises associated with World War II and its aftermath.[10]

The postwar periods offered some bouts of turbulence: the inflationary outbursts that accompanied the first oil shocks in the mid-1970s, the recessions associated with bringing down inflation in the early 1980s, the severe banking crises in the Nordic countries and Japan in the early 1990s, and the bursting of the dot-com bubble in the early 2000s. However, these episodes pale in comparison with their prewar counterparts and with the global contraction of 2008, which has been unparalleled (by a considerable margin) in the sixty-plus years since World War II (figure 16.3). Like its prewar predecessors, the 2008 episode has been both severe in magnitude and global in scope, as reflected by the large share of countries mired in crises. Stock market crashes have been nearly universal. Banking crises have emerged as asset price bubbles have burst and high degrees of leverage have become exposed. Currency crashes against the U.S. dollar in advanced economies took on the magnitudes and volatilities of crashes in emerging markets.

A growing body of academic literature, including contributions by McConnell and Perez-Quiros and Blanchard and Simon, had documented a post-mid-1980s decline in various aspects of macroeconomic volatility, presumably emanating from a global low-inflation environment. This had been termed "a Great Moderation" in the United States and elsewhere.[11] However, systemic crises and low levels of macroeconomic volatility do not travel hand in hand; the sharp increases in volatility that occurred during the Second Great Contraction, which began in 2007, are evident across asset markets, including real estate, stock prices, and exchange rates. They are also manifestly evident in the macroeconomic aggregates, such as those for output, trade, and employment. It remains to be seen how economists will assess the Great Moderation and its causes after the crisis recedes.

For many emerging markets, the Great Moderation was a fleeting event. After all, the debt crisis of the 1980s was as widespread and severe as the events of the 1930s (figure 16.3). These episodes, which affected Africa, Asia, and Latin America in varying degrees, often involved a combination of sovereign default, chronic inflation, and protracted banking crises. As the debt crisis of the 1980s settled, new eruptions emanated from the economies of Eastern Europe and the former Soviet Union in the early 1990s. The Mexican crisis of 1994–1995 and its repercussions in Latin America, the fierce Asian crisis that began in the summer of 1997, and the far-reaching Russian crisis of 1998 did not make for many quiet stretches in emerging markets. This string of crises culminated in Argentina's record default and implosion in 2001–2002.[12]

Until the crisis that began in the United States in the summer of 2007 and became global in scope a year later, emerging markets enjoyed a period of tranquility and even prosperity. During 2003–2007, world growth conditions were favorable, commodity prices were booming, and world interest rates were low, so credit was cheap. However, five years is too short a time span to contemplate extending the "Great Moderation" arguments to emerging markets; in effect, the events of the past two years have already rekindled volatility almost across the board.

Regional Observations

We next look at the regional profile of crises. In figures 16.2 and 16.3 we looked at averages weighted by country size. So that no single country will dominate the regional profiles, the remainder of this discussion focuses on unweighted simple averages for Africa, Asia, and Latin America. In figures 16.4–16.6 we show regional tallies for 1800–2008 for Asia and Latin America and for the post–World War II period for the more newly independent African states.

For Africa, the regional composite index of financial turbulence begins in earnest in the 1950s (figure 16.4), for only South Africa (1910) was a sovereign state prior to that period. However, we do have considerable coverage of prices and exchange rates for the years following World War I, so numerous preindependence crises (including some severe banking crises in South Africa) are dated and included for the colonial period. The index jumps from a low that is close to zero in the 1950s to a high in the 1990s. The thirteen African

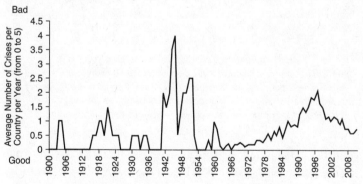

Figure 16.4. Varieties of crises: Africa, 1900–2008.
Source: The authors' calculations based on sources listed in appendixes A.1–A.3.

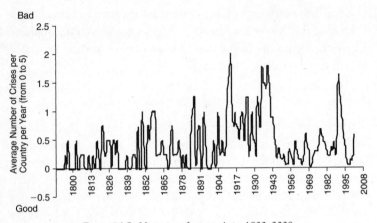

Figure 16.5. Varieties of crises: Asia, 1800–2008.
Source: The authors' calculations based on sources listed in appendixes A.1–A.3.

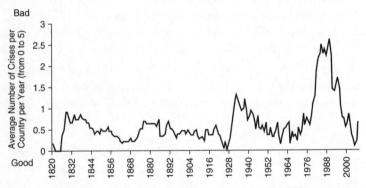

Figure 16.6. Varieties of crises: Latin America, 1800–2008.
Source: The authors' calculations based on sources listed in appendixes A.1–A.3.
Notes: The hyperinflations in Argentina, Bolivia, Brazil, Nicaragua, and Peru sharply increase in the index (reflected in the spike shown for the late 1980s and early 1990s) because all these episodes register a maximum reading of 5.

countries in our sample had, on average, two simultaneous crises during the worst years of the 1980s. In all cases, except that of Mauritius, which has neither defaulted on nor restructured its sovereign debts, the two crises could have been a pairing of any of our crisis varieties. The decline in the average number of crises in the 1990s reflected primarily a decline in the incidence of inflation crises and the eventual (if protracted) resolution of the decade-long debt crisis of the 1980s.

The regional composite index of financial turbulence for Asia (figure 16.5) spans 1800–2008, for China, Japan, and Thailand were independent nations throughout this period. Having gained independence almost immediately following World War II, the remaining Asian countries in the sample then join in the regional average. The profile for Asia highlights a point we have made on more than one occasion: the economic claim of the superiority of the "tigers" or "miracle economies" in the three decades before the 1997–1998 crisis was naïve in terms of the local history. The region had experienced several protracted bouts of economic instability by the international standards of the day. The most severe crisis readings occurred during the period bracketed by the two world wars. In that period, China saw hyperinflation, several defaults, more than one banking crisis, and countless currencies and currency conversions. Japan had numerous bouts of banking, inflation, and exchange rate crises, culminating in its default on its external debt during World War II, the freezing of bank deposits, and its near-hyperinflation (approaching 600 percent) at the end of the war in 1945.

Perhaps Latin America would have done better in terms of economic stability had the printing press never crossed the Atlantic (figure 16.6). Before Latin America's long struggle with high, hyper-, and chronic inflation took a dark turn in the 1970s, the region's average turbulence index reading was very much in line with the world average. Despite periodic defaults, currency crashes, and banking crises, the average never really surpassed one crisis per year, in effect comparing moderately favorably with those of other regions for long stretches of time. The rise of inflation (which began before the famous debt crisis of the 1980s, the "lost decade") would change the relative and absolute performance of the region until the second half of the 1990s. During Latin America's worst moments in the late 1980s —before the 1987 Brady plan (discussed earlier in box 5.3) restructured bad sovereign debts and while Argentina, Brazil, and Peru were mired in hyperinflation—as we can see from the index, the region experienced an average of almost three crises a year.[13]

Defining a Global Financial Crisis

Although the indexes of financial turbulence we have developed can be quite useful in assessing the severity of a global financial crisis, we need a broader-ranging algorithm to systematically delineate true crises so as to exclude, for example, a crisis that registers high on the global scale but affects only one large region. We propose the working definition of a global financial crisis found in box 16.1.

Global Financial Crises: Economic Effects

We next turn to two broad factors associated with global crises, both of which are present in the recent-vintage global contraction: first, the effects of the crisis on the level and the volatility of economic activity broadly defined and measured by world aggregates of equity prices, real GDP, and trade; and second, its relative synchronicity across countries, which is evident in asset markets as well as trends in trade, employment, and other economic sectoral statistics, such as

---

BOX 16.1
Global financial crises: A working definition

Broadly speaking, a global crisis has four main elements that distinguish it from a regional one or a less virulent multicountry crisis:

1. One or more global financial centers are mired in a systemic (or severe) crisis of one form or another. This "requirement" ensures that at least one affected country has a significant (although not necessarily dominant) share in world GDP. Crises in global financial centers also directly or indirectly affect financial flows to numerous other countries. An example of a financial center is a lender to other countries, as the United Kingdom was to "emerging markets" in the 1820s lending boom and the United States was to Latin America in the late 1920s.
2. The crisis involves two or more distinct regions.
3. The number of countries in crisis in each region is three or greater. Counting the number of affected countries (as opposed to the share of regional GDP affected by crisis) ensures that a crisis in a large country—such as Brazil in Latin America or China or Japan in Asia—is not sufficient to define the crisis episode.
4. Our composite GDP-weighted index average of global financial turbulence is at least one standard deviation above normal.

Selected episodes of global, multicountry, and regional economic crisis

Episode	Type	Global financial center(s) most affected	At least two distinct regions	Number of countries in each region
The crisis of 1825–1826	Global	United Kingdom	Europe and Latin America	Greece and Portugal defaulted, as did practically all of newly independent Latin America.
The panic of 1907	Global	United States	Europe, Asia, and Latin America	Notably France, Italy, Japan, Mexico, and Chile suffered from banking panics.
The Great Depression, 1929–1938	Global	United States and France	All regions	Widespread defaults and banking crises across all regions.
Debt crisis of the 1980s	Multicountry (developing countries and emerging markets)	United States (affected, but crisis was not systemic)	Developing countries in Africa, Latin America, and to a lesser extent Asia	Sovereign default, currency crashes, and high inflation were rampant.
The Asian crisis of 1997–1998	Multicountry, extending beyond Asia in 1998	Japan (affected, but by then it was five years into the resolution of its own systemic banking crisis)	Asia, Europe, and Latin America	Affected Southeast Asia initially. By 1998, Russia, Ukraine, Colombia, and Brazil were affected.
The Global Contraction of 2008	Global	United States, United Kingdom	All regions	Banking crises proliferated in Europe, and stock market and currency crashes versus the dollar cut across regions.

Source: Earlier parts of this book.

housing. The emphasis of our discussion is on the last two global crises, the Great Depression of the 1930s and the Second Great Contraction, for which documentation is most complete. Obviously, looking at this broad range of macroeconomic data gives us a much more nuanced picture of a crisis.

Global Aggregates

The connection between stock prices and future economic activity is hardly new. The early literature on turning points in the business cycle, such as the classic by Burns and Mitchell, documented the leading-indicator properties of share prices.[14] Synchronous (across-the-board) and large declines in equity prices (crashes) characterized the onset of the episode that became the Great Depression and somewhat more belatedly the recent global crisis. Figure 16.7 plots an index of global stock prices for 1929–1939 and for 2008–2009 (to the present). For the more recent episode, the index accounts for about 70 percent of world equity market capitalization and covers seven distinct regions and twenty-nine countries. Stock prices are deflated by world consumer prices. The data for 1928–1939 are constructed using median inflation rates for the sixty-six-country sample; for 2007–2009 they are taken from the end-of-period prices published in the *World Economic Outlook*.[15] The years 1928 and 2007 marked the cycle peak in these indices.

The decline in equity markets during 2008 and beyond match the scale (and the cross-country reach) of the 1929 crashes. It is worth noting that during the crisis of the 1930s equity ownership worldwide was far more limited than it has become in the twenty-first century; the growth of pension funds and retirement plans and the ascent of an urban population have increased the links between household wealth and equity markets.

In much the same spirit as figure 16.7, figure 16.8 plots real per capita GDP (weighted by world population) for various country groupings for the two global crises.[16] The aggregate for Europe corresponds to Maddison's twelve-country population-weighted aggregate;[17] the index for Latin America is comprised of the region's eight

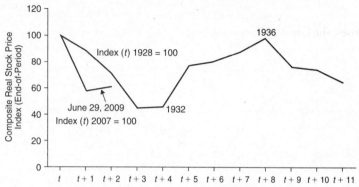

Figure 16.7. Global stock markets during global crises:
The composite real stock price index (end of period).
Sources: Global Financial Data (GFD) (n.d.); Standard and Poor's;
International Monetary Fund (various years), World Economic Outlook;
and the authors (details provided in appendix A.1).
Notes: The world composite stock price index was taken from GFD for 1928–1939
and from S&P for 2007–2009. The S&P Global 1200 index covers seven distinct
regions and twenty-nine countries and captures approximately 70 percent of the
world market capitalization. Stock prices are deflated by world consumer prices.
For 1928–1939 these have been constructed using median inflation rates for the
sixty-six-country sample; for 2007–2009 these have been taken from the World
Economic Outlook end-of-period prices. The years 1928 and 2007 marked the
cycle peak in these indexes. The year of the crisis is indicated by t.

largest countries. The year 1929 marked the peak in real per capita
GDP for all three country groupings. The current data come from the
World Economic Outlook. When all this information is taken together, it is difficult to reconcile the projected trajectory in real GDP,
particularly for emerging markets, and the developments of 2008
through early 2009 in equity markets.

As for trade, we offer two illustrations of its evolution during
the two global crises. The first of these (figure 16.9) is a reprint of an
old classic titled "The Contracting Spiral of World Trade: Month by
Month, January 1929–June 1933." This inward spiral appeared in the
World Economic Survey, 1932–1933, which in turn reprinted it from
another contemporary source.[18] The illustration documents the 67
percent decline in the value of trade as the Depression took hold. As

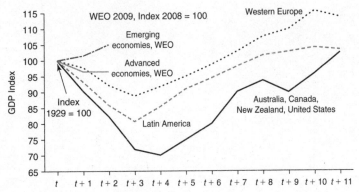

Figure 16.8. Real per capita GDP during global financial crises:
Multicountry aggregates (PPP weighted).
Sources: Maddison (2004); International Monetary Fund (various years),
World Economic Outlook; and the authors (details provided in appendix A.1).
Notes: The Europe aggregate corresponds to Maddison's twelve-country
population-weighted aggregate; the Latin America index is comprised
of the region's eight largest countries. The years 1929 and 2008 marked
the peak in real per capita GDP for all three country groupings.
The year of the crisis is indicated by *t*.

has been extensively documented, including by contemporaneous
sources, the collapse in international trade was only partially the
byproduct of sharp declines in economic activity, ranging from about
10 percent for Western Europe to about 30 percent for Australia,
Canada, New Zealand, and the United States.[19] The other destruc-
tive factor was the worldwide increase in protectionist policies in the
form of both trade barriers and competitive devaluations.

Figure 16.10 plots the value of world merchandise exports for
1928–2009. The estimate for 2009 uses the actual year-end level for
2008 as the average for 2009; this yields a 9 percent year-over-year
decline in 2009, the largest one-year drop since 1938.[20] Other large
post–World War II declines are in 1952, during the Korean War, and
in 1982–1983, when recession hit the United States and a 1930s-scale
debt crisis swept through the emerging world. Smaller declines occurred in 1958, the bottom of a recession in the United States; in 1998,
during the Asian financial crisis; and in 2001, after September 11.

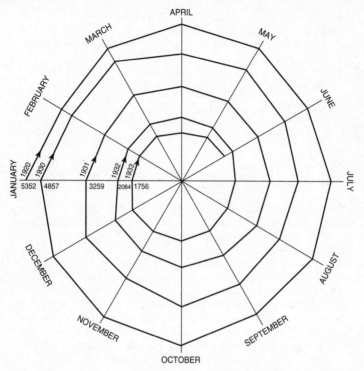

Figure 16.9. The contracting spiral of world trade month by month,
January 1929–June 1933.
*Source: Monatsberichte des Österreichischen Institutes für
Konjunkturforschung 4 (1933): 63.*

Cross-Country Synchronicity

The performance of the global aggregates provides evidence that a
crisis has affected a sufficiently large share of the world's population
and/or countries. However, because the information is condensed
into a single world index, it does not fully convey the synchronous
nature of global crises. To fill in this gap, we present evidence on the
performance of various economic indicators during the most recent
previous global crisis. Specifically, we present evidence on the
changes in unemployment and indexes of housing activity, exports,
and currency movements during 1929–1932.

265

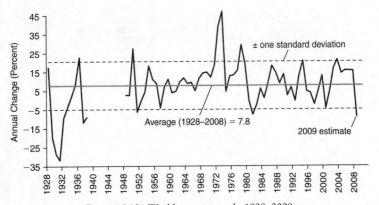

Figure 16.10. World export growth, 1928–2009.
Sources: Global Financial Data (GFD) (n.d.); League of Nations (various years),
World Economic Survey; International Monetary Fund (various years),
World Economic Outlook; and the authors (see notes).
Notes: No world aggregate is available during World War II. The estimate for
2009 uses the actual year-end level for 2008 as the average for 2009; this yields
a 9 percent year-over-year decline in 2009, the largest postwar drop. Other
large post–World War II declines were in 1952, during the Korean War, and
in 1982–1983, when recession hit the United States and a 1930s-scale debt
crisis swept through the emerging world. Smaller declines occurred in 1958,
the bottom of a recession in the United States; in 1998, during the Asian
financial crisis; and in 2001, after September 11.

The massive collapse in trade at the height of the Great Depression was already made plain by the two figures displaying world
aggregates. Figure 16.11 adds information on the widespread nature
of the collapse, which affected countries in all regions, low-, middle-,
and high-income alike. In other words, the world aggregates are truly
representative of the individual country experience and are not
driven by developments in a handful of large countries that are
heavily weighted in the world aggregates. Apart from wars that have
involved a significant share of the world either directly or indirectly
(including the Napoleonic Wars), such across-the-board synchronicity is not to be found in the data.

Cross-country synchronicity is not limited to variables for
which one would expect close cross-country co-movement, such as
international trade or exchange rates. The construction industry,

266

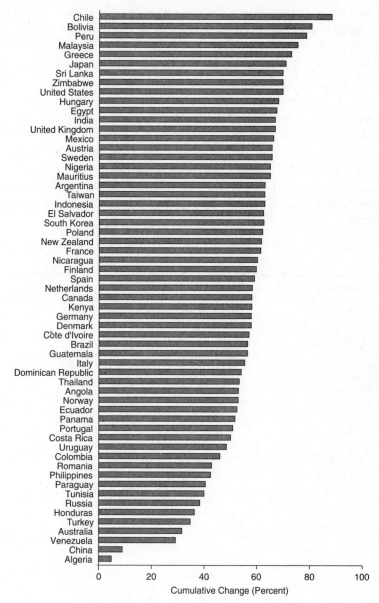

Figure 16.11. The collapse of exports, 1929–1932.
Sources: The individual country sources are provided in appendix A.1;
the authors' calculations were also used.

which lies at the epicenter of the recent boom-bust cycle in the United States and elsewhere, is usually best characterized as being part of the "nontraded sector." Yet the decline in housing-related construction activity during 1929–1932 was almost as synchronous as that seen in trade, as illustrated in table 16.1.

With both traded and nontraded sectors shrinking markedly and consistently across countries, the deterioration in unemployment reported in table 16.2 should come as no surprise. Unemployment increases almost without exception (no comparable 1929 data are available for Japan and Germany) by an average of 17 percentage points. As in the discussion of the aftermath of the postwar crises in the preceding chapter, the figures reflect differences in the defini-

TABLE 16.1
Indexes of total building activity in selected countries (1929 = 100)

Country	Indicator	1932
Argentina	Permits (area)	42
Australia	Permits (value)	23
Belgium	Permits (number)	93
Canada	Permits (value)	17
Chile	Permits (area)	56
Colombia	Buildings completed (area)	84
Czechoslovakia	Buildings completed (number)	88
Finland	Buildings completed (cubic space)	38
France	Permits (number)	81
Germany	Buildings completed (rooms)	36
Hungary	Buildings completed (number)	97
Netherlands	Buildings completed (dwellings)	87
New Zealand	Buildings completed (value)	22
South Africa	Buildings completed (value)	100
Sweden	Buildings completed (rooms)	119
United Kingdom	Permits (value)	91
United States	Permits (value)	18
Average		64

Memorandum item: September 2005 peak = 100:		
United States	Permits (number)	25[a]

Sources: League of Nations, *World Economic Survey* (various issues), Carter et al. (2006).
Note: Note the differences in the definition of the indicator from country to country.
[a]Through February 2009.

TABLE 16.2
Unemployment rates for selected countries, 1929–1932

Country	1929	1932	Increase
Australia	11.1	29.0	17.9
Austria	12.3	26.1	13.8
Belgium	4.3	39.7	35.4
Canada	5.7	22.0	16.3
Czechoslovakia	2.2	13.5	11.3
Denmark	15.5	31.7	16.2
Germany	n.a.	31.7	n.a.
Japan	n.a.	6.8	n.a.
Netherlands	7.1	29.5	22.4
Norway	15.4	30.8	15.4
Poland	4.9	11.8	6.9
Sweden	10.7	22.8	12.1
Switzerland	3.5	21.3	17.8
United Kingdom	10.4	22.1	11.7
United States[a]	3.2	24.9	21.7
Average	8.2	25.0	16.8

Sources: League of Nations (various issues), *World Economic Survey;* Carter et al. (2006).
Note: The figures reflect differences in the definition of unemployment and in the methods of compiling the statistics, so cross-country comparisons, particularly of the levels, are tentative.
[a]Annual averages.

tion of unemployment and in the methods of compiling the statistics; hence cross-country comparisons, particularly of the levels, are tentative.

Some Reflections on Global Crises

Here we pause to underscore why global financial crises can be so much more dangerous than local or regional ones. Fundamentally, when a crisis is truly global, exports no longer form a cushion for growth. In a global financial crisis, one typically finds that output, trade, equity prices, and other indicators behave qualitatively (if not quantitatively) much the same way for the world aggregates as they do in individual countries. A sudden stop in financing typically not only hits one country or region but to some extent impacts a large part of the world's public and private sectors.

Conceptually, it is not difficult to see that for a country to be "pulled" out of a postcrisis slump is far more difficult when the rest of the world is similarly affected than when exports offer a stimulus. Empirically, this is not a proposition that can be readily tested. We have hundreds of crises in our sample, but very few global ones, and, as noted in box 16.1, some of the earlier global crises were associated with wars, which complicates comparisons even further.

More definitively, it can be inferred from the evidence of so many episodes that recessions associated with crises (of any variety) are more severe in terms of duration and amplitude than the usual business cycle benchmarks of the post–World War II period in both advanced economies and emerging markets. Crises that are part of a global phenomenon may be worse still in the amplitude and volatility (if not duration) of the downturn. Until the most recent crisis, there had been no postwar global financial crisis; thus, by necessity the comparison benchmarks are prewar episodes. As to severity, the Second Great Contraction has already established several postwar records. The business cycle has evidently not been tamed.

The Sequencing of Crises: A Prototype

Just as financial crises have common macroeconomic antecedents in terms of asset prices, economic activity, external indicators, and so on, common patterns also appear in the sequencing (temporal order) in which crises unfold. Obviously not all crises escalate to the extreme outcome of a sovereign default. Yet advanced economies have not been exempt from their share of currency crashes, bouts of inflation, severe banking crises, and, in an earlier era, even sovereign default.

Investigating what came first, banking or currency crises, was a central theme of Kaminsky and Reinhart's "twin crises" work; they also concluded that financial liberalization often preceded banking crises; indeed, it helped predict them.[21] Demirgüç-Kunt and Detragiache, who employed a different approach and a larger sample, arrived at the same conclusion.[22] Reinhart examined the link between currency crashes and external default.[23] Our work here has investigated the connections between domestic and external debt crises, inflation crises and default (domestic or external), and banking crises and external default.[24] Figure 16.12 maps out a "prototypical" sequence of events yielded by this literature.

As Diaz-Alejandro narrates in his classic paper about the Chilean experience of the late 1970s and early 1980s, "Goodbye Financial Repression, Hello Financial Crash," financial liberalization simultaneously facilitates banks' access to external credit and more risky lending practices at home.[25] After a while, following a boom in lending and asset prices, weaknesses in bank balance sheets become manifest and problems in the banking sector begin.[26] Often these problems are more advanced in the shakier institutions (such as finance companies) than in the major banks.

The next stage in the crisis unfolds when the central bank begins to provide support for these institutions by extending credit to them. If the exchange rate is heavily managed (it does not need to be explicitly pegged), a policy inconsistency arises between supporting the exchange rate and acting as lender of last resort to troubled institutions. The numerous experiences in these studies suggest that (more often than not) the exchange rate objective is subjugated

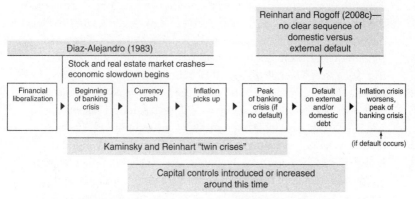

Figure 16.12. The sequencing of crises: A prototype.
Sources: Based on empirical evidence from Diaz-Alejandro (1985), Kindleberger (1989), Demirgüç-Kunt and Detragiache (1998), Kaminsky and Reinhart (1999), Reinhart (2002), and Reinhart and Rogoff (2004, 2008c), among others.

271

to the role of the central bank as lender of last resort. Even if central bank lending to the troubled financial industry is limited in scope, the central bank may be more reluctant to engage in an "interest rate defense" policy to defend the currency than would be the case if the financial sector were sound. This brings the sequence illustrated in figure 16.12 to the box labeled "Currency crash." The depreciation or devaluation of the currency, as the case may be, complicates the situation in (at least) three ways: (1) it exacerbates the problem of the banks that have borrowed in a foreign currency, worsening currency mismatches;[27] (2) it usually worsens inflation (the extent to which the currency crisis translates into higher inflation is highly uneven across countries, for countries with a history of very high and chronic inflation usually have a much higher and faster pass-through from exchange rates to prices);[28] and (3) it increases the odds of external and domestic default if the government has foreign currency–denominated debt.

At this stage, the banking crisis either peaks following the currency crash (if there is no sovereign credit crisis) or keeps getting worse as the crisis mounts and the economy marches toward a sovereign default (the next box in figure 16.12).[29] In our analysis of domestic and external credit events we have not detected a well-established sequence between these credit events. Domestic defaults have occurred before, during, and after external defaults, in no obvious pattern. As regards inflation, the evidence presented in chapter 9 all points in the direction of a marked deterioration in inflation performance after a default, especially a twin default (involving both domestic and foreign debt). The coverage of our analysis summarized here does not extend to the eventual crisis resolution stage.

We should note that currency crashes tend to be more serious affairs when governments have been explicitly or even implicitly fixing (or nearly fixing) the exchange rate. Even an implicit guarantee of exchange rate stability can lull banks, corporations, and citizens into taking on heavy foreign currency liabilities, thinking there is a low risk of a sudden currency devaluation that will sharply increase the burden of carrying such loans. In a sense, the collapse of a currency is a collapse of a government guarantee on which the private sector might have relied, and therefore it constitutes a default on an important promise. Of course, large swings in exchange rates can also be traumatic for a country with a clear and explicit regime of floating exchange rates, especially if there are substantial levels of foreign exchange debts and if imported intermediate goods play an important role in production. Still, the trauma is typically less, because it does not involve a loss of credibility for the government or the central bank. The persistent and recurring nature of financial crises in various guises through the centuries makes us skeptical about providing easy answers as to how to best avoid them. In our final chapter we sketch out some of the issues regarding the prospects for and measurement of graduation from these destabilizing boom-bust cycles.

Summary

This chapter has greatly extended our perspective of crises by illustrating quantitative measures of the global nature of a crisis, ranging from our composite index of global financial turbulence to comparisons of the aftermath of crises between the Great Depression of the past century and the recent Second Great Contraction. We have seen that by all measures, the trauma resulting from this contraction, the first global financial crisis of the twenty-first century, has been extraordinarily severe. That its macroeconomic outcome has been only the most severe global recession since World War II—and not even worse —must be regarded as fortunate.

- PART VI -

WHAT HAVE WE LEARNED?

There is nothing new except what is forgotten.
—Rose Bertin

REFLECTIONS ON EARLY WARNINGS, GRADUATION, POLICY RESPONSES, AND THE FOIBLES OF HUMAN NATURE

We have come to the end of a long journey that has taken us from the debt defaults and debasements of preindustrial Europe to the first global financial crisis of the twenty-first century—the Second Great Contraction. What has our quantitative tour of this history revealed that might help us mitigate financial crises in the future? In chapter 13, on the run-up to the 2007 subprime financial crisis, we argued that it would be helpful to keep track of some basic macroeconomic series on housing prices and debt and calibrate them against historical benchmarks taken from past deep financial crises. But can one say more? In this chapter we begin by briefly reviewing the nascent "early crisis warning system" literature. We acknowledge that it can claim only modest success to date, but based on the first results here, we would argue that there is tremendous scope to strengthen macroprudential supervision by improving the reporting of current data and by investing in the development of long-dated time series (our basic approach here) so as to gain more perspective on patterns and statistical regularities in the data.

For starters, cross-country data on debt that covers long spans of time would be particularly useful. Ideally, one would have decades or even centuries of data in order to perform statistical analysis. We have taken a significant step here by exploiting previously little-known data on public debt for more than sixty countries for nearly one hundred years (and in some cases longer). But for most countries our long-dated time series includes only central government debt, not state and provincial debt. It would be helpful to have broader measures that take into account the debt of quasi-state companies and implicit debt guarantees. It would also be extremely helpful to have long-dated time series on consumer, bank, and corporate debt. We recognize that gathering such information will be very difficult for most countries, but it is our firm belief that much more can be done than has been accomplished to date. And whereas the housing price series used here (in chapters 10, 13, 14, and 16) is a considerable improvement over earlier studies in making use of a broad range of countries, including emerging markets, it would be very useful to expand the data to include more countries and a longer time period.

The second section of this concluding chapter explores the potential role of multilateral financial institutions such as the International Monetary Fund in helping to gather and monitor data on domestic public debt, housing prices, and other matters. It is utterly remarkable that as of this writing no international agency with global reach is providing these data or pressuring member states to provide it. We argue that even with better data on risks, it would probably be extremely desirable to create a new independent international institution to help develop and enforce international financial regulations. Our argument rests not only on the need to better coordinate rules across countries but also on the need for regulators to be more independent of national political pressures.

In the third section of the chapter we revisit the theme of "graduation" that comes up again and again throughout the book. How can emerging markets graduate from a history of serial default on sovereign debt and from recurrent bouts of high inflation? A central conclusion is that graduation is a very slow process, and congratulations are all too often premature.

We conclude the chapter with a range of broader lessons.

On Early Warnings of Crises

In earlier chapters we described some of the characteristic antecedents of banking crises and links between various types of crises (for instance, between banking and external debt crises or between inflation and debt crises). It is beyond the scope of this book to en-gage in a full-fledged analysis of early warning systems to anticipate the onset of banking, currency, or debt crises. Following the famous Mexican crisis of 1994–1995 and the even better-known Asian cri-sis of 1997–1998, a sizable body of empirical literature emerged rep-resenting an attempt to ascertain the relative merits of various macroeconomic and financial indicators in accurately "signaling" a crisis ahead of time.[1] These works reviewed a large body of indica-tors and adopted a broad array of econometric strategies and crisis episodes, with some modest success. Notably, as we have already dis-cussed, the early literature had to be built on the very limited data-bases then available, which lacked key time series for many countries. In particular, data on real estate markets, a critical element of many bubble and overleverage episodes, are simply absent from most of the existing crisis warning literature because until now these data were not adequate.

Because the data set underlying the present book encom-passes the prerequisite information on residential housing prices for a large number of advanced economies and emerging markets, span-ning nearly all regions, we can now focus on filling in this important gap in the early warnings literature.[2] Our exercise, as regards hous-ing prices, is not meant to be definitive. Specifically, we followed the approach proposed by Kaminsky and Reinhart in several of their con-tributions, the so-called signals approach, to examine where in the pecking order of indicators housing prices fit.[3] Table 17.1 presents some of the highlights of the signals approach exercise for banking and currency crises. We did not revisit, update, or enlarge the sam-ple of crisis episodes with regard to the other indicators. Our contri-bution is to compare the performance of housing prices to that of the other indicators commonly found in this literature.

For banking crises, real housing prices are nearly at the top of the list of reliable indicators, surpassing the current account bal-ance and real stock prices by producing fewer false alarms. Monitor-ing developments in the prices of this asset has clear value added for helping us to anticipate potential banking crisis scenarios. For pre-dicting currency crashes, the link with the real estate price cycle is

TABLE 17.1

Early warning indicators of banking and currency crises: A summary

Indicator rank (best to worst)	Description	Frequency
Banking crises		
Best		
Real exchange rate	Deviations from trend	Monthly
Real housing prices[a]	Twelve-month (or annual) percentage change	Monthly, quarterly, annually (depending on country)
Short-term capital inflows/GDP	In percentage points	Annually
Current account balance/ investment	In percentage points	Annually
Real stock prices	Twelve-month percentage change	Monthly
Worst		
Institutional Investor (II) and Moody's sovereign ratings	Change in index	Biannually (II), monthly (Moody's)
Terms of trade	Twelve-month percentage change	Monthly
Currency crashes		
Best		
Real exchange rate	Deviations from trend	Monthly
Banking crisis	Dichotomous variable	Monthly or annually
Current account balance/GDP	In percentage points	Annually
Real stock prices	Twelve-month percentage change	Monthly
Exports	Twelve-month percentage change	Monthly
M2 (broad money)/ international reserves	Twelve-month percentage change	Monthly
Worst		
Institutional Investor (II) and Moody's sovereign ratings	Change in index	Biannually (II), monthly (Moody's)
Domestic-foreign interest differential (lending rate)[b]	In percentage points	Monthly

Sources: Kaminsky, Lizondo, and Reinhart (1998), Kaminsky and Reinhart (1999), Goldstein, Kaminsky, and Reinhart (2000), and the authors' calculations.

[a]This is the "novel" variable introduced here.

[b]This is not to be confused with a domestic-foreign interest rate differential such as that seen in the Emerging Market Bond Index spread.

not as sharp, and housing prices do not score as well as a proxy of overvaluation of the real exchange rate as does a banking crisis or the performance of the current account and exports.

The signals approach (or most alternative methods) will not pinpoint the exact date on which a bubble will burst or provide an obvious indication of the severity of the looming crisis. What this systematic exercise can deliver is valuable information as to whether an economy is showing one or more of the classic symptoms that emerge before a severe financial illness develops. The most significant hurdle in establishing an effective and credible early warning system, however, is not the design of a systematic framework that is capable of producing relatively reliable signals of distress from the various indicators in a timely manner. The greatest barrier to success is the well-entrenched tendency of policy makers and market participants to treat the signals as irrelevant archaic residuals of an outdated framework, assuming that old rules of valuation no longer apply. If the past we have studied in this book is any guide, these signals will be dismissed more often that not. That is why we also need to think about improving institutions.

The Role of International Institutions

International institutions can play an important role in reducing risk, first by promoting transparency in reporting data and second by enforcing regulations related to leverage.

It would also be extremely helpful to have better and clearer information on government debt and implicit government debt guarantees in addition to more transparent data on bank balance sheets. Greater transparency in accounting would not solve all problems, but it would certainly help. In enforcing transparency, there is a huge role for international institutions—institutions that have otherwise foundered for the past two decades seeking their place in the international order. For governments, the International Monetary Fund (IMF) could provide a public good by having an extremely rigorous standard for government debt accounting that included implicit guarantees and off–balance sheet items.

The IMF's 1996 initiative, the *Special Data Dissemination Standard*, provides a major first step, but much more can be done in this regard. One has only to look at how opaque the United States government's books have become during the 2007 financial crisis to see how helpful an outside standard would be. (The Federal Reserve alone has taken trillions of dollars of difficult-to-price private assets onto its books, but during the depths of the crisis it refused to disclose the composition of some of these assets even to the U.S. Congress. This assumption of assets was admittedly an extraordinarily delicate and sensitive operation, yet over the long run systematic transparency has to be the right approach.) The task of enforcing transparency is far more easily said than done, for governments have many incentives to obfuscate their books. But if the rules are written from outside and in advance of the next crisis, failing to follow the rules might be seen as a signal that would enforce good behavior. In our view, the IMF can play a more useful role by prodding governments into being forthcoming about their borrowing positions than it can by serving as a firefighter once governments have already gotten into trouble. Of course, the lesson of history is that the IMF's influence before a crisis is small relative to its role during a crisis.

We also strongly believe that there is an important role for an international financial regulatory institution. First, cross-border flows of capital continue to proliferate, often seeking light regulation as much as high rates of return. In order to have meaningful regulatory control over modern international financial behemoths, it is important to have some measure of coordination in financial regulation. Equally important, an international financial regulator can potentially provide some degree of political insulation from legislators who relentlessly lobby domestic regulators to ease up on regulatory rule and enforcement. Given that the special qualifications needed to staff such an institution are extremely different from those prevalent in any of the current major multilateral lending institutions, we believe an entirely new institution is needed.[4]

Graduation

Our analysis of the history of various types of financial crises raises many important questions (and provides considerably fewer answers). Possibly the most direct set of questions has to do with the theme of "graduation," a concept that was first introduced in our joint work with Savastano and that we have repeatedly emphasized throughout this book.[5] Why is it that some countries, such as France and Spain, managed to emerge from centuries of serial default on sovereign debt and eventually stopped defaulting, at least in a narrow technical sense? There is the prerequisite issue of what exactly is meant by graduation. The transition from "emerging market" to "advanced economy" status does not come with a diploma or a well-defined set of criteria to mark the upgrade. As Qian and Reinhart highlight, graduation can be defined as the attainment and subsequent maintenance of international investment-grade status; the emphasis here is on the maintenance part.[6] Another way of describing this criterion for graduation would be to say that the country has significantly and credibly reduced its chances of defaulting on its sovereign debt obligations. If it ever was a serial defaulter, it no longer is, and investors recognize it as such. Gaining access to capital markets is no longer a stop-and-go process. Graduation may also be defined as the achievement of some minimum threshold in terms of income per capita, a significant reduction in macroeconomic volatility, and the capacity to conduct countercyclical fiscal and monetary policies or, at a minimum, move away from the destabilizing procyclical policies that plague most emerging markets.[7] Obviously, these milestones are not unrelated.

If graduation were taken to mean total avoidance of financial crises of any kind, we would be left with no graduating class. As we have noted earlier, countries may "graduate" from serial default on sovereign debt and recurrent episodes of very high inflation, as the cases of Austria, France, Spain, and others illustrate. History tells us, however, that graduation from recurrent banking and financial crises is much more elusive. And it should not have taken the 2007 financial crisis to remind us. As noted in chapter 10, out of the sixty-six countries in our core sample, only a few had escaped banking crises since 1945, and by 2008 only one remained. Graduation from currency crashes also seems elusive. Even in the context of floating exchange rates, in which concerted speculative attacks on a peg are no longer an issue, the currencies of advanced economies do crash (i.e., experience depreciations in excess of 15 percent). Admittedly, whereas countries do not outgrow exchange rate volatility, those with more developed capital markets and more explicitly flexible exchange rate systems may be better able to weather currency crashes.

Once we adopt a definition of graduation that focuses on the terms on which countries can access international capital markets, the question that follows is how to make this concept operational. In other words, how do we develop a "quantitative" working measure of graduation? A solid definition of graduation should not be unduly influenced by "market sentiment." In the run-up to major crises in Mexico (1994), Korea (1997), and Argentina (2001), these countries had all been widely portrayed by the multilateral organizations and the financial markets as poster children for—sterling examples of—graduation.

Tackling this complex issue is beyond the scope of our endeavors here. Our aim is to provide a brief snapshot of what "debtors' club" (as defined in chapter 2) countries belong to and a "big picture" of how perceptions of the chances of sovereign default have changed during the past thirty years. To this end, table 17.2 lists all the countries in our sample (and their respective dates of independence). The third column presents the *Institutional Investor* sovereign ratings for sixty-two of the sixty-six countries in our sample for which ratings are available. It is safe to assume that with the notable exceptions of Hong Kong and Taiwan, all the countries that are not rated fall into club C (countries permanently shut out of international private capital markets). The next column shows the changes in the ratings from 1979 (the first year during which *Institutional Investor* published the results of their biannual survey of market participants) to March 2008.

Candidates for graduation should not only meet the criteria for "club A," with an *Institutional Investor* rating of 68 or higher, but should also show the "right slope." Specifically, these countries should

TABLE 17.2

Institutional Investor ratings of sixty-six countries: Upgrade or demotion, 1979–2008

Country	Year of independence (if after 1800)	*Institutional Investor* rating, 2008 (March)	Change in rating from 1979 to 2008 (+ indicates improvement)
Africa			
Algeria	1962	54.7	−3.9
Angola	1975	n.a.	
Central African Republic	1960	n.a.	
Côte d'Ivoire	1960	19.5	−28.7
Egypt	1831	50.7	16.8
Kenya	1963	29.8	−15.8
Mauritius*	1968	56.3	38.3
Morocco	1956	55.1	9.6
Nigeria	1960	38.3	−15.8
South Africa	1910	65.8	3.8
Tunisia	1957	61.3	11.3
Zambia	1964	n.a.	.
Zimbabwe	1965	5.8	−18.0
Asia			
China		76.5	5.4
Hong Kong*		n.a.	
India	1947	62.7	8.5
Indonesia	1949	48.7	−5.0
Japan		91.4	−5.5
Korea*	1945	79.9	8.7
Malaysia*	1957	72.9	2.6
Myanmar	1948	n.a.	
The Philippines	1947	49.7	4.0
Singapore*	1965	93.1	14.2
Taiwan*	1949	n.a.	
Thailand*		63.1	8.4
Europe			
Austria		94.6	8.9
Belgium*	1830	91.5	5.7
Denmark*		94.7	19.4
Finland*	1917	94.9	20.0
France	943	94.1	3.0
Germany		94.8	−3.5
Greece	1829	81.3	18.7
Hungary	1918	66.8	4.2

(continued)

TABLE 17.2 Continued

Country	Year of independence (if after 1800)	*Institutional Investor* rating, 2008 (March)	Change in rating from 1979 to 2008 (+ indicates improvement)
Europe (*continued*)			
Italy		84.1	10.3
The Netherlands*		95.0	5.3
Norway*	1905	95.9	7.0
Poland	1918	73.0	23.5
Portugal		84.8	32.8
Romania	1878	58.4	3.6
Russia		69.4	−9.4
Spain		89.6	19.3
Sweden		94.8	10.6
Turkey		52.0	37.2
United Kingdom*		94.0	3.4
Latin America			
Argentina	1816	41.9	−20.5
Bolivia	1825	30.3	−1.3
Brazil	1822	60.6	4.3
Chile	1818	77.4	23.2
Colombia	1819	54.7	−6.0
Costa Rica	1821	52.3	7.6
Dominican Republic	1845	36.1	−0.3
Ecuador	1830	30.9	−22.3
El Salvador	1821	46.6	33.7
Guatemala	1821	41.3	19.7
Honduras	1821	31.5	12.4
Mexico	1821	69.3	−2.5
Nicaragua	1821	19.3	8.9
Panama	1903	57.1	11.6
Paraguay	1811	29.7	−13.7
Peru	1821	57.7	27.0
Uruguay	1811	48.8	7.8
Venezuela	1830	43.1	−29.3
North America			
Canada*	1867	94.6	1.1
United States*		93.8	−5.1
Oceania			
Australia*	1901	91.2	3.5
New Zealand*	1907	88.2	10.0

Sources: Institutional Investor (various years), the authors' calculations, and Qian and Reinhart (2009).
Notes: An asterisk (*) denotes no history of sovereign external default or rescheduling; n.a., not available.

show an overall improvement in their ratings from thirty years ago. Countries like Turkey have shown a substantial improvement in their ratings over time, but their current status still falls below the threshold of club A—advanced economy status. Others, such as Mexico on the basis of its 2008 score, meet club A criteria but have seen a deterioration in their rating from what it was in 1979. Figure 17.1 plots the change in the *Institutional Investor* ratings (the last column of table 17.2) and highlights the countries with the potential for graduation. These include Chile, China, Greece, Korea, and Portugal (Malaysia and Poland are more borderline cases whose most recent ratings are just below the threshold for club A). Absent from this list are African countries and practically all of Latin America. This exercise is meant to be illustrative rather than definitive, for the question of who graduates from "emerging market or developing" status and why should remain at the forefront of development economics.

Some Observations on Policy Responses

The persistent and recurrent nature of the this-time-is-different syndrome is itself suggestive that we are not dealing with a challenge that can be overcome in a straightforward way. In its different guises, this syndrome has surfaced at one time or another in every region. No country, irrespective of its global importance, appears immune to it. The fading memories of borrowers and lenders, policy makers and academics, and the public at large do not seem to improve over time, so the policy lessons on how to "avoid" the next blow-up are at best limited. Danger signals emanating from even a well-grounded early warning system may be dismissed on the grounds that the old rules of valuation no longer apply and that the "Lucas critique" is on our side. (The Lucas critique, named for Robert Lucas, known for his work on macroeconomic policy making, says that it is naïve to try to predict the effects of a change in economic policy entirely on the basis of relationships observed in historical data, especially highly aggregated historical data.)

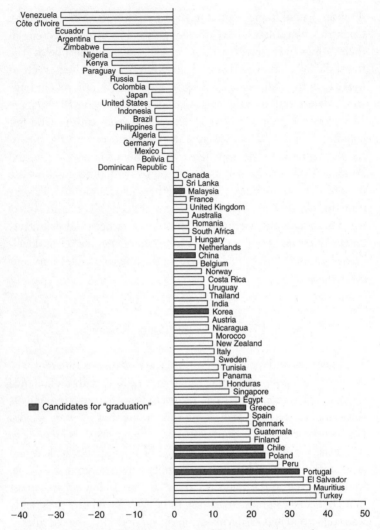

Figure 17.1. Change in *Institutional Investor* sovereign credit
ratings of sixty-six countries, 1979–2008.
Sources: Qian and Reinhart (2009) and sources cited therein.
Note: Malaysia and Poland are included as graduation candidates,
but these are "borderline" cases.

Even if crises are inevitable, there must at least be some basic insights that we can gather from such an extensive review of financial folly. We have already discussed the importance of developing better time series data for studying the history of financial crises, the central premise of this book. In what follows we highlight some further insights.

First, as regards mitigating and managing debt and inflation crises:

- Having a complete picture of government indebtedness is critical, for there is no meaningful *external* debt sustainability exercise that does not take into account the magnitude and features of outstanding *domestic* government debt, ideally including contingent liabilities.
- Debt sustainability exercises must be based on plausible scenarios for economic performance, because the evidence offers little support for the view that countries simply "grow out" of their debts. This observation may limit the options for governments that have inherited high levels of debt. Simply put, they must factor in the possibility of "sudden stops" in capital flows, for these are a recurrent phenomenon for all but the very largest economies in the world.
- The inflationary risks to monetary policy frameworks (whether the exchange rate is fixed or flexible) also seem to be linked in important ways to the levels of domestic debt. Many governments have succumbed to the temptation to inflate away domestic debt.

Second, policy makers must recognize that banking crises tend to be protracted affairs. Some crisis episodes (such as those of Japan in 1992 and Spain in 1977) were stretched out even longer by the authorities by a lengthy period of denial. Fiscal finances suffer mightily as government revenues shrink in the aftermath of crises and bailout costs mount. Our extensive coverage of banking crises, however, says little about the much-debated issue of the efficacy of stimulus packages as a way of shortening the duration of the crisis and cushioning the downside of the economy as a banking crisis unfolds. Pre–World War II banking crises were seldom met with counter-cyclical fiscal policies. The postwar period has witnessed only a handful of severe banking crises in advanced economies. Before 2007, explicit stimulus measures were a part of the policy response only in the Japanese crisis. In the numerous severe banking crises in emerging markets, fiscal stimulus packages were not an option, because governments were shut out of access to international capital markets. Increases in government spending in these episodes primarily reflected bailout outlays and markedly rising debt servicing costs. It is dangerous to draw conclusions about the effectiveness of fiscal stimulus packages from a single episode. However, the surge in government debt following a crisis is an important factor to weigh when considering how far governments should be willing to go to offset the adverse consequences of the crisis on economic activity. This message is particularly critical to countries with a history of debt intolerance, which may meet debt servicing difficulties even at relatively moderate levels of debt.

Third, on graduation, the greatest policy insight is that premature self-congratulations may lead to complacency and demotion to a lower grade. Several debt crises involving default or near-default occurred on the heels of countries' ratings upgrades, joining the OECD (e.g., Mexico, Korea, Turkey), and being generally portrayed as the poster children of the international community (e.g., Argentina in the late 1990s prior to its meltdown in late 2001).

The Latest Version of the This-Time-Is-Different Syndrome

Going into the recent financial crisis, there was a widespread view that debtors and creditors had learned from their mistakes and that financial crises were not going to return for a very long time, at least in emerging markets and developed economies. Thanks to better-informed macroeconomic policies and more discriminating lending practices, it was argued, the world was not likely to see a major wave of defaults again. Indeed, in the run-up to the recent financial crisis, an oft-cited reason as to why "this time is different" for the emerging markets was that their governments were relying more on domestic debt financing.

But celebrations may be premature. They are certainly un-informed by the history of the emerging markets. Capital flow and de-fault cycles have been around since at least 1800, if not before in other parts of the globe. Why they would end anytime soon is not obvious.

In the run-up to the recent crisis, in the case of rich coun-tries one of the main this-time-is-different syndromes had to do with a belief in the invincibility of modern monetary institutions. Central banks became enamored with their own versions of "inflation tar-geting," believing that they had found a way both to keep inflation low and to optimally stabilize output. Though their successes were founded on some solid institutional progress, especially the indepen-dence of the central banks, those successes seem to have been over-sold. Policies that appeared to work perfectly well during an all-encompassing boom suddenly did not seem at all robust in the event of a huge recession. Market investors, in turn, relied on the central banks to bail them out in the event of any trouble. The famous "Greenspan put" (named after Federal Reserve Chairman Alan Greenspan) was based on the (empirically well-founded) belief that the U.S. central bank would resist raising interest rates in response to a sharp upward spike in asset prices (and therefore not undo them) but would react vigorously to any sharp fall in asset prices by cutting interest rates to prop them up. Thus, markets believed, the Federal Reserve provided investors with a one-way bet. That the Federal Re-serve would resort to extraordinary measures once a collapse started has now been proven to be a fact. In hindsight, it is now clear that a single-minded focus on inflation can be justified only in an environ-ment in which other regulators are able to ensure that leverage (bor-rowing) does not become excessive.

The lesson of history, then, is that even as institutions and policy makers improve, there will always be a temptation to stretch the limits. Just as an individual can go bankrupt no matter how rich she starts out, a financial system can collapse under the pressure of greed, politics, and profits no matter how well regulated it seems to be.

Technology has changed, the height of humans has changed, and fashions have changed. Yet the ability of governments and investors to delude themselves, giving rise to periodic bouts of euphoria that usually end in tears, seems to have remained a constant. No careful reader of Friedman and Schwartz will be surprised by this lesson about the ability of governments to mismanage financial markets, a key theme of their analysis.[8] As for financial markets, Kindleberger wisely titled the first chapter of his classic book "Financial Crisis: A Hardy Perennial."[9]

We have come full circle to the concept of financial fragility in economies with massive indebtedness. All too often, periods of heavy borrowing can take place in a bubble and last for a surprisingly long time. But highly leveraged economies, particularly those in which continual rollover of short-term debt is sustained only by confidence in relatively illiquid underlying assets, seldom survive forever, particularly if leverage continues to grow unchecked. This time may seem different, but all too often a deeper look shows it is not. Encouragingly, history does point to warning signs that policy makers can look at to assess risk—if only they do not become too drunk with their credit bubble–fueled success and say, as their predecessors have for centuries, "This time is different."

Data Appendixes

APPENDIX A.1
MACROECONOMIC TIME SERIES

This appendix covers the macroeconomic time series used; a separate appendix (appendix A.2) is devoted to the database on government debt.

Abbreviations of Frequently Used Sources and Terms

Additional sources are listed in the tables that follow.

BNB	Banque Nationale de Belgique
DIA	Díaz et al. (2005)
ESFDB	European State Finance Database
GDF	World Bank, *Global Development Finance* (various issues)
GFD	Global Financial Data
GNI	Gross national income
GPIHG	Global Price and Income History Group
IFS	International Monetary Fund, *International Financial Statistics* (various issues)
II	*Institutional Investor*
IISH	International Institute of Social History
KRV	Kaminsky, Reinhart, and Végh (2003)
Lcu	local currency units
MAD	Maddison (2004)
MIT	Mitchell (2003a, 2003b)
NNP	Net national product

OXF   Oxford Latin American Economic History Database
RR   Reinhart and Rogoff (years as noted)
TED   Total Economy Database
WEO   International Monetary Fund, *World Economic Outlook* (various issues)

TABLE A.1.1
Prices: Consumer or cost-of-living indexes (unless otherwise noted)

Country	Period covered	Sources	Commentary
Algeria	1869–1884	Hoffman et al. (2002)	Wheat prices
	1938–2007	GFD, WEO	
Angola	1914–1962	MIT	
	1991–2007	WEO	
Argentina	1775–1812	Garner (2007)	Buenos Aires only
	1864–1940	Williamson (1999)	
	1884–1913	Flandreau and Zumer (2004)	
	1900–2000	OXF	
	1913–2000	DIA	
	1913–2007	GFD, WEO	
Australia	1818–1850	Butlin (1962), Vanplew (1987), GPIHG	New Wales, food prices
	1850–1983	Shergold (1987), GPIHG	Sydney, food
	1861–2007	GFD, WEO	
Austria	1440–1800	Allen (2001)	Vienna
	1800–1914	Hoffman et al. (2002)	Wheat prices
	1880–1913	Flandreau and Zumer (2004)	
	1919–2007	GFD, WEO	
Belgium	1462–1913	Allen (2001)	Antwerp
	1835–2007	GFD, WEO	
Bolivia	1936–2007	GFD, WEO	
Brazil	1763–1820	Garner (n.d.)	Rio de Janeiro only
	1830–1937	Williamson (1999)	Rio de Janeiro only
	1861–2000	DIA	
	1912–2007	GFD, WEO	

TABLE A.1.1 Continued

Country	Period covered	Sources	Commentary
Canada	1867–1975	Statistics Canada (StatCan)	
	1910–2007	GFD, WEO	
Central African Republic	1956–1993	MIT	
	1980–2007	WEO	
Chile	1754–1806	Garner (2007)	Santiago only
	1810–2000	DIA	
	1900–2000	OXF	
	1913–2007	GFD, WEO	
China	1644–2000	Lu and Peng (2006)	Rice prices
	1867–1935	Hsu	Wholesale prices
	1926–1948	GFD, WEO	
	1978–2007		
Colombia	1863–1940	Williamson (1999)	
	1900–2000	OXF	
	1923–2007	GFD, WEO	
Costa Rica	1937–2007	GFD, WEO	
Côte d'Ivoire	1951–2007	GFD, WEO	
Denmark	1748–1800	Hoffman et al. (2002)	Wheat prices
	1815–2007	GFD, WEO	
Dominican Republic	1942–2000	OXF	
	1980–2007	WEO	
Ecuador	1939–2007	GFD, WEO	
Egypt	1859–1941	Williamson (2000a)	
	1913–2007	GFD, WEO	
	1915–1999	GFD	
El Salvador	1937–2000	OXD	
	1980–2007	WEO	
Finland	1860–2001	Finnish Historical National Accounts	
	1980–2007	WEO	
France	1431–1786	Allen (2001)	
	1840–1913		
	1807–1935	Dick and Floyd (1997)	Retail prices
	1840–2007	GFD, WEO	

(*continued*)

TABLE A.1.1 Continued

Country	Period covered	Sources	Commentary
Germany	1427–1765	Allen (2001)	Munich
	1637–1855	Hoffman et al. (2002)	Wheat prices
	1820–2007	GFD, WEO	
Greece	1833–1938	Kostelenos et al. (2007)	GDP deflator
	1922–2007	GFD, WEO	
Ghana	1949–2007	GFD, WEO	
Guatemala	1938–2000	OXD	
	1980–2007	WEO	
Honduras	1938–2000	OXD	
	1980–2007	WEO	
Hungary	1923–2007	GFD, WEO	
India	1866–2000	DIA	
	1873–1939	Williamson (2000b)	
	1913–2007	GFD, WEO	
Indonesia	1820–1940	Williamson (2000b)	
	1948–2007	GFD, WEO	
Italy	1548–1645	Allen (2001)	Naples
	1734–1806		
	1701–1860	deMaddalena (1974)	Wheat prices, Milan
	1861–2007	GFD, WEO	
Korea	1690–1909	Jun and Lewis (2002)	Rice prices in the southern region of Korea
	1906–1939	Williamson (2000b)	
	1948–2007	GFD, WEO	
Japan	1600–1650	Kimura (1987)	Rice prices, Osaka
	1818–1871	Bassino and Ma (2005)	Rice prices, Osaka
	1860–1935	Williamson (2000b)	
	1900–2007	GFD, WEO	
Kenya	1947–2007	GFD, WEO	
Malaysia	1948–2007	GFD, WEO	
Mauritius	1946–2007	GFD, WEO	

TABLE A.1.1 Continued

Country	Period covered	Sources	Commentary
Mexico	1786–1821	Garner (2007)	Zacatecas
	1877–1940	Williamson (1999)	
	1918–2007	GFD, WEO	
Morocco	1939–2007	GFD, WEO	
Myanmar (Burma)	1870–1940	Williamson (2000b)	
	1939–2007	GFD, WEO	
The Netherlands	1500–1800	Van Zanden (2005)	
	1800–1913	Van Riel (2009)	
	1880–2007	GFD, WEO	
New Zealand	1857–2004	Statistics New Zealand	
	1980–2007	WEO	
Nicaragua	1937–2007	GFD, WEO	
Nigeria	1953–2007	GFD, WEO	
Norway	1516–2005	Grytten (2008)	
	1980–2007	WEO	
Panama	1939–2000	OXD	
	1980–2007	WEO	
Paraguay	1938–2007	GFD, WEO	
	1750–1816	Garner (2007)	Potosi
Peru	1790–1841	Garner (2007)	Lima
	1800–1873	DIA	
	1913–2000		
	1980–2007	WEO	
The Philippines	1899–1940	Williamson (2000b)	
	1937–2007	GFD, WEO	
Poland	1701–1815	Hoffman et al. (2002)	Oat prices, Warsaw
	1816–1914	Allen (2001)	Warsaw
	1921–1939	GFD, WEO	
	1983–2007		
Portugal	1728–1893	Hoffman et al. (2002)	Wheat prices
	1881–1997	Bordo et al. (2001)	
	1980–2007	WEO	

(continued)

TABLE A.1.1 Continued

Country	Period covered	Sources	Commentary
Romania	1779–1831	Hoffman et al. (2002)	Wheat prices, Wallachia
	1971–2007	WEO	
Russia	1853–1910	Borodkin (2001)	Wheat and rye flour prices, St. Petersburg
	1880–1913	Flandreau and Zumer (2004)	
	1917–1924	GFD, WEO	
	1927–1940		
	1944–1972		
	1991–2007		
Singapore	1948–2007	GFD, WEO	
South Africa	1895–2007	GFD, WEO	
Spain	1500–1650	Hamilton (1969)	Valencia
	1651–1800	Hoffman et al. (2002)	Prices of wheat, eggs, and linen
	1800–2000	DIA	
	1980–2000	WEO	
Sri Lanka	1939–2007	GFD, WEO	
Sweden	1732–1800	Hoffman et al. (2002)	Wheat prices
	1800–2000	Edvinsson (2002)	
	1980–2007	WEO	
Taiwan	1897–1939	Williamson (2000b)	
	1980–2007	WEO	
Thailand (Siam)	1820–1941	Williamson (2000b)	
	1948–2007	GFD, WEO	
Tunisia	1939–2007	GFD, WEO	
Turkey	1469–1914	Pamuk (2005)	Istanbul
	1854–1941	Williamson (2000a)	
	1922–2007	GFD, WEO	
United Kingdom	1450–1999	Van Zanden (2002)	Southern England
	1781–2007	GFD, WEO	
United States	1720–1789	Carter et al. (2006)	Wholesale prices

TABLE A.1.1 Continued

Country	Period covered	Sources	Commentary
	1774–2003	Carter et al. (2006)	
	1980–2007	WEO	
Uruguay	1870–1940	Williamson (1999)	
	1929–2000	OXF	
	1980–2007	WEO	
Venezuela	1830–2002	Baptista (2006)	
	1914–2007	GFD, WEO	
Zambia	1938–2007	GFD, WEO	
Zimbabwe	1920–1970	MIT	
	1930–2007	GFD, WEO	

TABLE A.1.2
Modern nominal exchange rates (domestic currency units per U.S. dollar
and other currencies noted)

Country	Period covered	Source	Other relevant rates
Algeria	1831–2007	GFD, IFS	French franc, euro
Angola	1921–2007	GFD, IFS	
Argentina	1880–1913	Flandreau and Zumer (2004)	French franc
	1885–2007	GFD, IFS	
Australia	1835–2007	GFD, IFS	U.K. pound
Austria	1814–2007	GFD, IFS	U.K. pound, German mark
Belgium	1830–2007	GFD, IFS	French franc
Bolivia	1863–2007	GFD, IFS	
Brazil	1812–2007	GFD, IFS	U.K. pound
Canada	1858–2007	GFD, IFS	U.K. pound

(*continued*)

TABLE A.1.2 Continued

Country	Period covered	Source	Other relevant rates
Central African Republic	1900–2007	GFD, IFS	French franc
Chile	1830–1995	Braun et al. (2000)	U.K. pound
	1878–2007	GFD, IFS	
China	1848–2007	GFD, IFS	U.K. pound
Colombia	1900–2000	OXF	U.K. pound
	1919–2007	GDF, IFS	
Costa Rica	1921–2007	GDF, IFS	
Denmark	1864–2007	GDF, IFS	U.K. pound, German mark
Dominican Republic	1905–2007	GDF, IFS	
Ecuador	1898–2000	OXF, Pick (various years)	
	1980–2007	IFS	
Egypt	1869–2007	GFD, IFS	U.K. pound
El Salvador	1870–2007	GFD, IFS	
Finland	1900–2007	GFD, IFS	German mark
France	1619–1810	ESFDB, Course of the Exchange	U.K. pound
	1800–2007	GFD, IFS	U.K. pound, German mark
Germany	1698–1810	ESFDB, Course of the Exchange	U.K. pound
	1795–2007	GFD, IFS	
Greece	1872–1939	Lazaretou (2005)	U.K. pound, German mark
	1901–2007	GFD, IFS	
Guatemala	1900–2007	GFD, IFS	
Honduras	1870–2007	GFD, IFS	
Hungary	1900–2007	GFD, IFS	Austrian schilling
India	1823–2007	GFD, IFS	U.K. pound
Indonesia	1876–2007	GFD, IFS	Dutch guilder

TABLE A.1.2 Continued

Country	Period covered	Source	Other relevant rates
Italy	1816–2007	GFD, IFS	U.K. pound, German mark
Japan	1862–2007	GFD, IFS	U.K. pound
Kenya	1898–2007	GFD, IFS	U.K. pound
Korea	1905–2007	GFD, IFS	Japanese yen
Malaysia	1900–2007	GFD, IFS	U.K. pound
Mauritius	1900–2007	GFD, IFS	U.K. pound
Mexico	1814–2007	GFD, IFS	U.K. pound, French franc
	1823–1999	GFD	
Morocco	1897–2007	GFD, IFS	French franc, euro
Myanmar (Burma)	1900–2007	GFD, IFS	U.K. pound
The Netherlands	1698–1810	ESFDB, Course of the Exchange	U.K. pound
	1792–2007	GFD, IFS	German mark
New Zealand	1892–2007	GFD, IFS	U.K. pound
Nicaragua	1912–2007	GFD, IFS	
Nigeria	1900–2007	GFD, IFS	U.K. pound
Norway	1819–2007	GFD, IFS	Swedish krona, German mark
Panama	1900–2007	GFD, IFS	
Paraguay	1900–2000	OXD	Argentine peso
	1980–2007	IFS	
Peru	1883–2007	GFD, IFS	U.K. pound
The Philippines	1893–2007	GFD, IFS	Spanish peseta
Poland	1916–2007	GFD, IFS	
Portugal	1750–1865	Course of the Exchange	Dutch grooten
	1794–2007	GDF, IFS	U.K. pound, German mark

(*continued*)

TABLE A.1.2 Continued

Country	Period covered	Source	Other relevant rates
Romania	1814–2007	GFD	
	1900–2000	OXF, IFS	
	1921–2007	GDF, IFS	
Singapore	1834–2007	GFD, IFS	U.K. pound
South Africa	1900–2007	GFD, IFS	U.K. pound
Spain	1814–2007	GFD, IFS	German mark
Sri Lanka	1900–2007	GFD, IFS	U.K. pound
Sweden	1814–2007	GDF, IFS	U.K. pound, German mark
Taiwan	1895–2007	GDF, IFS	U.K. pound, Japanese yen
Thailand (Siam)	1859–2007	GFD, IFS	U.K. pound
Tunisia	1900–2007	GFD, IFS	French franc
Turkey	1859–2007	GFD, IFS	U.K. pound
United Kingdom	1619–1810	ESFDB, Course of the Exchange	French franc
	1660–2007	GFD, IFS	
United States	1660–2007	GFD, IFS	
Uruguay	1900–2007	GFD, IFS	
Venezuela	1900–2007	GFD, IFS	
Zambia	1900–2007	GFD, IFS	U.K. pound
Zimbabwe	1900–2007	GFD, IFS	U.K. pound

TABLE A.1.3
Early silver-based exchange rates (domestic currency units per U.K. penny)

Country	Period covered	Source	Currency, commentary
Austria	1371–1860	Allen and Unger (2004)	Kreuzer, Vienna
Belgium	1349–1801	Korthals Altes (1996)	Hoet
France	1258–1789	Allen and Unger (2004)	Livre tournois
Germany	1350–1830	Allen and Unger (2004)	Composite pfennig
Italy	1289–1858	Malanima (n.d.)	Lira fiorentina
Netherlands	1366–1800	Allen and Unger (2004), Van Zanden (2005)	Composite
Portugal	1750–1855	Godinho (1955)	Reis
Russia	1761–1840	Lindert and Mironov (n.d.)	Common ruble
Spain	1351–1809	Allen and Unger (2004)	Composite
Sweden	1523–1573	Söderberg (2004)	Mark ortug
Turkey	1555–1914	Ozmucur and Pamuk (2002)	Akche

TABLE A.1.4
The silver content of currencies

Country	Period covered	Sources	Currency, commentary
Austria	1371–1860	Allen and Unger (2004)	Kreuzer, Vienna
Belgium	1349–1801	Korthals Altes (1996)	Hoet
France	1258–1789	Allen (2001), Allen and Unger (2004)	Livre tournois
Germany	1350–1798	Allen (2001), Allen and Unger (2004)	Pfennig, Frankfurt
	1417–1830	Allen (2001), Allen and Unger (2004)	Pfennig, Augsburg
Italy	1289–1858	Malanima (n.d.)	Lira fiorentina
The Netherlands	1366–1575	Allen and Unger (2004)	Flemish grote
	1450–1800	Van Zanden (2005)	Guilder
Portugal	1750–1855	Godinho (1955)	Reis
Russia	1761–1840	Lindert and Mironov (n.d.)	Common ruble
	1761–1815		Assignatzia
Spain	1351–1650	Allen and Unger (2004)	Dinar, Valencia
	1501–1800		Vellon maravedis, New Castile
	1630–1809	Allen and Unger (2004)	Real
Sweden	1523–1573	Soderberg (2004)	Mark ortug
Turkey	1555–1914	Ozmucur and Pamuk (2002)	Akche
United Kingdom	1261–1918	Allen and Unger (2004)	Penny
United States	1800–1979	Allen and Unger (2004)	Dollar

TABLE A.1.5
Index of nominal and real gross national product and output (domestic currency units)

Country	Period covered	Source	Commentary
Algeria	1950–2007	GFD, WEO, IFS	
Angola	1962–2007	GFD, WEO, IFS	
Argentina	1884–1913	Flandreau and Zumer (2004)	Nominal
	1875–2000	DIA	Index of total production (1995 = 100)
	1900–2000	OXF	Real (base = 1970)
	1900–2007	GFD, WEO	
Australia	1798–2007	GFD, WEO	Nominal
	1820–2000	DIA	Index of total production (1995 = 100)
Belgium	1835–2007	BNB, Centre d'études économiques de la Katholieke Universiteit Leuven	Nominal
Bolivia			
Brazil	1861–2007	GFD, WEO	Nominal
	1850–2000	DIA	Index of total production (1995 = 100)
	1900–2000	OXF	(Base = 1970)
Canada			
Chile	1810–2000	DIA	Index of total production (1995 = 100)
China (NNP)	1962–1999	GFD	
Colombia	1900–2000	OXF	Real (base = 1970)
	1925–1999	GFD	
Costa Rica	1947–1999	GFD	
Côte d' Ivoire			

(continued)

TABLE A.1.5 Continued

Country	Period covered	Source	Commentary
Denmark	1818–1975	Nordic Historical National Accounts	
Egypt	1886–1945	Yousef (2002)	
	1952–2007	GFD, WEO	
	1821–1859	Landes (1958)	Cotton output
Finland	1860–2001	Nordic Historical National Accounts	
Greece	1833–1939	Kostelenos et al. (2007)	
	1880–1913	Flandreau and Zumer (2004)	
GNI	1927–1999	GFD	
	1948–1999	GFD	
India	1900–1921	GFD	
	1948–2007	GFD, WEO	
	1861–1899	Brahmananda (2001)	Real, per capita
	1820–2000	DIA	Index of total production
Indonesia	1815–1913	Van Zanden (2006)	Java
	1910–1970	Bassino and Van der Eng (2006)	
	1921–1939	GFD	
	1951–1999	GFD	
	1911–1938	GFD	
	1953–1999	GFD	
Korea	1911–1940	Cha and Kim (2006)	Thousand yen, GNI also calculated
GNI	1953–1999	GFD	
Malaysia	1910–1970	Bassino and Van der Eng (2006)	
	1949–1999	GFD	
Mexico	1820–2000	DIA	Index of total production (1995 = 100)

TABLE A.1.5 Continued

Country	Period covered	Source	Commentary
Mexico (*continued*)	1900–2000	OXF	
	1900–2000	OXF	Real (base = 1970)
	1925–1999	GFD	
Myanmar (Burma)	1913–1970	Bassino and Van der Eng (2006)	
	1950–1999	GFD	
The Netherlands	1800–1913	National Accounts of the Netherlands	
Norway	1830–2003	Grytten (2008)	
Peru	1900–2000	OXF	Real (base = 1970)
	1900–2000	OXF	Nominal
	1942–1999	GFD	
The Philippines	1910–1970	Bassino and Van der Eng (2006)	
	1946–1997	GFD, WEO	
Russia	1885–1913	Flandreau and Zumer (2004)	Nominal
GNI	1928–1940	GFD	
	1945–1995	GFD	
	1979–1997	GFD	
	1992–1999	GFD	Production
South Africa	1911–1999	GFD	
Sri Lanka	1900–1970	Bassino and Van der Eng (2006)	
Sweden	1720–2000	Edvinsson (2002)	Real, per capita
	1800–2000	Edvinsson (2002)	Nominal and real
Taiwan	1910–1970	Bassino and Van der Eng (2006)	
Thailand (Siam)	1946–2007	GFD, WEO	
	1910–1970	Bassino and Van der Eng (2006)	
Turkey	1923–2005	GFD	Nominal
	1950–1999	GFD	
United Kingdom	1830–1999	GFD	GNI
	1948–1999	GFD	

(*continued*)

TABLE A.1.5 Continued

Country	Period covered	Source	Commentary
United States	1790–2002	Carter et al. (2006)	Real, per capita
	1948–1999	GFD	
Uruguay	1935–1999	GFD	
	1955–2000	OXF	
	1900–2000	OXF	Real (base = 1970)
GNI	1955–1999	GFD	
Venezuela	1830–2002	Baptista (2006)	
	1900–2000	OXF	Real (base = 1970)
	1950–2007	GFD, WEO	

TABLE A.1.6
Gross national product (PPP in constant dollars)

Country	Period covered	Source	Commentary
Algeria	1950–2005	MAD, TED	
	1820–2005	RR (2008a)	Interpolation 1821–1949
Angola	1950–2005	MAD, TED	
Argentina	1875–2000	DIA	Base = 1996
	1900–2005	MAD, TED	
	1870–2005	RR (2008a)	Interpolation 1871–1899
Australia	1820–2006	MAD, TED	
Austria	1870–2006	MAD, TED	
	1820–2006	RR (2008a)	Interpolation 1821–1869
Belgium	1846–2006	MAD, TED	
	1820–2006	RR (2008a)	Interpolation 1821–1845
Bolivia	1945–2005	MAD, TED	
	1936–2005	RR (2008a)	Interpolation 1936–1944
Brazil	1820–2000	DIA	Base = 1996
	1870–2005	MAD, TED	
	1820–2005	RR (2008a)	Interpolation 1821–1869
Canada	1870–2006	MAD, TED	
	1820–2006	RR (2008a)	Interpolation 1821–1869
Central African Republic	1950–2003	MAD	
Chile	1810–2000	DIA	Base = 1996
	1820–2005	MAD, TED	
China	1929–1938	MAD, TED	
	1950–2006		
Colombia	1900–2005	MAD, TED	
Costa Rica	1920–2005	MAD, TED	
Denmark	1820–2006	MAD, TED	
Dominican Republic	1950–2005	MAD, TED	
	1942–2005	RR (2008a)	Interpolation 1942–1949

(continued)

TABLE A.1.6 Continued

Country	Period covered	Source	Commentary
Ecuador	1939–2005	MAD, TED	
	1900–2000	OXF	Base = 1970
	1900–2005	RR (2008a)	Interpolation 1900–1938
Egypt	1950–2005	MAD, TED	
	1820–2005	RR (2008a)	Interpolation 1821–1949
El Salvador	1900–2000	OXF	Base = 1970
Finland	1860–2006	MAD, TED	
	1820–2006	RR (2008a)	Interpolation 1821–1859
France	1820–2006	MAD, TED	
Germany	1850–2006	MAD, TED	
	1820–2006	RR (2008a)	Interpolation 1821–1849
Greece	1921–2006	MAD, TED	
	1820–2006	RR (2008a)	Interpolation 1821–1920
Guatemala	1920–2005	MAD, TED	
Honduras	1920–2005	MAD, TED	
Hungary	1824–2006	MAD, TED	
	1870–2006	RR (2008a)	Interpolation 1871–1923
India	1884–2006	MAD, TED	
	1820–2006	RR (2008a)	Interpolation 1821–1883
Indonesia	1870–2005	MAD, TED	
	1820–2005	RR (2008a)	Interpolation 1821–1869
Japan	1870–2006	MAD, TED	
	1820–2006	RR (2008a)	Interpolation 1821–1869
Kenya	1950–2005	MAD, TED	
Korea	1911–2006	MAD, TED	
	1820–2006	RR (2008a)	Interpolation 1821–1910
Malaysia	1911–2005	MAD, TED	
	1820–2006	RR (2008a)	Interpolation 1821–1910
Mauritius	1950–2005	MAD, TED	
Mexico	1900–2006	MAD, TED	
	1820–2006	RR (2008a)	Interpolation 1821–1899

TABLE A.1.6 Continued

Country	Period covered	Source	Commentary
Morocco	1950–2005	MAD, TED	
	1820–2005	RR (2008a)	Interpolation 1821–1949
Myanmar (Burma)	1950–2005	MAD, TED	
	1820–2005	RR (2008a)	Interpolation 1821–1949
Panama	1945–2005	MAD, TED	
	1939–2005	RR (2008a)	Interpolation 1939–1944
Paraguay	1939–2005	MAD, TED	
Peru	1895–2005	MAD, TED	
The Philippines	1902–2005	MAD, TED	
	1870–2005	RR (2008a)	Interpolation 1871–1901
Poland	1929–1938	MAD, TED	
	1950–2006		
	1870–2005	RR (2008a)	Interpolation 1871–1928
Portugal	1865–2006	MAD, TED	
	1820–2006	RR (2008a)	Interpolation 1821–1864
Romania	1926–1938	MAD, TED	
	1950–2006		
Russia	1928–2006	MAD, TED	
Singapore	1950–2005	MAD, TED	
	1820–2005	RR (2008a)	Interpolation 1821–1949
South Africa	1950–2005	MAD, TED	
	1905–2005	RR (2008a)	Interpolation 1905–1949
Spain	1850–2006	MAD, TED	
	1820–2005	RR (2008a)	Interpolation 1821–1849
Sweden	1820–2006	MAD, TED	
Thailand (Siam)	1950–2005	MAD, TED	
	1820–2005	RR (2008a)	Interpolation 1821–1949
Tunisia	1950–2005	MAD, TED	
	1820–2005	RR (2008a)	Interpolation 1821–1949
Turkey	1923–2005	MAD, TED	

(*continued*)

TABLE A.1.6 Continued

Country	Period covered	Source	Commentary
United Kingdom	1830–2006	MAD, TED	
	1820–2006	RR (2008a)	Interpolation 1821–1829
United States	1870–2006	MAD, TED	
	1820–2006	RR (2008a)	Interpolation 1821–1869
Uruguay	1870–2005	MAD, TED	
Venezuela	1900–2005	MAD, TED	
	1820–2005	RR (2008a)	Interpolation 1821–1899
Zambia	1950–2005	MAD, TED	
Zimbabwe	1950–2005	MAD, TED	
	1919–2005	MAD, TED	

Note: The information is also available on a per capita basis.

TABLE A.1.7

Central government expenditures and revenues
(domestic currency units unless otherwise noted)

Country	Period covered	Sources	Commentary
Algeria	1834–1960	MIT	Revenues begin in 1830
	1964–1975		
	1994–1996		
	1963–2003	KRV	
Angola	1915–1973	MIT	
	1980–2003	KRV	
Argentina	1864–1999	MIT	
	1880–1913	Flandreau and Zumer (2004)	
	1963–2003	KRV	
Australia	1839–1900	MIT	Revenues begin in 1824, for New South Wales and other provinces circa 1840
	1901–1997	MIT	Commonwealth
	1965–2003	KRV	

TABLE A.1.7 Continued

Country	Period covered	Sources	Commentary
Austria	1791–1993	MIT	Missing data for World Wars I and II
	1965–2003	KRV	
Belgium	1830–1993		Missing data for World War I
	1965–2003	KRV	
Bolivia	1888–1999	MIT	Revenues begin in 1885
	1963–2003	KRV	
Brazil	1823–1994	Instituto Brasileiro de de Geografia e Estatística, MIT	
	1980–2003	KRV	
Canada	1806–1840	MIT	Lower Canada
	1824–1840		Upper Canada
	1867–1995		Canada
	1963–2003	KRV	
Central African Republic	1906–1912	MIT	
	1925–1973		
	1963–2003	KRV	
Chile	1810–1995	Braun et al. (2000)	Base = 1995
	1857–1998	MIT	
	1963–2003	KRV	
China	1927–1936	Cheng (2003)	Nationalist government
	1963–2003	KRV	
Colombia	1905–1999	MIT	
	1963–2003	KRV	
Costa Rica	1884–1999	MIT	
	1963–2003	KRV	
Côte d'Ivoire	1895–1912	MIT	
	1926–1999		
	1963–2003	KRV	
Denmark	1853–1993	MIT	
	1965–2003	KRV	

(continued)

TABLE A.1.7 Continued

Country	Period covered	Sources	Commentary
Dominican Republic	1905–1999	MIT	
	1963–2003	KRV	
Ecuador	1884–1999	MIT	
	1979–2003	KRV	
Egypt	1821–1879	Landes (1958)	
	1852–1999	MIT	
	1963–2003	KRV	
El Salvador	1883–1999	MIT	
	1963–2003	KRV	
Finland	1882–1993	MIT	
	1965–2003	KRV	
France	1600–1785	ESFDB	
	1815–1993	MIT	
	1965–2003	KRV	
Germany (Prussia)	1688–1806	ESFDB	
Germany	1872–1934	MIT	Revenues end in 1942
	1946–1993		West Germany
	1979–2003	KRV	
Greece	1885–1940	MIT	Expenditure begins in 1833 and again in 1946
	1954–1993		
	1963–2003	KRV	
Guatemala	1882–1999	MIT	
	1963–2003	KRV	
Honduras	1879–1999	MIT	
	1963–2003	KRV	
Hungary	1868–1940	MIT	
India	1810–2000	MIT	
	1963–2003	KRV	
Indonesia	1821–1940	Mellegers (2006)	Netherlands East Indies, florins, high government

TABLE A.1.7 Continued

Country	Period covered	Sources	Commentary
	1816–1939	MIT	
	1959–1999		
	1963–2003	KRV	
Italy	1862–1993	MIT	
	1965–2003	KRV	
Japan	1868–1993	MIT	
	1963–2003	KRV	
Kenya	1895–2000	MIT	
	1970–2003	KRV	
Korea	1905–1939	MIT	Japanese yen
	1949–1997		South Korea
	1963–2003	KRV	
Malaysia	1883–1938	MIT	Malaya
	1946–1999		
	1963–2003	KRV	
Mauritius	1812–2000	MIT	
	1963–2003	KRV	
Mexico	1825–1998	MIT	
	1963–2003	KRV	
Morocco	1938–2000	MIT	Revenues also 1920–1929
	1963–2003	KRV	
Myanmar (Burma)	1946–1999	MIT	
	1963–2003	KRV	
The Netherlands	1845–1993	MIT	
	1965–2003	KRV	
New Zealand	1841–2000	MIT	
	1965–2003	KRV	
Nicaragua	1900–1999	MIT	
	1963–2003	KRV	
Nigeria	1874–1998	MIT	
	1963–2003	KRV	

(continued)

TABLE A.1.7 Continued

Country	Period covered	Sources	Commentary
Norway	1850–1992	MIT	
	1965–2003	KRV	
Panama	1909–1996	MIT	
	1963–2003	KRV	
Paraguay	1881–1900	MIT	Revenues through 1902
	1913–1993		
	1963–2003	KRV	
Peru	1846–1998	MIT	
	1963–2003	KRV	
The Philippines	1901–2000	MIT	Missing data for World War II
	1963–2003	KRV	
Poland	1922–1937	MIT	
	1947–1993		Expenditure only
Portugal	1879–1902	MIT	
	1917–1992		
	1975–2003	KRV	
Romania	1883–1992	MIT	Expenditure begins in 1862
Russia	1769–1815	ESFDB	
	1804–1914	MIT	
	1924–1934		
	1950–1990		
	1931–1951	Condoide (1951)	National budget
Singapore	1963–2000	MIT	
South Africa	1826–1904	MIT	Natal began in 1850
	1905–2000		
	1963–2003	KRV	
Spain	1520–1553	ESFDB	Not continuous
	1753–1788		
	1850–1997	MIT	
	1965–2003	KRV	
Sri Lanka	1811–2000	MIT	
	1963–2003	KRV	

318

TABLE A.1.7 Continued

Country	Period covered	Sources	Commentary
Sweden	1881–1993	MIT	
	1980–2003	KRV	
Taiwan	1898–1938	MIT	
	1950–2000		
Thailand (Siam)	1891–2000	MIT	Revenue began in 1851
	1963–2003	KRV	
Tunisia	1909–1954	MIT	
	1965–1999		
	1963–2003	KRV	
Turkey	1923–2000	MIT	
	1963–2003	KRV	
United Kingdom	1486–1815	ESFDB	
	1791–1993	MIT	
	1963–2003	KRV	
United States	1789–1994	MIT	
	1960–2003	KRV	
Uruguay	1871–1999	MIT	
	1963–2003	KRV	
Venezuela	1830–1998	MIT	
	1963–2003	KRV	
Zambia	1963–2003	KRV	
Zimbabwe	1894–1997	MIT	
	1963–2003	KRV	

TABLE A.1.8
Total exports and imports (local currency units and U.S. dollar, as noted)

Country	Period covered	Sources	Currency, commentary
Algeria	1831–2007	GFD, WEO	
Angola	1891–2007	GFD, WEO	
Argentina	1864–2007	GFD, WEO	Lcu
	1885–2007	GFD, WEO	U.S. dollar
	1880–1913	Flandreau and Zumer (2004)	Exports
Australia	1826–2007	GFD, WEO	
Austria	1831–2007	GFD, WEO	
Belgium	1846–2007	GFD, WEO	
	1816–2007	GFD, WEO	U.S. dollar
Bolivia	1899–1935	GFD	Lcu
	1899–2007		U.S. dollar
Brazil	1821–2007	GFD, WEO	
	1880–1913	Flandreau and Zumer (2004)	Exports
Canada	1832–2007	GFD, WEO	Lcu
	1867–2007		U.S. dollar
Chile	1857–1967	GFD, WEO	Lcu
China	1865–1937	GFD, WEO	Lcu
	1950–2007		
Colombia	1835–1938		Lcu
	1919–2007	GFD, WEO	U.S. dollar
Costa Rica	1854–1938	GFD, WEO	Lcu
	1921–2007		U.S. dollar
Côte d'Ivoire	1892–2007	GFD, WEO	Lcu
	1900–2007		U.S. dollar
Denmark	1841–2007	GFD, WEO	Exports begin in 1818, lcu
	1865–2007		U.S. dollar
Ecuador	1889–1949	GFD, WEO	Lcu
	1924–2007		U.S. dollar
Egypt	1850–2007	GFD, WEO	Lcu
	1869–2007		U.S. dollar

TABLE A.1.8 Continued

Country	Period covered	Sources	Currency, commentary
El Salvador	1859–1988	GFD, WEO	Exports begin in 1854, lcu
	1870–2007		U.S. dollar
Finland	1818–2007	GFD, WEO	Lcu
	1900–2007		U.S. dollar
France	1800–2007	GFD, WEO	
Germany	1880–2007	GFD, WEO	
Ghana	1850–2007	GFD, WEO	Lcu
	1900–2007		U.S. dollar
Greece	1849–2007	GFD, WEO	Lcu
	1900–2007		U.S. dollar
Guatemala	1851–2007	GFD, WEO	
Honduras	1896–2007	GFD, WEO	
India	1832–2007	GFD, WEO	
Indonesia	1823–1974	GFD, WEO	Lcu
	1876–2007		U.S. dollar
Italy	1861–2007	GFD, WEO	
Japan	1862–2007	GFD, WEO	
Kenya	1900–2007	GFD, WEO	
Korea	1886–1936	GFD, WEO	Lcu
	1905–2007		U.S. dollar
Malaysia	1905–2007	GFD, WEO	Includes Singapore until 1955
Mauritius	1833–2007	GFD, WEO	Lcu
	1900–2007		U.S. dollar
Mexico	1797–1830	GFD, WEO	U.K. pound
	1872–2007		Lcu
	1797–1830		U.S. dollar
	1872–2007		
Morocco	1947–2007	GFD, WEO	
Myanmar (Burma)	1937–2007	GFD, WEO	
The Netherlands	1846–2007	GFD, WEO	

(continued)

TABLE A.1.8 Continued

Country	Period covered	Sources	Currency, commentary
Nicaragua	1895–2007	GFD, WEO	
Norway	1851–2007	GFD, WEO	
Panama	1905–2007	GFD, WEO	Lcu
Paraguay	1879–1949 1923–2007	GFD, WEO	U.S. dollar
Peru	1866–1952 1882–2007	GFD, WEO	Lcu U.S. dollar
The Philippines	1884–2007	GFD, WEO	
Poland	1924–2007	GFD, WEO	
Portugal	1861–2007	GFD, WEO	
Romania	1862–1993 1921–2007	GFD, WEO	Lcu U.S dollar
Russia	1802–1991 1815–2007	GFD, WEO	Lcu U.S. dollar
Singapore	1948–2007	GFD, WEO	
South Africa	1826–2007 1900–2007	GFD, WEO	Lcu U.S. dollar
Spain	1822–2007	GFD, WEO	
Sri Lanka	1825–2007 1900–2007	GFD, WEO	Lcu U.S. dollar
Sweden	1832–2007	GFD, WEO	
Taiwan	1891–2007	GFD, WEO	
Thailand (Siam)	1859–2007	GFD, WEO	
Turkey	1878–2007	GFD, WEO	
United Kingdom	1796–2007	GFD, WEO	
United States	1788–2007	GFD, WEO	
Uruguay	1862–1930 1899–2007	GFD, WEO	
Venezuela	1830–2007 1900–2007	GFD, WEO	
Zambia	1908–2007	GFD, WEO	
Zimbabwe	1900–2007	GFD, WEO	

TABLE A.1.9
Global indicators and financial centers

Country	Series	Period covered	Sources
United Kingdom	Current account balance/ GDP	1816–2006	Imlah (1958), MIT, United Kingdom National Statistics
	Consol rate	1790–2007	GFD, Bank of England
	Discount rate	1790–2007	GFD, Bank of England
United States	Current account balance/ GDP	1790–2006	Carter et al. (2006), WEO
	60- to 90-day commercial paper	1830–1900	Carter et al. (2006)
	Discount rate	1915–2007	GFD, Board of Governors of the Federal Reserve
	Federal funds rate	1950–2007	Board of Governors of the Federal Reserve
	Long-term bond	1798–2007	Carter et al. (2006), Board of Governors of the Federal Reserve
World	Commodity prices, nominal and real	1790–1850	Gayer, Rostow, and Schwartz (1953)
		1854–1990	Boughton (1991)
		1862–1999	*Economist*
		1980–2007	WEO
	Sovereign external default dates	1341–2007	Suter (1992), Purcell and Kaufman (1993), Reinhart, Rogoff, and Savastano (2003a), MacDonald (2006), Standard and Poor's (various issues)

TABLE A.1.10
Real house prices

Country	Period covered	Source	Commentary
Argentina	1981–2007	Reporte Immobiliario	Average value of old apartments, Buenos Aires
Colombia	1997:Q1–2007:Q4	Departamento Administrativo Nacional de Estadistica	New housing price index, total twenty-three municipalities
Finland	1983:Q1–2008:Q1	StatFin Online Service	Dwellings in old blocks of flats, Finland
	1970–2007	Bank for International Settlements	House price index, Finland
Hong Kong	1991:7–2008:2	Hong Kong University	Real estate index series, Hong Kong
Hungary	2000–2007	Otthon Centrum	Average price of old condominiums, Budapest
Iceland	2000:3–2008:4	Statistics Iceland	House price index, Iceland
Indonesia	1994:Q1–2008:Q1	Bank of Indonesia	Residential property price index, new houses, new developments, big cities
Ireland	1996:Q1–2008:Q1	ESRI, Permanent TSB	House prices, standardized, Ireland
Japan	1955:H1–2007:H2	Japan Real Estate Institute	Land prices, urban, residential index, Japan
Malaysia	2000:Q1–2007:Q4	Bank Negara	House price index, Malaysia
Norway	1970–2007	Bank for International Settlements	House price index, all dwellings, Norway
	1819–2007	Norges Bank	Housing prices, Norway
The Philippines	1994:Q4–2007:Q4	Colliers International: Philippines	Prime three-bedroom condominiums, Makati Central Business District

TABLE A.1.10 Continued

Country	Period covered	Source	Commentary
South Korea	1986:1–2006:12	Kookmin Bank	Housing price index
	2007:Q1–2008:Q1	Kookmin Bank	Housing price index
Spain	1990:Q1–2008:Q1	Banco de España	House price index, appraised housing, Spain
	1970–2007	Bank for International Settlements	House price index, appraised housing, Spain
Thailand	1991:Q1–2008:Q4	Bank of Thailand	House price index, single detached house
United Kingdom	1952:1–2008:4	Nationwide	Average house price, U.K.
	1970–2007	Bank for International Settlements	House price index, U.K.
United States	1890–2007	Standard and Poor's	Case-Shiller national price index, U.S.
	1987:Q1–2008:Q2	Standard and Poor's	Case-Shiller national price index, U.S.

TABLE A.1.11
Stock market indexes (equity prices) (local currency and U.S. dollars)

Country	Period covered	Country	Period covered
Argentina	1967–2008	Korea	1962–2008
Australia	1875–2008	Malaysia	1970–2008
Austria	1922–2008	Mexico	1930–2008
Belgium	1898–2008	The Netherlands	1919–2008
Brazil	1954–2008	New Zealand	1931–2008
Canada	1914–2008	Norway	1918–2008
Chile	1927–2008	Pakistan	1960–2008
Colombia	1929–2008	Peru	1932–2008
Denmark	1915–2008	The Philippines	1952–2008
Finland	1922–2008	Portugal	1931–2008
France	1856–2008	Singapore	1966–2008
Germany	1856–2008	South Africa, Union of	1910–2008
Greece	1952–2008	Spain	1915–2008
Hong Kong	1962–2008	Sweden	1913–2008
India	1921–2008	Switzerland	1910–2008
Ireland	1934–2008	Taiwan	1967–2008
Israel	1949–2008	United Kingdom	1800–2008
Italy	1906–2008	United States	1800–2008
Japan	1915–2008	Venezuela	1937–2008
Kenya	1964–2008	Zimbabwe	1968–2008

Source: Global Financial Data.

APPENDIX A.2
PUBLIC DEBT

This appendix covers the government debt series used, while appendix A.1 is devoted to the database on macroeconomic time series.

Abbreviations of Frequently Used Sources and Terms

Additional sources are listed in the tables that follow.

CLYPS	Cowan, Levy-Yeyati, Panizza, Sturzenegger (2006)
ESFDB	European State Finance Data Base
GDF	World Bank, *Global Development Finance*
GFD	Global Financial Data
IFS	International Monetary Fund, *International Financial Statistics* (various issues)
Lcu	local currency units
LM	Lindert and Morton (1989)
LofN	League of Nations, *Statistical Yearbook* (various years)
MAR	Marichal (1989)
MIT	Mitchell (2003a, 2003b)
RR	Reinhart and Rogoff (year as noted)
UN	United Nations, *Statistical Yearbook* (various years)
WEO	International Monetary Fund, *World Economic Outlook* (various issues)

TABLE A.2.1
Public debentures: External government bond issues

Country	Period covered	Sources	Commentary
Argentina	1824–1968	LM, MAR	Includes first loan
	1927–1946	UN	
Australia	1857–1978	LM, Page (1919)	
	1927–1946	UN	
Bolivia	1864–1930	MAR	
	1927–1946	UN	
Brazil	1843–1970	Bazant (1968), LM, MAR, Summerhill (2006)	Includes first loan
	1928–1946	UN	
Canada	1860–1919	LM	
	1928–1946	UN	
Chile	1822–1830	LM, MAR	Includes first loan
	1928–1946	UN	
China	1865–1938	Huang (1919), Winkler (1928)	
Colombia	1822–1929	MAR	
	1928–1946	UN	
Costa Rica	1871–1930	MAR	
Egypt	1862–1965	Landes (1958), LM	Includes first loan
	1928–1946	UN	
El Salvador	1922–1930	MAR	
	1928–1946	UN	
Greece	1824–1932	Levandis (1944)	Includes first loan (independence loan)
	1928–1939	UN	
Guatemala	1856–1930	MAR	
	1928–1939	UN	
Honduras	1867–1930	MAR	
India	1928–1945	UN	
Japan	1870–1965	LM	Includes first loan
	1928–1939	UN	

328

TABLE A.2.1 Continued

Country	Period covered	Sources	Commentary
Mexico	1824–1946	Bazant (1968), LM, MAR	Includes first loan
	1928–1944	UN	
Panama	1923–1930	UN	
	1928–1945	UN	
Peru	1822–1930	MAR	Includes first loan
	1928–1945	UN	
Russia	1815–1916	Miller (1926), Crisp (1976), LM	
South Africa	1928–1946	UN	
Thailand (Siam)	1928–1947	UN	
Turkey	1854–1965	Clay (2000), LM	Includes first loan
	1933–1939	UN	
Uruguay	1871–1939	MAR	
	1928–1947	UN	
Venezuela	1822–1930	MAR	Includes first loan
	1928–1947	UN	

TABLE A.2.2
Total (domestic plus external) public debt

Country	Period covered	Source	Commentary
Argentina	1863–1971	Garcia Vizcaino (1972)	Lcu
	1914–1981	LofN, UN	Lcu
	1980–2005	GFD, Jeanne and Guscina (2006)	
Australia	1852–1914	Page (1919)	
	1914–1981	LofN, UN	Lcu
	1980–2007	Australian Office of Financial Management	Lcu
Austria	1880–1913	Flandreau and Zumer (2004)	Lcu
	1945–1984	UN	Lcu
	1970–2006	Austrian Federal Financing Agency	Euro
Belgium	1830–2005	BNB, Centre d'études économiques de la KUL	Euro
Bolivia	1914–1953	LofN, UN	Lcu
	1968–1981		
	1991–2004	CLYPS	U.S. dollar
Brazil	1880–1913	Flandreau and Zumer (2004)	Lcu
	1923–1972	LofN, UN	Lcu
	1991–2005	GFD, Jeanne and Guscina (2006)	
Canada	1867–2007	Statistics Canada, Bank of Canada	Lcu
Chile	1827–2000	Diaz et al. (2005)	Lcu
	1914–1953	LofN, UN	Lcu
	1990–2007	Ministerio de Hacienda	U.S. dollar
China	1894–1950	Cheng (2003), Huang (1919), RR (2008c)	
	1981–2005	GFD, Jeanne and Guscina (2006) (2006)	
Colombia	1923–2006	Contraloria General de la Republica	Lcu
Costa Rica	1892–1914	Soley Güell (1926)	Lcu
	1914–1983	LofN, UN	Lcu
	1980–2007	CLYPS, Ministerio de Hacienda	U.S. dollar
Côte d'Ivoire	1970–1980	UN	Lcu

TABLE A.2.2 Continued

Country	Period covered	Source	Commentary
Denmark	1880–1913	Flandreau and Zumer (2004)	Lcu
	1914–1975	LofN, UN	Lcu
	1990–2007	Danmarks National Bank	Lcu
Dominican Republic	1914–1952	LofN, UN	Lcu
Ecuador	1914–1972	LofN, UN	Lcu
	1990–2006	Ministry of Finance	U.S. dollar
Egypt	1914–1959	LofN, UN	Lcu
	2001–2005	Ministry of Finance	Lcu
El Salvador	1914–1963, 1976–1983	LofN, UN	Lcu
	1990–2004	CLYPS	U.S. dollar
	2003–2007	Banco Central de Reserva	U.S. dollar
Finland	1914–1983	LofN, UN	Lcu
	1978–2007	State Treasury Finland	Lcu
France	1880–1913	Flandreau and Zumer (2004)	Lcu
	1913–1972	LofN, UN	Lcu
	1999–2007	Ministère du Budget, des comptes public	Lcu
Germany	1880–1913	Flandreau and Zumer (2004)	Lcu
	1914–1983	LofN, UN	Lcu
	1950–2007	Bundesbank	Lcu
Greece	1869–1893	Levandis (1944)	Not continuous, Lcu
	1880–1913	Flandreau and Zumer (2004)	Lcu
	1920–1983	LofN, UN	Lcu
	1993–2006	OECD	
Guatemala	1921–1982	LofN, UN	Lcu
	1980–2005	CLYPS	U.S. dollar
Honduras	1914–1971	LofN, UN	Lcu
	1980–2005	CLYPS	U.S. dollar
Hungary	1913–1942	LofN, UN	Lcu
	1992–2005	Jeanne and Guscina (2006)	

(continued)

331

TABLE A.2.2 Continued

Country	Period covered	Source	Commentary
India	1840–1920	Statistical Abstract Relating to British India	
	1913–1983	LofN, UN	Lcu
	1980–2005	Jeanne and Guscina (2006)	
Indonesia	1972–1983	UN	Lcu
	1998–2005	Bank Indonesia, GDF	
Italy	1880–1913	Flandreau and Zumer (2004)	Lcu
	1914–1894	LofN, UN	Lcu
	1982–2007	Dipartamento del Tesoro	Lcu
Japan	1872–2007	Historical Statistics of Japan, Bank of Japan	Lcu
Kenya	1911–1935	Frankel (1938)	U.K. pound
	1961–1980	LofN, UN	Lcu
	1997–2007	Central Bank of Kenya	Lcu
Korea	1910–1938	Mizoguchi and Umemura (1988)	Yen
	1970–1984	LofN, UN	
	1990–2004	Jeanne and Guscina (2006)	
Malaysia	1947–1957	UN	Lcu
	1976–1981		
	1980–2004	Jeanne and Guscina (2006)	
Mauritius	1970–1984	LofN, UN	Lcu
	1998–2007		Lcu
Mexico	1814–1946	Bazant (1968)	Not continuous
	1914–1979	LofN, UN	Lcu
	1980–2006	Direccion General de la Deuda Publica	
Morocco	1965–1980	UN	Lcu
The Netherlands	1880–1914	Flandreau and Zumer (2004)	Lcu
	1914–1977	LofN, UN	Lcu
	1914–2008	Dutch State Treasury Agency	Lcu
New Zealand	1858–2006	Statistics New Zealand, New Zealand Treasury	Lcu
Nicaragua	1914–1945	LofN, UN	Lcu
	1970–1983		
	1991–2005	CLYPS	U.S. dollar

TABLE A.2.2 Continued

Country	Period covered	Source	Commentary
Norway	1880–1914	Flandreau and Zumer (2004)	Lcu
	1913–1983	LofN, UN	Lcu
	1965–2007	Ministry of Finance	Lcu
Panama	1915–1983	LofN, UN	U.S. dollar
	1980–2005	CLYPS	U.S. dollar
Paraguay	1927–1947	LofN, UN	Lcu
	1976–1982		
	1990–2004	CLYPS	U.S. dollar
Peru	1918–1970	LofN, UN	Lcu
	1990–2005	CLYPS	U.S. dollar
The Philippines	1948–1982	LofN, UN	Lcu
	1980–2005	GFD, Jeanne and Guscina (2006)	
Poland	1920–1947	LofN, UN	
	1994–2004	GFD, Jeanne and Guscina (2006)	
Portugal	1851–1997	Instituto Nacional Estadisticas–Portuguese Statistical Agency	
	1914–1975	LofN, UN	Lcu
	1980–2007	Banco de Portugal	In euros from 1999
Russia	1880–1914	Crisp (1976), Flandreau and Zumer (2004)	French franc and lcu
	1922–1938	LofN, UN	Lcu
	1993–2005	Jeanne and Guscina (2006)	
Singapore	1969–1982	UN	Lcu
	1986–2006	Monetary Authority	Lcu
South Africa	1859–1914	Page (1919)	U.K. pound
	1910–1982	LofN, UN	Lcu
	1946–2006	South Africa Reserve Bank	Lcu
Spain	1504–1679	ESFDB	Not continuous
	1850–2001	Estadisticas Historicas de España: Siglos XIX–XX	Lcu
	1999–2006	Banco de España	Euro
Sri Lanka	1861–1914	Page (1919)	U.K. pound
	1950–1983	UN	Lcu
	1990–2006	Central Bank of Sri Lanka	Lcu

(continued)

TABLE A.2.2 Continued

Country	Period covered	Source	Commentary
Sweden	1880–1913	Flandreau and Zumer (2004)	
	1914–1984	LofN, UN	Lcu
	1950–2006	Riksgälden	Lcu
Thailand (Siam)	1913–1984	LofN, UN	Lcu
	1980–2006	Jeanne and Guscina (2006), Bank of Thailand	
Tunisia	1972–1982	LofN, UN	Lcu
	2004–2007	Central Bank of Tunisia	Lcu
Turkey	1933–1984	LofN, UN	Lcu
	1986–2007	Turkish Treasury	U.S. dollar
United Kingdom	1693–1786	Quinn (2004)	Total funded debt
	1781–1915	Page (1919), Bazant (1968)	1787–1815, not continuous
	1850–2007	U.K. Debt Management Office	
United States	1791–2007	Treasury Direct	
Uruguay	1914–1947	LofN, UN	Lcu
	1972–1984		
	1999–2007	Banco Central del Uruguay	U.S. dollar
Venezuela	1914–1982	LofN, UN	
	1983–2005	Jeanne and Guscina (2006)	
Zimbabwe	1924–1936	Frankel (1938)	U.K. pound
	1969–1982	UN	

TABLE A.2.3
External public debt

Country	Period covered	Source	Commentary
Algeria	1970–2005	GFD	U.S. dollar
Angola	1989–2005	GFD	U.S. dollar
Argentina	1863–1971	Garcia Vizcaino (1972)	Lcu
	1914–1981	LofN, UN	Lcu
	1970–2005	GFD	U.S. dollar
Australia	1852–1914	Page (1919)	
	1914–1981	LofN, UN	Lcu
	1980–2007	Australian Office of Financial Management	Lcu
Austria	1945–1984	UN	Lcu
	1970–2006	Austrian Federal Financing Agency	Euro
Belgium	1914–1981	LofN, UN	Lcu
	1992–2007		
Bolivia	1914–1953	LofN, UN	Lcu
	1968–1981		
	1970–2005	GFD	
	1991–2004	CLYPS	U.S. dollar
Brazil	1824–2000	Instituto Brasileiro de Geografia e Estatistica	U.K. pound and U.S. dollar
	1923–1972	LofN, UN	Lcu
	1970–2005	GFD	U.S. dollar
	1991–2005	Jeanne and Guscina (2006)	U.S. dollar
Canada	1867–2007	Statistics Canada, Bank of Canada	Lcu
Central African Republic	1970–2005	GFD	U.S. dollar
Chile	1822–2000	Díaz et al. (2005)	Lcu
	1970–2005	GFD	U.S. dollar
	1822–1930	RR (2008c)	Estimated from debentures
China	1865–1925	RR (2008c)	Estimated from debentures
	1981–2005	GFD	U.S. dollar

(*continued*)

TABLE A.2.3 Continued

Country	Period covered	Source	Commentary
Colombia	1923–2006	Contraloria General de la Republica	Lcu
Costa Rica	1892–1914	Soley Güell (1926)	Lcu
	1914–1983	LofN, UN	Lcu
	1980–2007	CLYPS, Ministerio de Hacienda	U.S. dollar
Côte d'Ivoire	1970–2005	GFD	U.S. dollar
Dominican Republic	1914–1952	LofN, UN	Lcu
	1961–2004	Banco de la Republica	U.S. dollar
Ecuador	1914–1972	LofN, UN	Lcu
	1970–2005	GFD	U.S. dollar
	1990–2007	Ministry of Finance	U.S. dollar
Egypt	1862–1930	RR	Estimated from debentures
	1914–1959	LofN, UN	Lcu
	1970–2005	GFD	U.S. dollar
France	1913–1972	LofN, UN	Lcu
	1999–2007	Ministère du Budget, des comptes public	Lcu
Germany	1914–1983	LofN, UN	Lcu
Greece	1920–1983	LofN, UN	Lcu
Guatemala	1921–1982	LofN, UN	Lcu
	1970–2005	GFD	U.S. dollar
	1980–2005	CLYPS	U.S. dollar
Honduras	1914–1971	LofN, UN	Lcu
	1970–2005	GDF	U.S. dollar
	1980–2005		U.S. dollar
Hungary	1913–1942	LofN, UN	Lcu
	1982–2005	GDF	U.S. dollar
	1992–2005	Jeanne and Guscina (2006)	
India	1840–1920	Statistical Abstract Relating to British India (various years)	
	1913–1983	LofN, UN	Lcu
	1980–2005	Jeanne and Guscina (2006)	

TABLE A.2.3 Continued

Country	Period covered	Source	Commentary
Indonesia	1972–1983	UN	Lcu
	1970–2005	GDF	U.S. dollar
Italy	1880–1913	Flandreau and Zumer (2004)	Lcu
	1914–1984	LofN, UN	Lcu
	1982–2007	Dipartamento del Tesoro	Lcu
Japan	1872–2007	Historical Statistics of Japan, Bank of Japan	Lcu
	1910–1938	Mizoguchi and Umemura (1988)	Yen
Kenya	1961–1980	LofN, UN	Lcu
	1970–2005	GDF	U.S. dollar
	1997–2007	Central Bank of Kenya	Lcu
Korea	1970–1984	LofN, UN	Lcu
	1970–2005	GDF	U.S. dollar
	1990–2004	Jeanne and Guscina (2006)	U.S. dollar
Malaysia	1947–1957	LofN, UN	Lcu
	1976–1981		
	1970–2005	GDF	U.S. dollar
	1980–2004	Jeanne and Guscina (2006)	
Mauritius	1970–1984	LofN, UN	Lcu
	1970–2005	GDF	U.S. dollar
	1998–2007	Bank of Mauritius	Lcu
Mexico	1814–1946	Bazant (1968)	Not continuous
	1820–1930	RR (2008c)	Estimated from debentures
	1914–1979	LofN, UN	Lcu
	1970–2005	GDF	U.S. dollar
	1980–2006	Direccion General de la Deuda Publica	
Morocco	1965–1980	UN	Lcu
	1970–2005	GDF	U.S. dollar
The Netherlands	1880–1914	Flandreau and Zumer (2004)	Lcu
	1914–1977	LofN, UN	Lcu
	1914–2008	Dutch State Treasury Agency	Lcu
New Zealand	1858–2006	Statistics New Zealand, New Zealand Treasury	Lcu

(continued)

337

TABLE A.2.3 Continued

Country	Period covered	Source	Commentary
Nicaragua	1914–1945	LofN, UN	Lcu
	1970–1983		
	1970–2005	GDF	U.S. dollar
	1991–2005	CLYPS	U.S. dollar
Norway	1880–1914	Flandreau and Zumer (2004)	Lcu
	1913–1983	LofN, UN	Lcu
	1965–2007	Ministry of Finance	Lcu
Panama	1915–1983	LofN, UN	U.S. dollar
	1980–2005	CLYPS	U.S. dollar
Paraguay	1927–1947	LofN, UN	Lcu
	1976–1982		
	1970–2005	GFD	U.S. dollar
	1990–2004	CLYPS	U.S. dollar
Peru	1822–1930	RR (2008c)	Estimated from debentures
	1918–1970	LofN, UN	Lcu
	1990–2005	CLYPS	U.S. dollar
	1970–2005	GFD	U.S. dollar
The Philippines	1948–1982	LofN, UN	Lcu
	1970–2005	GFD	U.S. dollar
Poland	1920–1947	LofN, UN	Lcu
	1986–2005	GFD	U.S. dollar
Portugal	1851–1997	Instituto Nacional Estadisticas–Portuguese Statistical Agency	
	1914–1975	LofN, UN	Lcu
	1980–2007	Banco de Portugal	In euros from 1999
Russia	1815–1917	RR (2008c)	
	1922–1938	LofN, UN	Lcu
	1993–2005	Jeanne and Guscina (2006)	
Singapore	1969–1982	UN	Lcu
South Africa	1859–1914	Page (1919)	U.K. pound
	1910–1983	LofN, UN	Lcu
	1946–2006	South Africa Reserve Bank	Lcu
Spain	1850–2001	Estadisticas Historicas de España: Siglos XIX–XX	Lcu
	1999–2006	Banco de España	Euro

TABLE A.2.3 Continued

Country	Period covered	Source	Commentary
Sri Lanka	1950–1983	UN	Lcu
	1970–2005	GFD	U.S. dollar
	1990–2006	Central Bank of Sri Lanka	Lcu
Sweden	1914–1984	LofN, UN	Lcu
	1950–2006	Riksgälden	Lcu
Thailand (Siam)	1913–1984	LofN, UN	Lcu
	1970–2005	GFD	U.S. dollar
	1980–2006	Jeanne and Guscina (2006), Bank of Thailand	Lcu
Tunisia	1970–2005	GFD	U.S. dollar
	2004–2007	Central Bank of Tunisia	Lcu
	1972–1982	LofN, UN	Lcu
Turkey	1854–1933	RR (2008c)	Estimated from debentures
	1933–1984	LofN, UN	Lcu
	1970–2005	GFD	U.S. dollar
	1986–2007	Turkish Treasury	U.S. dollar
United Kingdom	1914–2007	LofN, UN	Lcu
Uruguay	1871–1930	RR (2008c)	Estimated from debentures
	1914–1947, 1972–1984	LofN, UN	Lcu
	1970–2005	GFD	U.S. dollar
	1980–2004	CLYPS	U.S. dollar
Venezuela	1822–1842	RR (2008c)	Estimated from debentures, U.S. dollar
	1914–1982	LofN, UN	Lcu
Zambia	1970–2005	GFD	
Zimbabwe	1969–1982	UN	Lcu
	1970–2005	GFD	U.S. dollar

TABLE A.2.4
Domestic public debt

Country	Period covered	Source	Commentary
Argentina	1863–1971	Garcia Vizcaino (1972)	Lcu
	1914–1981	LofN, UN	Lcu
	1980–2005	GFD, Jeanne and Guscina (2006)	
Australia	1914–1981	LofN, UN	Lcu
	1980–2007	Australian Office of Financial Management	Lcu
Austria	1945–1984	UN	Lcu
	1970–2006	Austrian Federal Financing Agency	Euro
Belgium	1914–1983	LofN, UN	Lcu
	1992–2007	BNB, Centre d'études économiques de la KUL	
Bolivia	1914–1953	LofN, UN	Lcu
	1968–1981		
	1991–2004	CLYPS	U.S. dollar
Brazil	1923–1972	LofN, UN	Lcu
	1991–2005	GFD, Jeanne and Guscina (2006)	
Canada	1867–2007	Statistics Canada, Bank of Canada	Lcu
Chile	1827–2000	Díaz et al. (2005)	Lcu
	1914–1953	LofN, UN	Lcu
	1914–1946	UN	
	1990–2007	Ministerio de Hacienda	U.S. dollar
China	1894–1949	RR (2008c)	Lcu
Colombia	1923–2006	Contraloria General de la Republica	Lcu
Costa Rica	1892–1914	Soley Güell (1926)	Lcu
	1914–1983	LofN, UN	Lcu
	1980–2007	CLYPS, Ministerio de Hacienda	U.S. dollar
Côte d'Ivoire	1970–1980	UN	Lcu
Denmark	1914–1975	LofN, UN	Lcu
	1990–2007	Danmarks Nationalbank	Lcu

TABLE A.2.4 Continued

Country	Period covered	Source	Commentary
Dominican Republic	1914–1952	LofN, UN	Lcu
Ecuador	1914–1972	LofN, UN	Lcu
	1990–2006	Ministry of Finance	U.S. dollar
Egypt	1914–1959	LofN, UN	Lcu
	2001–2005	Ministry of Finance	Lcu
France	1913–1972	LofN, UN	Lcu
	1999–2007	Ministère du Budget, des comptes public	Lcu
Greece	1920–1983	LofN, UN	Lcu
	1912–1941	UN	
Guatemala	1921–1982	LofN, UN	Lcu
	1980–2005	CLYPS	U.S. dollar
Honduras	1914–1971	LofN, UN	Lcu
	1980–2005		U.S. dollar
Hungary	1913–1942	LofN, UN	Lcu
	1992–2005	Jeanne and Guscina (2006)	
India	1840–1920	Statistical Abstract Relating to British India (various years)	
	1913–1983	LofN, UN	Lcu
	1980–2005	Jeanne and Guscina (2006)	
Indonesia	1972–1983	UN	Lcu
	1998–2005	Bank Indonesia, GDF	
Italy	1880–1913	Flandreau and Zumer (2004)	Lcu
	1882–2007	Dipartamento del Tesoro	Lcu
	1894–1914	LofN, UN	Lcu
Japan	1872–2007	Historical Statistics of Japan, Bank of Japan	Lcu
	1914–1946	UN	
Kenya	1961–1980	LofN, UN	Lcu
	1997–2007	Central Bank of Kenya	Lcu
Korea	1970–1984	LofN, UN	Lcu
	1990–2004	Jeanne and Guscina (2006)	Lcu

(*continued*)

TABLE A.2.4 Continued

Country	Period covered	Source	Commentary
Malaysia	1947–1957	LofN, UN	Lcu
	1976–1981		
	1980–2004	Jeanne and Guscina (2006)	
Mauritius	1970–1984	LofN, UN	Lcu
	1998–2007	Bank of Mauritius	Lcu
Mexico	1814–1946	Bazant (1968)	Not continuous
	1914–1979	LofN, UN	Lcu
	1980–2006	Direccion General de la Deuda Publica	
Morocco	1965–1980	UN	Lcu
The Netherlands	1880–1914	Flandreau and Zumer (2004)	Lcu
	1914–1977	LofN, UN	Lcu
	1914–2008	Dutch State Treasury Agency	Lcu
New Zealand	1858–2006	Statistics New Zealand, New Zealand Treasury	Lcu
Nicaragua	1914–1945	LofN, UN	Lcu
	1970–1983		
	1991–2005	CLYPS	U.S. dollar
Norway	1880–1914	Flandreau and Zumer (2004)	Lcu
	1913–1983	LofN, UN	Lcu
	1965–2007	Ministry of Finance	Lcu
Panama	1915–1983	LofN, UN	U.S. dollar
	1980–2005	CLYPS	U.S. dollar
Paraguay	1927–1947	LofN, UN	Lcu
	1976–1982		
	1990–2004	CLYPS	U.S. dollars
Peru	1918–1970	LofN, UN	Lcu
	1990–2005	CLYPS	U.S. dollar
The Philippines	1948–1982	LofN, UN	Lcu
	1980–2005	GFD, Jeanne and Guscina (2006)	
Poland	1920–1947	LofN, UN	Lcu
	1994–2004	Jeanne and Guscina (2006)	Lcu

TABLE A.2.4 Continued

Country	Period covered	Source	Commentary
Portugal	1851–1997	Instituto Nacional Estadisticas– Portuguese Statistical Agency	Lcu
	1914–1975	LofN, UN	Lcu
	1980–2007	Banco de Portugal	In euros from 1999
Russia	1922–1938	LofN, UN	Lcu
	1993–2005	Jeanne and Guscina (2006)	
Singapore	1969–1982	UN	Lcu
	1986–2006	Monetary Authority	Lcu
South Africa	1859–1914	Page (1919)	U.K. pound
	1910–1983	LofN, UN	Lcu
	1946–2006	South Africa Reserve Bank	Lcu
Spain	1850–2001	Estadisticas Historicas de España: Siglos XIX–XX	Lcu
	1999–2006	Banco de España	Euro
Sri Lanka	1950–1983	UN	Lcu
	1990–2006	Central Bank of Sri Lanka	Lcu
Sweden	1914–1984	LofN, UN	Lcu
	1950–2006	Riksgälden	Lcu
Thailand (Siam)	1913–1984	LofN, UN	Lcu
	1980–2006	Jeanne and Guscina (2006), Bank of Thailand	Lcu
Tunisia	1972–1982	UN	Lcu
	2004–2007	Central Bank of Tunisia	Lcu
Turkey	1933–1984	LofN, UN	Lcu
	1986–2007	Turkish Treasury	U.S. dollar
United Kingdom	1914–2007	LofN, UN	Lcu
United States	1791–2007	Treasury Direct	Lcu
Uruguay	1914–1947	LofN, UN	Lcu
	1972–1984		
	1980–2004	CLYPS	U.S. dollar
Venezuela	1914–1982	LofN, UN	Lcu
	1983–2005	Jeanne and Guscina (2006)	Lcu
Zimbabwe	1969–1982	UN	Lcu

APPENDIX A.3
DATES OF BANKING CRISES

TABLE A.3.1

Banking crisis dates and capital mobility, 1800–2008

High-income countries		Middle-income countries		Low-income countries	
Country(ies)	Beginning year	Country(ies)	Beginning year	Country(ies)	Beginning year
Capital mobility: Low–moderate, 1800–1879					
France	1802				
France	1805				
United Kingdom	1810				
Sweden	1811				
Denmark	1813				
Spain, United States	1814				
United Kingdom	1815				
United States	1818				
United Kingdom, United States	1825				
United States	1836				
Canada, United Kingdom	1837				
United Kingdom	1847				
Belgium	1848				
United Kingdom, United States	1857			India	1863
Italy, United Kingdom	1866				
Austria, United States	1873	Peru	1873		
		South Africa	1877		
Capital mobility: High, 1880–1914					
Germany	1880				
France	1882	Mexico	1883		
United States	1884				
Denmark	1885				
Italy	1887				
France	1889				

TABLE A.3.1 Continued

High-income countries		Middle-income countries		Low-income countries	
Country(ies)	Beginning year	Country(ies)	Beginning year	Country(ies)	Beginning year
Portugal, United Kingdom, United States	1890	Argentina,* Brazil, Chile, Paraguay, South Africa	1890		
Germany, Italy, Portugal	1891				
Australia	1893	Uruguay	1893		
The Netherlands, Sweden	1897				
Norway	1898	Chile	1899		
Finland	1900	Brazil	1900		
Germany, Japan	1901				
Denmark, France, Italy, Japan, Sweden, United States	1907	Mexico	1907		
		Chile	1908		
		Mexico	1913	India	1913
Belgium, France,* Italy, Japan, the Netherlands, Norway,* United Kingdom, United States	1914	Argentina,* Brazil*	1914		
Capital mobility: Low, 1915–1919					
		Chile*	1915		
Capital mobility: Moderate, 1920–1929					
Portugal*	1920	Mexico	1920		
Finland, Italy, the Netherlands,* Norway*	1921			India	1921
Canada, Japan, Taiwan	1923	China	1923		
Austria	1924				
Belgium,* Germany*	1925	Brazil, Chile*	1926		
Japan, Taiwan	1927				
United States*	1929	Brazil, Mexico*	1929	India	1929
Capital Mobility: Low, 1930–1969					
France, Italy	1930				
Austria, Belgium, Finland, Germany,* Greece, Norway, Portugal,* Spain,* Sweden,* Switzerland	1931	Argentina,* Brazil, China, Czechoslovakia, Estonia, Hungary, Latvia, Poland, Romania, and Turkey	1931		

(*continued*)

TABLE A.3.1 Continued

High-income countries		Middle-income countries		Low-income countries	
Country(ies)	Beginning year	Country(ies)	Beginning year	Country(ies)	Beginning year
Belgium*	1934	Argentina, China	1934		
Italy	1935	Brazil	1937		
Belgium,* Finland	1939			India*	1947
		Brazil	1963		
Capital mobility: Moderate, 1970–1979					
		Uruguay	1971		
United Kingdom	1974	Chile*	1976	Central African Republic	1976
Germany, Israel, Spain	1977	South Africa	1977		
		Venezuela	1978		
Capital mobility: High, 1980–2007					
		Argentina,* Chile,* Ecuador, Egypt	1980		
		Mexico, the Philippines Uruguay	1981		
Hong Kong, Singapore	1982	Colombia, Turkey	1982	Congo (Democratic Republic of), Ghana	1982
Canada, Korea, Kuwait Taiwan	1983	Morocco, Peru, Thailand	1983	Equatorial Guinea, Niger	1983
United Kingdom, United States	1984			Mauritania	1984
		Argentina,* Brazil,* Malaysia*	1985	Guinea, Kenya	1985
Denmark, New Zealand, Norway	1987	Bolivia, Cameroon, Costa Rica, Nicaragua	1987	Bangladesh, Mali, Mozambique, Tanzania	1987
		Lebanon, Panama	1988	Benin, Burkina Faso, Central African Republic, Côte d'Ivoire, Madagascar, Nepal, Senegal	1988
Australia	1989	Argentina,* El Salvador, South Africa, Sri Lanka	1989		
Italy	1990	Algeria, Brazil,* Egypt, Romania	1990	Sierra Leone	1990
Czech Republic, Finland, Greece, Sweden, United Kingdom	1991	Georgia, Hungary, Poland, Slovak Republic	1991	Djibouti, Liberia, Sao Tome	1991
Japan	1992	Albania, Bosnia-Herzegovina, Estonia, Indonesia	1992	Angola, Chad, China, Congo, Kenya, Nigeria	1992

TABLE A.3.1 Continued

High-income countries		Middle-income countries		Low-income countries	
Country(ies)	Beginning year	Country(ies)	Beginning year	Country(ies)	Beginning year
Macedonia, Slovenia	1993	Cape Verde, Venezuela	1993	Guinea, Eritrea, India, Kyrgyz Republic, Togo	1993
Capital mobility: High, 1980–2007					
France	1994	Armenia, Bolivia, Bulgaria, Costa Rica, Jamaica, Latvia, Mexico,* Turkey	1994	Burundi, Congo (Republic of), Uganda	1994
United Kingdom	1995	Argentina, Azerbaijan, Brazil, Cameroon, Lithuania, Paraguay, Russia, Swaziland,	1995	Guinea-Bissau, Zambia, Zimbabwe	1995
		Croatia, Ecuador, Thailand	1996	Myanmar, Yemen	1996
Taiwan	1997	Indonesia, Korea,* Malaysia, Mauritius, the Philippines, Ukraine	1997	Vietnam	1997
		Colombia,* Ecuador, El Salvador, Russia	1998		
		Bolivia, Honduras, Peru	1999		
		Nicaragua	2000		
		Argentina,* Guatemala	2001		
		Paraguay, Uruguay	2002		
		Dominican Republic	2003		
		Guatemala	2006		
Iceland, Ireland, United States, United Kingdom	2007				
Austria, Spain	2008				

Note: Appendix A.4 contains more information on episodes listed in this table and includes some selected milder episodes. An asterisk (*) denotes that the episode in question was associated with an output collapse as defined by Barro and Ursua (2008). However, many of the countries in our extended sample are not covered by Barro and Ursua.

APPENDIX A.4
HISTORICAL SUMMARIES
OF BANKING CRISES

TABLE A.4.1
Banking crises: Historical summaries, 1800–2008

Country	Brief summary	Year	Source
Albania	After the July 1992 cleanup, 31 percent of "new" banking system loans were nonperforming. Some banks faced liquidity problems due to a logjam of interbank liabilities.	1992	Caprio and Klingebiel (2003)
Algeria	Circulation limits led to suspended specie payments. Lack of mortgage banking institutes led banks to secure loans based on real estate; many were foreclosed to escape loss.	August 1870	Conant (1915), Reinhart and Rogoff (2008a)
	The share of banking system non-performing loans reached 50 percent.	1990–1992	Caprio and Klingebiel (2003)
Angola	Two state-owned commercial banks had insolvency problems.	1992–1996	Caprio and Klingebiel (2003)
Argentina	The operation of National Bank of the Argentine Republic was suspended; high levels of foreign debt, domestic credit, and imports led to reserve losses; the peso fell 27 percent, but the crisis was brief and had relatively little impact on industrial production.	January 1885	Conant (1915), Bordo and Eichengreen (1999)
	Banks made extensive loans, and real estate prices rose dramatically with the excess issue of bank notes. Land	July 1890–1891	Bordo and Eichengreen (1999), Conant (1915)

TABLE A.4.1 Continued

Country	Brief summary	Year	Source
	prices fell by 50 percent; and Bank of the Nation could not pay its dividend, leading to a run; and the peso fell 36 percent both years. In July 1890, every bank of issue was suspended, sending gold up 320 percent. In December 1890, the Bank of the Argentine Nation replaced the old Bank of the Nation.		
	Bad harvests and European demands for liquidity due to the war led to bank runs, with private banks losing 45 percent of deposits in two years.	1914	Conant (1915), Bordo and Eichengreen (1999), Nakamura and Zarazaga (2001)
	The gold standard was ended, with insolvent loans building.	1931	della Paolera and Taylor (1999), Bordo et al. (2001)
	Huge loans to the government and nonperforming assets had been building for many years; finally all were taken over by the new Central Bank.	1934	della Paolera and Taylor (1999), Bordo et al. (2001)
	The failure of a large private bank (Banco de Intercambio Regional) led to runs on three other banks. Eventually more than seventy institutions—representing 16 percent of commercial bank assets and 35 percent of finance company assets—were liquidated or subjected to central bank intervention.	March 1980–1982	Kaminsky and Reinhart (1999), Bordo et al. (2001), Caprio and Klingebiel (2003)
	In early May, the government closed a large bank, leading to large runs, which led the government to freeze dollar deposits on May 19.	May 1985	Kaminsky and Reinhart (1999)
	Nonperforming assets accounted for 27 percent of aggregate portfolios and 37 percent of state banks' portfolios. Failed banks held 40 percent of financial system assets.	1989–1990	Bordo et al. (2001), Caprio and Klingebiel (2003)
	The Mexican devaluation led to a run on the banks, which resulted in an 18 percent decline in deposits between December and March. Eight	1995	Bordo et al. (2001), Reinhart (2002), Caprio and Klingebiel (2003)

(continued)

349

TABLE A.4.1 Continued

Country	Brief summary	Year	Source
	banks suspended operations, and three banks collapsed. Through the end of 1997, 63 of 205 banking institutions were closed or merged.		
	In March 2001, a bank run started due to a lack of public confidence in government policy actions. In late November 2001, many banks were on the verge of collapsing, and partial withdrawal restrictions were imposed (*corralito*) and fixed-term deposits (CDs) were reprogrammed to stop outflows from banks (*corralon*). In December 2002, the *corralito* was lifted. In January 2003, one bank was closed, three banks were nationalized, and many others were reduced in size.	March 2001	Caprio and Klingebiel (2003), Jácome (2008)
Armenia	The Central Bank closed half the active banks; large banks continued to suffer from a high level of non-performing loans. The savings bank was financially weak.	August 1994–1996	Caprio and Klingebiel (2003)
Australia	A domestic lending boom showed the deteriorated quality of bank assets; a land boom and unregulated banking system led to speculation. Closure of Mercantile Bank in Australia and the Federal Bank of Australia meant that British deposits ran off. Bank share prices fell heavily, banks retrenched and stopped long-term loans, and many closed. The depression of the 1890s followed.	January 1893	Conant (1915), Bordo and Eichengreen (1999)
	Two large banks received capital from the government to cover losses.	1989–1992	Bordo et al. (2001), Caprio and Klingebiel (2003)
Austria	There was speculation in the economy; the crash of the Vienna Stock Exchange led firty-two banks and forty-four provincial banks to fail.	May 1873–1874	Conant (1915)

TABLE A.4.1 Continued

Country	Brief summary	Year	Source
	There were difficulties in the major bank; liquidation began in June.	1924	Bernanke and James (1990)
	The second-largest bank failed and merged with the major bank.	November 1929	Bernanke and James (1990)
	Creditanstalt failed, and there was a run of foreign depositors.	May 1931	Bernanke and James (1990)
Azerbaijan	Twelve private banks closed; three large state-owned banks were deemed insolvent, and one faced serious liquidity problems.	1995	Caprio and Klingebiel (2003)
Bangladesh	Four banks, accounting for 70 percent of credit, had 20 percent non-performing loans. From the late 1980s, the entire private and public banking system was technically insolvent.	1987–1996	Bordo et al. (2001), Caprio and Klingebiel (2003)
Belarus	Many banks were undercapitalized; forced mergers burdened some banks with poor loan portfolios.	1995	Caprio and Klingebiel (2003)
Belgium	There were two rival banks: the Bank of Belgium (created in 1835) and the Société Générale. Fear of war led to credit contraction. The Société tried to bankrupt the Bank of Belgium by redeeming large amounts of credit, weakening both. There were runs on Bank of Belgium; it did not suspend payment but appealed to the treasury for assistance.	December 1838–1839	Conant (1915)
	The Bank of Belgium resigned its function as state depository to the Société Générale; the Société felt the impact of the crisis and abandoned all branches except that at Antwerp.	1842	Conant (1915)
	The Société Générale suspended payments and lost the right of issue after the government demanded reform. The National Bank of Belgium was created.	February 1848	Conant (1915)

(continued)

TABLE A.4.1 Continued

Country	Brief summary	Year	Source
	There was public fear due to state decisions and burdens, but the Bank of Belgium reassured people by continuing payments (it raised the discount rate and placed restrictions on acceptance of commercial paper) —at great cost to commerce and the bank.	July 1870–1871	Conant (1915)
	Worldwide investors dumped assets and withdrew liquidity, pushing prices down and threatening financial institutions with failure. Stock exchanges around the world collapsed.	1914	Bordo et al. (2001)
	Systemic deflation led to a funding crisis.	1925–1926	Johnson (1998), Bordo et al. (2001)
	Rumors about the imminent failure of the Bank of Brussels, the largest bank, led to withdrawals from all banks. Later, expectations of devaluations led to withdrawals of foreign deposits.	May 1931	Bernanke and James (1990), Bordo et al. (2001)
	Failure of the Banque Belge de Travail developed into a general banking and exchange crisis.	1934	Bernanke and James (1990), Bordo et al. (2001)
	The cconomy was slowly recovering, although the prospect of war hampered investment decisions. Foreign exchange and gold reserves diminished dramatically.	1939	Bordo et al. (2001)
Benin	All three commercial banks collapsed, and 80 percent of banks' loan portfolios were nonperforming.	1988–1990	Caprio and Klingebiel (2003)
Bolivia	In October 1987, the central bank liquidated two of twelve state commercial banks; seven more reported large losses. In total, five banks were liquidated. Banking system nonperforming loans reached 30 percent in 1987 and 92 percent by mid-1988.	October 1987–1988	Kaminsky and Reinhart (1999), Caprio and Klingebiel (2003)
	Two banks, with 11 percent of banking system assets, closed in 1994. In 1995, four of fifteen domestic banks, with	1994	Caprio and Klingebiel (2003)

TABLE A.4.1 Continued

Country	Brief summary	Year	Source
	30 percent of banking system assets, experienced liquidity problems and suffered a high level of nonperforming loans.		
	One small bank (with a market share of 4.5 percent of deposits) was intervened and resolved.	1999	Jácome (2008)
Bosnia and Herzegovina	The banking system suffered from a high level of nonperforming loans due to the breakup of the former Yugoslavia and the civil war.	1992–?	Caprio and Klingebiel (2003)
Botswana	Banks merged, liquidated, or recapitalized.	1994–1995	Caprio and Klingebiel (2003)
Brazil	There was a large amount of government borrowing and currency speculation; the government continually issued more notes. The National Bank of Brazil and Bank of the U.S. of Brazil merged into the Bank of the Republic of the U.S. of Brazil. The new bank retired the government's paper notes. Turmoil in the financial sector led to a decline in output.	December 1890–1892	Conant (1915), Bordo and Eichengreen (1999)
	There was a civil war and currency depreciation. A loan from Rothschild's in London helped, with an agreement made on settling the country's debt.	1897–1898	Conant (1915), Bordo and Eichengreen (1999)
	Inelastic coffee exports could not respond to currency depreciation; there was concentrated industry, limited competition, and slowed recovery from deflation. Liquidity injection did not help; deposits ran off, and loans were recalled.	1900–1901	Conant (1915), Bordo and Eichengreen (1999)
	Payments were suspended due to the difficulty of international remittance.	1914	Brown (1940), Bordo et al. (2001)
	The treasury supported large budget deficits by issuing notes for discount at the Banco de Brasil. High inflation and public dissatisfaction led to the	1923	Triner (2000), Bordo et al. (2001)

(continued)

TABLE A.4.1 Continued

Country	Brief summary	Year	Source
	reestablishment of the gold standard, and a new government reorganized the Banco de Brasil, making it the central bank. However, it failed to operate independent of political control. The banking sector contracted by 20 percent in the next three years due to diminished money supply.		
	Overaccumulation of capital came at the expense of urban workers, and the economic structures could not adjust to accommodate these pressures by changing wages. The economic crisis led to a political one, and a military coup resulted.	1963	Bordo et al. (2001)
	Three large banks (Comind, Maison Nave, and Auxiliar) were taken over by the government.	November 1985	Kaminsky and Reinhart (1999)
	Deposits were converted to bonds.	1990	Bordo et al. (2001), Caprio and Klingebiel (2003)
	In 1994, seventeen small banks were liquidated, three private banks were intervened, and eight state banks were placed under administration. The Central Bank intervened in or put under temporary administration forty-three financial institutions, and banking system nonperforming loans reached 15 percent by the end of 1997. Private banks returned to profitability in 1998, but public banks did not begin to recover until 1999.	July 1994–1996	Kaminsky and Reinhart (1999), Bordo et al. (2001), Caprio and Klingebiel (2003)
Brunei	Several financial firms and banks failed.	1986	Caprio and Klingebiel (2003)
Bulgaria	In 1995, about 75 percent of banking system loans were substandard. There was a banking system run in early 1996. The government stopped providing bailouts, prompting the closure of nineteen banks accounting for one-	1995–1997	Caprio and Klingebiel (2003)

TABLE A.4.1 Continued

Country	Brief summary	Year	Source
	third of sector assets. The surviving banks were recapitalized by 1997.		
Burkina Faso	Banking system nonperforming loans were estimated at 34 percent.	1988–1994	Caprio and Klingebiel (2003)
Burundi	Banking system nonperforming loans were estimated at 25 percent in 1995, and one bank was liquidated.	1994–1995	Caprio and Klingebiel (2003)
Cameroon	In 1989, banking system nonperforming loans reached 60–70 percent. Five commercial banks were closed and three restructured.	1987–1993	Caprio and Klingebiel (2003)
	At the end of 1996, nonperforming loans were 30 percent of total loans. Two banks were closed and three restructured.	1995–1998	Caprio and Klingebiel (2003)
Canada	The Bank of Upper Canada and Gore Bank suspended specie payments; a rebellion in Lower Canada led to suspension of payments.	1837	Conant (1915)
	A bank in Western Canada suspended payments, leading to financial panic. The Bank of Upper Canada failed; there was rapid growth in Ontario, and the bank lost capital in land speculation in 1857; it abandoned safe banking practices and made loans to lawyers, politicians, and the gentry.	September 1866	Conant (1915)
	There were several bank failures and a depression from 1874 to 1879.	September 1873	Conant (1915)
	Ontario Bank failed due to speculation in the N.Y. stock market; shareholders lost their entire investments.	October 1906	Conant (1915)
	A current account deficit and a crop failure meant that eastern banks were unwilling to ship funds west; banks raised their loan rates, cut lending, and limited credit to farmers. There was a short but sharp recession; Canadian banks borrowed dominion	January 1908	Conant (1915), Bordo and Eichengreen (1999)

(*continued*)

TABLE A.4.1 Continued

Country	Brief summary	Year	Source
	notes, and banks increased their note issue.		
	The Royal Bank acquired the Bank of British Honduras and Bank of British Guiana.	1912	Conant (1915)
	The Home Bank of Canada, with over seventy branches, failed due to bad loans.	1923	Kryzanowski and Roberts (1999), Bordo et al. (2001)
	Fifteen members of the Canadian Deposit Insurance Corporation, including two banks, failed.	1983–1985	Bordo et al. (2001), Caprio and Klingebiel (2003)
Cape Verde	At the end of 1995, commercial banks' nonperforming loans reached 30 percent.	1993	Caprio and Klingebiel (2003)
Central African Republic	Four banks were liquidated.	1976–1982	Caprio and Klingebiel (2003)
	The two largest banks, with 90 percent of assets, were restructured. Banking system nonperforming loans reached 40 percent.	1988–1999	Caprio and Klingebiel (2003)
Chad	The banking sector experienced solvency problems.	1980s	Caprio and Klingebiel (2003)
	Private sector nonperforming loans reached 35 percent.	1992	Caprio and Klingebiel (2003)
Chile	The bank currency system and gold standard were completely wrecked by the threat of war with the Argentine Republic. On July 5, growing exports of gold and the Bank of Chile's refusal to honor gold drafts led to a run on banks at Santiago and general suspicion of gold drafts. The government issued irredeemable paper money, constantly increasing the monetary supply for the next ten years, leading to a period of inflation and overspeculation.	July 1898	Conant (1915), Bordo and Eichengreen (1999)
	There were four years of inflationary measures following a stock market crash; the peso fell 30 percent during	1907	Conant (1915), Bordo and Eichengreen (1999)

TABLE A.4.1 Continued

Country	Brief summary	Year	Source
	the crisis, and the government loaned treasury notes to banks to prevent a financial sector crisis. Data concerning the ensuing recession are unavailable.		
	The entire mortgage system became insolvent.	1976	Bordo et al. (2001), Caprio and Klingebiel (2003)
	Three banks began to lose deposits; interventions began two months later. Interventions occurred in four banks and four nonbank financial institutions, accounting for 33 percent of outstanding loans. In 1983, there were seven more bank interventions and one *financiera*, accounting for 45 percent of financial system assets. By the end of 1983, 19 percent of loans were nonperforming.	1980	Kaminsky and Reinhart (1999), Bordo et al. (2001), Caprio and Klingebiel (2003)
China	Failure of a major silk-trading company in Shanghai led to the bankruptcies of many local banks.	1883	Cheng (2003)
	The postwar depression led many banks to fail.	1923–1925	Young (1971)
	Shanghai closed all Chinese banks for the duration of the war.	1931	Cheng (2003)
	The flight of silver led to a huge economic downturn and financial crisis; the two major banks came under government control and were reorganized.	1934–1937	Cheng (2003)
	China's four large state-owned commercial banks, with 68 percent of banking system assets, were deemed insolvent. Banking system nonperforming loans were estimated at 50 percent.	1997–1999	Caprio and Klingebiel (2003)
Colombia	Banco Nacional became the first of six major banks and eight financial companies to be intervened, accounting for 25 percent of banking system assets.	July 1982–1987	Kaminsky and Reinhart (1999), Bordo et al. (2001), Caprio and Klingebiel (2003)

(*continued*)

TABLE A.4.1 Continued

Country	Brief summary	Year	Source
	Many banks and financial institutions failed; capitalization ratios and liquidity decreased dramatically, and the total assets of the financial industry contracted by more than 20 percent.	April 1998	Reinhart (2002), Jácome (2008)
Congo, Democratic Republic of	The banking sector experienced solvency problems.	1982	Caprio and Klingebiel (2003)
	Four state-owned banks were insolvent; a fifth was recapitalized with private participation.	1991–1992	Caprio and Klingebiel (2003)
	Nonperforming loans reached 75 percent. Two state-owned banks liquidated, and two privatized. In 1997, twelve banks had serious financial difficulties.	1994–?	Caprio and Klingebiel (2003)
Congo, Republic of	A crisis began in 1992. In 2001–2002, two large banks were restructured and privatized. The remaining insolvent bank was being liquidated.	1992–?	Caprio and Klingebiel (2003)
Costa Rica	In 1987, public banks accounting for 90 percent of banking system loans were in financial distress, with 32 percent of loans considered uncollectable.	1987	Caprio and Klingebiel (2003), Bordo et al. (2001)
	The third largest bank, Banco Anglo Costarricense, a state-owned institution with 17 percent of deposits, was closed.	1994–1997	Bordo et al. (2001), Caprio and Klingebiel (2003), Jácome (2008)
Côte d'Ivoire	Four large banks (with 90 percent of banking system loans) were affected; three or four were insolvent, and six government banks closed.	1988–1991	Bordo et al. (2001), Caprio and Klingebiel (2003)
Croatia	Five banks, accounting for about half of banking system loans, were deemed insolvent and taken over by the Bank Rehabilitation Agency.	1996	Caprio and Klingebiel (2003)
Czechoslovakia	Withdrawal of foreign deposits sparked domestic withdrawals but no general banking panic.	July 1931	Bernanke and James (1990)

TABLE A.4.1 Continued

Country	Brief summary	Year	Source
Czech Republic	There have been several bank closings since 1993. In 1994–1995, 38 percent of banking system loans were non-performing.	1991–?	Caprio and Klingebiel (2003)
Denmark	The government declared that it could not redeem Deposit Bank's Courant notes at their original value; this was a form of bankruptcy that diminished its public debt because notes were held by the people. The new Royal Bank was established; Courantbank, Specie Bank, and Deposit Bank were abolished.	January 1813	Conant (1915)
	A financial crisis led to the National bank to assume central bank responsibilities through the 1860s.	1857	Jonung and Hagberg (2002)
	Industrial Bank diverted half its capital stock to cover its losses; two provincial banks failed, leading to a lull in the banking business.	1877	Conant (1915), Jonung and Hagberg (2002)
	National Bank intervened to provide support for commercial and savings banks.	1885	Jonung and Hagberg (2002)
	An important bank failure led to suspension of Freeholders' Bank and bank runs on other institutions. The National Bank helped alleviate panic; it took on the five remaining banks and suspended the banks' liabilities.	February 1902	Conant (1915)
	Turbulence in the world markets and Germany and nonperforming assets led to decreased confidence. A consortium of five leading banks assisted and guaranteed the liabilities of weak banks, leading to a quick recovery.	1907	Conant (1915), Bordo and Eichengreen (1999), Jonung and Hagberg (2002)
	Banking crises lasted for many years due to reckless lending during the war and the international downswing in prices in the early 1920s.	1921	Bordo et al. (2001), Jonung and Hagberg (2002)
	The banks suffered liquidity problems that lasted until the gold standard was abandoned.	1931	Bordo et al. (2001)

(continued)

359

TABLE A.4.1 Continued

Country	Brief summary	Year	Source
	Two small banks collapsed, which shook the banking system, leading to moves to curb bank lending. The cumulative losses over 1990–1992 were 9 percent of loans; forty of sixty problem banks were merged.	March 1987–1992	Kaminsky and Reinhart (1999), Bordo et al. (2001), Caprio and Klingebiel (2003)
Djibouti	Two of six commercial banks ceased operations, and other banks experienced difficulties.	1991–1993	Caprio and Klingebiel (2003)
Dominican Republic	The third largest bank, with a market share of 7 percent of assets, was intervened.	1996	Jácome (2008)
	The 2003 banking crisis started with the intervention of the third largest bank, with a market share of 10 percent. Deposit withdrawals had already started by mid-2002 following allegations of fraud resulting from the discovery of hidden liabilities recorded in a parallel bank. Immediately afterward, the crisis extended to two other institutions (with an additional 10 percent of market share) featuring similar inappropriate accounting practices.	2003	Jácome (2008)
Ecuador	A program for exchanging domestic for foreign debt was implemented to bail out the banking system.	1981	Bordo et al. (2001), Caprio and Klingebiel (2003)
	A medium-sized bank, Banco de los Andes, with a market share of 6 percent of deposits, was intervened and then purchased by another private bank.	1994	Jácome (2008)
	Authorities intervened in several small financial institutions; by the end of 1995, thirty financial societies (*sociedades financieras*) and seven banks were receiving extensive liquidity support. In	1996	Bordo et al. (2001), Caprio and Klingebiel (2003)

TABLE A.4.1 Continued

Country	Brief summary	Year	Source
	early 1996, the fifth largest commercial bank was intervened.		
	Banks amounting to 60 percent of the banking system were intervened, taken over, or closed. Seven financial institutions, accounting for 25–30 percent of commercial banking assets, were closed in 1998–1999. In March 1999, bank deposits were frozen for six months. By January 2000, sixteen financial institutions, accounting for 65 percent of the assets, had either been closed (twelve) or taken over (four) by the governments. All deposits were unfrozen by March 2000.	April 1998–1999	Caprio and Klingebiel (2003), Jácome (2008)
Egypt	A crisis developed due to credit abuse and the issue of new securities.	March 1907	Conant (1915)
	There was a run on the Cairo and Alexandria branches of German banks.	July 1931	Bernanke and James (1990)
	The government closed several large investment companies.	January 1980–1981	Bordo et al. (2001), Reinhart (2002), Caprio and Klingebiel (2003)
	Four public banks were given capital assistance.	January 1990–1995	Bordo et al. (2001), Reinhart (2002), Caprio and Klingebiel (2003)
El Salvador	Nine state-owned commercial banks had nonperforming loans averaging 37 percent.	1989	Caprio and Klingebiel (2003)
	After a sharp stop in economic growth in 1996 associated with a terms-of-trade deterioration (a decline in coffee prices), the financial system was stressed from 1997 onward. A small- to medium-sized institution (Banco Credisa), with a 5 percent market share, was closed.	1998	Jácome (2008)

(continued)

TABLE A.4.1 Continued

Country	Brief summary	Year	Source
Equatorial Guinea	Two of the country's largest banks were liquidated.	1983–1985	Caprio and Klingebiel (2003)
Eritrea	Most of the banking system was insolvent.	1993	Caprio and Klingebiel (2003)
Estonia	Two medium-sized banks failed; the ensuing panic lasted until January 1931.	November 1930	Bernanke and James (1990)
	There were waves of general bank runs.	September 1931	Bernanke and James (1990)
	Insolvent banks accounted for 41 percent of financial system assets. Five banks' licenses were revoked, and two major banks were merged and nationalized while two more merged and were converted to a loan recovery agency.	1992–1995	Caprio and Klingebiel (2003)
	The Social Bank, with 10 percent of financial system assets, failed.	1994	Caprio and Klingebiel (2003)
	Three banks failed.	1998	Caprio and Klingebiel (2003)
Ethiopia	The government-owned bank was restructured, and nonperforming loans taken over.	1994–1995	Caprio and Klingebiel (2003)
Finland	A crisis in Russia and the Balkans and export prices put the finance sector at risk. The Bank of Finland extended loans and note issues, but the growth rate of real GDP still fell by 4 percent.	1900	Bordo and Eichengreen (1999)
	The country fared better than other Nordic countries because its currency was already severely devalued, which also eased economic recovery.	1921	Bordo et al. (2001), Jonung and Hagberg (2002)
	A recession began in 1929; many banks were stuck with large losses, which led to bankruptcies; the Bank of Finland facilitated loans and mergers.	1931	Bordo et al. (2001), Jonung and Hagberg (2002)

TABLE A.4.1 Continued

Country	Brief summary	Year	Source
	Financial stability was maintained, and GDP growth did not suffer much.	1939	Bordo et al. (2001), Jonung and Hagberg (2002)
	A large bank (Skopbank) collapsed on September 19 and was intervened. Savings banks were badly affected; the government took control of three banks that together accounted for 31 percent of system deposits.	September 1991–1994	Kaminsky and Reinhart (1999), Bordo et al. (2001), Jonung and Hagberg (2002), Caprio and Klingebiel (2003)
France	The Bank of France experienced a serious crisis.	1802	Conant (1915)
	The Bank of France had a debt of 68 million francs with only 0.782 million francs in specie; it used commercial paper, government bonds, and credit to buy specie (from the Spanish treasury). This occurred after the formation of a third coalition against France during preparations for Austerlitz; the victory at Austerlitz (December 2, 1805) restored much confidence.	September 1805–1806	Conant (1915)
	There were bankruptcies in Alsace.	December 1827–1828	Conant (1915)
	There were severe runs on banks in Paris after the Bank of Belgium failed.	December 1838–1839	Conant (1915)
	On March 24, 1848, notes from the Bank of France and departmental banks were declared legal tender; the need for a uniform paper currency led to the consolidation of local banks with the Bank of France (April 27 and May 2).	February 1848–1850	Conant (1915)
	There was a French panic after cotton speculation.	January 1864	Conant (1915)
	A French crisis developed after the failure of Credit Mobilier.	November 1867–1868	Conant (1915)

(*continued*)

TABLE A.4.1 Continued

Country	Brief summary	Year	Source
	Branches of the Bank of France suspended their operations. After surrender, Germany suspended the Bank of Strasburg, and the Bank of Prussia replaced the Bank of France in Alsace-Lorraine.	May 1871	Conant (1915)
	Speculation and financial innovation led to problems among banks; the Bank of France extended loans to smaller banks and borrowed from the Bank of England to replenish its reserves. Growth fell by 5 percent that year and failed to recover to the previous trend for a long time.	February 1882	Conant (1915), Bordo and Eichengreen (1999)
	A French financier attempted to corner the copper market, while the Comptoir d'Escompte discounted copper warrants; the product limits broke down and copper prices fell, so the Comptoir suffered heavy losses. The head committed suicide, leading to a run; sound assets could not satisfy liquidity demands. Comptoir appealed to the Bank of France for help; growth fell by 14 percent during the crisis.	March 1889	Conant (1915), Bordo and Eichengreen (1999)
	There was a French banking panic; there had been a depression in Bourse since the beginning of the Russo–Japanese War.	February 1904	Conant (1915)
	Trouble in the United States raised the global demand for gold and money; a majority of France's losses were in silver to its colonies. As a result, the visible impact on GDP growth was mild.	1907	Conant (1915), Bordo and Eichengreen (1999)
	Two major banks failed, and there were runs on provincial banks.	1930–1932	Bernanke and James (1990), Bordo et al. (2001)

TABLE A.4.1 Continued

Country	Brief summary	Year	Source
	Crédit Lyonnaise had serious solvency problems.	1994–1995	Bordo et al. (2001), Caprio and Klingebiel (2003)
Gabon	One bank temporarily closed in 1995.	1995	Caprio and Klingebiel (2003)
Gambia	In 1992, a government bank was restructured and privatized.	1985–1992	Caprio and Klingebiel (2003)
Georgia	Most large banks were virtually insolvent. About one-third of banking system loans were nonperforming.	1991	Caprio and Klingebiel (2003)
Germany	Hamburg Bank was rescued by the Austrian National Bank; this restored confidence and dispelled the crisis; Hamburg Bank repaid its loan in six months.	1857	Conant (1915)
	Triggered by Russia's crisis, stock prices in Berlin fell by 61 percent; the problem hit mortgage banks first, but discount banks provided liquidity. Dresdner Creditanstalt, the Bank of Leipzig, and Leipzig Bank failed. There was a modest slowdown in the rate of growth.	1901	Conant (1915), Bordo and Eichengreen (1999)
	There were twin crises in which banks were recapitalized or their deposits guaranteed by the government. Bank runs exacerbated troubles building since mid-1930; many banks were unable to make payments, and there was a bank holiday.	1931	Bernanke and James (1990), Bordo et al. (2001), Temin (2008)
	Giro institutions faced problems.	1977	Caprio and Klingebiel (2003)
Ghana	Seven out of eleven banks were insolvent; the rural banking sector was affected.	1982–1989	Bordo et al. (2001), Caprio and Klingebiel (2003)

(continued)

365

TABLE A.4.1 Continued

Country	Brief summary	Year	Source
	Nonperforming loans increased from 11 percent to 27 percent; two state-owned banks were in bad shape, and three others were insolvent.	1997	Bordo et al. (2001), Caprio and Klingebiel (2003)
Greece	The country defaulted on external debt and left the gold standard in place.	1931	Bordo et al. (2001)
	Localized problems required significant injections of public funds.	1991–1995	Bordo et al. (2001), Reinhart (2002), Caprio and Klingebiel (2003)
Guatemala	Two small state-owned banks had a high level of nonperforming operations and closed in the early 1990s.	1991	Caprio and Klingebiel (2003)
	Three small banks (Banco Empresarial, Promotor, and Metropolitano), with a market share of 7 percent of deposits, were intervened and later closed for not observing solvency requirements.	2001	Jácome (2008)
	The third largest bank, Bancafe (with 9 percent of deposits), was closed, followed by another small bank, Banco del Comercio (with 1 percent of deposits), a few months later.	2006	Jácome (2008)
Guinea	Six banks (with 99 percent of system deposits) were deemed insolvent.	1985	Caprio and Klingebiel (2003)
	Two banks were insolvent, and one other had serious financial difficulties, accounting for 45 percent of the market total.	1993–1994	Caprio and Klingebiel (2003)
Guinea-Bissau	At the end of 1995, 45 percent of commercial banks' loan portfolios were nonperforming.	1995	Caprio and Klingebiel (2003)
Honduras	A small bank, Bancorp, with 3 percent of deposits, was closed in September.	1999	Jácome (2008)

TABLE A.4.1 Continued

Country	Brief summary	Year	Source
	A small bank, Banhcreser, with 3 percent of market share, was closed.	2001	Jácome (2008)
	Two small banks, Banco Sogerin and Banco Capital, were intervened and taken over by the deposit insurance institution.	2002	Jácome (2008)
Hong Kong	Nine deposit-taking companies failed.	1982	Bordo et al. (2001), Caprio and Klingebiel (2003)
	Seven banks were liquidated or taken over.	1983–1986	Bordo et al. (2001), Caprio and Klingebiel (2003)
	One large investment bank failed.	1998	Caprio and Klingebiel (2003)
Hungary	There was a run on Budapest banks; there were foreign withdrawals and a bank holiday.	July 1931	Bernanke and James (1990)
	By the second half of 1993, eight banks (with 25 percent of financial system assets) were deemed insolvent.	1991–1995	Caprio and Klingebiel (2003)
Iceland	One of three state-owned banks became insolvent.	1985–1986	Bordo et al. (2001), Caprio and Klingebiel (2003)
	The government injected capital into the state-owned commercial bank.	1993	Bordo et al. (2001), Caprio and Klingebiel (2003)
India	The Bank of Bengal could not meet the demands for financing, which resulted in increased capitalization.	1863	Scutt (1904), Reinhart and Rogoff (2008a)
	There were crop failures and excessive obligations to European banks; silver replaced much of the gold.	April 1908	Conant (1915)
	The nonperforming assets of twenty-seven public banks were estimated at 20 percent in 1995.	1993–1996	Bordo et al. (2001), Caprio and Klingebiel (2003)

(continued)

TABLE A.4.1 Continued

Country	Brief summary	Year	Source
Indonesia	A large bank (Bank Summa) collapsed, triggering runs on three smaller banks.	November 1992	Kaminsky and Reinhart (1999)
	Nonperforming assets accounted for 14 percent of banking system assets, with more than 70 percent in state banks.	1994	Bordo et al. (2001), Caprio and Klingebiel (2003)
	Through May 2002, Bank Indonesia closed 70 banks and nationalized 13 out of 237. Nonperforming loans were 65–75 percent of total loans at the peak of the crisis and fell to about 12 percent in February 2002.	1997–2002	Caprio and Klingebiel (2003)
Ireland	There was a run on most Irish banks; Agricultural Bank failed in November.	November 1836–1837	Conant (1915)
	Tipperary Joint Stock Bank failed upon discovery that one director (John Sadlier) had systematically robbed the bank and falsified accounts.	February 1856	Conant (1915)
Israel	Almost the entire banking sector was affected, representing 60 percent of stock market recapitalization. The stock exchange closed for eighteen days, and bank share prices fell more than 40 percent.	1977–1983	Bordo et al. (2001), Caprio and Klingebiel (2003)
	Stocks of the four largest banks collapsed and were nationalized by the state.	October 1983	Reinhart (2002)
Italy	National Bank suspended specie due to the expectation of the Austro-Prussian War.	June 1866–1868	Conant (1915)
	Tiber Bank, the Italian Mortgage Bank Society, and the Naples Building Association were taken over by National Bank.	1887	Conant (1915)

TABLE A.4.1 Continued

Country	Brief summary	Year	Source
	There was a real estate boom and bust, bringing banks with it. A tariff war with France raised interest rates and helped to prick the land bubble. Growth slowed and did not pick up for five years.	1891	Bordo and Eichengreen (1999)
	The government overhauled the banking system by merging several banks and authorized expansions of credit, triggering a currency crisis. The lira depreciated, but the recessionary impact was mild.	January 1893	Conant (1915), Bordo and Eichengreen (1999)
	Financial speculation and mounting difficulties in New York, London, and Paris in 1906 put pressure on interest rates and pricked the financial bubble. A sharp drop in output followed.	1907	Bordo and Eichengreen (1999)
	Savings banks were on the verge of collapse; they were rescued by the three main issuing banks, which also supported industry during the war.	1914	Teichova et al. (1997), Bordo et al. (2001)
	The third and fourth largest banks became insolvent, partly due to overtrading during and after the war.	1921	Bordo et al. (2001)
	There were withdrawals from the largest banks; a panic ensued until April, when the government reorganized many institutions and took over bad industrial assets.	December 1930–1931	Bernanke and James (1990), Bordo et al. (2001)
	There were agricultural bank closures and savings and commercial bank mergers to such an extent that the Italian banking system appeared completely reorganized.	1935	Teichova et al. (1997), Bordo et al. (2001)
	Fifty-eight banks, with 11 percent of lending, merged with other institutions.	1990–1995	Bordo et al. (2001), Caprio and Klingebiel (2003)

(*continued*)

TABLE A.4.1 Continued

Country	Brief summary	Year	Source
Jamaica	A merchant banking group was closed.	1994–1997	Bordo et al. (2001), Caprio and Klingebiel (2003)
	FINSAC, a government resolution agency, assisted five banks, five life insurance companies, two building societies, and nine merchant banks.	1995–2000	Caprio and Klingebiel (2003)
Japan	The National Bank Act forced banks to accept the government's paper notes, causing nine or ten banks to fail.	1872–1876	Conant (1915)
	Deflationary measures depressed trade, and four national banks failed, five suspended operations, and ten were consolidated.	1882–1885	Conant (1915)
	There were trade deficits and reserve losses as well as significant output losses; growth fell by 6 percent in one year.	1901	Bordo and Eichengreen (1999)
	The Tokyo stock market crashed in early 1907, and there was global uncertainty; the Bank of Japan intervened for some banks and let other banks fail. The recession was severe.	1907	Bordo and Eichengreen (1999)
	Japan went off the gold standard.	1917	Bordo et al. (2001), Flath (2005)
	A Tokyo earthquake led to bad debts that shook the Bank of Tokyo and Chosen. They were restructured with government aid.	September 1923	Bernanke and James (1990)
	A banking panic led to tighter regulation. The failure of Tokyo Watanabe bank led to runs and a wave of failures; fifteen banks were unable to make their payments. The government's unwillingness to bail out the banks led to more uncertainty and other runs. The crisis resulted in bank consolidations.	April 1927	Bernanke and James (1990), Bordo et al. (2001)

TABLE A.4.1 Continued

Country	Brief summary	Year	Source
	Banks suffered from a sharp decline in stock market and real estate prices. In 1995, estimates of nonperforming loans were $469–1,000 billion or 10–25 percent of GDP; at the end of 1998 they were estimated at $725 billion or 18 percent of GDP; and in 2002 they were 35 percent of total loans. Seven banks were nationalized, sixty-one financial institutions closed, and twenty-eight institutions merged.	1992–1997	Bordo et al. (2001), Caprio and Klingebiel (2003)
Jordan	The third largest bank failed.	August 1989–1990	Caprio and Klingebiel (2003)
Kenya	Fifteen percent of financial system liabilities faced liquidity and solvency problems.	1985–1989	Caprio and Klingebiel (2003)
	There were interventions in two local banks.	1992	Caprio and Klingebiel (2003)
	There were serious solvency problems with banks accounting for more than 30 percent of financial system assets.	1993–1995	Caprio and Klingebiel (2003)
	Nonperforming loans reached 19 percent.	1996	Caprio and Klingebiel (2003)
Korea	Financial deregulation led to an increase in the number of banks.	January 1986	Shin and Hahm (1998), Reinhart (2002)
	Through May 2002, five banks were forced to exit the market through a "purchase and assumption formula," 303 financial institutions (215 of them credit unions) shut down, and four banks were nationalized. Banking system nonperforming loans peaked between 30 and 40 percent and fell to about 3 percent by March 2002.	July 1997	Bordo et al. (2001), Reinhart (2002), Caprio and Klingebiel (2003)

(*continued*)

TABLE A.4.1 Continued

Country	Brief summary	Year	Source
Kuwait	About 40 percent of loans were nonperforming by 1986.	1983	Caprio and Klingebiel (2003)
Kyrgyz Republic	About 80–90 percent of banking system loans were doubtful. Four small banks closed in 1995.	1993	Caprio and Klingebiel (2003)
Lao People's Democratic Republic	Some banks experienced problems.	Early 1990s	Caprio and Klingebiel (2003)
Latvia	There was a run on banks with German connections; two large banks were hit especially hard.	July 1931	Bernanke and James (1990)
	Between 1995 and 1999, thirty-five banks saw their licenses revoked, were closed, or ceased operations.	1994–1999	Caprio and Klingebiel (2003)
Lebanon	Four banks became insolvent, and eleven resorted to Central Bank lending.	1988–1990	Caprio and Klingebiel (2003)
Lesotho	One of four commercial banks had nonperforming loans.	1988	Caprio and Klingebiel (2003)
Liberia	Seven out of eleven banks were not operational, accounting for 60 percent of bank assets.	1991–1995	Caprio and Klingebiel (2003)
Lithuania	In 1995, twelve small banks out of twenty-five banks were liquidated; three private banks (29 percent of banking system deposits) failed, and three state-owned banks were deemed insolvent.	1995–1996	Caprio and Klingebiel (2003)
Macedonia	About 70 percent of banking system loans were nonperforming. The government took over banks' foreign debt and closed the second largest bank.	1993–1994	Caprio and Klingebiel (2003)
Madagascar	Twenty-five percent of bank loans were deemed unrecoverable.	1988	Caprio and Klingebiel (2003)

TABLE A.4.1 Continued

Country	Brief summary	Year	Source
Malaysia	There were runs on some branches of a large domestic bank following the collapse of a related bank in Hong Kong. Insolvent institutions accounted for 3 percent of financial system deposits; marginally recapitalized and possibly insolvent institutions accounted for another 4 percent.	July 1985–1988	Kaminsky and Reinhart (1999), Bordo et al. (2001), Caprio and Klingebiel (2003)
	The finance company sector was restructured, and the number of finance institutions was reduced from thirty-nine to ten through mergers. Two finance companies were taken over by the Central Bank, including the largest independent finance company. Two banks—accounting for 14 percent of financial system assets—were deemed insolvent and were to be merged with other banks. Nonperforming loans peaked between 25 and 35 percent of banking system assets but fell to 10.8 percent by March 2002.	September 1997	Bordo et al. (2001), Reinhart (2002), Caprio and Klingebiel (2003)
Mali	The nonperforming loans of the largest bank reached 75 percent.	1987–1989	Caprio and Klingebiel (2003)
Mauritania	In 1984, five major banks had nonperforming assets in 45–70 percent of their portfolios.	1984–1993	Caprio and Klingebiel (2003)
Mauritius	The Central Bank closed two out of twelve commercial banks for fraud and irregularities.	1997	Caprio and Klingebiel (2003)
Mexico	The Mexican government borrowed widely and then suspended payments (June 1885); foreign investments fell, leading to a credit crisis and bank runs, and banks stopped	1883	Conant (1915)

(continued)

TABLE A.4.1 Continued

Country	Brief summary	Year	Source
	lending. National Bank and Mercantile Bank merged into National Bank of Mexico (Banamex) in 1884 to meet the government's demand for a loan.		
	National Bank absorbed Mexican Mercantile Bank, its main competitor.	1893	Conant (1915)
	There was a severe credit shortage due to the U.S. crash; banks could not collect debts; the Mexican Central Bank and many state banks failed. Other banks survived with federal assistance or by merging. The failures caused many bankruptcies and prevented economic activity. The government cautioned against overexpansion of credit; in February a circular warned against unsafe loans, and restrictions were imposed in June.	February 1908	Conant (1915)
	Payments were suspended after a run on the major banks.	1929	Bernanke and James (1990)
	There was capital flight; the government responded by nationalizing the private banking system.	1981–1982	Bordo et al. (2001)
	The government took over the banking system.	September 1982–1991	Kaminsky and Reinhart (1999), Caprio and Klingebiel (2003)
	Several financial institutions that held Ajustabonos were hurt by the rise in real interest rates in the second half of 1992.	October 1992	Kaminsky and Reinhart (1999)
	In 1994, nine banks were intervened and eleven participated in the loan/purchase recapitalization programs of thirty-four commercial banks. The nine banks accounted for 19 percent of financial system assets and were deemed insolvent. One percent of bank assets were owned by foreigners, and by 1998,	1994–1997	Bordo et al. (2001), Caprio and Klingebiel (2003), Jácome (2008)

TABLE A.4.1 Continued

Country	Brief summary	Year	Source
	18 percent of bank assets were held by foreign banks.		
Morocco	The banking sector experienced problems.	1983	Caprio and Klingebiel (2003)
Mozambique	The main commercial bank experienced solvency problems, which were apparent after 1992.	1987–1995	Caprio and Klingebiel (2003)
Myanmar	The largest state-owned commercial bank was reported to have large nonperforming loans.	1996–?	Caprio and Klingebiel (2003)
Nepal	In early 1988, the reported arrears of three banks, accounting for 95 percent of the financial system, averaged 29 percent of assets.	1988	Caprio and Klingebiel (2003)
The Netherlands	The Bank of Amsterdam closed by government decree; liquidation began in January and lasted many years.	December 1819–1829	Conant (1915)
	Discount rates were volatile and eventually reached a crisis high.	1897	Bordo et al. (2001), Homer and Sylla (1991)
	Temporary closure of the Amsterdam Exchange led to a sharp acceleration in the evolution of banking. Large commercial banks replaced older institutions, and many banks were taken over or replaced.	1914	't Hart et al. (1997), Bordo et al. (2001)
	Scores of banks failed, and many others experienced serious problems. The banking crisis resulted in banks' working more closely together and in more centralization. Banks financed industry more heavily after the war; after the crisis, industrial growth stalled.	1921	't Hart et al. (1997), Bordo et al. (2001)
	The major bank, Amsterdamsche Bank, took over another large bank, Noordhollandsch Landbouwcrediet.	1939	Bordo et al. (2001)

(continued)

375

TABLE A.4.1 Continued

Country	Brief summary	Year	Source
New Zealand	One large state-owned bank, with 25 percent of banking assets, experienced solvency problems, with a high percentage of non-performing loans.	1987–1990	Bordo et al. (2001), Caprio and Klingebiel (2003)
Nicaragua	Banking system nonperforming loans reached 50 percent in 1996.	1987–1996	Caprio and Klingebiel (2003)
	Four out of eleven banks, representing about 40 percent of deposits, were intervened and sold to other financial institutions.	2000–2002	Jácome (2008)
Niger	In the mid-1980s, banking system nonperforming loans reached 50 percent. Four banks liquidated, three restructured in the late 1980s, and more restructured in 2002.	1983–?	Caprio and Klingebiel (2003)
Nigeria	In 1993, insolvent banks had 20 percent of banking system assets and 22 percent of deposits. In 1995, almost half the banks reported being in financial distress.	1992–1995	Bordo et al. (2001), Caprio and Klingebiel (2003)
	Distressed banks had 4 percent of banking system assets.	1997	Bordo et al. (2001), Caprio and Klingebiel (2003)
Norway	There was real estate speculation; the bubble burst when interest rates increased, and many banks failed. The Bank of Norway stepped in and prevented the crisis from spreading.	1898	Jonung and Hagberg (2002)
	Reckless lending during the war and the global downswing in the early 1920s causes bank instability.	1921–1923	Bordo et al. (2001), Jonung and Hagberg (2002)
	Norway abandoned the gold standard; the Norges Bank provided much support to smaller banks to prevent a systemic crisis. The situation was more successfully managed than the 1921 crisis.	1931	Bordo et al. (2001), Øksendal (2007)

TABLE A.4.1 Continued

Country	Brief summary	Year	Source
	Legislation introducing a tax on bank deposits led to many withdrawals.	1936	Bernanke and James (1990)
	Two regional savings banks failed. The banks were eventually merged and bailed out. The Central Bank provided special loans to six banks suffering from the recession of 1985–1986 and from problem real estate loans. The state took control of the three largest banks, with 85 percent of banking system assets.	1987–1993	Kaminsky and Reinhart (1999), Bordo et al. (2001), Jonung and Hagberg (2002), Caprio and Klingebiel (2003)
Panama	In 1988, the banking system had a nine-week banking holiday. The financial position of most state-owned and private commercial banks was weak, and fifteen banks ceased operations.	1988–1989	Caprio and Klingebiel (2003)
Papua New Guinea	Eighty-five percent of savings and loan associations ceased operations.	1989–?	Caprio and Klingebiel (2003)
Paraguay	The Bank of Paraguay and River Plate Bank suspended payments, and there was a severe run; gold prices increased 300 percent, and banks eventually liquidated.	1890	Conant (1915)
	The Government Superintendency intervened in most domestic private and public banks and in a number of finance companies by the end of 1998, including the largest bank and savings and loan institution. By the end of 1999, the banks were mostly foreign-owned, with over 80 percent of bank assets in foreign hands. All banks were deemed sound in 2000. Two banks, with about 10 percent of deposits, were intervened and closed in 1997. A medium-sized bank, with 6.5 percent of deposits, was closed in 1998.	1995–1999	Bordo et al. (2001), Caprio and Klingebiel (2003), Jácome (2008)

(continued)

377

TABLE A.4.1 Continued

Country	Brief summary	Year	Source
	The third largest bank, with nearly 10 percent of deposits, was intervened and closed.	2002	Caprio and Klingebiel (2003), Jácome (2008)
Peru	Gold coinage was suspended, and the country had a silver standard for twenty-five years.	1872–1873	Conant (1915), Reinhart and Rogoff (2008a)
	Two large banks failed. The rest of the system suffered from high levels of nonperforming loans and financial disintermediation following the nationalization of the banking system in 1987.	April 1983–1990	Kaminsky and Reinhart (1999), Bordo et al. (2001), Caprio and Klingebiel (2003)
	Capital outflows triggered a domestic credit crunch that unveiled solvency problems in a number of banks, including Banco Wiese, Banco Latino (16.7 percent and 3 percent of market share, respectively), and other smaller financial institutions. Bank resolution was applied to two banks (with nearly 21 percent of deposits). Instability also affected another six small banks (with 6.5 percent of deposits).	1999	Jácome (2008)
The Philippines	The commercial paper market collapsed, triggering bank runs and the failure of nonbank financial institutions and thrift banks. There were problems in two public banks accounting for 50 percent of banking system assets, 6 private banks accounting for 12 percent of banking system assets, 32 thrifts accounting for 53 percent of thrift banking assets, and 128 rural banks.	January 1981–1987	Kaminsky and Reinhart (1999), Bordo et al. (2001), Caprio and Klingebiel (2003)
	One commercial bank, 7 of 88 thrifts, and 40 of 750 rural banks were placed under receivership. Banking system nonperforming loans reached 12 percent by November 1998 and were expected to reach 20 percent in 1999.	July 1997–1998	Reinhart (2002), Caprio and Klingebiel (2003)

TABLE A.4.1 Continued

Country	Brief summary	Year	Source
Poland	Bank runs caused three large banks to stop payments; the bank shakeout lasted until 1927.	July 1926–1927	Bernanke and James (1990)
	There was a run on banks, especially those associated with Austrian Creditanstalt, representing spread of the Austrian crisis.	June 1931	Bernanke and James (1990)
	In 1991, seven of nine treasury-owned commercial banks (90 percent of credit), the Bank for Food Economy, and the cooperative banking system experienced solvency problems.	1991	Caprio and Klingebiel (2003)
Portugal	The Bank of Lisbon suspended payments; it had experienced a consistently troubled career because of its ties to the Portuguese government.	1828	Conant (1915)
	The Bank of Lisbon lost all credit, could not redeem its notes, and reorganized into the Bank of Portugal.	May 1846–1847	Conant (1915)
	Large budget deficits, the Barings crisis, and the Brazilian revolution led to currency depreciation. The government reneged on some domestic debt and renegotiated foreign debt to reduce interest payments. The crisis had a large impact on growth.	1890	Conant (1915), Bordo and Eichengreen (1999)
	Bank failures were common in the postwar economy.	1920	Bordo et al. (2001)
	Multiple bank failures occurred.	1923	Bordo et al. (2001)
	Portugal abandoned the gold standard.	1931–1932	Bordo et al. (2001)
Romania	German-controlled banks and other banks collapsed; there were heavy runs on banks.	July 1931	Bernanke and James (1990)

(continued)

TABLE A.4.1 Continued

Country	Brief summary	Year	Source
	In 1990, nonperforming loans reached 25–30 percent in the six main state-owned banks.	1990	Caprio and Klingebiel (2003)
Russia	The Bank of Russia closed in April; specie payments were suspended and never resumed. A permanent treasury deficit meant that several loans were necessary, and there was a hopeless credit situation.	April 1862–1863	Conant (1915)
	Skopine community bank garnered deposits from all over the empire but kept low reserves; the bubble burst in 1875 when it could not pay its deposits. There was limited communal banking after that.	1875	Conant (1915), Reinhart and Rogoff (2008a)
	Joint-stock commercial banks were loaded with nonperforming assets; many small banks failed, although large ones were protected by the state bank.	1896	Cameron (1967)
	The interbank loan market stopped working due to concerns about connected lending in many new banks.	August 1995	Caprio and Klingebiel (2003)
	Nearly 720 banks, representing half of those in operation, were deemed insolvent. The banks accounted for 4 percent of sector assets and 32 percent of retail deposits. Eighteen banks, holding 40 percent of sector assets and 41 percent of household deposits, were in serious difficulties and needed rescue.	1998–1999	Caprio and Klingebiel (2003)
Rwanda	One well-connected bank closed.	1991	Caprio and Klingebiel (2003)
Santo Domingo	The National Bank failed after unsuccessfully trying to adopt the gold standard; bank notes were not accepted anywhere.	1894	Conant (1915)

TABLE A.4.1 Continued

Country	Brief summary	Year	Source
Sao Tome and Principe	At the end of 1992, 90 percent of the monobank's loans were non-performing. In 1993, the monobank liquidated, and two new banks were licensed and took over most assets. In 1994, credit operations at one new bank were suspended.	1991	Caprio and Klingebiel (2003)
Scotland	Western Bank failed due to reckless banking practices. The bank made various bad loans to four firms; when discovered, the accounts were stopped and the firms closed. There was a panic on the stock exchange; depositors withdraw their accounts, and the bank failed.	October 1857–1858	Conant (1915)
	The City of Glasgow Bank failed due to the falsification of books for three years, with loans made to four firms; the failure ruined share-holders but not creditors.	September 1878–1880	Conant (1915)
	Bank of Scotland absorbed Caledo-nian Bank, and North of Scotland Bank absorbed Town and Country Bank.	March 1908	Conant (1915)
Senegal	In 1988, 50 percent of loans were nonperforming. Six commercial banks and one development bank (with 20–30 percent of financial system assets) closed.	1988–1991	Bordo et al. (2001), Caprio and Klingebiel (2003)
Sierra Leone	In 1995, 40–50 percent of banking system loans were nonperforming, undergoing bank recapitalization and restructuring.	1990	Caprio and Klingebiel (2003)
Singapore	Nonperforming loans rose to $200 million or 0.6 percent of GDP.	1982	Bordo et al. (2001), Caprio and Klingebiel (2003)

(*continued*)

TABLE A.4.1 Continued

Country	Brief summary	Year	Source
Slovakia	In 1997, unrecoverable loans were estimated at 101 billion crowns—about 31 percent of loans and 15 percent of GDP.	1991	Caprio and Klingebiel (2003)
Slovenia	Three banks (with two-thirds of banking system assets) were restructured.	1993–1994	Caprio and Klingebiel (2003)
South Africa	Trust Bank experienced problems.	December 1977–1978	Bordo et al. (2001), Reinhart (2002), Caprio and Klingebiel (2003)
	Some banks experienced problems.	1989	Caprio and Klingebiel (2003)
Spain	During the Peninsular War, Spain was occupied by France, and the Bank of St. Charles was essentially dead after 1814.	1814–1817	Conant (1915)
	The Bank of St. Charles reorganized into the Bank of Ferdinand.	July 1829	Conant (1915)
	The Bank of Isabella II (created by the government to punish the Bank of Ferdinand in 1844) and the Bank of Ferdinand consolidated into one, the Bank of Ferdinand. The Bank of Ferdinand bore the Bank of Isabella's debts and was completely at the mercy of the state. In 1848, with the cash reserve of the bank decreasing, circulation increasing, the government demanded more loans, the bank was a victim of theft and embezzlement. The government reorganized the bank into the Bank of Spain to resemble Bank of England.	February 1846–1847	Conant (1915)
	A number of Catalonian universal banks became insolvent, which eventually led to the failure of the most prominent and oldest credit	1920–1923	Bordo et al. (2001)

TABLE A.4.1 Continued

Country	Brief summary	Year	Source
	institutions, with the severest impact on Barcelona.		
	Two major banks failed.	1924–1925	Bernanke and James (1990), Bordo et al. (2001)
	The country avoided the worst of the Great Depression by staying off the gold standard; it experienced runs, but the Bank of Spain could lend freely as a lender of last resort.	1931	Bordo et al. (2001), Temin (2008)
	The Bank of Spain began rescuing a number of smaller banks. In 1978–1983, 24 institutions were rescued, 4 were liquidated, 4 were merged, and 20 small and medium-sized banks were nationalized. These 52 banks out of 110, representing 20 percent of banking system deposits, were experiencing solvency problems.	1977–1985	Kaminsky and Reinhart (1999), Bordo et al. (2001), Caprio and Klingebiel (2003)
Sri Lanka	State-owned banks, comprising 70 percent of the banking system, were estimated to have nonperforming loans of 35 percent.	1989–1993	Caprio and Klingebiel (2003)
Swaziland	The Central Bank took over three other banks.	1995	Caprio and Klingebiel (2003)
Sweden	Depreciation of gold led to the Bullion Report (similar to the Report on Irish Currency of 1804).	January 1811	Conant (1915)
	There were severe banking crises.	1876–1879	Jonung and Hagberg (2002)
	The Riksbank Act made the Riksbank the central bank and gave it exclusive rights to issue bank notes.	1897	Bordo et al. (2001), Jonung and Hagberg (2002)
	There was a lending boom, and decreasing confidence in the stability of the banking system led to bank runs. Reserves depreciated,	1907	Bordo and Eichengreen (1999), Jonung and Hagberg (2002)

(*continued*)

TABLE A.4.1 Continued

Country	Brief summary	Year	Source
	but Riksbank extended loans to national banks. Output was negatively affected, but the economy recovered quickly.		
	One of severest banking crises in Swedish banking history occurred following a steep recession.	1922–1923	Jonung and Hagberg (2002)
	Banks tied to the financier Ivar Kreuger suffered after his death; the banks suffered large losses, but depositors were protected by the government and did not suffer from the failures.	1931–1932	Bordo et al. (2001), Jonung and Hagberg (2002)
	The Swedish government rescued Nordbanken, the second largest bank. Nordbanken and Gota Bank, with 22 percent of banking system assets, were insolvent. Sparbanken Foresta, accounting for 24 percent of banking system assets, intervened. Five of the six largest banks, accounting for over 70 percent of banking system assets, experienced difficulties.	November 1991–1994	Kaminsky and Reinhart (1999), Bordo et al. (2001), Jonung and Hagberg (2002), Caprio and Klingebiel (2003)
Switzerland	Switzerland could not obtain its supply of coin from France; bank clients rushed to redeem their notes for coin; the banks cut down discounts and loans, which led to an economic downturn.	July 1870–1871	Conant (1915)
	There was a wave of bank failures and consolidations.	1910–1913	Vogler (2001)
	Swiss banks were badly shaken by the German banking crisis; total assets shrank, and many banks restructured.	1931	Bordo et al. (2001), Vogler (2001)
	There was continued distress due to pressures from America and the Great Depression and due to the German banking crisis of 1931.	1933	Bordo et al. (2001), Vogler (2001)

TABLE A.4.1 Continued

Country	Brief summary	Year	Source
Taiwan	Four trust companies and eleven corporations failed.	1983–1984	Bordo et al. (2001), Caprio and Klingebiel (2003)
	The failure of Changua Fourth sparked runs on other credit unions.	July 1995	Bordo et al. (2001), Caprio and Klingebiel (2003)
	Banking system nonperforming loans were estimated at 15 percent at the end of 1998.	1997–1998	Bordo et al. (2001), Caprio and Klingebiel (2003)
Tajikistan	One of largest banks became insolvent, and one small bank closed.	1996–?	Caprio and Klingebiel (2003)
Tanzania	In 1987, the main financial institutions had arrears amounting to half their portfolios. The National Bank of Commerce, with 95 percent of banking system assets, became insolvent in 1990.	1987	Caprio and Klingebiel (2003)
Thailand	Following the stock market crash, one of the largest finance companies failed. The bailout of the financial sector began.	March 1979	Kaminsky and Reinhart (1999)
	Large losses in a finance company led to runs and government intervention. Authorities intervened in fifty finance and security firms and five commercial banks, with about 25 percent of financial system assets; three commercial banks (with 14 percent of commercial bank assets) were deemed insolvent.	October 1983–1987	Kaminsky and Reinhart (1999), Bordo et al. (2001), Caprio and Klingebiel (2003)
	As of May 2002, the Bank of Thailand shut down fifty-nine of ninety-one financial companies (13 percent of financial system assets and 72 percent of finance company assets) and one of fifteen domestic banks and nationalized four banks. A publicly owned assets manage-	May 1996	Bordo et al. (2001), Reinhart (2002), Caprio and Klingebiel (2003)

(*continued*)

385

TABLE A.4.1 Continued

Country	Brief summary	Year	Source
	ment company held 29.7 percent of financial system assets as of March 2002. Nonperforming loans peaked at 33 percent of total loans and were reduced to 10.3 percent of total loans in February 2002.		
Togo	The banking sector experienced solvency problems.	1993–1995	Caprio and Klingebiel (2003)
Trinidad and Tobago	Several financial institutions faced solvency problems, and three government-owned banks merged.	1982–1993	Caprio and Klingebiel (2003)
Tunisia	Most commercial banks were under-capitalized.	1991–1995	Caprio and Klingebiel (2003)
Turkey	There were runs on branches of German banks in the wake of the German crisis.	July 1931	Bernanke and James (1990)
	Three banks were merged with the state-owned Agriculture Bank and then liquidated; two large banks were restructured.	1982–1985	Bordo et al. (2001), Caprio and Klingebiel (2003)
	The start of the war led to massive withdrawals and a run on banks, prompting the government to guarantee all deposits.	January 1991	Kaminsky and Reinhart (1999)
	Three banks failed in April.	April 1994	Bordo et al. (2001), Caprio and Klingebiel (2003)
	Two banks closed, and nineteen banks have been taken over by the Savings Deposit Insurance Fund.	2000	Caprio and Klingebiel (2003)
Uganda	During 1994–1998, half the banking system faced solvency problems. During 1998–2002, various banks recapitalized and privatized or closed.	1994–2002	Caprio and Klingebiel (2003)
Ukraine	By 1997, 32 of 195 banks were being liquidated, while 25 others were undergoing financial rehabilitation. Bad loans amounted to 50–65 per-	1997–1998	Caprio and Klingebiel (2003)

TABLE A.4.1 Continued

Country	Brief summary	Year	Source
	cent of assets, even in some leading banks. In 1998, banks were further hit by the government's decision to restructure its debt.		
United Kingdom	There was mass speculation due to Napoleon's Berlin Decree. Many new country banks issued notes; excessive issue led to a severe fall on the London exchange; the treasury rescued the banks on April 11, 1811.	1810	Conant (1915)
	A good harvest and low prices led to speculation; a general depression of property prices affected production industries. Eighty-nine country banks went bankrupt; three hundred to five hundred ceased business, and there was an increased demand for Bank of England notes.	1815–1817	Conant (1915)
	Speculation in real and imaginary investments financed by unregulated country banking caused a bubble in stocks and Latin American foreign sovereign debt, followed by a stock market crash; six London banks closed (including Henry Thornton's Bank), and sixty country banks closed; there was a panic in London.	April 1825–1826	Conant (1915)
	Three banks failed in March 1837; the Bank of England gave generous advances to other banks to prevent a panic, but still they drifted toward bankruptcy. The country raised the discount rate and borrowed from France and Germany.	March 1837–1839	Conant (1915)
	The Irish Potato Famine and the railroad mania led to a steady drain on bullion; reduced resources led to a panic. Firms overextended	April 1847–1848	Conant (1915)

(continued)

TABLE A.4.1 Continued

Country	Brief summary	Year	Source
	into railroad endeavors and sugar plantations; they began failing, which led to bank failures.		
	The discovery of Australian and Californian gold fields led to massive speculation and then collapse, paralyzing finances throughout world (the crisis spread from the United States to Europe, South America, and the Far East). Most banks suspended operations; the Bank of England was the only source of a discount.	August 1857	Conant (1915)
	The Bank Act of 1844 was suspended to deal with the panic; demands were paid in gold. The Joint Stock Discount company failed, and various industries provided discounts.	May 1866	Conant (1915)
	There was a provincial bank crisis: the West of England and South Wales District Bank failed (December 9), and the City of Glasgow Bank failed (October 2) due to depressed confidence.	October 1878	Conant (1915)
	The House of Baring's portfolio was mostly in securities in Argentina and Uruguay. The Buenos Aires Water Supply and Drainage Company loan failed, but the Bank of England, assisted by the Bank of France and Russia, organized a rescue, which prevented Barings from failing. A short and mild recession followed.	November 1890	Conant (1915), Bordo and Eichengreen (1999)
	There was a "secondary" banking crisis.	1974–1976	Bordo et al. (2001), Caprio and Klingebiel (2003)
	Johnson Matthey Bankers failed.	1984	Caprio and Klingebiel (2003)
	The Bank of Credit and Commerce International failed.	1991	Caprio and Klingebiel (2003)
	Barings failed.	1995	Caprio and Klingebiel (2003)

388

TABLE A.4.1 Continued

Country	Brief summary	Year	Source
United States	State banks suspended specie payments due to the War of 1812, paralyzing the treasury's operations.	August 1814	Conant (1915)
	Forty-six banks were rendered insolvent due to demands for specie by Second Bank of the United States.	1818–1819	Conant (1915)
	Preceding England's crisis, the Bank of the United States and all other banks were brought to the verge of suspension.	January 1825	Conant (1915)
	Three banks failed; the Bank of England gave generous advances to other banks to prevent a panic. The failures began in New Orleans and New York and spread to other cities' banks.	1836–1838	Conant (1915)
	Second Bank of the United States liquidated; lenders were repaid, but shareholders lost all interest; twenty-six local banks failed.	March 1841	Conant (1915)
	The discovery of Australian and Californian gold fields led to massive speculation and then collapse, paralyzing finances throughout the world (the crisis spread from the United States to Europe, South America, and the Far East). Most banks suspended operations; the Bank of England was the only source of discount.	August 1857	Conant (1915)
	The government suspended specie payments until 1879, driving up the price of gold (which peaked in 1864) and all other retail items.	December 1861	Conant (1915)
	There was a U.S. panic due to the Civil War.	April 1864	Conant (1915)
	The Philadelphian banking firm Jay Cooke and Company failed, triggering a recession that lasted until 1877.	September 1873	Conant (1915)

(continued)

TABLE A.4.1 Continued

Country	Brief summary	Year	Source
	Weak commodity prices and a series of brokerage firm failures led to bank runs and suspended payments, mostly in the New York region. The output effects were mild.	May 1884	Conant (1915), Bordo and Eichengreen (1999)
	Monetary uncertainty and a stock market crash led to bank runs. Political action was taken to ameliorate the crisis; there was a severe decline in output, but the economy recovered quickly.	1890	Conant (1915), Bordo and Eichengreen (1999)
	There were global credit restrictions and domestic financial excesses, increasing the number of state banks, and a rising ratio of deposits to cash reserves set the stage for a crisis. Real estate and stock speculation bubbles burst; the crisis spread from New York nationwide. The growth rate fell by 9 percent per year. J. P. Morgan, the Bank of Montreal, and the treasury of New York replenished liquidity.	March 1907	Conant (1915), Bordo and Eichengreen (1999)
	The New York Stock Exchange closed until December in response to the war; however, a banking crisis was avoided by flooding the country with emergency currency to prevent hasty withdrawals.	July 1914	Bordo et al. (2001)
	During the Great Depression, thousands of banks closed; failures were correlated with particular Federal Reserve districts. The Bank of the USA failed in December 1930; between August 1931 and January 1932, 1,860 banks failed.	1929–1933	Bernanke and James (1990), Bordo et al. (2001)
	There were 1,400 savings and loan and 1,300 bank failures.	1984–1991	Bordo et al. (2001), Caprio and Klingebiel (2003)

TABLE A.4.1 Continued

Country	Brief summary	Year	Source
Uruguay	The National Bank failed.	1893	Conant (1915)
	There was a run on banks to redeem bank notes due to a government decree to reduce the circulation of notes.	September 1898	Conant (1915)
	Banco Mercantil failed. A wave of bank mergers and bankruptcies developed, driven by high real interest rates.	March 1971	Kaminsky and Reinhart (1999)
	A large-scale run on banks came in the wake of the Argentine devaluation, which marked the end of the Argentine *tablita*. The institutions affected accounted for 30 percent of financial system assets; insolvent banks accounted for 20 percent of financial system deposits.	March 1981–1984	Kaminsky and Reinhart (1999), Bordo et al. (2001), Caprio and Klingebiel (2003)
	The government-owned mortgage bank was recapitalized in December 2001. The banking system had 33 percent of its deposits withdrawn in the first seven months of 2002. In 2002, four banks (with 33 percent of total bank assets) were closed, and fixed-term deposits (CDs) were restructured and their maturity extended.	2002	Caprio and Klingebiel (2003), Jácome (2008)
Venezuela	There were notable bank failures in 1978, 1981, 1982, 1985, and 1986.	1978–1986	Bordo et al. (2001), Caprio and Klingebiel (2003)
	There were runs on Banco Latino, the country's second largest bank, which closed in January 1994. Insolvent banks accounted for 35 percent of financial system deposits. Authorities intervened in seventeen of forty-seven banks that held 50 percent of deposits, nationalized nine banks, and closed seven more in 1994. The government intervened in five more banks in 1995.	October 1993–1995	Kaminsky and Reinhart (1999), Bordo et al. (2001), Caprio and Klingebiel (2003), Jácome (2008)

(*continued*)

TABLE A.4.1 Continued

Country	Brief summary	Year	Source
Vietnam	Two of four large state-owned commercial banks (with 51 percent of banking system loans) were deemed insolvent; the remaining two experienced significant solvency problems. Several joint stock companies were in severe financial distress. Banking system nonperforming loans reached 18 percent in late 1998.	1997–?	Caprio and Klingebiel (2003)
Yemen	Banks suffered from extensive nonperforming loans and heavy foreign currency exposure.	1996–?	Caprio and Klingebiel (2003)
Zambia	Meridian Bank, with 13 percent of commercial bank assets, became insolvent.	1995	Caprio and Klingebiel (2003)
Zimbabwe	Two of five commercial banks had a high level of nonperforming loans.	1995	Bordo et al. (2001), Caprio and Klingebiel (2003)

NOTES

Preface

1. Notably those of Winkler (1928), Wynne (1951), and Marichal (1989).
2. More recently, there was Ferguson's (2008) excellent and equally engaging history of the foundations of currency and finance. See also MacDonald (2006).

Preamble: Some Initial Intuitions on Financial Fragility and the Fickle Nature of Confidence

1. See Shleifer and Vishny (1992) and Fostel and Geanakoplos (2008) for interesting technical analyses of how changing fortunes of optimists and pessimists can drive leverage cycles.
2. Classic articles on multiple equilibria and financial fragility include those of Diamond and Dybvig (1983) and Allen and Gale (2007) on bank runs, Calvo (1988) on public debt, and Obstfeld (1996) on exchange rates. See also Obstfeld and Rogoff (1996), chapters 6 and 9.
3. See Buchanan and Wagner (1977).
4. Krugman (1979).
5. See, for instance, North and Weingast (1988) and also Ferguson (2008).
6. See Bernanke (1983) and Bernanke and Gertler (1990), for example.
7. We term the recent global crisis the "Second Great Contraction" in analogy with Friedman and Schwartz's (1963) depiction of the 1930's Great Depression as "The Great Contraction." *Contraction* provides an apt description of the wholesale collapse of credit markets and asset prices that has marked the depth of these traumatic events, along with, of course, contracting employment and output.

Chapter 1   Varieties of Crises and Their Dates

1. See Reinhart and Rogoff (2004).
2. Frankel and Rose (1996).
3. Ibid.; Kaminsky and Reinhart (1999).
4. See Kaminsky and Reinhart (1999) for the construction of thresholds to date equity price crashes and Reinhart and Rogoff (2008b) for a depiction of the behavior of real estate prices on the eve of banking crises in industrialized economies.

5. See Kaminsky and Reinhart (1999), Caprio and Klingebiel (2003), Caprio et al. (2005), and Jácome (2008). For the period before World War II, Willis (1926), Kindleberger (1989), and Bordo et al. (2001) provide multicountry coverage on banking crises.

6. See Camprubri (1957) for Peru, Cheng (2003) and McElderry (1976) for China, and Noel (2002) for Mexico.

7. This is not meant to be an exhaustive list of the scholars who have worked on historical sovereign defaults.

8. Notably, that supplied by Lindert and Morton (1989), Suter (1992), Purcell and Kaufman (1993), and MacDonald (2006). Of course, required reading in this field includes Winkler (1933) and Wynne (1951). Important further readings include Eichengreen (1991a, 1991b, 1992), and Eichengreen and Lindert (1989).

9. At present, Honduras has remained in default since 1981.

10. Apparently an old saw in the marketplace is "More money has been lost because of four words than at the point of a gun. Those words are 'This time is different.'"

11. For example, during the mid-1990s Thailand claimed not to have a dollar peg but rather a peg to an (unspecified) basket of currencies. Investors could clearly see, however, that the basket did not contain much besides the dollar; the exchange rate of baht to dollars fluctuated only within narrow bands.

12. Central banks typically lose money in any unsuccessful intervention to prop up the currency because they are selling hard currency (e.g., dollars) in exchange for the local currency (e.g., baht). When the exchange rate for the local currency collapses, the intervening central bank suffers a capital loss.

Chapter 2   Debt Intolerance

1. Later, in chapter 8, we use new historical data on domestic public debt in emerging markets and find that it is a significant factor in some cases. However, introducing this consideration does not fundamentally change the remarkable phenomenon of serial default examined here.

2. The figures for Japan's level of debt relative to GDP are from International Monetary Fund, *World Economic Outlook*, October 2008.

3. Following the World Bank for some purposes, we divide developing countries according to their level of per capita income into two broad groups: middle-income countries (those with a GNP per capita in 2005 higher than US$755) and low-income countries. Most (but not all) emerging market economies with substantial access to private external financing are middle-income countries. Similarly, most (though not all) of the low-income countries do not have access to private capital markets and rely primarily on official sources of external funding.

4. Note that many of these default episodes lasted several years, as discussed in chapter 8.

5. Note that tables 2.1 and 2.2 measure *gross* total external debt because debtor governments have little capacity to tax or otherwise confiscate private citizens' assets held abroad. For example, when Argentina defaulted on US$95 billion of external debt in 2001, its citizens held foreign assets abroad estimated by some commentators at about US$120–150 billion. This phenomenon is not uncommon and was the norm in the debt crises of the 1980s.

6. Using an altogether different approach, an International Monetary Fund (2002) study on debt sustainability came up with external debt thresholds for developing countries (excluding the highly indebted poorest countries) that were in the neighborhood of 31 to 39 percent, depending on whether official financing was included or not. The results, which we will present later, suggest that country-specific thresholds for debt-intolerant countries should probably be even lower.

7. For particulars about the survey, see the September 2002 issue of *Institutional Investor* and their Web site. Though not critical to our following analysis, we interpret the ratings reported in each semiannual survey as capturing the risk of near-term default within one to two years.

8. One can use secondary market prices of external commercial bank debt, which are available for the time since the mid-1980s, to provide a measure of expected repayment for a number of emerging market countries. However, the Brady debt restructurings of the 1990s converted much of this bank debt to bond debt, so from 1992 onward the secondary market prices would have to be replaced by the Emerging Market Bond Index (EMBI) spread, which remains the most commonly used measure of risk at present. These market-based indicators introduce a serious sample selection bias: almost all the countries in the EMBI, and all the countries for which there is secondary debt price data for the 1980s, had a history of adverse credit events, leaving the control group of nondefaulters approximately the null set.

9. See the debt glossary (box 1.1) for a brief explanation of the various concepts of debt used in this study.

10. This exercise updates the work of Reinhart, Rogoff, and Savastano (2003a), who used thresholds based on a smaller sample of countries over 1979–2002.

11. Prasad, Rogoff, Wei, and Kose (2003) found that during the 1990s, economies that were de facto relatively financially open experienced, on average, a rise in consumption volatility relative to output volatility, contrary to the premise that the integration of capital markets spreads country-specific output risk. Prasad et al. also argue that the cross-country empirical evidence on the effects of capital market integration on growth shows only weak positive effects at best, and arguably none.

12. See Kaminsky, Reinhart, and Végh (2004) on this issue.

13. Of course, it was not always so. Prior to the 1980s, many governments viewed allowing foreign direct investment (FDI) as equivalent to mortgaging their futures, and hence preferred debt finance. And where FDI was more dominant (e.g., in oil and natural resources investment in the 1950s and 1960s), many countries eventually ended up seizing foreigners' operations later on, again leading to considerable trauma. Thus FDI should not be regarded as a panacea for poor growth performance.

14. Rogoff (1999) and Bulow and Rogoff (1990) argue that the legal systems of creditor countries should be amended so they no longer tilt capital flows toward debt.

15. The issues of debt reduction and debt reversal are taken up in box 5.3.

Chapter 3   A Global Database on
Financial Crises with a Long-Term View

1. Detailed citations are in our references and data appendix.

2. See Williamson's "regional" papers (1999, 2000a, 2000b). These regional papers provided time series for numerous developing countries for the mid-1800s to before World War II.

3. For OXLAD, see http://oxlad.qeh.ox.ac.uk/. See also Williamson (1999, 2000a, 2000b).

4. See http://gpih.ucdavis.edu/ and http://www.iisg.nl/hpw/. Although our analysis of inflation crises begins in 1500, many of the price series begin much earlier.

5. HSOUS is cited in the references as Carter et al. (2006); Garner's Economic History Data Desk is available at http://home.comcast.net/~richardgarner04/.

6. Reinhart and Rogoff (2004).

7. See Richard Bonney's European State Finance Database (ESFDB), available at http://www.le.ac.uk/hi/bon/ESFDB/frameset.html.

8. Allen and Unger's time series, *European Commodity Prices 1260–1914*, is available at http://www2.history.ubc.ca/unger/htm_files/new_grain.htm. Sevket Pamuk has constructed comparable series for Turkey through World War I (see http://www.ata.boun.edu.tr/sevket%20pamuk.htm).

9. See Maddison (2004). The TED is available at http://www.ggdc.net/.

10. PPP is calculated using Geary-Khamis weights. The Geary-Khamis dollar, also known as the international dollar, is a hypothetical unit of currency that has the same purchasing power that the U.S. dollar had in the United States at a given point in time. The year 1990 is used as a benchmark year for comparisons that run through time. The Geary-Khamis dollar shows how much a local currency unit is worth within the country's borders. It is used to make comparisons both between countries and over time.

11. There are exceptions. For instance, Rodney Edvinsson's careful estimates for Sweden from 1720 to 2000 or HSOUS for the United States beginning in 1790 offers a basis from which to examine earlier economic cycles and their relation to crises.

12. It is well known that revenues are intimately linked to the economic cycle.

13. See, for example, calculations in the background material to Reinhart and Rogoff (2004), available on the authors' Web pages.

14. See Mitchell (2003a, 2003b) and Kaminsky, Reinhart, and Végh (2004).

15. See Brahmananda (2001), Yousef (2002), and Baptista (2006).

16. These numbers are a lower bound because they do not include the many sovereign defaults prior to 1800 and, as regards domestic defaults, we have only begun to skim the surface; see Reinhart and Rogoff (2008c).

17. This description comes from the IMF's Web site, http://www.imf.org/external/data.htm: "Download time series data for GDP growth, inflation, unemployment, payments balances, exports, imports, external debt, capital flows, commodity prices, more."

18. For some countries, such as the Netherlands, Singapore, and the United States, practically all public debt is domestic.

19. For Australia, Ghana, India, Korea, and South Africa, among others, we have put together debt data for much of the colonial period.

20. See Miller (1926), Wynne (1951), Lindert and Morton (1989), and Marichal (1989).

21. Flandreau and Zumer (2004) are an important data source for Europe, 1880–1913.

22. Even under these circumstances, they continue to be a useful measure of gross capital inflows; the earlier sample included relatively little private external borrowing or bank lending.

23. Indonesia prior to 1972 is a good example of a country where this exercise was particularly useful.

24. Jeanne and Guscina (2006) compiled detailed data on the composition of domestic and external debt for nineteen important emerging markets for 1980–2005; Cowan et al. (2006) performed a similar exercise for all the developing countries of the Western Hemisphere for 1980–2004. See Reinhart, Rogoff, and Savastano (2003a) for an early attempt to measure domestic public debt for emerging markets.

25. http://www.imf.org/.

26. The fact that some of the world's poorest countries often fail to fully repay their debts to official lenders cannot be construed as a financial crisis in the conventional sense, because the official lenders often continue to provide aid nevertheless. See Bulow and Rogoff (2005) for a discussion of the related issue of whether multilateral development banks would be better structured as outright aid agencies.

Chapter 4 A Digression on the Theoretical Underpinnings of Debt Crises

1. During the late 1920s, Stalin's collectivization of farms led to mass starvation, and Russia needed money to import grain. As a result, in 1930 and 1931 the country sold some of its art treasures to foreigners, including the British oil magnate Calouste Gulbenkian and the American banker Andrew Mellon. But Stalin surely did not contemplate using any of the proceeds to repay old Tsarist debts.

2. See Persson and Tabellini (1990) and Obstfeld and Rogoff (1996) for literature surveys.

3. Tomz (2007).

4. See Eaton and Gersovitz (1981).

5. If countries simply borrow ever greater amounts without ever repaying, levels of debt relative to income must eventually explode provided the world (risk-adjusted) real interest rate exceeds the country's long-term real growth rate, which generally appears to be the case both in practice and under reasonable theoretical restrictions.

6. More generally, the game theoretic approach to reputation detailed by Eaton and Gersovitz typically admits to a huge variety of equilibria (outcomes), all of which can be rationalized by the same reputation mechanism.

7. See Bulow and Rogoff (1989b).

8. See Bulow and Rogoff (1989a).

9. Bulow and Rogoff (1989b) present a simple example based on a tariff war; Cole and Kehoe (1996) place this argument in a more general setting.

10. Borensztein et al. (1998) examine the empirics of the relationship of FDI and economic growth.

11. See Diamond and Rajan (2001).

12. See Jeanne (2009).

13. See Sachs (1984).

14. See, for example, Obstfeld and Rogoff (1996, chapter 6).

15. See Bulow and Rogoff (1988a, 1989a).

16. The citizens of a creditor country (outside of banks) may realize gains from trade just as the citizens of the debtor country do. Or, in the case of an international lending agency such as the IMF, creditors and debtors may be able to induce payments based on the IMF's fear that a default will lead to contagion to other borrowers.

17. See Jayachandran and Kremer (2006).

18. See, for example, Broner and Ventura (2007).

19. See Barro (1974).

20. See North and Weingast (1988).

21. See Kotlikoff, Persson, and Svensson (1988).

22. See Tabellini (1991).

23. For example, see Barro and Gordon (1983).

Chapter 5 Cycles of Sovereign Default on External Debt

1. MacDonald (2006); Ferguson (2008).

2. Cipolla (1982).

3. North and Weingast (1988); Weingast (1997).

4. Carlos et al. (2005).

5. Kindleberger (1989) is among the few scholars who emphasize that the 1950s still has to be viewed as a financial crisis era.

6. This comparison weights defaulting countries by share of world income. On an un-weighted basis (so that, for example, the poorest countries in Africa and South Asia receive the same weight as Brazil or the United States), the period from the late 1960s until 1982 saw an even lower percentage of independent countries in default.

7. Kindleberger (1989) emphasizes the prevalence of default after World War II, though he does not provide quantification.

8. Note that in figure 5.2 the debt crises of the 1980s do not loom as large as the previous cycle of defaults, for only middle- and low-income countries faced default in the 1980s while, in addition to emerging market economies, several advanced economies defaulted during the Great Depression and several more defaulted during World War II.

9. Calvo (1998) credits the late Rudy Dornbusch, who quotes the old banking adage, "It is not the speed that kills you. It is the sudden stop" (Dornbusch et al. 1995).

10. Reinhart, Rogoff, and Savastano (2003b) illustrated that countries with a history of external defaults also had a poor inflation track record.

11. Fisher (1933).

12. Domestic defaults produce even worse inflation outcomes; see chapter 9.

13. See Calvo, Leiderman, and Reinhart (1993); Dooley et al. (1996); and Chuhan et al. (1998) for earlier papers quantifying the role of external factors influencing capital flows to emerging markets and their access to credit markets. On predicting defaults with domestic and some global factors, see Manasse and Roubini (2005).

14. See Kaminsky, Reinhart, and Végh (2004) and Aguiar and Gopinath (2007).

15. See the work of Reinhart and Reinhart (2009), who document the common occurrence of "capital inflow bonanzas" in the years preceding debt crises in emerging markets. It is of note that this analysis also shows that capital flow bonanzas precede banking crises in both advanced and emerging market economies.

16. For a fuller account of the episode, see Baker (1994).

17. Hale (2003).

18. Box 5.3 summarizes some of the results in Reinhart, Rogoff, and Savastano (2003a), which presents empirical evidence of this "quick-to-releverage" pattern.

19. Reinhart, Rogoff, and Savastano (2003a).

Chapter 6   External Default through History

1. See Reinhart, Rogoff, and Savastano (2003a); they thank Harold James for this observation.

2. Winkler (1933), p. 29. One wonders if Thomas Jefferson read those words, in that he subsequently held that "the tree of liberty must be refreshed from time to time with the blood of patriots and tyrants."

3. Macdonald (2006).

4. Ibid.

5. Kindleberger (1989).

6. Reinhart, Rogoff, and Savastano (2003a).

7. For example, see Mauro et al. (2006).

8. Latin American states were not the only ones borrowing at this time. Greece (still engaged in its struggle for independence), Portugal, and Russia were also issuing and placing pound-denominated bonds in London.

9. For a fascinating fact-based account of this enterprise that reads like fiction, see David Sinclair's 2004 book, *The Land That Never Was: Sir Gregor MacGregor and the Most Audacious*

Fraud in History. Of the 250 settlers who crossed the Atlantic en route to Poyais (which was supposedly on the Bay of Honduras, site of the present Belize), only 50 survived to tell the tale.

10. MacGregor was also able to raise an additional £40,000 through various channels for a total of £200,000, well above the £163,000 raised by the nonfictional Federation of Central American States during the 1822–1825 lending boom.

Chapter 7   The Stylized Facts of Domestic Debt and Default

1. Reinhart, Rogoff, and Savastano (2003a) drew on national sources to develop a data set for selected developing countries and emerging markets covering the years 1990–2002. More recently, Jeanne and Guscina (2006) provided detailed data on domestic debt for nineteen important emerging markets from 1980 to 2005. Cowan et al. (2006) provided data for all the countries in the Western Hemisphere from 1980 (or 1990) to 2004. Reinhart and Rogoff (2008a) described a companion database covering a broad range of related variables, including external debt, on which we also draw here.

2. Domestic public debt has never amounted to much in a few Latin American countries (Uruguay stands out in this regard), and public debt markets are virtually nonexistent in the CFA African countries (originally the *Colonies françaises d'Afrique*).

3. Of course, during the early years of the interwar period, many countries pegged their currencies to gold.

4. It should also be noted that until the past ten to fifteen years, most countries' external debt was largely public debt. Private external borrowing has become more significant only over the past couple of decades; see Prasad et al. (2003). Arellano and Kocherlakota (2008) developed a model of the relationship between private debt and external government default.

5. See chapter 12 for a discussion of the aftermath and consequences of high inflation.

6. See Calvo (1991) on these "perilous" practices.

7. See Barro (1974).

8. See Woodford (1995) on the former, Diamond (1965) on the latter.

9. For example, Tabellini (1991) or Kotlikoff et al. (1988).

10. Including a handful of very recent domestic defaults, the sample can in fact be extended to more than seventy domestic defaults.

11. Brock (1989). The average reserve requirements for developing countries in Brock's sample from 1960 to early 1980s ran at about 0.25, more than three times that for advanced economies.

12. Another subtle type of default is illustrated by the Argentine government's treatment of its inflation-indexed debt in 2007. Most impartial observers agree that during this period, Argentina's official inflation rate considerably understated its actual inflation because of government manipulation. This understatement represented a partial default on index-linked debt by any reasonable measure, and it affected a large number of bondholders. Yet Argentina's de facto domestic bond default did not register heavily in the external press or with rating agencies.

Chapter 8   Domestic Debt

1. One of the best standard sources is Maddison (2004).

2. For instance, Bulow and Rogoff (1988b); Reinhart, Rogoff, and Savastano (2003a).

3. See Reinhart, Rogoff, and Savastano (2003a).

4. For example, the Kolmogorov-Smirnov test rejects the hypothesis that the two frequency distributions are equal at the 1 percent level.

5. See Gavin and Perotti (1997) and Kaminsky, Reinhart, and Végh (2004) for evidence on procyclical macroeconomic policies. See also Aguiar and Gopinath (2007) for a model in which the procyclical behavior of the current account can be rationalized by the high ratio of permanent to transitory shocks in emerging markets.

6. Of course, today's rich countries experienced much the same problems in earlier eras—when they, too, were serial defaulters and they, too, exhibited highly procyclical fisal policy.

7. See Cagan (1956). Seignorage revenue is simply the real income a government can realize by exercising its monopoly on printing currency. The revenue can be broken down into the quantity of currency needed to meet the growing transactions demand at constant prices and the remaining growth, which causes inflation, thereby lowering the purchasing power of existing currency. The latter effect is generally referred to as the inflation tax. In a classic paper, Sargent (1982) includes data on central banks' holdings of treasury bills after World War I for five countries (Austria, Czechoslovakia, Germany, Hungary, and Poland). But of course, these debts are essentially a wash on the consolidated government balance sheet.

8. See Dornbusch and Fischer (1993).

9. Of course, the possibility of using unanticipated inflation to default on nominal debt is well understood in the theoretical literature, such as Barro (1983).

10. The case of Brazil is exceptional in that some of the debt was indexed to inflation, although lags in the indexation scheme still made it possible for the government to largely inflate away the debt with a high enough rate of inflation. Indeed, this appears to be exactly what happened, for the country lurched in and out of hyperinflation for many years.

11. Calvo and Guidotti (1992) developed a model of the optimal maturity structure of nominal debt whereby the government trades off flexibility (the option to inflate away long-term debt when under financial duress) versus its high credibility for maintaining a low inflation rate (achieved by having very short-term debt, which is more difficult to inflate away).

Chapter 9   Domestic and External Default

1. It should also be noted that other economic indicators (besides inflation and per capita GDP growth, which we examine in detail) would provide a richer answer to the broad question of how bad conditions have to be before a country should contemplate default. (Specifically, the impacts of domestic versus foreign default on social indicators relating to poverty, health, income distribution, and so on, are, in principle, bound to be quite different.)

2. It is hardly surprising that inflation rises in the aftermath of external default, especially given the typical massive exchange rate depreciation.

3. We have excluded Bolivia's 1982 domestic default from these averages, because inflation peaked at over 11,000 percent in the year before $(t-1)$ the domestic default.

4. Reinhart and Savastano (2003) discuss the forcible conversion of foreign currency bank deposits (as was also seen in Argentina in 2002) during the hyperinflations in Bolivia and Peru.

5. The United States, of course, is the modern exception. Virtually all U.S. debt is domestic (as the Carter bonds have matured). Yet about 40 percent is held by nonresidents (mostly central banks and other official institutions), and all is dollar denominated. Thus, inflation in the United States would also affect nonresidents.

6. The huge spike in external defaults in the 1820s was due to the much-studied first wave of sovereign defaults of the newly independent Latin American countries. But Greece and Portugal also defaulted at that time.

7. See figure 9.6.

8. Drazen (1998).

9. See Alesina and Tabellini (1990).

10. Beyond simply reporting debt data, international financial institutions such as the International Monetary Fund and the World Bank can also help with disseminating information on best practices (see, for example, the institutional evolution discussed in Wallis and Weingast 1988).

Chapter 10   Banking Crises

1. See Gorton (1988) and Calomiris and Gorton (1991) on banking panics before World War II; Sundararajan and Baliño (1991) for several case studies of emerging markets; and Jácome (2008) on banking crises in Latin America.

2. Studies that encompass episodes in both advanced and emerging economies include those of Demirgüç-Kunt and Detragiache (1998), Kaminsky and Reinhart (1999), and Bordo et al. (2001).

3. See, for instance, Agénor et al. (2000).

4. Reinhart and Rogoff (2008a, 2008c) show that output growth typically decelerates in advance of a crisis.

5. See Diamond and Dybvig (1983).

6. Ibid.

7. See Bernanke and Gertler (1990).

8. See Kiyotaki and Moore (1997).

9. See, for example, Bernanke and Gertler (1995).

10. See Bernanke et al. (1999).

11. This refers to default on external debt. The widespread abrogation of gold clauses and other forms of restructuring—on domestic debt—by the United States and other developed economies during the Great Depression of the 1930s are considered sovereign defaults on domestic debt (debt issued under domestic law).

12. As we have already acknowledged, our accounting of financial crises in poorer countries may be incomplete, especially for earlier periods, despite our best efforts.

13. To be precise, the advanced countries experienced 7.2 crises, on average, versus 2.8 for emerging market countries.

14. See Obstfeld and Taylor (2004).

15. See Kaminsky and Reinhart (1999).

16. See Demirgüç-Kunt and Detragiache (1998). See also Drees and Pazarbasioglu (1998) for an insightful discussion of the Nordic experience with financial liberalization.

17. See Caprio and Klingebiel (1996).

18. To define a capital flow bonanza, Reinhart and Reinhart (2009) settled on an algorithm that provided uniform treatment across countries but was flexible enough to allow for significant cross-country variation in the current account. Like Kaminsky and Reinhart (1999), they selected a threshold to define bonanzas that is common across countries (in this case, the 20th percentile of the sample). This threshold included most of the better known episodes in the literature but was not so inclusive as to label as a bonanza a more "routine" deterioration in the current account. Because the underlying frequency distributions vary widely across countries, the common threshold produces quite disperse country-specific cutoffs. For instance, in the case of relatively closed India, the cutoff to define a bonanza is a ratio of current account deficit

to GDP in excess of 1.8 percent, while for trade-oriented Malaysia the comparable cutoff is a ratio of deficit to GDP of 6.6 percent.

19. Reinhart and Reinhart performed comparable exercises for currency, debt, and inflation crises.

20. See Reinhart and Reinhart (2009).

21. See Mendoza and Terrones (2008). See also the work of Kaminsky and Reinhart (1999), who also examined the growth in real credit available to the private sector around both banking and currency crises.

22. See Reinhart and Rogoff (2008b). Each year refers to the beginning of the crisis.

23. See Bordo and Jeanne (2002).

24. See Gerdrup (2003).

25. Historical comparisons are hard to come by, because most real housing price series are of recent vintage, but we do include in this category two older episodes: that of the United States during the Great Depression and that of Norway at the turn of the century (1898).

26. See the work of Ceron and Suarez (2006), who estimate its average duration at six years.

27. For example, Agénor et al. (2000) provide evidence that output and real consumption are far more volatile in emerging markets; Kaminsky, Reinhart, and Végh (2003) present evidence that the amplitude of the cycle in real government spending is orders of magnitude greater in emerging markets.

28. This notion is consistent with the fact that house prices are far more inertial than equity prices.

29. See Philippon (2007).

30. See Frydl (1999) and Norges Bank (2004). See also Sanhueza (2001), Hoggarth et al. (2005), and Caprio et al. (2005).

31. A similar problem plagues work on determining the effectiveness of foreign exchange intervention by measuring the profitability of such market purchases or sales. The results depend significantly on the width of the time window and on implicit assumptions of the cost of financing. See Neely (1995).

32. See Vale (2004).

33. See, for instance, Frydl (1999), Kaminsky and Reinhart (1999), and especially Rajan et al. (2008), who examine the output consequences of the credit channel following banking crises using micro data. We note that, of the cases of output collapses studied by Barro and Ursúa (2008), virtually all are associated with banking crises.

34. Revenues (from Mitchell, 2003a, 2003b) are deflated by consumer price indexes; the numerous sources of these data are given on a country-by-country and period-by-period basis in appendix A.2.

35. Indeed, in some important cases, such as that of Japan, the accelerated debt buildup goes on for more than a decade, so the three-year cutoff grossly understates the longer-term consequences.

36. Note that figure 10.10 gives the percentage of change in debt rather than debt relative to GDP in order not to distort the numbers by the large falls in GDP that sometimes accompany crises. However, the same basic message comes across looking at debt relative to GDP instead. Note that the calculations are based on total central government debt.

37. An important question is how rare banking crises, through sudden changes in market liquidity, might amplify the effects on asset prices, as analyzed by Barro (2009).

Chapter 11   Default through Debasement

1. See, for example, Sargent and Velde (2003). Ferguson (2008) provides an insightful discussion of the early roots of money.
2. See Winkler (1928).
3. MacDonald (2006).

Chapter 12   Inflation and Modern Currency Crashes

1. Végh (1992) and Fischer et al. (2002) are essential readings for discussions of the literature on relatively modern inflation crises.
2. The dates in table 12.2 extend back prior to the time of independence for many countries, including, for example, Malaysia.
3. China, which invented the printing press well ahead of Europe, famously experienced episodes of high inflation created by paper currency in the twelfth and thirteen centuries. (For more on this subject, see, for example, Fischer et al. 2002.) These episodes are in our database as well.
4. Reinhart and Rogoff (2002).
5. Cagan (1956).
6. At the time of this writing, the "official" inflation rate in Argentina is 8 percent; informed estimates place it at 26 percent.
7. Reinhart, Rogoff, and Savastano (2003b).
8. The following section examines in detail the experience of countries that have recorded large declines in their degree of domestic dollarization, including in the context of disinflations.
9. Reinhart and Rogoff (2004) show that countries with dual exchange rate systems tend to have worse average growth performances and vastly worse inflation performances.
10. This pattern was particularly common in the second half of the 1990s among the transition economies (e.g., Azerbaijan, Belarus, Lithuania, and Russia) but was also present in other countries and periods—for instance, in Bolivia and Peru in the early 1980s and in Egypt in the mid-1990s.
11. See Bufman and Leiderman (1992).
12. See Dornbusch and Werner (1994).

Chapter 13   The U.S. Subprime Crisis

1. As indicated in note 7 to the preamble, we use the term "Second Great Contraction" after Friedman and Schwartz's (1963) depiction of the 1930s as "The Great Contraction." See also Felton and Reinhart (2008, 2009), who use the term "First Global Financial Crisis of the 21st Century."
2. See chapter 10 for further discussion.
3. We have explored this issue further in chapter 10.
4. Although China's heavy-handed capital controls shielded it from contagious currency crashes during Asia's turmoil, they did not protect it from a systemic and costly banking crisis emanating primarily from large-scale lending to inefficient and bankrupt state-owned enterprises.

5. Figure 13.1 does not fully capture the extent of the present upsurge in financial crises, for Ireland and Iceland (both of which are experiencing banking crises at the time of this writing) are not part of our core sixty-six-country sample.

6. The Case-Shiller index is described by Robert Shiller (2005) and in recent years has been published monthly in conjunction with Standard and Poor's (as described at their Web site, www.standardandpoors.com). The Case-Shiller index focuses on resales of the same houses and therefore is arguably a more accurate gauge of price movements than indexes that look at all sales. Of course, there are many biases even in the Case-Shiller index (e.g., it is restricted to major metropolitan areas). Nevertheless, it is widely regarded as the most accurate gauge of changes in housing prices in the United States.

7. The Case-Shiller index appears to paint a quite plausible history of housing prices, but as a caveat we note that construction of the series required a significant number of assumptions to interpolate data missing for some intervals, particularly prior to World War II.

8. The current account balance is basically a broader measure of the trade balance—imports minus exports—extended to include investment returns. Note that the current account represents the sum of both government and private borrowing flows from abroad; it is not the same thing as the government deficit. It is perfectly possible for the government to be running a fiscal deficit and yet for the current account to be in surplus, provided the private savings compensate.

9. Greenspan (2007).

10. *Economist Magazine,* "The O'Neill Doctrine," lead editorial, April 25, 2002.

11. Bernanke (2005).

12. See Philippon (2007).

13. Securitization of mortgages involves the bunching and repackaging of mortgage pools to transform highly idiosyncratic individual loans into more standardized products. Thus, to the extent that the U.S. current account was being driven by superior U.S. financial innovation, there was also nothing to worry about. Or so top U.S. financial regulators maintained.

14. See Obstfeld and Rogoff (2001, 2005, 2007).

15. Obstfeld and Rogoff (2001).

16. Roubini and Setser (2004).

17. Krugman (2007). Wile E. Coyote is the hapless character from Chuck Jones's *Road Runner* cartoons. His schemes invariably fail, and, as he runs off a cliff, there is a moment or two before the recognition sets in that nothing is below him.

18. See Obstfeld and Rogoff (2009) for a more detailed discussion of the literature; see also Wolf (2008).

19. Dooley et al. (2004a, 2004b).

20. Cooper (2005).

21. Hausmann and Sturzenegger (2007).

22. Curcuru et al. (2008) argue that the "dark matter" hypothesis is at odds with the data.

23. See Bernanke and Gertler (2001).

24. Bordo and Jeanne (2002), Bank for International Settlements (2005).

25. See Rolnick (2004).

26. We first noted the remarkable similarities between the 2007 U.S. subprime crisis and other deep financial crises in Reinhart and Rogoff (2008b), first circulated in December 2007. By the time of this writing, of course, the facts overwhelmingly support this reading of events.

Our sources have included Caprio and Klingebiel (1996 and 2003), Kaminsky and Reinhart (1999), and Caprio et al. (2005).

27. Later we look at some alternative metrics for measuring the depth of these financial crises, arguing that the traditional measure—fiscal costs of the bank cleanup—is far too narrow.

28. See, for example, Kaminsky, Lizondo, and Reinhart (1998) and Kaminsky and Reinhart (1999).

29. For the United States, as earlier in this chapter, house prices are measured by the Case-Shiller index. The remaining house price data were made available by the Bank for International Settlements and are described by Gregory D. Sutton (2002). Of course, there are many limitations to the international housing price data; they typically do not have the long history that allows for a richer comparison across business cycles. Nevertheless, they probably reasonably capture our main variable of interest, peak-to-trough falls in the price of housing, even if they perhaps exaggerate the duration of the fall, because they are relatively slow to reflect changes in underlying market prices.

30. For the United States, the index is the S&P 500.

31. According to Reinhart and Reinhart (2009), during 2005–2007 the U.S. episode qualified as a "capital flow bonanza" (i.e., a period of abnormally large capital inflows, which is a different way of saying above-average borrowing from abroad).

32. In principle, the rise in real public debt is determined by taking the rise in nominal public debt and adjusting for the rise that represents inflation in all prices.

33. See the conclusions of Reinhart and Reinhart (2008), who explain these changes in interest rates and exchange rates as anomalies for the United States—because the United States is too big to fail.

Chapter 14   The Aftermath of Financial Crises

1. Also included in the comparisons are two prewar episodes in developed countries for which we have housing price and other relevant data.

2. To be clear, peak-to-trough calculations are made on an individual series-by-series basis. The trough and peak dates are those nearest the crisis date and refer to the local (rather than global) maximum or minimum, following much the same approach pioneered by Burns and Mitchell (1946) in their classic study of U.S. business cycles. So for example, in the case of Japan's equity prices, the trough is the local bottom in 1995, even though the subsequent recovery in the equity market left prices well below their prior peak before the crisis (and that the subsequent troughs would see prices at lower levels still).

3. In chapter 10, we looked at financial crises in sixty-six countries over two hundred years, emphasizing the broad parallels between emerging markets and developing countries, including, for example, the nearly universal run-up in government debt.

4. The historical average, which is shaded in black in the diagram, does not include the ongoing crises.

5. Notably, widespread "underemployment" in many emerging markets and the vast informal sector are not fully captured in the official unemployment statistics.

6. Again, see Calvo (1998) and Dornbusch et al. (1995).

7. See International Monetary Fund (various years), *World Economic Outlook*, April 2002, chapter 3.

8. Other noteworthy comparisons and parallels to the Great Depression are presented in Eichengreen and O'Rourke (2009).

Chapter 15   The International
Dimensions of the Subprime Crisis

1. The IMF, of course, is effectively the global lender of last resort for emerging markets, which typically face severe strains in floating new debt during a crisis. Given the quadrupling of IMF resources agreed to at the April 2, 2009, London meeting of the Group of 20 heads of state (including those of the largest rich countries and the major emerging markets), world market panic about the risks of sovereign default have notably abated. The IMF guarantees apply only to government debt, however, and risk spreads on the corporate debt of emerging markets remain elevated as of mid-2009, with rates of corporate default continuing to rise. It remains to be seen to what extent, if any, these debt problems will spill over to governments through bailouts, as they often have in the past.

2. Kaminsky, Reinhart, and Végh (2003); quote on p. 55, emphasis ours.

3. Bordo and Murshid (2001), Neal and Weidenmier (2003). Neal and Weidenmier emphasize that periods of apparent contagion can be more readily interpreted as responses to common shocks, an issue we return to in the context of the recent crisis. But perhaps the bottom line as regards a historical perspective on financial contagion is best summarized by Bordo and Murshid, who conclude that there is little evidence to suggest that cross-country linkages are tighter in the aftermath of a financial crisis for the recent period as opposed to 1880–1913, the earlier heyday of globalization in financial markets that they study.

4. Table 15.1 does not include the bunching of other "types" of crises, such as the wave of sovereign defaults during 1825 or the currency crashes or debasements of the Napoleonic Wars. Again, the indexes developed in chapter 16 will allow us to capture this kind of bundling of crises across both countries and types of crises.

5. See Neal and Weidenmier (2003) and Reinhart and Rogoff (2008a).

6. Owing to the opaqueness of balance sheets in many financial institutions in these countries, the full extent of exposure is, as yet, unknown.

7. See Reinhart and Reinhart (2009) for a full listing of episodes of capital inflow bonanzas.

Chapter 16   Composite Measures of Financial Turmoil

1. Kaminsky and Reinhart (1999).

2. The tally would come to six varieties of crises if we included currency debasement. We do not follow this route for two reasons: first, there are far fewer sources of data across countries (about a dozen or so) on the metallic content of their currencies; second, the printing press displaced debasement and decoupled currencies in circulation from a metallic base with the rise of fiat money. Because the period we analyzed for the turbulence composite was after 1800 (when our dating of banking crises begins in earnest), the exclusion of debasement crises is not as troublesome as for 1300–1799, when debasement was rampant.

3. This goes back to the dichotomous measures of crises that we (and most studies) employ. Of course, it is possible to consider additional gradations of crises to capture some measure of severity.

4. As noted, one could easily refine this measure to include three categories, say, high inflation (above 20 percent but less than 40), very high inflation (above 40 percent but less than 1,000), and hyperinflation (1,000 percent or higher).

5. Namely, crash episodes associated with international financial crises and turbulence (mostly in advanced economies).

6. Our list of economic crises does not include a growth collapse crisis as defined by Barro and Ursúa (2008, 2009), which is an episode in which per capita GDP falls cumulatively by 10 percent or more. An important share of the crisis episodes we identify are candidates for this definition as well. We examine this issue later. Nor does our composite index of financial turbulence necessarily include all "sudden stop" episodes as defined by Guillermo Calvo and co-authors in several contributions (see references). The reader will recall that a sudden stop is an episode in which there is an abrupt reversal in international capital flows, often associated with loss of capital market access. It is noteworthy that most systemic banking crises past and present (the 2007 U.S. subprime crisis is an exception) have been associated with sudden stops. The same could be said of sovereign external defaults.

7. Barro and Ursúa (2009). They identify 195 stock market crashes for twenty-five countries (eighteen advanced economies and seven emerging markets) over 1869–2006.

8. Samuelson (1966).

9. The reader will recall from earlier chapters that our sixty-six-country sample accounts for about 90 percent of world GDP.

10. It is important to note that Austria, Germany, Italy, and Japan remained in default for varying durations after the end of the war.

11. See McConnell and Perez-Quiros (2000) and Blanchard and Simon (2001).

12. As in nearly all previous historical crises in Argentina, the 2001–2002 episode was followed by a crisis in its small neighbor, Uruguay.

13. The hyperinflation episodes are the most notorious, obviously, but the share of countries in the region with an annual inflation rate above 20 percent, thereby meeting our threshold for a crisis, hit a peak of nearly 90 percent in 1990!

14. Burns and Mitchell (1946). For more recent treatments of the early warning properties of equity markets in the context of crises, see Kaminsky et al. (1998), Kaminsky and Reinhart (1999), and Barro and Ursúa (2009).

15. International Monetary Fund (various years), *World Economic Outlook*.

16. Eichengreen and O'Rourke (2009) add trade to highlight the similarities while noting the difference in monetary policy response (specifically, central bank discount rates).

17. Maddison (2004).

18. League of Nations (various years), *World Economic Survey*.

19. See, for example, League of Nations (1944).

20. Although we have reliable trade data for most countries during World War II, there are sufficient missing entries to make the calculation of the world aggregate not comparable to other years during 1940–1947.

21. Kaminsky and Reinhart (1999).

22. Demirgüç-Kunt and Detragiache (1998).

23. Reinhart (2002).

24. Reinhart and Rogoff (2004) also examined the relationship between currency crashes and inflation as well as the timing of currency crashes and capital control (specifically, dual or multiple exchange rates).

25. Diaz-Alejandro (1985).

26. In contrast to other studies of banking crises, Kaminsky and Reinhart (1999) provide two dates for each banking crisis episode—the beginning of a banking crisis and the later peak.

27. See Goldstein and Turner (2004).

28. See Reinhart, Rogoff, and Savastano (2003a).

29. The second and third effects of the depreciation or devaluation of the currency listed earlier are less of an issue for advanced economies.

Chapter 17   Reflections on Early
Warnings, Graduation, Policy Responses,
and the Foibles of Human Nature

1. On indicators for risk of currency crises, see Kaminsky, Lizondo, and Reinhart (1998); Berg and Pattillo (1999); Bussiere and Mulder (2000); Berg et al. (2004); Bussiere and Fratzscher (2006); and Bussiere (2007) and sources cited therein. For banking crises, see Demirgüç-Kunt and Detragiache (1998, 1999). For the twin crises (indicators of when a country is at risk of a joint banking and currency crisis), see Kaminsky and Reinhart (1999) and Goldstein, Kaminsky, and Reinhart (2000).

2. Ideally, one would also want comparable price data for commercial real estate, which played a particularly important role in the asset bubbles in Japan and other Asian economies in the run-up to their major banking crises.

3. Kaminsky, Lizondo, and Reinhart (1998) and Kaminsky and Reinhart (1999). The signals approach, described in detail by Kaminsky, Lizondo, and Reinhart (1998), ranks indicators according to their "noise-to-signal" ratios. When an indicator sends a signal (waves a red flag) and a crisis occurs within the following two-year window, it is an accurate signal; if no crisis follows the signal, it is a false alarm or noise. Hence the best indicators are those with the lowest noise-to-signal ratio.

4. We have argued the case for an international financial regulator in Reinhart and Rogoff (2008d).

5. See Reinhart, Rogoff, and Savastano (2003a).

6. Qian and Reinhart (2009).

7. See Kaminsky, Reinhart, and Végh (2004).

8. Friedman and Schwartz (1963).

9. See Kindleberger (1989).

REFERENCES

Agénor, Pierre-Richard, John McDermott, and Eswar Prasad. 2000. "Macro-economic Fluctuations in Developing Countries: Some Stylized Facts." *World Bank Economic Review* 14: 251–285.

Aguiar, Mark, and Gita Gopinath. 2007. "Emerging Market Business Cycles: The Cycle Is the Trend." *Journal of Political Economy* 115 (1): 69–102.

Alesina, Alberto, and Guido Tabellini. 1990. "A Positive Theory of Fiscal Deficits and Government Debt." *Review of Economic Studies* 57: 403–414.

Allen, Franklin, and Douglas Gale. 2007. *Understanding Financial Crises*. Oxford: Oxford University Press.

Allen, Robert C. 2001. "The Great Divergence: Wages and Prices from the Middle Ages to the First World War." *Explorations in Economic History* 38 (4): 411–447.

———. n.d. *Consumer Price Indices, Nominal/Real Wages and Welfare Ratios of Building Craftsmen and Labourers, 1260–1913*. Oxford, England: Oxford University Press. Available at http://www.iisg.nl/hpw/data.php# europe.

Allen, Robert C., and Richard W. Unger. 2004. *European Commodity Prices, 1260–1914*. Oxford, England: Oxford University Press. Available at http://www2.history.ubc.ca/unger.

Arellano, Cristina, and Narayana Kocherlakota. 2008. "Internal Debt Crises and Sovereign Defaults." NBER Working Paper 13794. National Bureau of Economic Research, Cambridge, Mass. February.

Baker, Melvin. 1994. *The Second Squires Administration and the Loss of Responsible Government, 1928–1934*. Available at http://www.ucs.mun.ca/~melbaker/1920s.htm.

Bank for International Settlements. 2005. *Annual Report*. Basel: Bank for International Settlements.

Baptista, Asdrúbal. 2006. *Bases Cuantitativas de la Economía Venezolana, 1830–2005*. Caracas: Ediciones Fundación Polar.

Barro, Robert. 1974. "Are Government Bonds Net Wealth?" *Journal of Political Economy* 82 (6): 1095–1117.

————. 1983. "Inflationary Finance under Discretion and Rules." *Canadian Journal of Economics* 16 (1): 1–16.

————. 2009. "Rare Disasters, Asset Prices and Welfare Costs." *American Economic Review* 99 (1): 243–264.

Barro, Robert J., and David B. Gordon. 1983. "A Positive Theory of Monetary Policy in a Natural Rate Model." *Journal of Political Economy* 91 (August): 589–610.

Barro, Robert, and José F. Ursúa. 2008. "Macroeconomic Crises since 1870." NBER Working Paper 13940. National Bureau of Economic Research, Cambridge, Mass. April.

————. 2009. "Stock-Market Crashes and Depressions." NBER Working Paper 14760. National Bureau of Economic Research, Cambridge, Mass. February.

Bassino, Jean-Pascal, and Debin Ma. 2005. "Japanese Unskilled Wages in International Perspective, 1741–1913." *Research in Economic History* 23: 229–248.

Bassino, Jean-Pascal, and Pierre van der Eng. 2006. "New Benchmark of Wages and GDP, 1913–1970." Mimeo. Montpellier University, Montpellier, France.

Bazant, Jan. 1968. *Historia de la Deuda Exterior de Mexico: 1823–1946*. Mexico City: El Colegio de México.

Berg, Andrew, and Catherine Pattillo. 1999. "Predicting Currency Crises: The Indicators Approach and an Alternative." *Journal of International Money and Finance* 18: 561–586.

Berg, Andrew, Eduardo Borensztein, and Catherine Pattillo. 2004. "Assessing Early Warning Systems: How Have They Worked in Practice?" International Monetary Fund Working Paper 04/52. International Monetary Fund, Washington, D.C.

Bernanke, Ben S. 1983. "Nonmonetary Effects of the Financial Crisis in the Propagation of the Great Depression." *American Economic Review* 73 (June): 257–276.

―――. 2005. "The Global Saving Glut and the U.S. Current Account Deficit." Speech given at the Homer Jones Lecture, St. Louis, Mo., April 14. Available at http://www.federalreserve.gov/boarddocs/speeches/2005/20050414/default.htm.

Bernanke, Ben S., and Mark Gertler. 1990. "Financial Fragility and Economic Performance." *Quarterly Journal of Economics* 105 (February): 87–114.

―――. 1995. "Inside the Black Box: The Credit Channel of Monetary Policy Transmission." *Journal of Economic Perspectives* 9 (Fall): 27–48.

―――. 2001. "Should Central Banks Respond to Movements in Asset Prices?" *American Economic Review* 91 (2): 253–257.

Bernanke, Ben S., and Harold James. 1990. "The Gold Standard, Deflation, and Financial Crisis in the Great Depression: An International Comparison." NBER Working Paper 3488. National Bureau of Economic Research, Cambridge, Mass. October.

Bernanke, Ben S., Mark Gertler, and Simon Gilchrist. 1999. "The Financial Accelerator in a Quantitative Business Cycle Framework." In *Handbook of Macroeconomics,* vol. 1A, ed. John Taylor and Michael Woodford. Amsterdam: North-Holland.

Blanchard, Olivier, and John Simon. 2001. "The Long and Large Decline in U.S. Output Volatility." *Brookings Papers on Economic Activity* 1: 135–164.

Bonney, Richard. n.d. European State Finance Database. Available at http://www.le.ac.uk/hi/bon/ESFDB/frameset.html.

Bordo, Michael D. 2006. "Sudden Stops, Financial Crises and Original Sin in Emerging Countries: Déjà vu?" NBER Working Paper 12393. National Bureau of Economic Research, Cambridge, Mass. July.

Bordo, Michael, and Barry Eichengreen. 1999. "Is Our Current International Economic Environment Unusually Crisis Prone?" In *Capital Flows and the International Financial System.* Sydney: Reserve Bank of Australia Annual Conference Volume.

Bordo, Michael, and Olivier Jeanne. 2002. "Boom-Busts in Asset Prices, Economic Instability, and Monetary Policy." NBER Working Paper 8966. National Bureau of Economic Research, Cambridge, Mass. June.

Bordo, Michael D., and Antu Panini Murshid. 2001. "Are Financial Crises Becoming Increasingly More Contagious? What Is the Historical Evidence?" In *International Financial Contagion: How It Spreads and How It Can Be Stopped*, ed. Kristin Forbes and Stijn Claessens. New York: Kluwer Academic. Pp. 367–406.

Bordo, Michael, Barry Eichengreen, Daniela Klingebiel, and Maria Soledad Martinez-Peria. 2001. "Is the Crisis Problem Growing More Severe?" *Economic Policy* 16 (April): 51–82.

Borensztein, Eduardo, José De Gregorio, and Jong-Wha Lee. 1998. "How Does Foreign Direct Investment Affect Economic Growth?" *Journal of International Economics* 45 (1): 115–135.

Borodkin, L. I. 2001. " Inequality of Incomes in the Period of Industrial Revolution: Is Universal Hypothesis about Kuznets's Curve?" *Russian Political Encyclopedia*. Moscow: Rosspen.

Bouchard, Léon. 1891. *Système financier de l'ancienne monarchie*. Paris: Guillaumin.

Boughton, James. 1991. "Commodity and Manufactures Prices in the Long Run." International Monetary Fund Working Paper 91/47. International Monetary Fund, Washington, D.C. May.

Brahmananda, P. R. 2001. *Money, Income and Prices in 19th Century India*. Dehli: Himalaya.

Braun, Juan, Matias Braun, Ignacio Briones, and José Díaz. 2000. "Economía Chilena 1810–1995, Estadisticas Historicas." Pontificia Universidad Católica de Chile Documento de Trabajo 187. Pontificia Universidad Católica de Chile, Santiago. January.

Brock, Philip. 1989. "Reserve Requirements and the Inflation Tax." *Journal of Money, Credit and Banking* 21 (1): 106–121.

Broner, Fernando, and Jaume Ventura. 2007. "Globalization and Risk Sharing." CREI Working Paper. Centre de Recerca en Economia Internacional, Barcelona. July.

Brown, William Adams. 1940. *The International Gold Standard Reinterpreted, 1914–1940*. New York: National Bureau of Economic Research

Buchanan, James, and Richard Wagner. 1977. *Democracy in Deficit: The Political Legacy of Lord Keynes*. Amsterdam: Elsevier.

Bufman, Gil, and Leonardo Leiderman. 1992. "Simulating an Optimizing

Model of Currency Substitution." *Revista de Análisis Económico* 7 (1): 109–124.

Bulow, Jeremy, and Kenneth Rogoff. 1988a. "Multilateral Negotiations for Rescheduling Developing Country Debt: A Bargaining-Theoretic Framework." *IMF Staff Papers* 35 (4): 644–657.

———. 1988b. "The Buyback Boondoggle." *Brookings Papers on Economic Activity* 2: 675–698.

———. 1989a. "A Constant Recontracting Model of Sovereign Debt." *Journal of Political Economy* 97: 155–178.

———. 1989b. "Sovereign Debt: Is to Forgive to Forget?" *American Economic Review* 79 (March): 43–50.

———. 1990. "Cleaning Up Third-World Debt without Getting Taken to the Cleaners." *Journal of Economic Perspectives* 4 (Winter): 31–42.

———. 2005. "Grants versus Loans for Development Banks." *American Economic Review* 95 (2): 393–397.

Burns, Arthur F., and Wesley C. Mitchell. 1946. *Measuring Business Cycles*. National Bureau of Economic Research Studies in Business Cycles 2. Cambridge, Mass.: National Bureau of Economic Research.

Bussiere, Matthieu. 2007. "Balance of Payments Crises in Emerging Markets: How 'Early' Were the Early Warning Signals?" European Central Bank Working Paper 713. European Central Bank, Frankfurt. January.

Bussiere, Matthieu, and Marcel Fratzscher. 2006. "Towards a New Early Warning System of Financial Crises." *Journal of International Money and Finance* 25 (6): 953–973.

Bussiere, Matthieu, and Christian Mulder. 2000. "Political Instability and Economic Vulnerability." *International Journal of Finance and Economics* 5 (4): 309–330.

Butlin, N. G. 1962. *Australian Domestic Product, Investment and Foreign Borrowing, 1861–1938/39*. Cambridge: Cambridge University Press.

Cagan, Philip. 1956. "The Monetary Dynamics of Hyperinflation in Milton Friedman." In *Studies in the Quantity Theory of Money*, ed. Milton Friedman. Chicago: University of Chicago Press. Pp. 25–117.

Calomiris, Charles, and Gary Gorton. 1991. "The Origins of Banking Panics: Models, Facts, and Bank Regulation." In *Financial Markets and Financial Crises*, ed. R. Glenn Hubbard. Chicago: University of Chicago Press for the National Bureau of Economic Research.

Calvo, Guillermo. 1988. "Servicing the Public Debt: The Role of Expectations." *American Economic Review* 78 (September): 647–661.

———. 1989. "Is Inflation Effective for Liquidating Short-Term Nominal Debt?" International Monetary Fund Working Paper 89/2. International Monetary Fund, Washington, D.C. January.

———. 1991. "The Perils of Sterilization." *IMF Staff Papers* 38 (4): 921–926.

———. 1998. "Capital Flows and Capital Market Crises: The Simple Economics of Sudden Stops." *Journal of Applied Economics* 1 (1): 35–54.

Calvo, Guillermo A., and Pablo Guidotti. 1992. "Optimal Maturity of Nominal Government Debt: An Infinite Horizon Model." *International Economic Review* 33 (November): 895–919.

Calvo, Guillermo A., Leonardo Leiderman, and Carmen M. Reinhart. 1993. "Capital Inflows and Real Exchange Rate Appreciation in Latin America: The Role of External Factors." *IMF Staff Papers* 40 (1): 108–151.

Calvo, Guillermo A., Alejandro Izquierdo, and Rudy Loo-Kung. 2006. "Relative Price Volatility under Sudden Stops: The Relevance of Balance Sheet Effects." *Journal of International Economics* 9 (1): 231–254.

Cameron, Rondo E. 1967. *Banking in the Early Stages of Industrialization: A Study in Comparative Economic History.* New York: Oxford University Press.

Camprubi Alcázar, Carlos. 1957. *Historia de los Bancos en el Perú, 1860–1879.* Lima: Editorial Lumen.

Caprio, Gerard Jr., and Daniela Klingebiel. 1996. "Bank Insolvency: Bad Luck, Bad Policy, or Bad Banking?" In *Annual World Bank Conference on Development Economics, 1996,* ed. Boris Pleskovic and Joseph Stiglitz. Washington, D.C.: World Bank. Pp. 79–104.

———. 2003. "Episodes of Systemic and Borderline Financial Crises." Mimeo. Washington, D.C.: World Bank. Available at http://go.world bank.org/5DYGICS7B0 (Dataset 1). January.

Caprio, Gerard, Daniela Klingebiel, Luc Laeven, and Guillermo Noguera. 2005. "Banking Crisis Database." In *Systemic Financial Crises,* ed. Patrick Honohan and Luc Laeven. Cambridge: Cambridge University Press.

Carlos, Ann, Larry Neal, and Kirsten Wandschneider. 2005. "The Origin of National Debt: The Financing and Re-Financing of the War of the Spanish Succession." University of Colorado Working Paper. University of Colorado, Boulder.

Carter, Susan B., Scott Gartner, Michael Haines, Alan Olmstead, Richard

Sutch, and Gavin Wright, eds. 2006. *Historical Statistics of the United States: Millennial Edition*. Cambridge: Cambridge University Press. Available at http://hsus.cambridge.org/HSUSWeb/HSUSEntryServlet.

Ceron, Jose, and Javier Suarez. 2006. "Hot and Cold Housing Markets: International Evidence." CEMFI Working Paper 0603. Center for Monetary and Financial Studies, Madrid. January.

Cha, Myung Soo, and Nak Nyeon Kim. 2006. "Korea's First Industrial Revolution, 1911–40." Naksungdae Institute of Economic Research Working Paper 2006-3. Naksungdae Institute of Economic Research, Seoul. June.

Cheng, Linsun. 2003. *Banking in Modern China: Entrepreneurs, Professional Managers, and the Development of Chinese Banks, 1897–1937*. Cambridge: Cambridge University Press.

Chuhan, Punam, Stijn Claessens, and Nlandu Mamingi. 1998. "Equity and Bond Flows to Asia and Latin America: The Role of Global and Country Factors." *Journal of Development Economics* (55): 123–150.

Cipolla, Carlo. 1982. *The Monetary Policy of Fourteenth Century Florence*. Berkeley: University of California Press.

Clay, C. G. A. 2000. *Gold for the Sultan: Western Bankers and Ottoman Finance 1856–1881: A Contribution to Ottoman and International Financial History*. London and New York: I. B. Tauris.

Cole, Harold L., and Patrick J. Kehoe. 1996. "Reputation Spillover across Relationships: Reviving Reputation Models of Debt." Staff Report 209. Federal Reserve Bank of Minneapolis.

Conant, Charles A. 1915. *A History of Modern Banks of Issue*. 5th ed. New York: G. P. Putnam's Sons.

Condoide, Mikhail V. 1951. *The Soviet Financial System: Its Development and Relations with the Western World*. Columbus: Ohio State University.

Cooper, Richard. 2005. "Living with Global Imbalances: A Contrarian View." Policy brief. Institute for International Economics, Washington, D.C.

Correlates of War. Militarized Interstate Disputes Database. http://correlates ofwar.org/.

Course of the exchange. Reported by John Castaing. Available at http://www .le.ac.uk/hi/bon/ESFDB/NEAL/neal.html.

Cowan, Kevin, Eduardo Levy-Yeyati, Ugo Panizza, and Federico Sturzenegger. 2006. "Sovereign Debt in the Americas: New Data and Stylized Facts." Working Paper 577. Research Department, Inter-American Development Bank, Washington, D.C. Available at http://www.iadb.org/res/pub_desc.cfm?pub_id=DBA-007.

Crisp, Olga. 1976. *Studies in the Russian Economy before 1914*. London: Macmillan.

Curcuru, Stephanie, Charles Thomas, and Frank Warnock. 2008. "Current Account Sustainability and Relative Reliability." *NBER International Seminar on Macroeconomics 2008*. Chicago: University of Chicago Press for the National Bureau of Economic Research.

Della Paolera, Gerardo, and Alan M. Taylor. 1999. "Internal versus External Convertibility and Developing-Country Financial Crises: Lessons from the Argentine Bank Bailout of the 1930s." NBER Working Paper 7386. National Bureau of Economic Research, Cambridge, Mass. October.

de Maddalena, Aldo. 1974. *Prezzi e Mercedi a Milano dal 1701 al 1860*. Milan: Banca Commerciale Italiana.

Demirgüç-Kunt, Asli, and Enrica Detragiache. 1998. "The Determinants of Banking Crises in Developing and Developed Countries." *IMF Staff Papers* 45: 81–109.

———. 1999. "Financial Liberalization and Financial Fragility." In *Annual World Bank Conference on Development Economics, 1998*, ed. Boris Pleskovic and Joseph Stiglitz. Washington, D.C.: World Bank.

Diamond, Douglas, and Philip H. Dybvig. 1983. "Bank Runs, Deposit Insurance, and Liquidity." *Journal of Political Economy* 91 (3): 401–419.

Diamond, Douglas, and Raghuram Rajan. 2001. "Liquidity Risk, Liquidity Creation and Financial Fragility: A Theory of Banking." *Journal of Political Economy* 109 (April): 287–327.

Diamond, Peter A. 1965. "National Debt in a Neoclassical Growth Model." *American Economic Review* 55 (5): 1126–1150.

Díaz, José B., Rolf Lüders, and Gert Wagner. 2005. "Chile, 1810–2000, La República en Cifras." Mimeo. Instituto de Economía, Pontificia Universidad Católica de Chile, Santiago. May.

Diaz-Alejandro, Carlos. 1983. "Stories of the 1930s for the 1980s." In *Financial Policies and the World Capital Market: The Problem of Latin American Countries*, ed. Pedro Aspe Armella, Rudiger Dornbusch, and Maurice Obstfeld. Chicago: University of Chicago Press for the National Bureau of Economic Research. Pp. 5–40.

———. 1984. "Latin American Debt: I Don't Think We Are in Kansas Anymore." *Brookings Papers in Economic Activity* 2: 355–389.

———. 1985. "Goodbye Financial Repression, Hello Financial Crash." *Journal of Development Economics* 19 (1–2): 1–24.

Dick, Trevor, and John E. Floyd. 1997. "Capital Imports and the Jacksonian Economy: A New View of the Balance of Payments." Paper presented at the Third World Congress of Cliometrics, Munich, Germany, July.

Dooley, Michael, Eduardo Fernandez-Arias, and Kenneth Kletzer. 1996. "Recent Private Capital Inflows to Developing Countries: Is the Debt Crisis History?" *World Bank Economic Review* 10 (1): 27–49.

Dooley, Michael, David Folkerts-Landau, and Peter Garber. 2004a. "An Essay on the Revived Bretton Woods System." *International Journal of Finance & Economics* 9 (4): 307–313.

———. 2004b. "The Revived Bretton Woods System: The Effects of Periphery Intervention and Reserve Management on Interest Rates and Exchange Rates in Center Countries." NBER Working Paper 10332. National Bureau of Economic Research, Cambridge, Mass. March.

Dornbusch, Rudiger, and Stanley Fischer. 1993. "Moderate Inflation." *World Bank Economic Review* 7 (1): 1–44.

Dornbusch, Rudiger, Ilan Goldfajn, and Rodrigo O. Valdés. 1995. "Currency Crises and Collapses." *Brookings Papers on Economic Activity* 26 (2): 219–293.

Dornbusch, Rudiger, and Alejandro Werner. 1994. "Mexico: Stabilization, Reform, and No Growth." *Brookings Papers on Economic Activity* 1: 253–315.

Drazen, Allan. 1998. "Towards a Political Economy Theory of Domestic Debt." In *The Debt Burden and Its Consequences for Monetary Policy*, ed. G. Calvo and M. King. London: Macmillan.

Drees, Burkhard, and Ceyla Pazarbasioglu. 1998. "The Nordic Banking Crisis: Pitfalls in Financial Liberalization." IMF Occasional Paper 161. International Monetary Fund, Washington, D.C.

Eaton, Jonathan, and Mark Gersovitz. 1981. "Debt with Potential Repudiation: Theory and Estimation." *Review of Economic Studies* 48 (2): 289–309.

Economist Magazine. 2002. "The O'Neill Doctrine." Lead editorial, April 25.

Edvinsson, Rodney. 2002. "Growth, Accumulation, Crisis: With New Macroeconomic Data for Sweden 1800–2000." Ph.D. dissertation, University of Stockholm, Sweden.

Eichengreen, Barry. 1991a. "Historical Research on International Lending and Debt." *Journal of Economic Perspectives* 5 (Spring): 149–169.

———. 1991b. "Trends and Cycles in Foreign Lending." In *Capital Flows in the World Economy*, ed. H. Siebert. Tübingen: Mohr. Pp. 3–28.

———. 1992. *Golden Fetters: The Gold Standard and the Great Depression 1919–1939*. New York: Oxford University Press.

Eichengreen, Barry, and Peter H. Lindert, eds. 1989. *The International Debt Crisis in Historical Perspective*. Cambridge, Mass.: MIT Press.

Eichengreen, Barry, and Kevin O'Rourke. 2009. "A Tale of Two Depressions." June 4. Available at http://www. voxeu.org.

European State Finance Database. Available at http://www.le.ac.uk/hi/bon/ESFDB/.

Felton, Andrew, and Carmen M. Reinhart. 2008. *The First Global Financial Crisis of the 21st Century*. London: VoxEU and Centre for Economic Policy Research. July. Available at http://www.voxeu.org/index.php?q=node/1352.

———. 2009. *The First Global Financial Crisis of the 21st Century, Part 2: June–December, 2008*. London: VoxEU and Centre for Economic Policy Research. Available at http://www.voxeu.org/index.php?q=node/3079.

Ferguson, Niall. 2008. *The Ascent of Money: A Financial History of the World*. New York: Penguin Press.

Fischer, Stanley, Ratna Sahay, and Carlos A. Végh. 2002. "Modern Hyper- and High Inflations." *Journal of Economic Literature* 40 (3): 837–880.

Fisher, Irving. 1933. "Debt-Deflation Theory of Great Depressions." *Econometrica* 1 (4): 337–357.

Flandreau, Marc, and Frederic Zumer. 2004. *The Making of Global Finance, 1880–1913*. Paris: Organisation of Economic Co-operation and Development.

Flath, David. 2005. *The Japanese Economy*. 2nd ed. Oxford: Oxford University Press.

Fostel, Ana, and John Geanakoplos. 2008. "Leverage Cycles and the Anxious Economy." *American Economic Review* 98 (4): 1211–1244.

Frankel, Jeffrey A., and Andrew K. Rose. 1996. "Currency Crashes in Emerging Markets: An Empirical Treatment." *Journal of International Economics* 41 (November): 351–368.

Frankel, S. Herbert. 1938. *Capital Investment in Africa: Its Course and Effects*. London: Oxford University Press.

Friedman, Milton, and Anna J. Schwartz. 1963. *A Monetary History of the United States, 1867–1960*. Princeton, N.J.: Princeton University Press.

Frydl, Edward J. 1999. "The Length and Cost of Banking Crises." International Monetary Fund Working Paper 99/30. International Monetary Fund, Washington, D.C. March.

Garcia Vizcaino, José. 1972. *La Deuda Pública Nacional*. Buenos Aires: EU-DEBA Editorial Universitaria de Buenos Aires.

Garner, Richard. 2007. "Late Colonial Prices in Selected Latin American Cities." Working Memorandum. Available at http://home.comcast.net/~richardgarner04/.

———. n.d. "Economic History Data Desk: Economic History of Latin America, United States and New World, 1500–1900." Available at http://home.comcast.net/~richardgarner04/.

Gavin, Michael, and Roberto Perotti. 1997. "Fiscal Policy in Latin America." *NBER Macroeconomics Annual* 12: 11–61.

Gayer, Arthur D., W. W. Rostow, and Anna J. Schwartz. 1953. *The Growth and Fluctuation of the British Economy, 1790–1850*. Oxford: Clarendon.

Gelabert, Juan. 1999a. "Castile, 1504–1808." In *The Rise of the Fiscal State in Europe, c. 1200–1815*, ed. R. J. Bonney. Oxford: Oxford University Press.

———. 1999b. "The King's Expenses: The Asientos of Philip III and Philip IV of Spain. In *Crises, Revolutions and Self-Sustained Growth: Essays in European Fiscal History, 1130–1830*, ed. W. M. Ormrod, M. M. Bonney, and R. J. Bonney. Stamford, England: Shaun Tyas.

Gerdrup, Karsten R. 2003. "Three Episodes of Financial Fragility in Norway since the 1890s." Bank for International Settlements Working Paper 142. Bank for International Settlements, Basel, Switzerland. October.

Godinho, V. Magalhaes. 1955. *Prix et Monnaies au Portugal, 1750–1850*. Paris: Librairie Armand Colin.

Global Financial Data. n.d. *Global Financial Data*. Available at https://www.globalfinancialdata.com/.

Global Price and Income History Group. Available at http://gpih.ucdavis.edu.

Goldstein, Morris. 2003. "Debt Sustainability, Brazil, and the IMF." Working Paper WP03-1. Institute for International Economics, Washington, D.C.

Goldstein, Morris, and Philip Turner. 2004. *Controlling Currency Mismatches in Emerging Markets*. Washington, D.C.: Institute for International Economics.

Goldstein, Morris, Graciela L. Kaminsky, and Carmen M. Reinhart. 2000. *Assessing Financial Vulnerability*. Washington, D.C.: Institute for International Economics.

Gorton, Gary. 1988. "Banking Panics and Business Cycles." *Oxford Economic Papers* 40: 751–781.

Greenspan, Alan. 2007. *The Age of Turbulence*. London and New York: Penguin.

Groningen Growth and Development Centre and the Commerce Department. 2008. Total Economy Database. Available at http://www.ggdc.net.

Grytten, Ola. 2008. "The Economic History of Norway." In *EH.Net Encyclopedia*, ed. Robert Whaples. Available at http://eh.net/encyclopedia/article/grytten.norway.

Hale, David. 2003. "The Newfoundland Lesson: During the 1930s, Long before the IMF, the British Empire Coped with a Debt Crisis in a Small Country. This Is a Tale of the Choice between Debt and Democracy. It Shouldn't Be Forgotten." *International Economy* (Summer). Available at http://www.entrepreneur.com/tradejournals/article/106423908.html.

Hamilton, Earl. 1969. *War and Prices in Spain, 1651–1800*. New York: Russell and Russell.

Hausmann, Ricardo, and Federico Sturzenegger. 2007. "The Missing Dark Matter in the Wealth of Nations and Its Implications for Global Imbalances." *Economic Policy* 51: 469–518.

Hoffman, P. T., D. S. Jacks, P. Levin, and P. H. Lindert. 2002. "Real Inequality in Europe since 1500." *Journal of Economic History* 62 (2): 381–413.

Hoggarth, Glenn, Patricia Jackson, and Erlend Nier. 2005. "Banking Crises and the Design of Safety Nets." *Journal of Banking & Finance* 29 (1): 143–159.

Homer, Sidney, and Richard Sylla. 1991. *A History of Interest Rates*. New Brunswick, N.J., and London: Rutgers University Press.

Hsu, Leonard Shih-Lien. 1935. *Silver and Prices in China: Report of the Committee for the Study of Silver Values and Commodity Prices*. Shanghai: Commercial Press.

Huang, Feng-Hua. 1919. *Public Debts in China.* New York: MAS.

Imlah, A. H. 1958. *Economic Elements in the Pax Britannica.* Cambridge. Mass.: MIT Press.

Institutional Investor. Various years. *Institutional Investor.*

Instituto Brasileiro de Geografia e Estadistica. 2007. *Estadisticas Historicas de Brazil.* Rio de Janeiro: Instituto Brasileiro de Geografia e Estadistica.

Instituto Nacional de Estatistica (Portuguese Statistical Agency). 1998. *Estadisticas Historicas Portuguesas.* Lisbon: INE.

International Institute of Social History. n.d. Available at http://www.iisg.nl/.

International Monetary Fund. 2002. "Assessing Sustainability." Available at http://www.imf.org/external/np/pdr/sus/2002/eng/052802.htm.

―――. Various years. *International Financial Statistics.* Washington, D.C.: International Monetary Fund.

―――. Various years. *World Economic Outlook.* Washington, D.C.: International Monetary Fund.

Jácome, Luis. 2008. "Central Bank Involvement in Banking Crises in Latin America." International Monetary Fund Working Paper 08/135. International Monetary Fund, Washington, D.C. May.

Jayachandran, Seema, and Michael Kremer. 2006. "Odious Debt." *American Economic Review* 96 (March): 82–92.

Jeanne, Olivier. 2009. "Debt Maturity and the International Financial Architecture." *American Economic Review,* forthcoming.

Jeanne, Olivier, and Guscina, Anastasia. 2006. "Government Debt in Emerging Market Countries: A New Dataset." International Monetary Fund Working Paper 6/98. International Monetary Fund, Washington, D.C. April.

Johnson, H. Clark. 1998. *Gold, France, and the Great Depression: 1919–1935.* New Haven, Conn.: Yale University Press.

Jonung, L., and T. Hagberg. 2002. "How Costly Was the Crisis?" Työväen Akatemia, Kauniainen. September.

Jun, S. H., and J. B. Lewis. 2002. "Labour Cost, Land Prices, Land Rent, and Interest Rates in the Southern Region of Korea, 1690–1909." Working Memorandum. Academy of Korean Studies, Seoul. Available at http://www.iisg.nl/hpw/korea.php.

Kaminsky, Graciela L., and Carmen M. Reinhart. 1999. "The Twin Crises: The Causes of Banking and Balance-of-Payments Problems." *American Economic Review* 89 (3): 473–500.

Kaminsky, Graciela L., J. Saul Lizondo, and Carmen M. Reinhart. 1998. "Leading Indicators of Currency Crises." *IMF Staff Papers* 45 (1): 1–48.

Kaminsky, Graciela L., Carmen M. Reinhart, and Carlos A. Végh. 2003. "The Unholy Trinity of Financial Contagion." *Journal of Economic Perspectives* 17 (4): 51–74.

———. 2004. "When It Rains, It Pours: Procyclical Capital Flows and Policies." In *NBER Macroeconomics Annual 2004*, ed. Mark Gertler and Kenneth S. Rogoff. Cambridge, Mass: MIT Press. Pp. 11–53.

Kimura, M. 1987. "La Revolucion de los Precios en la Cuenca del Pacifico, 1600–1650." Mimeo. Universidad Nacional Autonoma de México, Mexico City.

Kindleberger, Charles P. 1989. *Manias, Panics and Crashes: A History of Financial Crises*. New York: Basic Books.

Kiyotaki, Nobuhiro, and John Moore. 1997. "Credit Cycles." *Journal of Political Economy* 105: 211–248.

Kohlscheen, Emanuel. 2007. "Why Are There Serial Defaulters? Evidence from Constitutions." *Journal of Law and Economics* 50 (November): 713–729.

Korthals Altes, W. L. 1996. *Van L Hollands tot Nederlandse f*. Amsterdam: Neha.

Kostelenos, George, S. Petmezas, D. Vasileiou, E. Kounaris, and M. Sfakianakis. 2007. "Gross Domestic Product, 1830–1939." In *Sources of Economic History of Modern Greece*. Athens: Central Bank of Greece.

Kotlikoff, Lawrence J., Torsten Persson, and Lars E. O. Svensson. 1988. "Social Contracts as Assets: A Possible Solution to the Time-Consistency Problem." *American Economic Review* 7: 662–677.

Krugman, Paul. 2007. "Will There Be a Dollar Crisis?" *Economic Policy* 51 (July): 437–467.

Kryzanowski, Lawrence, and Gordon S. Roberts. 1999. "Perspectives on Canadian Bank Insolvency during the 1930s." *Journal of Money, Credit & Banking* 31 (1): 130–136.

Landes, David S. 1958. *Bankers and Pashas: International Finance and Economic Imperialism in Egypt*. Cambridge, Mass.: Harvard University Press.

Lazaretou, Sophia. 2005. "The Drachma, Foreign Creditors, and the International Monetary System: Tales of a Currency during the 19th and the Early 20th Centuries." *Explorations in Economic History* 42 (2): 202–236.

League of Nations. 1944. *International Currency Experience: Lessons of the Interwar Period.* Geneva: League of Nations.

———. Various years. *Statistical Abstract.* Geneva: League of Nations.

———. Various years. *Statistical Yearbook, 1926–1944.* Geneva: League of Nations.

———. Various years. *World Economic Survey, 1926–1944.* Geneva: League of Nations.

Levandis, John Alexander. 1944. *The Greek Foreign Debt and the Great Powers, 1821–1898.* New York: Columbia University Press.

Lindert, Peter H., and Boris Mironov. n.d. Ag-Content of the Ruble. Available at http://gpih.ucdavis.edu/.

Lindert, Peter H., and Peter J. Morton. 1989. "How Sovereign Debt Has Worked." In *Developing Country Debt and Economic Performance,* vol. 1, ed. Jeffrey Sachs. Chicago: University of Chicago Press. Pp. 39–106.

Lu, Feng, and Kaixiang Peng. 2006. "A Research on China's Long Term Rice Prices: 1644–2000." *Frontiers of Economics in China* 1 (4): 465–520.

MacDonald, James. 2006. *A Free Nation Deep in Debt: The Financial Roots of Democracy.* New York: Farrar, Straus, and Giroux.

Maddison, Angus. 2004. *Historical Statistics for the World Economy: 1–2003 AD.* Paris: Organisation for Economic Co-operation and Development. Available at http://www.ggdc.net/maddison/.

Malanima, Paolo. n.d. *Wheat Prices in Tuscany, 1260–1860.* Available at http://www.iisg.nl/.

Mamalakis, Markos. 1983. *Historical Statistics of Chile.* Westport, Conn.: Greenwood.

Manasse, Paolo, and Nouriel Roubini. 2005. "'Rules of Thumb' for Sovereign Debt Crises." IMF Working Paper 05/42. International Monetary Fund, Washington, D.C.

Marichal, Carlos. 1989. *A Century of Debt Crises in Latin America: From Independence to the Great Depression, 1820–1930.* Princeton, N.J.: Princeton University Press.

Mauro, Paolo, Nathan Sussman, and Yishay Yafeh. 2006. *Emerging Markets and Financial Globalization: Sovereign Bond Spreads in 1870–1913 and Today.* London: Oxford University Press.

McConnell, Margaret, and Gabriel Perez-Quiros. 2000. "Output Fluctuations in the United States: What Has Changed since the Early 1980's?" *American Economic Review* 90 (5): 1464–1476.

McElderry, Andrea Lee. 1976. *Shanghai Old-Style Banks, 1800–1935: A Traditional Institution in a Changing Society.* Ann Arbor: Center for Chinese Studies, University of Michigan.

McGrattan, Ellen, and Edward Prescott. 2007. "Technology Capital and the U.S. Current Accounts." Working Paper 646. Federal Reserve Bank of Minneapolis. June.

Mellegers, Joost. 2006. "Public Finance of Indonesia, 1817–1940." Working Memorandum. Indonesian Economic Development, International Institute of Social History, Amsterdam.

Mendoza, Enrique G., and Marco Terrones. 2008. "An Anatomy of Credit Booms: Evidence from the Macro Aggregates and Micro Data." NBER Working Paper 14049. National Bureau of Economic Research, Cambridge, Mass. May.

Miller, Margaret S. 1926. *The Economic Development of Russia, 1905–1914.* London: P. S. King and Son.

Mitchell, Brian R. 2003a. *International Historical Statistics: Africa, Asia, and Oceania, 1750–2000.* London: Palgrave Macmillan.

———. 2003b. *International Historical Statistics: The Americas, 1750–2000.* London: Palgrave Macmillan.

Mizoguchi, Toshiyuki, and Mataji Umemura. 1988. *Basic Economic Statistics of Former Japanese Colonies, 1895–1938: Estimates and Findings.* Tokyo: Toyo Keizai Shinposha.

Moody's Investor Service. 2000. "Historical Default Rates of Corporate Bond Issuers, 1920–1999." *Moody's Investor Service Global Credit Research,* special comment, January.

Morris, Stephen, and Hyun Song Shin. 1998. "Unique Equilibrium in a Model of Self-Fulfilling Currency Attacks." *American Economic Review* 88 (June): 587–597.

Nakamura, Leonard I, and Carlos E. J. M. Zarazaga. 2001. Banking and Finance in Argentina in the Period 1900–35. Federal Reserve Bank of Philadelphia Working Paper 01-7. Federal Reserve Bank of Philadelphia, Pa. June.

Neal, Larry, and Marc Weidenmier. 2003. "Crises in the Global Economy from Tulips to Today: Contagion and Consequences." In *Globalization in Historical Perspective*, ed. Michael Bordo, Alan M. Taylor, and Jeffrey Williamson. Chicago: University of Chicago Press. Pp. 473–514.

Neely, Christopher. 1995. "The Profitability of U.S. Intervention in the Foreign Exchange Markets." *Journal of International Money and Finance* 14: 823–844.

Noel, Maurer. 2002. *The Power and the Money—The Mexican Financial System, 1876–1932*. Stanford, Calif.: Stanford University Press.

Norges Bank. 2004. "The Norwegian Banking Crisis." Ed. Thorvald G. Moe, Jon A. Solheim, and Bent Vale. Occasional Paper 33. Norges Bank, Oslo.

North, Douglass, and Barry Weingast. 1988. "Constitutions and Commitment: The Evolution of Institutions Governing Public Choice in Seventeenth Century England." In *Empirical Studies in Institutional Change*, ed. L. Alston, P. Eggertsson, and D. North. Cambridge: Cambridge University Press.

Nurkse, Ragnar. 1946. *The Course and Control of Inflation: A Revue of Monetary Experience in Europe after World War I*. Geneva: League of Nations.

Obstfeld, Maurice. 1994. "The Logic of Currency Crises." *Cahiers Economiques et Monetaires* 43: 189–213.

———. 1996. "Models of Currency Crises with Self-Sustaining Features." *European Economic Review* 40 (April): 1037–1048.

Obstfeld, Maurice, and Kenneth S. Rogoff. 1996. *Foundations of International Macroeconomics*. Cambridge, Mass.: MIT Press.

———. 2001. "Perspectives on OECD Capital Market Integration: Implications for U.S. Current Account Adjustment." In *Global Economic Integration: Opportunities and Challenges*. Federal Reserve Bank of Kansas City, Mo. March. Pp. 169–208.

———. 2005. "Global Current Account Imbalances and Exchange Rate Adjustments." *Brookings Papers on Economic Activity* 1: 67–146.

———. 2007. "The Unsustainable U.S. Current Account Position Revisited." In *G7 Current Account Imbalances: Sustainability and Adjustment*, ed. Richard Clarida. Chicago: University of Chicago Press.

———. 2009. "The US Current Account and the Global Financial Crisis." Draft of a paper prepared for the Ohlin Lectures in International Economics, Harvard University.

Obstfeld, Maurice, and Alan Taylor. 2004. *Global Capital Markets: Integration, Crisis, and Growth.* Japan–U.S. Center Sanwa Monographs on International Financial Markets. Cambridge: Cambridge University Press.

Øksendal, Lars. 2007. "Re-Examining Norwegian Monetary Policy in the 1930s." Manuscript. Department of Economics, Norwegian School of Economics and Business Administration, Bergen.

Oxford Latin American Economic History Database. Available at http://oxlad.qeh.ox.ac.uk/references.php.

Ozmucur, Suleyman, and Sevket Pamuk. 2002. "Real Wages and Standards of Living in the Ottoman Empire, 1489–1914." *Journal of Economic History* 62 (June): 292–321.

Page, William. 1919. *Commerce and Industry: Tables of Statistics for the British Empire from 1815.* London: Constable.

Pamuk, Sevket. 2005. "Prices and Wages in Istanbul, 1469–1914." Working Memorandum. International Institute of Social History, Amsterdam.

Persson, Torsten, and Guido Tabellini. 1990. *Macroeconomic Policy, Credibility and Politics.* London: Routledge.

Philippon, Thomas. 2007. "Why Has the U.S. Financial Sector Grown So Much? The Role of Corporate Finance." NBER Working Paper 13405. National Bureau of Economic Research, Cambridge, Mass. September.

Pick, Franz. Various years, 1955–1982. *Pick's Currency Yearbook.* New York: Pick.

Prasad, Eswar, Kenneth S. Rogoff, Shang-Jin Wei, and M. Ayhan Kose. 2003. "Effects of Financial Globalization on Developing Countries: Some Empirical Evidence." IMF Occasional Paper 220. International Monetary Fund, Washington, D.C.

Purcell, John F. H., and Jeffrey A. Kaufman. 1993. *The Risks of Sovereign Lending: Lessons from History.* New York: Salomon Brothers.

Qian, Rong, and Carmen M. Reinhart. 2009. "Graduation from Crises and Volatility: Elusive Goals." Working mimeograph. University of Maryland, College Park.

Quinn, Stephen. 2004. "Accounting for the Early British Funded Debt, 1693–1786." Working paper. Mimeograph. Texas Christian University.

Rajan, Raghuram, Enrica Detragiache, and Giovanni Dell'Ariccia. 2008. "The Real Effect of Banking Crises." *Journal of Financial Intermediation* 17: 89–112.

Reinhart, Carmen M. 2002. "Default, Currency Crises, and Sovereign Credit Ratings." *World Bank Economic Review* 16 (2): 151–170.

Reinhart, Carmen M., and Vincent R. Reinhart. 2008. "Is the U.S. Too Big to Fail?" VoxEU, November 17. Available at http://www.voxeu.com/ index.php?q=node/2568.

———. 2009. "Capital Flow Bonanzas: An Encompassing View of the Past and Present." In *NBER International Seminar in Macroeconomics 2008*, ed. Jeffrey Frankel and Francesco Giavazzi. Chicago: Chicago University Press for the National Bureau of Economic Research. Pp. 1–54.

Reinhart, Carmen M., and Kenneth S. Rogoff. 2002a. "FDI to Africa: The Role of Price Stability and Currency Instability." In *Annual World Bank Conference on Development Economics 2002: The New Reform Agenda*, ed. Boris Pleskovic and Nicholas Stern. Washington, D.C.: World Bank/ Oxford University Press. Pp. 247–282.

———. 2002b. "The Modern History of Exchange Rate Arrangements: A Reinterpretation." NBER Working Paper 8963. National Bureau of Economic Research, Cambridge, Mass. May.

———. 2004. "The Modern History of Exchange Rate Arrangements: A Reinterpretation." *Quarterly Journal of Economics* 119 (1): 1–48.

———. 2008a. "This Time Is Different: A Panoramic View of Eight Centuries of Financial Crises." NBER Working Paper 13882. National Bureau of Economic Research, Cambridge, Mass. March.

———. 2008b. "Is the 2007 U.S. Subprime Crisis So Different? An International Historical Comparison." *American Economic Review* 98 (2): 339–344.

———. 2008c. "The Forgotten History of Domestic Debt." NBER Working Paper 13946. National Bureau of Economic Research, Cambridge, Mass. April.

———. 2008d. "Regulation Should Be International." *Financial Times*, November 18.

———. 2009. "The Aftermath of Financial Crisis." *American Economic Review* 99 (2): 1–10.

Reinhart, Carmen M., and Miguel A. Savastano. 2003. "The Realities of Modern Hyperinflation." *Finance and Development*, June, 20–23.

Reinhart, Carmen M., Kenneth S. Rogoff, and Miguel A. Savastano. 2003a. "Debt Intolerance." *Brookings Papers on Economic Activity* 1 (Spring): 1–74.

———. 2003b. "Addicted to Dollars." NBER Working Paper 10015. National Bureau of Economic Research, Cambridge, Mass. October.

Rogoff, Kenneth. 1999. "Institutions for Reducing Global Financial Instability." *Journal of Economic Perspectives* 13 (Fall): 21–42.

Rolnick, Arthur J. 2004. "Interview with Ben S. Bernanke." *Region Magazine* (Minneapolis Federal Reserve), June. Available at http://www.minneapolisfed.org/publications_papers/pub_display.cfm?id=3326.

Roubini, Nouriel, and Brad Setser. 2004. "The United States as a Debtor Nation: The Sustainability of the US External Imbalances." Draft. New York University, New York. November.

Sachs, Jeffrey. 1984. *Theoretical Issues in International Borrowing*. Princeton Studies in International Finance 54. Princeton University, Princeton, N.J.

Samuelson, Paul. 1966. "Science and Stocks." *Newsweek*, September 19.

Sanhueza, Gonzalo. 2001. "Chilean Banking Crisis of the 1980s: Solutions and Estimation of the Costs." Central Bank of Chile Working Paper 104. Central Bank of Chile, Santiago.

Sargent, Thomas J. 1982. "The Ends of Four Big Hyperinflations." In *Inflation: Causes and Effects*, ed. Robert J. Hall. Chicago: University of Chicago Press.

Sargent, Thomas, and Francois Velde. 2003. *The Big Problem with Small Change*. Princeton, N.J.: Princeton University Press.

Scutt, G. P Symes. 1904. *The History of the Bank of Bengal*. Bengal: Bank of Bengal Press.

Shergold, Peter. 1987. "Prices and Consumption." In *Australian Historical Statistics*. Sydney: Fairfax, Syme and Weldon.

Shiller, Robert. 2005. *Irrational Exuberance*. 2nd ed. Princeton, N.J.: Princeton University Press.

Shin, Inseok, and Joon-Ho Hahm. 1998. "The Korean Crisis: Causes and Resolution." Korea Development Institute Working Paper. Prepared for the Korea Development Institute–East-West Center Conference on the Korean Crisis: Causes and Resolution, Hawaii. August.

Shleifer, Andrei, and Robert W. Vishny. 1991. "Liquidation Values and Debt Capacity: A Market Equilibrium Approach." *Journal of Finance* 47 (4): 1343–1366.

Sinclair, David. 2004. *The Land That Never Was: Sir Gregor MacGregor and the Most Audacious Fraud in History*. London: Headline.

Söderberg, Johan. 2004. "Prices in Stockholm: 1539–1620." Working Memorandum. International Institute of Social History, Amsterdam.

Soley Güell, Tomas. 1926. *Historia Monetaria de Costa Rica*. San Jose, Costa Rica: Imprenta Nacional.

Standard and Poor's Commentary. Various issues.

Summerhill, William. 2006. "Political Economics of the Domestic Debt in Nineteenth-Century Brazil." Working Memorandum. University of California, Los Angeles.

Sundararajan, Vasudevan, and Tomás Baliño. 1991. *Banking Crises: Cases and Issues*. Washington D.C.: International Monetary Fund.

Suter, Christian. 1992. *Debt Cycles in the World-Economy: Foreign Loans, Financial Crises, and Debt Settlements, 1820–1990*. Boulder, Colo.: Westview.

Sutton, Gregory D. 2002. "Explaining Changes in House Prices." *BIS Quarterly Review* (September): 46–55.

Tabellini, Guido. 1991. "The Politics of Intergenerational Redistribution." *Journal of Political Economy* 99 (April): 335–357.

Teichova, Alice, Ginette Kurgan–van Hentenryk, and Dieter Ziegler, eds. 1997. *Banking, Trade and Industry: Europe, America and Asia from the Thirteenth to the Twentieth Century*. Cambridge: Cambridge University Press.

Temin, Peter. 2008. "The German Crisis of 1931: Evidence and Tradition." *Cliometrica: Journal of Historical Economics and Econometric History* 2 (1): 5–17.

't Hart, Marjolein, Joost Jonker, and Jan Luiten van Zanden. 1997. *A Financial History of the Netherlands*. Cambridge: Cambridge University Press.

Tomz, Michael. 2007. *Reputation and International Cooperation: Sovereign Debt across Three Centuries*. Princeton, N.J.: Princeton University Press.

Total Economy Database. Available at http://www.conference-board.org/economics/database.cfm.

Triner, Gail D. 2000. *Banking and Economic Development: Brazil, 1889–1930*. New York: Palgrave Macmillan.

United Nations, Department of Economic Affairs. 1948. *Public Debt, 1914–1946*. New York: United Nations.

———. 1949. *International Capital Movements during the Inter-War Period*. New York: United Nations.

———. 1954. *The International Flow of Private Capital, 1946–1952*. New York: United Nations.

———. Various years. *Statistical Yearbook, 1948–1984*. New York: United Nations.

Vale, Bent. 2004. Chapter 1. In "The Norwegian Banking Crisis." Ed. Thorvald G. Moe, Jon A. Solheim, and Bent Vale. Occasional Paper 33. Norges Bank, Oslo.

Vanplew, W. 1987. *Australia: Historical Statistics*. Sydney: Fairfax, Syme and Weldon.

Van Riel, Arthur. 2009. "Constructing the Nineteeth-Century Cost of Living Deflator (1800–1913)." Working Memorandum. International Institute of Social History, Amsterdam.

Van Zanden, Jan Luiten. 2002. "Wages and the Cost of Living in Southern England (London), 1450–1700." Working Memorandum. International Institute of Social History, Amsterdam.

———. 2005. "What Happenned to the Standard of Living before the Industrial Revolution? New Evidence from the Western Part of the Netherlands." In *Living Standards in the Past: New Perspectives on Well-Being in Asia and Europe*, ed. Robert Allen, Tommy Bengtsson, and Martin Dribe. New York: Oxford University Press.

———. 2006. "Economic Growth in Java, 1815–1930: The Reconstruction of the Historical National Accounts of a Colonial Economy." Working Memorandum. International Institute of Social History, Amsterdam.

Végh, Carlos A. 1992. "Stopping High Inflation: An Analytical Overview." *IMF Staff Papers* 91 (107): 626–695.

Velasco, Andres. 1996. "Fixed Exchange Rates: Credibility, Flexibility and Multiplicity." *European Economic Review* 40 (April): 1023–1036.

Vogler R. 2001. "The Genesis of Swiss Banking Secrecy: Political and Economic Environment." *Financial History Review* 8 (1): 73–84.

Wallis, John, and Barry R. Weingast. 1988. "Dysfunctional or Optimal Institutions: State Debt Limitations, the Structure of State and Local Governments, and the Finance of American Infrastructure." In *Fiscal Challenges: An Interdisciplinary Approach to Budget Policy*, ed. Elizabeth Garrett, Elizabeth Graddy, and Howell Jackson. Cambridge: Cambridge University Press. Pp. 331–363.

Wall Street Journal. Various issues.

Wang, Yeh-chien. 1992. "Secular Trends of Rice Prices in the Yangze Delta, 1638–1935." In *Chinese History in Economic Perspective*, ed. Thomas G. Rawski and Lillian M. Li. Berkeley: University of California Press.

Weingast, Barry, 1997. "The Political Foundations of Democracy and the Rule of Law." *American Political Science Review* 91 (2): 245–263.

Williamson, Jeffrey G. 1999. "Real Wages, Inequality, and Globalization in Latin America before 1940." *Revista de Historia Economica* 17: 101–142.

———. 2000a. "Factor Prices around the Mediterranean, 1500–1940." In *The Mediterranean Response to Globalization before 1950*, ed. S. Pamuk and J. G. Williamson. London: Routledge. Pp. 45–75.

———. 2000b. "Globalization, Factor Prices and Living Standards in Asia before 1940." In *Asia Pacific Dynamism, 1500–2000*, ed. A. J. H. Latham and H. Kawakatsu. London: Routledge. Pp. 13–45.

Williamson, John. 2002. "Is Brazil Next?" International Economics Policy Briefs PB 02-7. Institute for International Economics, Washington, D.C.

Willis, Parker H., and B. H. Beckhart, eds. 1929. *Foreign Banking Systems*. New York: Henry Holt.

Winkler, Max. 1928. *Investments of United States Capital in Latin America*. Cambridge, Mass.: World Peace Foundation.

———. 1933. *Foreign Bonds: An Autopsy*. Philadelphia: Roland Sway.

Wolf, Martin. 2008. *Fixing Global Finance*. Baltimore, Md.: Johns Hopkins University Press.

Woodford, Michael. 1995. "Price-Level Determinacy without Control of a Monetary Aggregate." *Carnegie-Rochester Conference Series on Public Policy* 43: 1–46.

World Bank. Various years. *Global Development Finance*. Washington D.C.: World Bank.

Wynne, William H. 1951. *State Insolvency and Foreign Bondholders: Selected Case Histories of Governmental Foreign Bond Defaults and Debt Readjustments*, vol. II. London: Oxford University Press.

Young, Arthur Nichols. 1971. *China's Nation-Building Effort, 1927–1937: The Financial and Economic Record.* Stanford, Calif.: Stanford University Press.

Yousef, Tarik M. 2002. "Egypt's Growth Performance under Economic Liberalism: A Reassessment with New GDP Estimates, 1886–1945." *Review of Income and Wealth* 48: 561–579.

References: National Sources

Australian Office of Financial Management

Austrian Federal Financing Agency

BNB (Banque Nationale de Belgique)

Banco Central del Uruguay

Banco Central de Reserva (El Salvador)

Banco de España

Banco de la Republica (Dominican Republic)

Banco de Portugal

Bank of Canada

Bank of Indonesia

Bank of Japan

Bank of Mauritius

Bank of Thailand

Bundesbank (Germany)

Central Bank of Kenya

Central Bank of Sri Lanka

Central Bank of Tunisia

Contraloria General de la Republica (Colombia)

Danmarks Nationalbank

Dipartamento del Tesoro (Italy)

Direccion General de la Deuda Publica (Mexico)

Dutch State Treasury Agency

Estadisticas Historicas de Espana: Siglos XIX–XX (Spain)

Finnish Historical National Accounts

Historical Statistics of Japan

Historical Statistics of the United States

Instituto Brasileiro de Geografia e Estatística

Ministère du Budget, des comptes public (France)
Ministerio de Hacienda (Chile)
Ministerio de Hacienda (Costa Rica)
Ministry of Finance (Ecuador)
Ministry of Finance (Egypt)
Ministry of Finance (Norway)
Monetary Authority (Singapore)
National Accounts of the Netherlands
New Zealand Treasury
Nordic Historical National Accounts
Organisation for Economic Co-operation and Development (for Greece)
Riksgalden (National Debt Office, Sweden)
South Africa Reserve Bank
State Treasury (Finland)
Statistical Abstracts Relating to British India
Statistics Canada
Statistics New Zealand
Treasury Direct (United States)
Turkish Treasury
U.K. Debt Management Office

NAME INDEX

Page numbers for entries occurring in boxes are suffixed by a b; those for entries in figures, by an f; those for entries in notes, by an n, with the number of the note following; and those for entries in tables, by a t.

SUBJECT INDEX

Page numbers for entries occurring in boxes are suffixed by a b; those for entries in figures, by an f; those for entries in notes, by an n, with the number of the note following; and those for entries in tables, by a t.

Nordic countries: banking crises in, 206; countercyclical fiscal policy in, 224–25

North America: banking crises in, 147, 150t, 153t, 154t; data coverage of, 43, 46t; domestic public debt in, 104f; external default in, 100t; inflation crises after 1800 in, 185, 187t. *See also* Canada; United States

North American Free Trade Agreement (NAFTA), 19

Northern Rock bank, xl–xli

Norway: bailout costs in, 164; banking crises in, 159, 164, 226, 376–77t; domestic debt in, 126; duration of crises in, 235; housing prices in, 402n25; inflation crises in, 185

Oceania: banking crises in, 147, 150t, 153t, 154t; data coverage of, 43, 46t; domestic public debt in, 104f; external default in, 100t; inflation crises after 1800 in, 185, 187t. *See also* Australia; New Zealand

odious debt, 63–64

oil: nationalization of, 58; price shocks in, 206, 248, 255; surpluses of, 17

OPEC. *See* Organization of Petroleum Exporting Countries

Organization of Petroleum Exporting Countries (OPEC), 17, 58

output: in aftermath of crises, 224; data on, 307–10t; in Great Depression versus postwar crises, 234–37, 234f

Pakistan, de-dollarization in, 194f, 195–96

Panama: banking crises in, 377t; debt reversals in, 84b; inflation crises in, 185

panic of 1907: banking crises in, 205; contagion of, 242; in financial turbulence index, 255

paper currency: debasement of, 175; inflation after advent of, 35, 75–76, 181; inflation before advent of, 5; transition to, 175, 179

Papua New Guinea, banking crises in, 377t

Paraguay, banking crises in, 377–78t

partial default, 61–63; amount repaid in, 61–62; through inflation, 44, 75; reschedulings as form of, 62, 90–92; serial, 15; third parties in, 62, 397n16; and trade, 62, 397n16

peak-to-trough calculations, 405n2

Peru: banking crises in, 204, 378t; Brady bonds in, 84b, 85b; de-dollarization in, 196, 403n10; domestic debt in, 104–5; external default by, 94, 98

Peruzzi Bank, 69b

Philippines: banking crises in, 226, 378t; Brady bonds in, 84b, 85b; debt reversals in, 84b; duration of crises in, 235; external default by, 98; housing prices in, 159, 226

Pick's Currency Yearbooks, 36–37

Poland: banking crises in, 379t; Brady bonds in, 84b, 85b; de-dollarization in, 194f, 195–96; duration of crises in, 235; graduation in, 287; inflation crises in, 182, 185

policy makers: early warning system and, 281; recommendations to, 287–90; on U.S. current account balance, 208–15; on U.S. housing bubble, 212–13

political disunity, in public defaults, 53

Ponzi schemes, 55, 58

Portugal: banking crises in, 171, 379t; external default by, 87, 87t; graduation in, 287; international capital markets of 1800s in, 398n8

PPP. *See* purchasing power parity

presidential elections: 2002 Brazilian, 53; 2008 U.S., 53

press coverage, of U.S. subprime crisis, 199

prices: after currency debasements, 174; data on, 35–36, 296–301t

private debt: in debt intolerance, 26; in financial turbulence index, 251; lack of data on, 220; recent rise of, 399n4; and U.S. subprime crisis, 209, 212, 220

protectionism, during Great Depression, 264